THE WOLF AND THE

(The timing of the Millennium)

Written by: Gavin Paynter

PROLOGUE

During the Second World War, US General Douglas MacArthur was forced to leave the Philippines on orders from President Franklin Roosevelt in March 1942, when it became apparent that the country would soon succumb to the Japanese offensive. Deeply disappointed, MacArthur issued a statement to the press in which he promised his stranded men and the people of the Philippines, "I shall return", a promise that he would often repeat in public appearances.[1]

Two and a half years later MacArthur was poised to launch an invasion of the Philippines. On 20 October 1944, a few hours after his troops landed, he waded ashore onto the island of Leyte. That day, he made a radio broadcast in which he declared, "People of the Philippines, I have returned!"[2]

Figure 1: "I have returned" - The iconic photo of MacArthur returning to the Philippines

---

[1] http://www.history.com/this-day-in-history/macarthur-returns
[2] Ibid

By June 1945 MacArthur announced his offensive operations to be at an end. "I'm a little late," he told the men he had left behind in 1942 who survived to see his return, "but we finally came." [3]

Now if humans can make and keep promises of rescue and deliverance, how much more will Jesus keep the promise he made to return. Jesus promised his disciples that, after he was killed, he would rise again (Luke 18:33-34 [4]). This was a promise he kept when he rose from the dead on the third day.

But he also promised his disciples that after his departure, he would come again.

> "In my Father's house are many rooms; if it were not so, I would have told you. I am going there to prepare a place for you. And if I go and prepare a place for you, I will come back and take you to be with me that you also may be where I am." (John 14:2-3)

And later the disciples were reminded of his promise. As they gazed intently up into the sky as Jesus ascended from the Mount of Olives, suddenly two men dressed in white stood beside them.

> "Men of Galilee," they said, "why do you stand here looking into the sky? This same Jesus, who has been taken from you into heaven, will come back in the same way you have seen him go into heaven." (Acts 1:11)

Eschatology which comes from the Greek word ἔσχατος (transliterated 'eschatos' and meaning 'last') is a part of theology concerned with the last days or End Times, a large part of which is dedicated to the Second Coming of Christ. In the last century, eschatology has been studied and argued probably more than at any other time period in church history.

---

[3] Ibid
[4] Luke 18:33-34 "He will be handed over to the Gentiles. They will mock him, insult him, spit on him, flog him and kill him. On the third day he will rise again."'

But while most Christians believe in the future return of Jesus, there are several areas which are hot items of debate. The major areas of study and debate include:

a) The timing of Bible prophecy
   1. Futurism
   2. Preterism
   3. Historicism

b) The timing of the Millennium
   1. Premillennialism
   2. Amillennialism
   3. Postmillennialism

c) The timing of the Rapture
   1. Pre-Tribulationism
   2. Post-Tribulationism
   3. Mid-Tribulationism

In my former book (The Profile of The Antichrist - Part 1), [5] we considered the differences between Preterism, Historicism and Futurism in some detail, stating my own preference for the Futurist view. In this book, we will look at the second area of debate, namely the timing of the Millennium, with a stated preference for the Premillennial view. In the final chapter, we will very briefly consider the third area of debate, namely the timing of the Rapture, with a preference for the Pre-Tribulation view.

At the same time, we need always to recall the wise word of caution offered by D.L. Moody, when 19th century Premillennial ranks were beginning to splinter over the issue of the timing of Christ's return, saying, "Don't criticize if our watches don't agree about the time we know that he is coming." [6]

---

[5] The Profile of the Antichrist (Part 1) - Gavin Paynter
 https://www.amazon.com/Profile-Antichrist-Part-1-ebook/dp/B014854DKK
[6] The Company of the Preachers: Volume 2

CHAPTER 1: THE TIMING OF THE MILLENNIUM

What is the millennium?

The word 'millennium' is derived from the Latin 'mille' (thousand) and 'annum' (year). "The Millennium" in Bible prophecy refers specifically to a 1000-year golden age when Jesus, as the Jewish Messiah, will reign on earth from Jerusalem in fulfilment of the Old Testament prophecies.

Premillennialism, Amillennialism and Postmillennialism

There are three different views regarding the timing and duration of the Millennium.

a) Premillennialism

1. The Millennium is a future literal 1000-years reign by Christ.
2. Christ himself reigns on earth with his Church.
3. Christ returns after the Church Age (Pre, Mid or Post-Tribulation rapture), but before the Millennium.
4. Like the Church, Israel has a separate irrevocable covenant with God.
5. There are two resurrections separated by 1000 years.
6. Satan will be bound in the future age to come.
7. There will be a great apostasy before the return of Christ.
8. The Church and State should remain separate.

b) Amillennialism

1. The entire Church Age (starting at the cross) is the Millennium (not a literal 1000 years).
2. Christ reigns in heaven.
3. Christ returns after the figurative Millennium.
4. The church has replaced Israel.
5. There is one resurrection.
6. Satan is bound now in the current age.

7. There will be a brief apostasy before the return of Christ when Satan is loosed.
8. Historically supported a State Church.

c) Postmillennialism

1. The Millennium is a future (or current) literal (or figurative) 1000 years (or long period).
2. The Church will reign on earth.
3. Christ returns after the Millennium.
4. The Church has replaced Israel.
5. There is one resurrection.
6. Satan is or will be bound in the current age.
7. There will be a time of unprecedented revival before the return of Christ.
8. The Church should control the State.

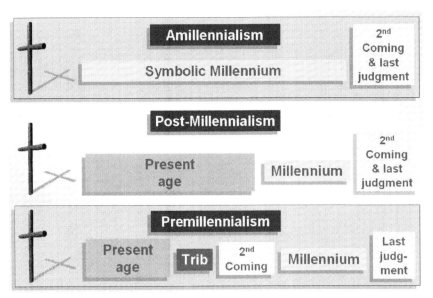

Figure 2: The Timing of the Millennium – for simplicity the differing views on the timing of the Rapture are not shown here under Premillennialism

Revelation 20:1-15 And I saw an angel coming down out of heaven... He seized ... Satan, and bound him for a thousand years. He threw him into the Abyss, and locked and sealed it over him, to keep him from deceiving the nations anymore until the thousand years were ended... I saw thrones on which were seated those who had been given authority to judge. And I saw the souls of those who had been beheaded because of their testimony about Jesus and because of the word of God. They had not worshiped the beast or his image and had not received his mark on their foreheads or their hands. They came to life and reigned with Christ a thousand years. (The rest of the dead did not come to life until the thousand years were ended.) This is the first resurrection. Blessed and holy are those who have part in the first resurrection. The second death has no power over them, but they will be priests of God and of Christ and will reign with him for a thousand years. When the thousand years are over... I saw a great white throne and him who was seated on it... And I saw the dead, great and small, standing before the throne, and books were opened. Another book was opened, which is the book of life. The dead were judged according to what they had done as recorded in the books... If anyone's name was not found written in the book of life, he was thrown into the lake of fire.

The Millennium is described above with clear detail regarding timing by the apostle John in Revelation 20. Hence, a summary of the plain and literal teaching of the passage is as follows:

Literal meaning	Rev 20
There are 2 resurrections.	20:5 This is the first resurrection.
The 2 resurrections are separated by 1000 years.	20:5 The rest of the dead did not come to life until the thousand years were ended.
During this 1000 years Jesus reigns on earth with his saints.	20:4 They came to life and reigned with Christ a thousand years.
These resurrected saints are immortal.	20:6 The second death has no power over them…
This follows a period when the Beast has ruled (Tribulation).	20:4 They had not worshiped the beast or his image and had not received his mark on their foreheads or their hands.
Those who are part of the first resurrection are blessed.	20:6 Blessed and holy are those who have part in the first resurrection.
Those who are part of the first resurrection will reign with Jesus.	20:6 … they will be priests of God and of Christ and will reign with him for a thousand years.
On the contrary, some at the second resurrection and Great White Throne judgment are cast into the lake of fire.	20:15 If anyone's name was not found written in the book of life, he was thrown into the lake of fire.
During this 1000-year period, Satan is bound in the Abyss.	20:2-3 He seized … Satan, and bound him for a thousand years. He threw him into the Abyss, and locked and sealed it over him…
This is a period where there is no spiritual deception.	20:3 … to keep him from deceiving the nations anymore until the thousand years were ended…

Table 1: The literal teaching of Revelation 20

This is in fact a precise summary of the Premillennial view. Both Amillennialists and Postmillennialists have to resort to an allegorical interpretation of Revelation 20 in order to make their view 'fit' a passage that in reality teaches the opposite.

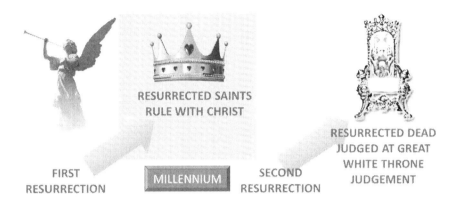

RESURRECTED SAINTS
RULE WITH CHRIST

RESURRECTED DEAD
JUDGED AT GREAT
WHITE THRONE
JUDGEMENT

FIRST
RESURRECTION

MILLENNIUM

SECOND
RESURRECTION

Figure 3: The 2 resurrections as detailed in Rev 20

Preterism, Historicism, Idealism and Futurism

In my former book, [7] we looked at the differences between Preterism, Historicism and Futurism. There are three main schools of thought (and one minority view) regarding the overall timing of End Time prophecy:

1) **Preterism** - holds that most or all of the Biblical prophecies concerning the End Times refer to events which actually happened in the 1st century AD.
2) **Historicism** - treats the prophecies of Daniel and Revelation as finding literal earthly fulfilment through the history of the church age.
3) **Futurism** - places the fulfilment of the prophecies of Daniel and Revelation mostly in the future as literal, physical, apocalyptic and global.
4) **Idealism** is a fourth minority view where prophecies are perpetually and cyclically fulfilled in a spiritual sense during the conflict between the Kingdom of God and the forces of

---

[7] Ibid

Satan throughout the time from the First Advent to the Second Coming of Christ.

There is no direct relationship between these schools of thought and the Millennial position held, but there are strong correlations.

a) Premillennialists are typically Futurist in outlook, though some adopt a mixture of Historicism and Futurism.
b) Amillennialists are generally associated with Preterism or Idealism.
c) Many Postmillennialists also adopt some form of Preterism. These viewpoints can easily coexist, as both reject a future apocalypse, with Preterism assigning it to the past instead. While Postmillennialists may also be Historicists, they are not likely to be Futurists, since they think the future is better, not worse. In contrast, a Futurist interpretation of the events in Revelation simply doesn't paint a picture of coming great revival - rather that of a coming great and fearful judgement.

Millennial view	Preterist	Historicist	Futurist	Idealist
Amillennial	**X**	X	X	**X**
Postmillennial	**X**	**X**		X
Premillennial		X	**X**	

Table 2: Possible Millennial views of Preterists, Historicists, Futurists and Idealists with the more likely ones in bold

CHAPTER 2: HISTORY OF MILLENNIAL VIEWS

1st century

Premillennialism, also called Millenarianism (from the Latin 'mille' for a thousand) or Chiliasm (from the Greek 'chilloi' for a thousand), was the original predominant church view in the 1st to 3rd century. Despite being a Postmillennialist, the renowned church historian Philip Schaff, honestly acknowledged that:

> The most striking point in the eschatology of the ante-Nicene age (AD 100-325) is the prominent chiliasm, or millenarianism, that is the belief of a visible reign of Christ in glory on earth with the risen saints for a thousand years, before the general resurrection and judgment. It was indeed not the doctrine of the church embodied in any creed or form of devotion, but a widely current opinion of distinguished teachers, such as Barnabas, Papias, Justin Martyr, Irenaeus, Tertullian, Methodius, and Lactantius. [8]

While Catholics generally hold to an Amillennial viewpoint, an article on a Catholic website acknowledges that:

> ... several early Christian writers - notably Papias, Justin Martyr, Irenaeus, Tertullian, Hippolytus, Methodius, Commodianus, and Lactanitus - were premillennialists who believed that Christ's Second Coming would lead to a visible, earthly reign. [9]

Christian writers who clearly held the Premillennial view in the first century AD were:

a) Papias
b) The author of the Epistle of Barnabas
c) (Possibly) Clement of Rome
d) (Possibly) Polycarp

---

[8] History of the Christian Church, Scribner, 1884; Vol. 2, p. 614
[9] Carl E. Olson
http://www.catholicculture.org/culture/library/view.cfm?recnum=5788

The sexta-septamillennial tradition

Many of these early theologians expressed their belief in Premillennialism through their acceptance of the sexta-septamillennial tradition. Based on Peter's statement that "with the Lord … a thousand years are like a day" (2 Pet 3:8), this is a belief that all human history will amount to a total of 7,000 years prior to the new creation. After 6,000 years of history, there will be a Sabbath for 1,000 years (the Millennial kingdom). We shall explore this idea in more detail later.

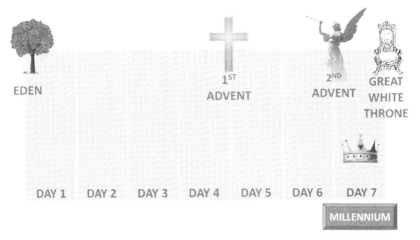

Figure 4: The sexta-septamillennial view of human history

The Epistle of Barnabas

The first editor of the Epistle of Barnabas, Hugo Menardus (1645) advocated the genuineness of its ascription to the Barnabas mentioned in the Book of Acts, but the general opinion today is that the apostle Barnabas was not the author. Some ascribe it to another Apostolic Father of the same name, Barnabas of Alexandria; while others simply attribute it to an unknown early Christian teacher. [10] The author of the epistle probably wrote between the years AD 70-131 and was a

---

[10] https://en.wikipedia.org/wiki/Epistle_of_Barnabas

Premillennialist, holding to the sexta-septamillennial scheme. He notes that "a day is with Him a thousand years" and that "in six days, that is, in six thousand years, all things will be finished". After that "His Son, coming [again], shall destroy the time of the wicked man" and "then shall He truly rest on the seventh day" which is the seventh 1000-year period. [11]

Papias

Papias (c. AD 70-163) of Hierapolis (modern Pamukkale in Turkey) is described by Irenaeus as "an ancient man who was a hearer of John and a companion of Polycarp". [12] He was acquainted with the daughters of Philip the evangelist, [13] who were mentioned in the Book of Acts. [14] He also knew many 'elders' who had heard the Twelve Apostles first-hand and it was based on his encounters and dialogue with them that he formulated his theology.[15] Papias writes, "For I did not think that information from the books would profit me as much as information from a living and surviving voice."[16]

---

[11] The Epistle of Barnabas, Ch. 15

[12] Against Heresies 5.33

[13] Eusebius writes, "The residence of the Apostle Philip with his daughters in Hierapolis has been mentioned above. We must now point out how Papias, who lived at the same time, relates that he had received a wonderful narrative from the daughters of Philip." (Ecclesiastical History, 3:39:8-9)

[14] Acts 21:8-9 Leaving the next day, we reached Caesarea and stayed at the house of Philip the evangelist, one of the Seven. He had four unmarried daughters who prophesied.

[15] Ecclesiastical History 3:39:3-4 - Papias writes, "I shall not hesitate also to put into ordered form for you, along with the interpretations, everything I learned carefully in the past from the elders and noted down carefully, for the truth of which I vouch. For unlike most people I took no pleasure in those who told many different stories, but only in those who taught the truth. Nor did I take pleasure in those who reported their memory of someone else's commandments, but only in those who reported their memory of the commandments given by the Lord to the faith and proceeding from the Truth itself. And if by chance anyone who had been in attendance on the elders arrived, I made enquiries about the words of the elders—what Andrew or Peter had said, or Philip or Thomas or James or John or Matthew or any other of the Lord's disciples, and whatever Aristion and John the Elder, the Lord's disciples, were saying."

[16] Ibid

According to early church historian Eusebius, Papias taught that "there will be a Millennium after the resurrection of the dead, when the kingdom of Christ will be set up in material form on this earth." [17] In circa 400 AD Jerome who, like Eusebius, was no friend of Premillennialism, also notes that Papias and many other notable early Christian writers, held a Premillennial view.

> He is said to have perpetuated a Jewish tradition of the thousand years, which Irenaeus and Apollinaris etc. follow, who say that the Lord will reign in the flesh with the saints after the resurrection. [18]

Many have criticized Papias because of certain fantastic elements in his description of the Millennium, as related later by Irenaeus. According to the latter, Papias wrote that:

> ...The days will come, in which vines shall grow, each having ten thousand branches, and in each branch ten thousand twigs, and in each true twig ten thousand shoots, and in each one of the shoots ten thousand clusters, and on every one of the clusters ten thousand grapes, and every grape when pressed will give five and twenty metretes of wine. And when any one of the saints shall lay hold of a cluster, another shall cry out, I am a better cluster, take me; bless the Lord through me... [19]

Thereafter Papias also attributes words to Jesus, that sound very apocryphal, namely:

> In like manner [the Lord declared] that a grain of wheat would produce ten thousand ears, and that every ear should have ten thousand grains, and every grain would yield ten pounds of clear, pure, fine flour; and that all other fruit-bearing trees, and seeds and grass, would produce in similar proportions. [20]

---

[17] Ecclesiastical History 3:39:13
[18] Illustrious Lives 18
[19] Against Heresies 5.33.3
[20] Ibid

But no matter what one thinks of Papias, because of his more bizarre ideas about the Millennium, the fact that he was a Chiliast proves the antiquity of the doctrine and invalidates the later arguments we encounter - claiming that Chiliasm originated with the heretic Cerinthus or other Gnostic sects.

Clement of Rome

Some have attempted to identify some Church Fathers, who were either silent on the matter of eschatology, or who said very little about it, as either Premillennialists or Amillennialists. While I agree that in this period of history it is more likely that they were Chiliast in outlook, I have considered it expedient to avoid making arguments from silence, [21] unless there is some evidence from contemporaries or those closer to the time (who may have had access to material not available today).

In reality Clement of Rome (AD 30-100) says too little on the matter to categorise him either way. Amazingly some have taken his silence as proof that he was not Premillennial in outlook. But Bethune-Baker wisely cautions, that although there is no reference to the Millennium in Clement and certain other early Fathers, "we are not justified in arguing from their silence that they did not hold it [i.e. millennialism]." [22]

The strongest argument for identifying Clement with Chiliasm comes from the 7th century father, Anastasius Sinaitia (AD 620-701), who makes this statement, which seems to indicate that Clement subscribed to the sexta-septamillennial view.

> And the fact that it was not said of the seventh day equally with the other days, 'And there was evening, and there was morning,' is a distinct indication of the consummation which is to take place in it before it is

---

[21] Jerome, Illustrious Lives 18 (c. 400)
[22] J. F. Bethune-Baker, An Introduction to the Early History of Christian Doctrine: To the Time of the Council of Chalcedon (London: Methuen & Co. Ltd, 1903), p. 69, n. 3

finished, as the fathers declare, especially St. Clement, and Irenaeus, and Justin the martyr and philosopher. [23]

'Consummation' in the above passage refers to 'completion' or 'attainment'. Thus, if Anastasius is correct, Clement saw the completion of all things in the seventh millennial day. We have no way of determining how Anastasius knew this though, as it is not evident in the extant writing of Clement (which amounts to a single epistle to the church of Corinth [24]).

Ignatius of Antioch

Again, the letters of Ignatius (c. 35 - c. 108 AD) were not intended to contain a complete outline of his theological views and so his outlook concerning the Millennium can only be guessed at - which some have still ventured to do, having him support both Premillennialism and Amillennialism, based on his silence on the issue.

Polycarp

Likewise, Polycarp (AD 69-155) says too little to make a call either way, at least based on his extant works alone. But Irenaeus wrote that he had listened to Polycarp 'attentively', noting whatever he taught and faithfully using this very same teaching himself. Irenaeus says that his own teaching conformed to that of Polycarp's and by implication to that of the apostles, and to that of the Asiatic churches, especially the Ephesian Church, which had been tutored by John himself. Irenaeus states:

> But Polycarp also was not only instructed by apostles, and conversed with many who had seen Christ, but was also, by apostles in Asia, appointed bishop of the Church in Smyrna, whom I also saw in my early youth, for he tarried [on earth] a very long time, and, when a very old

---

[23] Justin, Frag. XV, Comments by Anastasius
[24] Most scholars believe that the other writings attributed to him like the Second Epistle of Clement and Epistles on Virginity were the works of other authors.

man, gloriously and most nobly suffering martyrdom, departed this life, having always taught the things which he had learned from the apostles, and which the Church has handed down, and which alone are true. To these things all the Asiatic Churches testify, as do also those men who have succeeded Polycarp down to the present time...Then, again, the Church in Ephesus, founded by Paul, and having John remaining among them permanently until the times of Trajan, is a true witness of the tradition of the apostles.[25]

It seems no coincidence that the apostle John was very active in the Roman province of Asia, as was Polycarp - yet it is commonly accepted that Chiliasm was very prevalent in this area.[26] It also seems highly unlikely that Irenaeus would have deviated from the doctrine of his own mentor, on an issue that is clearly central to Irenaeus' eschatology. So, in view of the abundantly clear Premillennialism of Irenaeus, along with the fact that he faithfully followed the teachings of Polycarp, it is a reasonable assumption that Polycarp was a Chiliast, as indeed were all of the earliest Fathers whose eschatological position can be determined with any degree of certainty.

2nd century

Theologians who held to the Premillennial view during the second century were:

a) Justin Martyr
b) Melito
c) Tertullian

---

[25] Against Heresies 5.3.4

[26] E.g. The Catholic Encyclopedia calls Asia Minor "the principal seat of millenarian teachings", citing Irenaeus, Melito and The Montanists as examples. They also state "a large number of Christians of the post-Apostolic era, particularly in Asia Minor, yielded so far to Jewish apocalyptic as to put a literal meaning into these descriptions of St. John's Apocalypse; the result was that millenarianism spread and gained staunch advocates not only among the heretics but among the Catholic Christians as well."
http://www.newadvent.org/cathen/10307a.htm

d) Irenaeus

Justin Martyr

Justin Martyr (c. 100-165 AD) was an early Christian apologist, who was eventually martyred along with some of his students. Justin clearly describes himself as continuing in the Jewish belief of a temporary messianic kingdom prior to the eternal state.

> But I and others, who are right-minded Christians on all points, are assured that there will be a resurrection of the dead, and a thousand years in Jerusalem, which will then be built, adorned, and enlarged, the prophets Ezekiel and Isaiah and others declare. [27]

Justin also argues that the Book of Revelation was the work of John the apostle and that it supported this idea.

> And further, there was a certain man with us, whose name was John, one of the apostles of Christ, who prophesied, by a revelation that was made to him, that those who believed in our Christ would dwell a thousand years in Jerusalem; and that thereafter the general, and, in short, the eternal resurrection and judgment of all men would likewise take place. [28]

In later years we'll see that some (like Caius, Dionysius and Eusebius) would have to resort to questioning the authorship of Revelation, in an attempt to counteract the above argument.

Melito of Sardis

Melito (died AD 180) was the bishop of Sardis, in what was the Roman province of Asia (in modern Turkey). He was considered by his peers as a great authority due to his literary works, most of which have been lost. He is remembered especially for his

---

[27] 'Dialogue with Trypho' - Ch 80
[28] Ibid - Ch 81

work on developing the first Old Testament Canon. [29] Melito believed in a literal future Millennial reign of Christ on earth, [30] with both Jerome [31] and Gennadius [32] affirming that he was a Chiliast.

Irenaeus

Jerome saw Irenaeus (AD 140-202) as a Premillennialist, [33] which is hardly surprisingly, as that is clearly not an item of debate. This highly-respected church father, Irenaeus of Lyons, related how in his youth in Smyrna, he had often listened to Polycarp, the disciple of the apostle John. John was the author of the Book of Revelation and Irenaeus formulated his doctrine based on the apostolic teachings of John as related by Polycarp. [34] He is thus considered to be a second-generation disciple of John. Thus not only are the teachings of Irenaeus considered to be among the most important of early Christianity, they also provide important insight into John's teachings.

Irenaeus is best known for his work 'Adversus Haereses' (Against Heresies) written to refute the Gnostic heresies. In the fifth book, he concentrates largely on eschatology, expounding at great length on what is clearly Premillennial doctrine, replete

---

[29] Jerome, speaking of the Old Testament canon established by Melito, quotes Tertullian to the effect that he was esteemed as a prophet by many of the faithful. https://en.wikipedia.org/wiki/Melito_of_Sardis

[30] Ibid

[31] Comm. on Ezekiel 36

[32] De Dogm. Eccl., Ch. 52

[33] Illustrious Lives 18

[34] Irenaeus' letter to Florinus (4-6) - "For when I was a boy, I saw thee in lower Asia with Polycarp, moving in splendour in the royal court, and endeavouring to gain his approbation. I remember the events of that time more clearly than those of recent years. For what boys learn, growing with their mind, becomes joined with it; so that I am able to describe the very place in which the blessed Polycarp sat as he discoursed, and his goings out and his comings in, and the manner of his life, and his physical appearance, and his discourses to the people, and the accounts which he gave of his intercourse with John and with the others who had seen the Lord. And as he remembered their words, and what he heard from them concerning the Lord, and concerning his miracles and his teaching, having received them from eyewitnesses of the 'Word of life,' Polycarp related all things in harmony with the Scriptures."

with lengthy scriptural citations and assertions that the doctrine is the orthodox view. He writes that "John, therefore, did distinctly foresee the first 'resurrection of the just,' and the inheritance in the kingdom of the earth…" [35] In the context of his discussion of the earthly Millennial kingdom, he affirms that Papias and, by implication Polycarp and John, held to the Premillennial view of an earthly kingdom as well.

> And these things are borne witness to in the fourth book of the writings of Papias, the hearer of John, and a companion of Polycarp. [36]

Irenaeus believed that the purpose of ruling in an earthly kingdom was to enable the just "gradually to partake of the divine nature".

> … they are both ignorant of God's dispensations, and of the mystery of the resurrection of the just, and of the [earthly] kingdom which is the commencement of incorruption, by means of which kingdom those who shall be worthy are accustomed gradually to partake of the divine nature… it behooves the righteous first to receive the promise of the inheritance which God promised to the fathers, and to reign in it, when they rise again to behold God in this creation which is renovated…[37]

In further support of an earthly kingdom, he argues that it is fitting that we should receive our reward in the very creation wherein we suffered.

> For it is just that in that very creation in which they toiled or were afflicted, being proved in every way by suffering, they should receive the reward of their suffering; and that in the creation in which they were slain because of their love to God, in that they should be revived again; and

---

[35] Against Heresies 5.36
[36] Ibid 5.33.3
[37] Ibid 5.32.1

that in the creation in which they endured servitude, in that they should reign. [38]

Irenaeus emphasizes that these promises are not to be seen as fulfilled in our present age (as both Amillennialists and Postmillennialists do), but at the end of the age or "the consummation of the days".

> Then Daniel also says this very thing: And the kingdom and dominion, and the greatness of those under the heaven, is given to the saints of the Most High God, whose kingdom is everlasting, and all dominions shall serve and obey Him. Daniel 7:27 And lest the promise named should be understood as referring to this time, it was declared to the prophet: And come, and stand in your lot at the consummation of the days. Daniel 12:13 [39]

Tertullian

From Carthage in the Roman province of Africa, Tertullian (c. 160 - c. 220 AD) was an early apologist who produced an extensive amount of Christian literature in Latin. Some have called him "the father of Latin Christianity" [40] and "the founder of Western theology." He writes:

> But we do confess that a kingdom is promised to us upon the earth, although before heaven, only in another state of existence; inasmuch as it will be after the resurrection for a thousand years in the divinely-built city of Jerusalem, 'let down from heaven,' which the apostle also calls 'our mother from above'... [41]

Jerome attributed the viewpoint of Chiliasm, amongst others, to Tertullian.[42]

---

[38] Ibid
[39] Against Heresies 5.34.2
[40] Benham, William (1887). The Dictionary of Religion. p. 1013
[41] Against Marcion, 3:25
[42] Illustrious Lives 18

> He is said to have perpetuated a Jewish tradition of the thousand years… Tertullian also in the book On the Hope of the Faithful and Victorinus of Pettau and Lactantius are said to be of this opinion. [43]

Note that Jerome considered Tertullian's book "On the Hope of the Faithful" to be the strongest evidence that he was a Premillennialist. Unfortunately, the book is now lost, but Jerome, an opponent of Chiliasm, indirectly affirms that it looked forward to the Millennium, when Christ will rule with the saints. Furthermore, somewhere before AD 207, Tertullian joined the Montanists [44] who were well known for their Chiliasm (Premillennialism).[45]

3rd century

Theologians who held to the Premillennial view during the 3rd century AD were:

   a) Victorinus of Pettau
   b) Lactantius
   c) Commodianus
   d) Hippolytus of Rome
   e) Cyprian

Theologians who held to the Amillennial view were:

   a) Origen
   b) Caius of Rome

Victorinus of Pettau

We again recall that Jerome saw Victorinus as a Premillennialist. [46] Victorinus was martyred circa AD 303 during the persecutions of the Emperor Diocletian. His writings were clearly

---

[43] Ibid
[44] https://www.britannica.com/biography/Tertullian
[45] Ibid
[46] Jerome, Illustrious Lives 18

Premillennial, holding to the sexta-septamillennial view that the seven thousandth year of human history was a millennium of sabbatical rest. [47]

Lactantius

Jerome also regarded Lactantius as a Premillennialist. [48] Lactantius (c. 240 - c. 320 AD) was a Christian author who became an advisor to the Emperor Constantine, as well as a tutor to his son, Crispus. He correctly taught that the Millennium follows the judgement and resurrection.

> But He, when He shall have destroyed unrighteousness, and executed His great judgment, and shall have recalled to life the righteous, who have lived from the beginning, will be engaged among men a thousand years, and will rule them with most just command. [49]

He further states that the earth will be repopulated during the Millennium, being ruled by those who were part of the first resurrection.

> Then they who shall be alive in their bodies shall not die, but during those thousand years shall produce an infinite multitude, and their offspring shall be holy, and beloved by God; but they who shall be raised from the dead shall preside over the living as judges. [50]

---

[47] On the Creation of the World http://www.newadvent.org/fathers/0711.htm - "And in Matthew we read, that it is written Isaiah also and the rest of his colleagues broke the Sabbath Matthew 12:5 — that that true and just Sabbath should be observed in the seventh millenary of years. Wherefore to those seven days the Lord attributed to each a thousand years; for thus went the warning: In Your eyes, O Lord, a thousand years are as one day. Therefore in the eyes of the Lord each thousand of years is ordained, for I find that the Lord's eyes are seven. Zechariah 4:10 Wherefore, as I have narrated, that true Sabbath will be in the seventh millenary of years, when Christ with His elect shall reign."

[48] Jerome, Illustrious Lives 18

[49] The Divine Institutes, book 7, chapter 24

[50] Ibid

Thereafter God would establish his eternal kingdom after the 1000 years.

> But when the thousand years shall be completed, the world shall he renewed by God, and the heavens shall be folded together, and the earth shall be changed, and God shall transform men into the similitude of angels, and they... shall always be employed in the sight of the Almighty, and shall make offerings to their Lord, and serve Him for ever. [51]

The current Wikipedia article on Lactantius, states the following with regards to his prophetic exegesis:

> Like many writers in the first few centuries of the early church, Lactantius took a premillennialist view, holding that the second coming of Christ will precede a millennium or a thousand-year reign of Christ on earth. According to Charles E. Hill, "With Lactantius in the early fourth century we see a determined attempt to revive a more 'genuine' form of chiliasm." ... None of the fathers thus far had been more verbose on the subject of the millennial kingdom than Lactantius or more particular in describing the times and events preceding and following. He held to the literalist interpretation of the millennium, that the millennium originates with the second advent of Christ and marks the destruction of the wicked, the binding of the devil and the raising of the righteous dead. He depicted Jesus reigning with the resurrected righteous on this earth during the seventh thousand years prior to the general judgment. [52]

Commodianus

Commodianus, who lived circa 240 AD, was a Christian Latin poet, probably from North Africa, who may have ended his life as a bishop. Originally a heathen, he was converted to

---

[51] Ibid, chapter 26
[52] https://en.wikipedia.org/wiki/Lactantius

Christianity when advanced in years, and felt called upon to instruct the ignorant in the truth. He wrote:

> They shall come also who overcame cruel martyrdom under Antichrist, and they themselves live for the whole time, and receive blessings because they have suffered evil things; and they themselves marrying, beget for a thousand years. There are prepared all the revenues of the earth, because the earth renewed without end pours forth abundantly. [53]

Hippolytus and Cyprian

Hippolytus of Rome (AD 170-235) was the disciple of Irenaeus, who in turn learnt from Polycarp, the disciple of the apostle John. [54] So in a sense he is a third-generation disciple of John. Cyprian (AD 200-258) received a classical education in Carthage and was influenced in style and thinking by fellow Carthaginian, Tertullian. We will demonstrate later that both Cyprian and Hippolytus held to the Premillennial idea of a sexta-septamillennial view of history.

Origen

But in the 3rd century we also start to see the first shift away from Premillennialism. The Alexandrian Origen (AD 185-254) popularized the allegorical approach of interpreting Scripture, combining Christianity with the ideas of the Greek philosopher Plato. He spiritualized Bible passages and devalued anything material in favour of the spiritual. He thus laid a hermeneutical basis for the view that the promised kingdom of Christ was not an earthly kingdom, but rather a spiritual one.

Origen was the first to openly challenge and denounce Chiliasm (Premillennialism), regarding it as a 'Jewish' view. He wrote that

---

[53] The Instructions of Commodianus, ch 54
[54] Photios I of Constantinople describes Hippolytus in his Bibliotheca (cod. 121) as a disciple of Irenaeus, who was said to be a disciple of Polycarp, and from the context of this passage it is supposed that he suggested that Hippolytus styled himself in that same manner.

belief in a literal Millennium was "superficial", the result of laziness in thinking, indicative of an underlying desire for earthly indulgence, and due to one being overly committed to literalism ("being disciples of the letter alone").

> Certain persons, then, refusing the labour of thinking, and adopting a superficial view of the letter of the law, and yielding rather in some measure to the indulgence of their own desires and lusts, being disciples of the letter alone, are of opinion that the fulfilment of the promises of the future are to be looked for in bodily pleasure and luxury... And consequently they say, that after the resurrection there will be marriages, and the begetting of children, imagining to themselves that the earthly city of Jerusalem is to be rebuilt ... [55]

Caius of Rome

Caius was a Christian author in the early 3rd century. Little is known about him, but Eusebius tells us [56] that he held a disputation with Proclus, a Montanist leader at Rome. [57] The Montanists, while considered heretical by some, had the distinction of having the much-respected Tertullian joining their ranks. They were known for their Premillennialism and it was on this point that Caius took issue with them. The Catholic Encyclopedia notes:

> Additional light has been thrown on the character of Caius's dialogue against Proclus by Gwynne's publication of some fragments from the work of Hippolytus "Contra Caium" (Hermathena, VI, p. 397 sq.); from these it seems clear that Caius maintained that the Apocalypse of John was a work of the Gnostic Cerinthus.[58]

---

[55] Origen, de pricipiis, Book II chapter XI.2
[56] Ecclesiastical History 6:20
[57] Catholic Encyclopedia - Caius
[58] Ibid - http://www.newadvent.org/cathen/03144a.htm

Thus Caius' defence against Premillennialism was based on an argument that the Book of Revelation was written by a Gnostic heretic! Actually, Cerinthus was not just any heretic, he was the opponent of John, while the apostle was in Ephesus and was termed by John as "the enemy of the truth". [59] So attributing John's work to his enemy is undoubtedly the worst posthumous insult he could be given.

4th century

Theologians who held to the Premillennial view during the fourth century AD were:

a) Methodius of Olympus
b) Ambrosiaster
c) Apollinaris of Laodicea
d) Nepos
e) Coracion

Theologians who held to the Amillennial view were:

a) Eusebius
b) Dionysius of Alexandria
c) Tyconius
d) John Cassian
e) Gregory of Nyssa

Methodius of Olympus

According to Jerome, [60] Methodius was bishop first of Olympus in Lycia, then of Tyre, and died a martyr at Chalcis in Greece at

---

[59] Irenaeus mentions an anecdote about John, related by Polycarp, where John is said to have been so averse to Cerinthus, that on finding out that Cerinthus was inside a bathhouse, he fled the building, shouting "Let us flee, lest the building fall down; for Cerinthus, the enemy of the truth, is inside!" (Against Heresies 3.3.4) One tradition maintains that John wrote his first two epistles to counter Cerinthus' heresy.
[60] "De Viris Illustribus", 83

the end of the last Roman persecution (AD 311-312). [61] Roman Catholic scholar of patristics, Johannes Quasten, writes that Methodius was "one of the most distinguished adversaries of Origen". [62]

Again we see the sexta-septamillennial idea, when Methodius writes that "in the seventh thousand of years" that "resuming again immortal, we shall celebrate the great feast of true tabernacles in the new and indissoluble creation, the fruits of the earth having been gathered in, and men no longer begetting and begotten, but God resting from the works of creation." [63] After the 1000 years of rest, the eternal kingdom of God would be established.

> ... celebrate with Christ the millennium of rest... Then again from thence I... my body not remaining as it was before, but, after the space of a thousand years, changed from a human and corruptible form into angelic size and beauty, where at last we ... shall pass ... to greater and better things, ascending into the very house of God above the heavens...[64]

Ambrosiaster

Ambrosiaster is the name given to the author of a commentary on Paul's epistles written between AD 366 and 384. [65] J.N.D. Kelly (1909-1997), a prominent academic within the theological faculty of Oxford University writes:

> For Ambrosiaster, however, the collapse of the Roman empire was the sign of the approaching end of the world. Antichrist would then appear, only to be destroyed by

---

[61] Enrico Norelli (b. 1952), who lectures on the history of early Christianity at the University of Geneva.
[62] Johannes Quasten, Patrology (4 Volume Set), vol. 2, pp. 129-137
[63] Banquet of the Ten Virgins (Discourse 9), Chapter 1
http://www.newadvent.org/fathers/062309.htm
[64] Ibid, Chapter 5
[65] https://en.wikipedia.org/wiki/Ambrosiaster

divine power, and Christ would reign over His saints for a thousand years. [66]

Apollinaris of Laodicea

Apollinaris (c. 315-390 AD) was a bishop of Laodicea in Syria, a close friend and ally of Athanasius and best known as a noted opponent of the Arian (nontrinitarian) heresy. While his writings on the subject of Premillennialism have been lost, Basil of Caesarea, [67] Epiphanius [68] and Jerome, in his "Illustrious Lives", [69] all testify to his having been a Chiliast. In another work, Jerome again speaks of Irenaeus as the first, and Apollinaris as the last, of the Greek Millenarians; we therefore conclude that Apollinaris of Laodicea (of the 4th century) is meant and not Apollinaris Claudius (2nd century).[70] And yet again, Jerome says that Apollinaris replied to Dionysius of Alexandria (who we will look at shortly), defending the idea of the Millennium. [71]

Nepos, Coracion and Dionysius

Eusebius provides no exact date for the North African, Nepos, but writes of him:

> … Nepos, a bishop in Egypt… taught that the promises to the holy men in the Divine Scriptures should be understood in a more Jewish manner, and that there would be a certain millennium of bodily luxury upon this earth. As he thought that he could establish his private opinion by the Revelation of John, he wrote a book on this subject, entitled Refutation of Allegorists. [72]

After Nepos' death, his teaching continued to influence many people who read his book. Eusebius writes that in the district of

---

[66] Early Christian Doctrines (1978), p. 479
[67] Epist. CCLXIII, 4
[68] Haeres. LXX, 36
[69] Jerome, Illustrious Lives, 18
[70] In his Commentary in Ezekiel, Bk XI, chap. 36
[71] Prooem. in lib. XVIII. Comm. in Esaiam
[72] Ecclesiastical History, 7:24:1

Arsinoë there was such division, that churches had split over the issue. The Chiliast cause was championed by a man called Coracion, but Dionysius of Alexandria was eventually able to swing him and his followers over to his own contrary viewpoint.[73]

Dionysius (c. 190-265 AD) led the Alexandrian Catechetical School before becoming the Bishop of Alexandria. Much of what we know of him comes from the extensive correspondence he maintained that survived in the works of Eusebius. [74] It's interesting to read how Dionysius managed to quell this Egyptian support of Millennialism. As Nepos' arguments were based on the Apocalypse of John (or what we call the Book of Revelation), Dionysius' strategy was to discredit the book. He first notes that some (possibly a reference to Caius) had earlier tried to attribute its authorship to the Gnostic heretic Cerinthus, who they alleged had used John's name to give credibility to the work.

> Some before us have set aside and rejected the book altogether, criticising it chapter by chapter, and pronouncing it without sense or argument, and maintaining that the title is fraudulent. For they say that it is not the work of John, nor is it a revelation, because it is covered thickly and densely by a veil of obscurity. And they affirm that none of the apostles, and none of the saints, nor any one in the Church is its author, but that Cerinthus, who founded the sect which was called after him the Cerinthian, desiring reputable authority for his fiction, prefixed the name. [75]

But Dionysius admits that he "could not venture to reject the book, as many brethren hold it in high esteem", [76] so firstly he "proved that it is impossible to understand it according to the literal sense". [77] He then proceeded to ascribe it to another John

---

[73] Ibid
[74] https://orthodoxwiki.org/Dionysius_of_Alexandria
[75] Ecclesiastical History 7:25:1-3
[76] Ibid, 7:25:4
[77] Ibid, 7:25:6

- admitting that he was a "holy and inspired man" - but still not the apostle, [78] thereby robbing it of its apostolic authority.

> Therefore that he was called John, and that this book is the work of one John, I do not deny. And I agree also that it is the work of a holy and inspired man. But I cannot readily admit that he was the apostle, the son of Zebedee, the brother of James, by whom the Gospel of John and the Catholic Epistle were written.[79]

So there we have it - an early Premillennialist revival squashed by 'proving' that the apostle John never actually wrote the Book of Revelation!

Eusebius

Eusebius (c. 263-339 AD) was a Greek historian of Christianity, who became the bishop of Caesarea Maritima (in modern Israel) about AD 314. He wrote the first surviving history of the Church as a chronologically-ordered account, from the period of the apostles to his own era. He had the favour of the first Christian Roman Emperor, Constantine, and thus featured prominently at the Council of Nicaea in AD 325.

With persecution and martyrdom of Christians having been halted by Constantine and Christianity having a new-found position of favour in the Roman Empire, it was easy to accept the newer Amillennial position that Satan was bound and a figurative "Millennium" had begun, with Christ's rule over the nations through the Church. The Catholic Encyclopedia acknowledges this, while admitting too that Millenarianism was the doctrine of antiquity (a claim amazingly denied by some others).

> Moreover, the attitude of the Church towards the secular power had undergone a change with closer connection between her and the Roman empire. There is no doubt

---

[78] Ibid, 7:25:7
[79] Ibid, 7:7

that this turn of events did much towards weaning the Christians from the old millenarianism, which during the time of persecution had been the expression of their hopes that Christ would soon reappear and overthrow the foes of His elect. [80]

As a result, Eusebius was clearly hostile to the Premillennial views and seemingly 'blames' Papias for influencing Irenaeus and many others in this regard. And so, Eusebius writes of Papias:

> To these belong his statement that there will be a period of some thousand years after the resurrection of the dead, and that the kingdom of Christ will be set up in material form on this very earth..... But it was due to him that so many of the Church Fathers after him adopted a like opinion, urging in their own support the antiquity of the man; as for instance Irenæus and any one else that may have proclaimed similar views. [81]

Eusebius expanded on the idea that he had received from Dionysius of Alexandria regarding the authorship of the Book of Revelation, by attributing it to a fictitious "John the Elder" (or "John the Presbyter"). As Papias had identified one of his primary sources for his theology as "John the Elder", Eusebius set out to prove that this was a different person to John the Apostle. The argument was based on a claim that there were two tombs in Ephesus for John and thus one must be for "John the Apostle" and the other for "John the Elder". The second argument noted that Papias mentioned John twice in the same sentence and hence he seems to be referring to two different people. Papias had stated the following:

> And if by chance anyone who had been in attendance on the elders arrived, I made enquiries about the words of the elders - what Andrew or Peter had said, or Philip or Thomas or James or John or Matthew or any other of the

---

[80] http://www.newadvent.org/cathen/10307a.htm
[81] Ecclesiastical History 3:39:13

Lord's disciples, and whatever Aristion and John the Elder, the Lord's disciples, were saying." [82]

And so, Eusebius argues as follows:

It is worthwhile observing here that the name John is twice enumerated by him. The first one he mentions in connection with Peter and James and Matthew and the rest of the apostles, clearly meaning the evangelist; but the other John he mentions after an interval, and places him among others outside of the number of the apostles, putting Aristion before him, and he distinctly calls him a presbyter. This shows that the statement of those is true, who say that there were two persons in Asia that bore the same name, and that there were two tombs in Ephesus, each of which, even to the present day, is called John's. It is important to notice this. For it is probable that it was the second, if one is not willing to admit that it was the first that saw the Revelation, which is ascribed by name to John. And Papias, of whom we are now speaking, confesses that he received the words of the apostles from those that followed them, but says that he was himself a hearer of Aristion and the presbyter John. At least he mentions them frequently by name, and gives their traditions in his writings. These things we hope, have not been uselessly adduced by us. [83]

But the majority of church tradition squarely attributed all the Johannine books in the New Testament to a single author, namely the Apostle John. The Catholic Encyclopedia of the early 1900s argued that the distinction made by Eusebius "has no historical basis". [84] It related four main arguments in support of this: [85]

---

[82] Ecclesiastical History 3:39:3-4
[83] Ecclesiastical History 3:39
[84] St. John the Evangelist: The Alleged Presbyter John". Catholic Encyclopedia. NewAdvent.org
[85] https://en.wikipedia.org/wiki/John_the_Presbyter

1) The testimony of Eusebius is disputed, as his statement that Papias "was not himself a hearer and eye-witness of the holy apostles" is contradicted by a passage in Eusebius' Chronicle which expressly calls the Apostle John the teacher of Papias.
2) Eusebius' interpretation might derive from his opposition to Chiliasm and the Book of Revelation. Distinguishing between two persons called John, Eusebius could downgrade that book as the work of the Presbyter instead of the Apostle and also undermine Papias' reputation as a pupil of an Apostle.
3) In the fragment, Papias uses the same words - presbyter (or elder) and disciples of the Lord - both in reference to the Apostles and to the second John. The double occurrence of John is explained by Papias' "peculiar relationship" to John, from which he had learned some things indirectly and others directly.
4) Before Eusebius there exists no statement about a second John in Asia. Especially noteworthy in this context is Irenaeus, himself a pupil of Polycarp. In his book Against Heresies, Irenaeus mentions "Papias, the hearer of John, and a companion of Polycarp", [86] without indicating that this was another John other than "John, the disciple of the Lord, who also had leaned upon His breast [and] did himself publish a Gospel during his residence at Ephesus in Asia". [87]

Inadvertently Eusebius opened up a can of worms, because later authors would subsequently identify some epistles of John - and even his gospel - to the second "John the elder", if at any point these books caused problems with their theology, as Revelation did with Eusebius' theology. But at least Eusebius was inadvertently admitting that the plain teaching of Revelation (in particular chapter 20) was in alignment with the Premillennial view, in contrast to his own view. His best defence therefore is to question the canonicity of the book by removing the apostolic credentials of the author.

---

[86] Against Heresies 5.33
[87] Ibid 3.1

Tyconius

The Donatists lived in the Roman province of Africa and flourished in the 4th and 5th centuries. They were founded by the Berber Christian Donatus Magnus and had beliefs considered heretical by the churches of the Catholic tradition. Tyconius (active 370-390 AD), an African Donatist, was one of the earliest theologians to challenge Premillennialism. A major obstacle that opponents of Premillennialism needed to overcome was that Revelation 20 clearly speaks of two resurrections separated by a 1000-year rule of Christ on earth. And so Tyconius suggested an allegorical interpretation of this passage to escape the implications of the literal text. The 5th century Christian historian Gennadius of Marseille writes that Tyconius did not believe in a literal 1000-year Millennium and viewed the first resurrection of Rev 20:4 as being a spiritual resurrection, which was in reality the rising from baptismal waters. [88] As the Donatists were deemed heretics by the Catholic Church, it is ironic that it was Tyconius' interpretation of Revelation 20 which determined the Catholic Church's future exegesis of this passage.

John Cassian

Possibly due to the growing popularity of asceticism and monastic life, the monk John Cassian (AD 360-435) held a view gaining popularity at the time, which associated a literal earthly kingdom of Christ with carnality.

> Further also that recompense of reward, wherein the Lord promises a hundredfold in this life to those whose renunciation is perfect, and says: And everyone that has left house or brethren or sisters or father or mother or wife or children or lands for My name's sake, shall receive a hundredfold in the present time and shall inherit eternal life, Matthew 19:29 is rightly and truly taken in the same sense without any disturbance of faith. For many taking occasion by this saying, insist with crass intelligence that these things will be given carnally in the millennium, though they must certainly admit that age,

---

[88] De Viris Illustribis ("Of Famous Men") XVIII

which they say will be after the resurrection cannot possibly be understood as present. [89]

Gregory of Nyssa

Gregory of Nyssa (AD 335-394) was a theologian whose writings were influenced by Origen. He says something similar to John Cassian regarding the perceived Chiliast excesses and carnality.

> Do we promise the gluttony of the Millennium? Do we declare that the Jewish animal-sacrifices shall be restored? Do we lower men's hopes again to the Jerusalem below, imagining its rebuilding with stones of a more brilliant material? [90]

5th century

In the 5th century, along with the anti-Semitism that prevailed in the Church at this time, a Millennium which had anything to do with a suggested restoration of Israel was an unpopular idea now. Instead we have the growing support of Replacement Theology, which taught that the church had permanently replaced Israel in the plan of God. While Sulpicius Severus still held to the Premillennial view, notable theologians who advocated the Amillennial view were Jerome and Augustine.

Sulpicius Severus

Sulpicius Severus (AD 363-425), a native of Aquitania in modern-day France, is known for his chronicle of church history, as well as his biography of Martin of Tours. [91] According to the Catholic Encyclopedia:

> Jerome, himself a decided opponent of the millennial ideas, brands Sulpicius Severus as adhering to them, but

---

[89] Conference 24, Chapter 26 http://www.newadvent.org/fathers/350824.htm
[90] Letter 17 http://www.newadvent.org/fathers/291117.htm
[91] https://en.wikipedia.org/wiki/Sulpicius_Severus

in the writings of this author in their present form nothing can be found to support this charge. [92]

Jerome

Jerome (c. 340-420 AD) was an Illyrian Latin Christian theologian, historian, and Doctor of the Church, who is best remembered for the Vulgate, a Latin translation of the scriptures which became the standard Bible used for almost a thousand years. After Augustine, he is the second most prolific writer in ancient Latin Christianity. Jerome rejected Premillennialism because of the Jewishness of the idea [93] and dismissed the idea of a 1000-year kingdom of God on earth as a fable.

> But the saints shall never possess an earthly kingdom, but only a heavenly. Away, then, with the fable about a millennium! [94]

He removed the very foundation of Premillennialism by spiritualizing the Book of Revelation, but hesitated to condemn the doctrine outright as he acknowledged that "many ecclesiastical persons and martyrs affirm the same." [95] So this concession by Jerome, an opponent of Chiliasm, serves to bolster the case of those who attest to the prevalence of the Premillennial doctrine in the early church, by his admission that it was held by 'many', including those he held in high regard.

Augustine

Augustine (AD 354-430), who is often referred to as the 'Father of Amillennialism', popularized the views of Amillennialism in his famous book, De Civitate Dei ('The City of God'). He was the first to identify the Church with the Kingdom of God, believing that

---

[92] Catholic Encyclopedia - Millennium and Millenarianism - http://www.newadvent.org/cathen/10307a.htm

[93] In his Commentary on Isaiah 60.1, 66.20 - Jerome refers contemptuously to the Chiliasts as "our half-Jews who look for a ... future kingdom of 1000 years, in which all nations shall serve Israel".

[94] Commentary on Daniel, ch 7:17-18,

[95] Commentary on Jeremiah 19:10

Christ's Millennial rule was taking place through the offices and sacraments of the Church. To that effect, he wrote:

> The saints reign with Christ during the same thousand years, understood in the same way, that is, of the time of his first coming... Therefore, the church even now is the kingdom of Christ, and the kingdom of heaven. Accordingly, even now His saints reign with Him. [96]

In Augustine's theology, Revelation 20 is to be interpreted as follows:

- ❖ Jesus 'bound' Satan and restrained him from seducing the nations at Calvary.
- ❖ The saints currently reign with Christ in the Millennial kingdom of God, which presently exists.
- ❖ Satan will later be loosed for a 3½ year period, during which time the church will be severely persecuted.
- ❖ After this, Jesus will return. [97]

Augustine's position was not quite the same as many modern Amillennialists, in that he believed that the Millennium, although current, could still be exactly 1000 years in duration. He also held that the Antichrist would rule for a very precise 3½ year period. In "City of God" he pondered whether this rule of the Antichrist was included in the Millennium or if it was a distinct period.

> This last persecution by Antichrist shall last for three years and six months, as we have already said, and as is affirmed both in the book of Revelation and by Daniel the prophet. Though this time is brief, yet not without reason is it questioned whether it is comprehended in the thousand years in which the devil is bound and the saints reign with Christ, or whether this little season should be added over and above to these years. [98]

---

[96] The City of God (Book XX), chapter 9
[97] The City of God
[98] Ibid (Book XX), chapter 13

Augustine suggests that although the 1000 years may be an exact period, it might be a metaphor for the "whole duration of this world". Yet he still alludes to the sexta-septamillennial view (a very "Premillennial" idea) as a possible scenario.

> Now the thousand years may be understood in two ways, so far as occurs to me: either because these things happen in the sixth thousand of years or sixth millennium (the latter part of which is now passing), as if during the sixth day, which is to be followed by a Sabbath which has no evening, the endless rest of the saints, so that, speaking of a part under the name of the whole, he calls the last part of the millennium - the part, that is, which had yet to expire before the end of the world - a thousand years; or he used the thousand years as an equivalent for the whole duration of this world, employing the number of perfection to mark the fullness of time. [99]

Augustine even admits that he originally held the Chiliast (Premillennial) viewpoint and that it still would not be objectionable to him, were it not for the fact that the joy of the saints in this period is seemingly based on what he felt was carnal pleasure.

> And this opinion would not be objectionable, if it were believed that the joys of the saints in that Sabbath shall be spiritual, and consequent on the presence of God; for I myself, too, once held this opinion. But, as they assert that those who then rise again shall enjoy the leisure of immoderate carnal banquets, furnished with an amount of meat and drink such as not only to shock the feeling of the temperate, but even to surpass the measure of credulity itself, such assertions can be believed only by the carnal. They who do believe them are called by the spiritual Chiliasts, which we may literally reproduce by the name Millenarians. [100]

---

[99] Ibid (Book XX), chapter 7
[100] Ibid

The middle ages (5th - 15th century)

Very rapidly Amillennialism became the predominant view in the church. It is commonly held that in AD 431 the Premillennial view was condemned as superstitious at the Council of Ephesus, but it seems that those who allege this, use only secondary sources and that primary sources for that claim are absent. [101] And on that note, C. Cooper wrote:

> From the third to the fifth centuries Chiliasm was vigorously fought and ruthlessly put down, although it was not officially declared a heresy. It was all really rather awkward, because previously nearly everybody of note had been a Chiliast... Between Chiliasm and the charge of heresy stands the canonization of Justin the Martyr and Irenaeus. [102]

But Augustine's theology would dominate the church for over 1000 years. However, it must be noted that although the current Catholic Church still officially endorses Amillennialism, Catholic theologians, who are generally well-schooled in the writings of the Church Fathers, do not dispute the fact that Premillennialism

---

[101] An excellent article entitled "The Phantom Heresy: Did the Council of Ephesus (431) Condemn Chiliasm?" notes: "... when one attempts to start with the various secondary sources that make mention of a condemnation of Chiliasm by the Council of Ephesus and work backwards to the primary source, one is disappointed by what is ultimately found... As can be seen from the reconstruction of the history of the claim that the Council of Ephesus condemned Chiliasm in 431, the original source records no such condemnation, anathema, decree, or declaration. Cohn appears to have misunderstood or mistranslated his source in Gry (or failed to check Labbe directly!) and made the false assertion in his 1957 and 1961 editions of The Pursuit of the Millennium, but, apparently being corrected of his error, removed the statement from his 1970 edition. However, by then it was too late, for already others who had relied on the earlier editions were doomed to repeat the error without consulting either Gry or, more importantly, Labbe. Having been made by able scholars with a far-reaching influence in popular volumes, this error has now reproduced itself at the popular level with no hope for restraint."
https://bible.org/article/phantom-heresy-did-council-ephesus-431-condemn-chiliasm

[102] C. Cooper, "Chiliasm and the Chiliasts," Reformed Theological Review 29 (1970): 12.

was the predominant view in the early church. And so, one Catholic writer admits:

> True, several early Christian writers - notably Papias, Justin Martyr, Irenaeus, Tertullian, Hippolytus, Methodius, Commodianus, and Lactanitus - were premillennialists who believed that Christ's Second Coming would lead to a visible, earthly reign. But the premillennialism they embraced was quite different from that taught by modern dispensationalists. Catholic scholars acknowledge that some of the Fathers were influenced by the Jewish belief in an earthly Messianic kingdom, while others embraced millenarianism as a reaction to the Gnostic antagonism toward the material realm. [103]

Likewise, Catholic theologians generally acknowledge that the Amillennialism they endorse was popularised by Augustine.

> As far as the Millennium goes, we tend to agree with Augustine and, derivatively, with the Amillennialists. The Catholic position has thus historically been "Amillennial"... The Church has rejected the Premillennial position, sometimes called "millenarianism" (see the Catechism of the Catholic Church 676). In the 1940s the Holy Office judged that Premillennialism "cannot safely be taught," though the Church has not dogmatically defined this issue. [104]

Early reformers - 16th century

Amillennialism continued to be the predominant view of the early Magisterial Reformers, who maintained most of Augustine's opinions. The main issue that was scrutinized and re-examined by these Reformers was salvation by grace, not eschatology.

---

[103] Carl E. Olson
http:/catholicculture.org/culture/library/view.cfm?recnum=5788
[104] www.catholic.com

Martin Luther (1483-1546) was an Augustinian monk and claimed Augustine to be the greatest influence on theology after the Bible. So he agreed with Augustine, as he did on most issues, that the beginning of the 1000 years of Rev 20:1-10 was the beginning of the Christian era. He however saw the Millennium starting in AD 73 (which was when the Romans conquered Masada) and ending with the beginning of the papacy of Gregory VII (elected in AD 1073). Notice Luther was not strictly Amillennial because he took the 1000 years literally. Then for some unknown reason, he saw the 666 mark of the beast as additional years that he added to 1073 to come up with the year of Satan's release from his prison in the Abyss in the year 1739. Soon after, he believed Christ would defeat Satan and return. [105]

Like the Lutherans, the Reformed church spawned by Calvin and Zwingli also rejected Premillennialism. In 1553, in the 41st of the Anglican Articles, Thomas Cranmer (1489-1556) described the Millennium as a "fable of Jewish dotage", although this was omitted at a later time in the revision under Elizabeth (1563).

Many Reformed believers today still cling to Amillennialism, while proudly claiming a heritage from Augustinian theology (because this is where Calvin borrowed his deterministic views on predestination). Yet Augustine taught many things which Protestants see as heretical and distinctly Catholic, which they seem to have conveniently overlooked. For instance, besides Amillennialism and predestination, Augustine believed in:

❖ Purgatory and praying for the dead [106]

---

[105] http://library.dts.edu/pages/TL/Specialsc_bibles.shtml

[106] "That there should be some fire even after this life is not incredible, and it can be inquired into and either be discovered or left hidden whether some of the faithful may be saved, some more slowly and some more quickly in the greater or lesser degree in which they loved the good things that perish, through a certain purgatorial fire" (Handbook on Faith, Hope, and Charity 18:69); "We read in the books of the Maccabees [2 Macc. 12:43] that sacrifice was offered for the dead. But even if it were found nowhere in the Old Testament writings, the authority of the Catholic Church which is clear on this point is of no small weight, where in the prayers of the priest poured forth to the Lord God at his altar the commendation of the dead has its place" (The Care to be Had for the Dead 1:3).

- ❖ The perpetual virginity of Mary [107]
- ❖ Transubstantiation i.e. the real presence of Christ in the Eucharist [108]
- ❖ The Mass is a sacrifice [109]
- ❖ The necessity of the Lord's Supper for salvation [110]
- ❖ Baptismal regeneration [111]
- ❖ The necessity of baptism for forgiveness of sin [112]
- ❖ Pedo-baptism (baptism of infants) [113]

---

[107] Mary "remained a virgin in conceiving her Son, a virgin in giving birth to him, a virgin in carrying him, a virgin in nursing him at her breast, always a virgin." (Sermon 186); "Heretics called Antidicomarites are those who contradict the perpetual virginity of Mary and affirm that after Christ was born she was joined as one with her husband" (Heresies 56).

[108] "Christ was carried in his own hands when, referring to his own Body, he said, 'This is my Body' [Matt. 26:26]. For he carried that body in his hands" (Explanations of the Psalms 33:1:10); "That bread which you see on the altar, having been sanctified by the word of God, is the Body of Christ. That chalice, or rather, what is in that chalice, having been sanctified by the word of God, is the Blood of Christ" (Sermons 227); "What you see is the bread and the chalice; that is what your own eyes report to you. But what your faith obliges you to accept is that the bread is the Body of Christ and the chalice is the Blood of Christ." (ibid., 272).

[109] "In the sacrament he is immolated (sacrificed) for the people not only on every Easter Solemnity but on every day; and a man would not be lying if, when asked, he were to reply that Christ is being immolated (sacrificed)." (Letters 98:9).

[110] "[According to] Apostolic Tradition... the Churches of Christ hold inherently that without baptism and participation at the table of the Lord it is impossible for any man to attain either to the kingdom of God or to salvation and life eternal. This is the witness of Scripture too" (Forgiveness and the Just Deserts of Sin, and the Baptism of Infants 1:24:34).

[111] "Baptism washes away all, absolutely all, our sins, whether of deed, word, or thought, whether sins original or added, whether knowingly or unknowingly contracted" (Against Two Letters of the Pelagians 3:3:5).

[112] "There are three ways in which sins are forgiven: in baptism, in prayer, and in the greater humility of penance; yet God does not forgive sins except to the baptized" (Sermons to Catechumens, on the Creed 7:15); "[According to] Apostolic Tradition . . . the Churches of Christ hold inherently that without baptism and participation at the table of the Lord it is impossible for any man to attain either to the kingdom of God or to salvation and life eternal. This is the witness of Scripture too" (Forgiveness and the Just Deserts of Sin, and the Baptism of Infants 1:24:34).

[113] "It is this one Spirit who makes it possible for an infant to be regenerated... when that infant is brought to baptism; and it is through this one Spirit that the infant so presented is reborn." (Letters 98:2); "Likewise, whosoever says that those children who depart out of this life without partaking of that sacrament

- ❖ Unbaptised infants go to hell [114]
- ❖ Praying to saints [115]
- ❖ The value of relics [116]
- ❖ The authority of the Catholic Church [117]
- ❖ Apostolic Succession [118]

---

shall be made alive in Christ, certainly contradicts the apostolic declaration, and condemns the universal Church, in which it is the practice to lose no time and run in haste to administer baptism to infant children, because it is believed, as an indubitable truth, that otherwise they cannot be made alive in Christ." (A Treatise on the Origin of the Human Soul, Addressed to Jerome, Ch 7, #21).

[114] "If you want to be a Catholic, do not believe, do not say, and do not teach that infants carried off by death before they are baptized can attain the remission of original sin." (On the Soul and its Origin Book II). Augustine believed, although these infants are punished in hell, they will suffer only the "mildest condemnation" ("mitissima poena") (Enchiridion ad Laurentium 93 (PL 40, 275); cf. De pecc. mer. 1.16.21 (CSEL 60, 20f). He taught that there is no middle ground between heaven and hell. "There is no middle place left, where you can put babies" (Sermo 294.3 PL 38, 1337).

[115] "A Christian people celebrates together in religious solemnity the memorials of the martyrs, both to encourage their being imitated and so that it can share in their merits and be aided by their prayers" (Against Faustus the Manichean [AD 400]); "At the Lord's table we do not commemorate martyrs in the same way that we do others who rest in peace so as to pray for them, but rather that they may pray for us that we may follow in their footsteps" (Homilies on John 84).

[116] "For even now miracles are wrought in the name of Christ, whether by his sacraments or by the prayers or relics of his saints..." (City of God 22:8).

[117] "We must hold to the Christian religion and to communication in her Church, which is Catholic and which is called Catholic not only by her own members but even by all her enemies. For when heretics or the adherents of schisms talk about her, not among themselves but with strangers, willy-nilly they call her nothing else but Catholic. For they will not be understood unless they distinguish her by this name which the whole world employs in her regard" (The True Religion 7:12). "If you should find someone who does not yet believe in the gospel, what would you [Mani] answer him when he says, 'I do not believe'? Indeed, I would not believe in the gospel myself if the authority of the Catholic Church did not move me to do so" (Against the Letter of Mani Called 'The Foundation' 5:6).

[118] "If the very order of episcopal succession is to be considered, how much more surely, truly, and safely do we number them [the bishops of Rome] from Peter himself, to whom, as to one representing the whole Church, the Lord said, 'Upon this rock I will build my Church, and the gates of hell shall not conquer it.' Peter was succeeded by Linus, Linus by Clement... In this order of succession a Donatist bishop is not to be found" (Letters 53:1:2); "There are many other things which most properly can keep me in [the Catholic Church's] bosom. The unanimity of peoples and nations keeps me here. Her authority, inaugurated in miracles, nourished by hope, augmented by love, and confirmed

- ❖ The sacrament of penance (confession) [119]
- ❖ The Apocrypha is included in the canon of Scripture [120]

With their emphasis on "Sola Scriptura" (Scripture Alone), the Magisterial Reformers would have done well to go back to the 1st century New Testament on certain key issues, rather than only as far back as the 5th century Augustinian theology. As a result, Amillennialism and infant baptism crept into the Reformed and Lutheran theology as part of the Medieval baggage.

---

by her age, keeps me here. The succession of priests, from the very see of the Apostle Peter, to whom the Lord, after his resurrection, gave the charge of feeding his sheep [John 21:15-17], up to the present episcopate, keeps me here. And last, the very name Catholic, which, not without reason, belongs to this Church alone, in the face of so many heretics, so much so that, although all heretics want to be called 'Catholic,' when a stranger inquires where the Catholic Church meets, none of the heretics would dare to point out his own basilica or house" (Against the Letter of Mani Called 'The Foundation' 4:5).

[119] "When you shall have been baptized, keep to a good life in the commandments of God so that you may preserve your baptism to the very end. I do not tell you that you will live here without sin, but they are venial sins which this life is never without. Baptism was instituted for all sins. For light sins, without which we cannot live, prayer was instituted... But do not commit those sins on account of which you would have to be separated from the body of Christ. Perish the thought! For those whom you see doing penance have committed crimes, either adultery or some other enormities. That is why they are doing penance. If their sins were light, daily prayer would suffice to blot them out... In the Church, therefore, there are three ways in which sins are forgiven: in baptisms, in prayer, and in the greater humility of penance" (Sermon to Catechumens on the Creed 7:15, 8:16).

[120] "The whole canon of the Scriptures, however, in which we say that consideration is to be applied, is contained in these books: the five of Moses... and one book of Joshua... one of Judges; one little book which is called Ruth... then the four of Kingdoms, and the two of Paralipomenon... There are also others too, of a different order... such as Job and Tobit and Esther and Judith and the two books of Maccabees, and the two of Esdras... Then there are the Prophets, in which there is one book of the Psalms of David, and three of Solomon... But as to those two books, one of which is entitled Wisdom and the other of which is entitled Ecclesiasticus and which are called `of Solomon' because of a certain similarity to his books, it is held most certainly that they were written by Jesus Sirach. They must, however, be accounted among the prophetic books, because of the authority which is deservedly accredited to them" (Christian Instruction 2:8:13).

18th - 21st century: Postmillennialism

Postmillennialism is the view that the Millennium begins in the present age between the two advents of Christ. It holds that the advance of the Gospel will bring in a glorious age of righteousness, along with social and intellectual progress, before Christ returns. According to the New World Encyclopedia:

> Postmillennialism was first expressed by certain Reformed and Puritan scholars in the early seventeenth century and adhered to by many particularly during the English Civil War.[121]

Postmillennialism became popular in the 18th century. The beginnings of modern Postmillennialism are usually associated with the works of Daniel Whitby, who is considered by many to have systematised the teaching. Whitby (1638-1726) was a priest in the Church of England. Clarence Larkin wrote of Whitby's Postmillennialism:

> … Daniel Whitby… claimed that in reading the promises made to the Jews in the Old Testament of their restoration as a nation, and the re-establishment of the Throne of David, he was led to see that these promises were spiritual and applied to the Church. This view he called a 'New Hypothesis.' … His 'New Hypothesis' was that by the preaching of the Gospel Mohammedanism would be overthrown, the Jews converted, the Papal Church with the Pope (Antichrist) would be destroyed, and there would follow a 1000 years of righteousness and peace known as the Millennium; at the close of which there would be a short period of Apostasy, ending in the return of Christ. [122]

Whitby was known as an Arminian and also had evidence of Unitarian (antitrinitarian) tendencies. The extent of his departure from conventional Trinitarian opinion was not revealed till the posthumous publication in April 1727 of his Last Thoughts, which

---

[121] http://www.newworldencyclopedia.org/entry/Millennialism
[122] Clarence Larkin, "Dispensational Truth", Chapter II

he calls his 'retractation,' and which 'clearly shows his Unitarianism'.[123][124] Interestingly, although Whitby was known as a staunch anti-Calvinist Unitarian, today the Postmillennialism he espoused is commonly associated with Trinitarian Calvinist, specifically Reconstructionist churches.[125]

The Great Awakenings

During the waves of Great Awakenings in the 18th and 19th century, Postmillennialists felt they were justified in believing that the last days would be marked by a great sustained revival. The most famous Postmillennialist of the 18th century was undoubtedly the very influential American Puritan preacher, Jonathan Edwards (1703-1758), who played a critical role in the First Great Awakening.

Figure 5: Jonathan Edwards

Called the father of modern Revivalism, Charles Finney (1792-1875) was an American Presbyterian minister and leader in the Second Great Awakening in the US, who likewise saw the great revivals of his age as vindication for his Postmillennial beliefs.

Postmillennialism was a dominant theological belief among American Protestants who promoted social reform in the 19th

---

[123] "Whitby, Daniel". Dictionary of National Biography (1885-1900)
[124] Letter of 17 July 1727 by Samuel Crellius, in 'Thesaurus Epistolicus La-Crozianus,' quoted in Robert Wallace's Anti-trinitarian Biography, 1850, iii. 471
[125] https://en.wikipedia.org/wiki/Daniel_Whitby

and 20th century. [126] This interest in the social gospel was motivated by the idea that their efforts would expedite the start of the millennial golden age. While the First Great Awakening is considered to be a precursor to the American Revolutionary War, the Second Great Awakening was instrumental in promoting abolitionism, temperance, women's rights and prison reform. [127]

Figure 6: Charles Finney

George M. Fredrickson, a professor of US History at Stanford University from 1984 until 2002, writes:

> The belief that a religious revival and the resulting improvement in human faith and morals would eventually usher in a thousand years of peace and justice antecedent to the Second Coming of Christ was an impetus to the promotion of Progressive reforms, as historians have frequently pointed out. [128]

[126] https://en.wikipedia.org/wiki/Postmillennialism
[127] http://www.newworldencyclopedia.org/entry/Millennialism
[128] "The Coming of the Lord: The Northern Protestant Clergy and the Civil War Crisis," Religion and the American Civil War, (1998), 115

19th century decline

But Fredrickson notes that, while during the Second Great Awakening of the 1830s, some Postmillennialists expected the Millennium to arrive in a few years; by the 1840s the great day had receded to the distant future, and Post-Millennialism became the religious dimension of the broader American middle-class ideology of steady moral and material progress. [129] Then the American Civil War burst the bubble for many Postmillennialists, both in the North and South.

20th century decline and resurgence

But the 20th century did not prove to be any kinder to Postmillennialism. For obvious reasons it almost died out, after the two world wars put a damper on the optimism of this view. The world was not continually improving, as some once thought; in fact the 20th century was one of the most violent periods in human history. According to Associated Press, the century came to a close with a third of the world's 193 nations embroiled in conflict, nearly twice the Cold War level. The National Defence Council Foundation listed 65 conflicts in 1999 alone, up from 60 the year before. [130] During the course of the century, an estimated 191 million people lost their lives directly or indirectly as a result of conflict, and well over half of them were civilians.[131]

Yet amazingly, despite the ongoing conflicts, lawlessness and terrorism all over the world, the last few decades have witnessed a renewed revival of Postmillennialism in the form of Dominion Theologies like Reconstructionism and Kingdom Now theology, which teach that the world is getting progressively better and that worldly dominion is in the process of being passed to Christians.

---

[129] Fredrickson, "The Coming of the Lord" - 115.
[130] Tom Raum, Associated Press - 1 Jan 1999
[131] World Health Organisation

Resurgence of premillennialism

Historic Premillennialism

Despite the overwhelming Amillennialism of the medieval age, according to the New World Encyclopedia, "in spite of its condemnation, there was always an undercurrent of premillennialism during the Medieval period among individuals such as the Italian monk and theologian Joachim of Fiore (c. 1135-1202)".[132] But although, in his Summa Theologica, Thomas Aquinas rebutted Joachim's theories, in The Divine Comedy, Dante placed him in paradise. [133]

The Catholic Church also suppressed radical Premillennial groups such as the Franciscan Spirituals in the 13th and 14th centuries and the Taborites in the 15th century. The latter were a group inspired by the teachings of the Czech reformer, Jan Hus (c.1369-1415), who had been burnt as a heretic in 1415. [134] The theological thinking of the Taborites strongly influenced the foundation and rise of the Unity of the Brethren in 1457, known in English as the Moravian Church.[135] Despite the lingering influence of Augustinian theology on the early reformers, many of the Anabaptists along with the Moravians and Huguenots were Premillennial. Premillennialism was also adopted among some Puritans during the Post-Reformation era. [136]

German Calvinist Johann H. Alsted (1588-1638) advocated Premillennialism, in spite of Calvin's opposition, and his work was adopted by the Anglican, Joseph Mede. [137] Mede (1586-1639) was an English scholar educated at Christ's College, Cambridge, where he became a Fellow from 1613. Although he is mainly remembered as a Biblical scholar, he was also a naturalist, Egyptologist, scholar of the Hebrew language and lecturer of Greek. [138] Mede was the most popular Premillennialist

[132] http://www.newworldencyclopedia.org/entry/Millennialism
[133] https://en.wikipedia.org/wiki/Joachim_of_Fiore
[134] http://www.newworldencyclopedia.org/entry/Millennialism
[135] https://en.wikipedia.org/wiki/Taborite
[136] http://www.theopedia.com/premillennialism
[137] http://www.newworldencyclopedia.org/entry/Millennialism
[138] https://en.wikipedia.org/wiki/Joseph_Mede

of his age, being called the "prince of Millenarians" by Rev. David Brown (co-author of the Jamieson-Fausset-Brown Commentary). Mede's ideas were still somewhat of a mix between Futurism and Historicism; it was only later that Historicism would be dismissed altogether by most Premillennialists.

In the New World the Puritan minister Thomas Shepard (1604-1649). was a Premillennialist; [139] while father and son American Puritan preachers, Increase and Cotton Mather, openly proclaimed a belief in a literal Millennium; with Increase Mather (1639-1723) writing:

> That which presseth me so, as that I cannot gainsay (*deny*) the Chiliastical opinion, is that I take these things for Principles, and no way doubt but that they are demonstrable. (1) That the thousand apocalyptical years are not passed but future. (2) That the coming of Christ to raise the dead and to judge the earth will be within much less than this thousand years. (3) That the conversion of the Jews will not be till this present state of the world is near unto its end. (4) That, after the Jews' conversion there will be a glorious day for the elect upon earth, and that this day shall be a very long continuance.[140]

Other Premillennialists in this 17th to 18th century were the Bohemian Brethren in Germany and the Independents and Fifth Monarchists in England. [141] The 18th century Lutheran Pietist, Johann Albrecht Bengel was instrumental in making Premillennialism more respectable, and he influenced the Moravian leader Count Zinzendorf. [142]

---

[139] http://www.newworldencyclopedia.org/entry/Millennialism
[140] Increase Mather, The Mystery of Israel's Salvation Explained and Applied quoted in Charles Ryrie, The Basis of the Premillennial Faith, (1953), 31-32.
[141] The Fifth Monarchists took their name from the prophecy in Daniel that four monarchies (Babylonia, Persia, Greece and Rome) would precede the kingdom of Christ. The calendar year 1666 (1000 + 666) loomed large on the near horizon and was deemed significant by them. They denounced Cromwell as standing in the way of Christ's Millennial rule.
[142] http://www.newworldencyclopedia.org/entry/Millennialism

While some have claimed that the Wesley brothers were Postmillennialists, the writings of Charles Wesley indicate a precise Premillennial view, including the restoration of the Jews in their land, along with their conversion, and a physical millennial reign of Christ from Jerusalem, all preceded by a period of trial on earth. In a letter in 1754 he writes:

> As for the events themselves it is only proper at this time to mention in general, that they are the conversion of God's ancient people the Jews, their restoration to their own land; the destruction of the Romish Antichrist and of all the other adversaries of Christ's kingdom; the inbringing of the fullness of the Gentiles, and the beginning of that long and blessed Period when peace, righteousness and felicity are to flourish over the whole earth. Then Christ the Lord of hosts shall reign in Mount Sion, and in Jerusalem and before his Elders gloriously... But O! dreadful days that are coming on the earth before the last of the above-mentioned events, I mean before the long and blessed period takes place. There is a long train of dreadful judgments coming on the earth, more dreadful that ever it yet beheld. [143]

And he certainly did not hold the optimistic view of end times common to Postmillennialists, when in a note to Grace Murray he includes the words, "Fear not: in six troubles the Lord hath saved you. A little more suffering, and the end cometh, and the Lord and bridegroom of our souls." [144]

In the first half of the 19th century, Premillennialism was a popular view among English Evangelicals, even within the Anglican church. The English essayist, historian, and politician Thomas Macaulay (1800-1859) observed this and wrote, "Many Christians believe that the Messiah will shortly establish a kingdom on the earth, and visibly reign over all its inhabitants."

---

[143] "Premillennialism in the early writings of Charles Wesley Kenneth" - G. C. Newport - The Journal of the Wesleyan Theological Society, Vol 32, No 1, Spring, 1997
[144] Ibid

[145] Throughout the 19th century, Premillennialism continued to gain wider acceptance in both the US and in Britain, particularly among the Plymouth Brethren, Christadelphians, Church of God, Christian Israelite Church and even in the Mormon sect. The Catholic Apostolic Church, known as Irvingites, who originated in England around 1831 and later spread to Germany and the US, were Premillennial in outlook.

Although Seventh-day Adventists are said to belong to the Premillennial school, not only are they Historicist in outlook, they also teach that the Millennial reign of Christ takes place in heaven instead of on Earth. The similarity to Premillennialism lies only in their placement of the Millennium after the Second Advent.

The Catholic Encyclopedia acknowledges that "Some Catholic theologians of the nineteenth century championed a moderate, modified millenarianism, especially in connection with their explanations of the Apocalypse". [146]

Dispensational Premillennialism

According to an article on Theopedia:

> The greatest development and spread of premillennialism since the early church came in the late 1800's - early 1900's with the rise of US Fundamentalism and Dispensationalism. Starting in the British Isles and spreading to America, premillennialism (in its dispensational form) has become prominent in the Evangelical faith. [147]

---

[145] Quoted by Robert K. Whalen, "Premillennialism" in The Encyclopedia of Millennialism and Millennial Movements, Ed. Richard A. Landes (New York: Routledge, 2000), 331.
[146] http://www.newadvent.org/cathen/10307a.htm - Examples cited are "Pagani (The End of the World, 1856), Schneider (Die chiliastische Doktrin, 1859), Rohling (Erklärung der Apokalypse des hl. Iohannes, 1895; Auf nach Sion, 1901), Rougeyron Chabauty (Avenir de l'Église catholique selon le Plan Divin, 1890)".
[147] http://www.theopedia.com/premillennialism

Dispensation		
1	Noah	Government
2	Moses	Law
3	Aaron	Priesthood
4	Kingly	Manasseh
5	Spirit	Gentile

Table 3: Dispensational covenants of Darby

Figure 7: John Nelson Darby

John Nelson Darby (AD 1800-1882), Anglican founder of the Plymouth Brethren, is regarded by many as the father of modern Dispensationalism. This view is the belief in a system of historical progression, consisting of a series of dispensations, where God deals with man in a particular way during that period or age.

D. L. Moody, Harry Ironsides, along with most of the Baptist and Brethren churches, Bible colleges and seminaries started to recognize Premillennial Dispensationalism as the most accurate view of Biblical prophecy. The dispensational form of Premillennialism was propagated on the academic level with Lewis Sperry Chafer's 8-volume 'Systematic Theology' and on the popular level largely through C.I. Scofield's Reference Bible, which was an annotated, and widely circulated, study Bible first published in 1909. Like John Nelson Darby, Scofield (1843-1921) had been trained as a lawyer and his correspondence Bible study course formed the basis for his Reference Bible. [148]

---

[148] https://en.wikipedia.org/wiki/C._I._Scofield

	Dispensation	Scripture
1	Innocence	Gen 1:28 [149]
2	Conscience	Gen 3:23 [150]
3	Human Government	Gen 8:20 [151]
4	Promise	Gen 12:1 [152]
5	Law	Ex 19:8 [153]
6	Grace	John 1:17 [154]
7	Kingdom	Eph 1:10 [155]

Table 4: Dispensational covenants of Scofield

Figure 8: C.I. Scofield

In the early 1900's Clarence Larkin (1850-1924), an American Baptist pastor and teacher, published many books and useful charts outlying the Premillennial view. Many modern Premillennial prophecy teachers got their basic knowledge directly or indirectly from Larkin and Scofield. In the 20th century, Dispensationalism became the most popular eschatological perspective in the US. The formation of the Jewish state in 1948 further vindicated the belief in the restoration of Israel espoused by Dispensationalists.

---

[149] Gen 1:28 God blessed them and said to them, "Be fruitful and increase in number; fill the earth and subdue it. Rule over the fish in the sea and the birds in the sky and over every living creature that moves on the ground."

[150] Gen 3:23 So the LORD God banished him from the Garden of Eden to work the ground from which he had been taken.

[151] Gen 8:20 Then Noah built an altar to the LORD and, taking some of all the clean animals and clean birds, he sacrificed burnt offerings on it.

[152] Gen 12:1 The LORD had said to Abram, "Go from your country, your people and your father's household to the land I will show you.

[153] Ex 19:8 The people all responded together, "We will do everything the LORD has said." So Moses brought their answer back to the LORD.

[154] John 1:17 For the law was given through Moses; grace and truth came through Jesus Christ.

[155] Eph 1:10 to be put into effect when the times reach their fulfilment--to bring unity to all things in heaven and on earth under Christ.

	Scofield	Larkin
1	Innocence	Edenic
2	Conscience	Antediluvian
3	Human Government	Postdiluvian
4	Promise	Patriarchal
5	Law	Legal
6	Grace	Ecclesiastical
7	Kingdom	Messianic
8		The fullness of times

Table 5: Dispensational covenants of Larkin versus Scofield

Figure 9: Clarence Larkin [156]

Dallas Theological Seminary

According to the New World Encyclopedia, more than 200 Bible institutes and seminaries in the US, most notably Dallas Theological Seminary, have endorsed Dispensationalism. [157] The latter seminary, located in Texas, was founded in 1924 by Dr. Lewis Sperry Chafer (1871-1952), and is renowned for popularizing Dispensationalism. [158] Besides Chafer himself, many recent popular proponents of Dispensationalism were associated with DTS, including:

1) J. Dwight Pentecost (1915-2014) who wrote the excellent prophetic handbook "Things To Come: A Study in Biblical Eschatology", was Distinguished Professor of Bible Exposition, Emeritus, at DTS.

---

[156] Picture from Clarence Larkin Estate website
[157] http://www.newworldencyclopedia.org/entry/Millennialism
[158] https://en.wikipedia.org/wiki/Dallas_Theological_Seminary

Figure 10: Lewis Sperry Chafer

2) John Walvoord (1910-2002), the president of DTS from 1952 to 1986, earned a reputation as one of the most influential Dispensational theologians of the 20th century. [159]

3) Charles Ryrie (1926-2016), who served as professor of systematic theology and dean of doctoral studies at DTS, was a notable advocate of Dispensationalism.[160] Considered one of the most influential theologians of the 20th century [161] he was the editor of The Ryrie Study Bible by Moody Publishers, containing more than 10,000 of his explanatory notes endorsing Dispensationalism. First published in 1978, it has sold more than 2 million copies. [162]

4) Charles Lee Feinberg (1909-1995), an American Biblical scholar and professor of Semitics and Old Testament, was an authority on the Jewish history, languages and customs of the Old Testament and also on Bible prophecy. He joined the faculty of DTS as professor of Old Testament in 1934. [163] Feinberg authored many books promoting classic Dispensationalism.

[159] https://en.wikipedia.org/wiki/John_Walvoord
[160] https://en.wikipedia.org/wiki/Charles_Caldwell_Ryrie
[161] Ellwell, Walter (1993). Handbook of Evangelical Theologians. Baker.
[162] http://moodypublishers.com/pub_authorDetail.aspx?id=41798&aid=511 Charles C Ryrie
[163] https://en.wikipedia.org/wiki/Charles_L._Feinberg

5) Hal Lindsey (b. 1929) is a popular Dispensationalist author who graduated from DTS with a Master of Theology degree, majoring in the New Testament and early Greek literature.[164]

	Ryrie	Darby
1	Paradisaical state	
2	Noah	Noah (Government)
3	Abraham	
4	Israel - under Law	Moses (Law)
5	Israel - under priests	Aaron (Priesthood)
6	Israel - under kings	Kingly (Manasseh)
7	Gentiles	Spirit (Gentiles)
8	Spirit	
9	Millennium	

Table 6: Dispensational covenants of Ryrie versus Darby

Figure 11: Charles Ryrie

Pentecostal and Charismatics

From only one million in AD 1900, Pentecostals and Charismatics have mushroomed to 524 million affiliated (with unaffiliated believers, 602 million). As Pentecostals generally accept the Dispensational Premillennialism view, the rapid expansion of the Pentecostal movement in the 20th and 21st centuries, has further advanced Premillennialism into the churches of Asia, Africa and South America.

---

[164] https://en.wikipedia.org/wiki/Hal_Lindsey

During the 1970s, the Pre-Tribulation rapture viewpoint, held by many Dispensational Premillennialists, was popularized through the movie "A Thief in the Night" released in 1972, which has reportedly been seen by over 300 million people around the world. [165] Dispensationalism became popular in wider circles, in part due to the books of Hal Lindsey, in particular "The Late Great Planet Earth", which has reportedly sold between 15 and 35 million copies. The book compared end-time prophecies with then-current events, attempting to broadly predict future scenarios leading up to the Pre-Tribulation rapture and the subsequent Second Coming of Jesus to establish his Millennial reign.

More recently, the 'Left Behind' series of 17 best-selling novels by Tim Lahaye and Jerry Jenkins further popularised the viewpoint. First published 1995-2007, many books in the series have been on the New York Times best-seller list, with some even topping the list. Total sales for the series surpassed 65 million copies. To date, the series has been adapted into 4 films.

---

[165] http://christianitytoday.com/ct/2012/marchweb-only/originalleftbehind.html

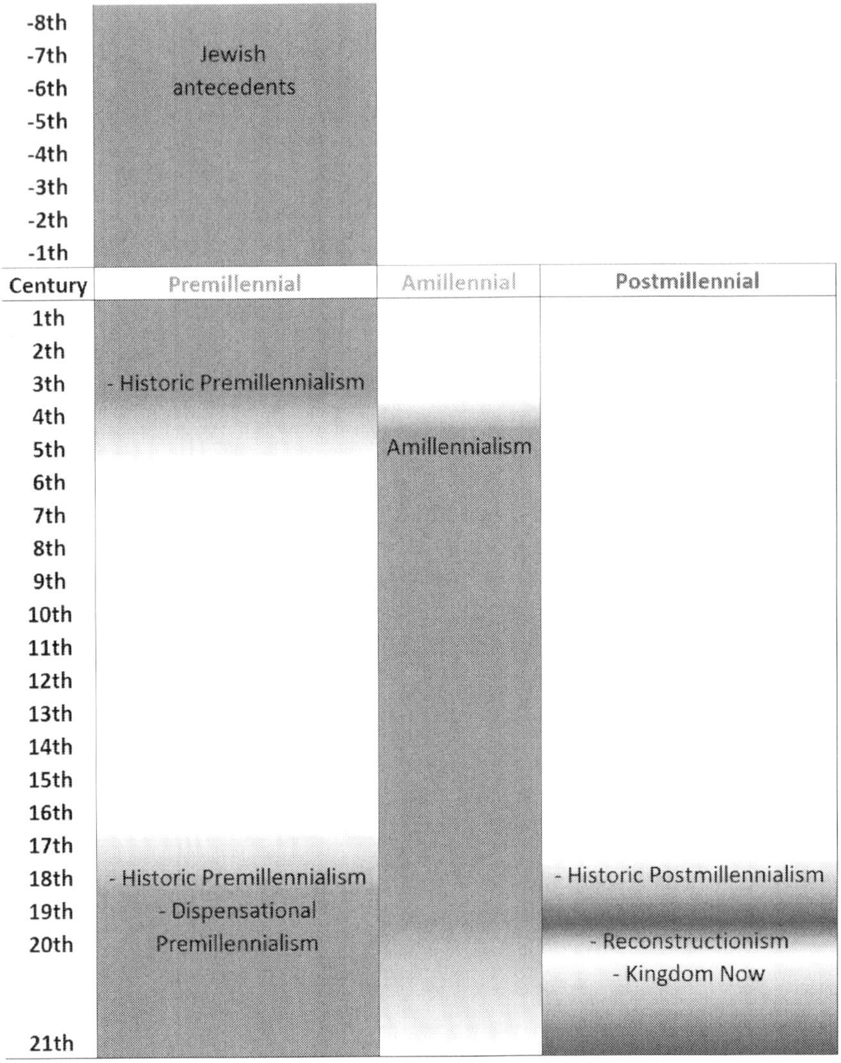

Century	Premillennial	Amillennial	Postmillennial
-8th	Jewish antecedents		
-7th			
-6th			
-5th			
-4th			
-3th			
-2th			
-1th			
1th			
2th			
3th	- Historic Premillennialism		
4th			
5th		Amillennialism	
6th			
7th			
8th			
9th			
10th			
11th			
12th			
13th			
14th			
15th			
16th			
17th			
18th	- Historic Premillennialism		- Historic Postmillennialism
19th	- Dispensational		
20th	Premillennialism		- Reconstructionism - Kingdom Now
21th			

Figure 12: History of Millennial views

CHAPTER 3: AMILLENNIALISM

In Latin, the prefix 'a' indicates a negative or 'no'. Thus the term "Amillennialism" (no-millennium) which appears to have been coined in the 1930s, is probably misleading, as it would seem to indicate that proponents do not believe in a Millennium of any sorts. In reality they do believe in a figurative Millennium, but hold that it is not a literal 1000-year period. Accordingly, the 1000 years in Revelation 20 is viewed as simply a number symbolic of "a very long time". Amillennialists generally believe that:

- ❖ The millennial age has already begun, being identical with the Church age.
- ❖ Christ's reign during the Millennium is spiritual in nature.
- ❖ The binding of Satan has already occurred at the cross, so that "he might not deceive the nations any longer" (Rev 20:3) by preventing the spread of the gospel.
- ❖ Israel has been permanently set aside and replaced for all time and God's current plan of salvation involves only the Church (Replacement Theology).
- ❖ The current millennial age is one of both the triumph of the spiritual kingdom of God and the corresponding rise of evil in opposition.
- ❖ At the end of the Church Age, after a brief apostasy when Satan is released, Christ will return in final judgment and establish a permanent reign in the new heaven and new earth.

Amillennialism is the official view of Catholics, but is also common in the Eastern Orthodox Church and among some Protestant denominations like the Lutheran, Reformed and Anglican churches. It started to decline in Protestant circles after the rise of Postmillennialism in the 18th century and the resurgence of Premillennialism in the 19th century, regaining some prominence after World War II. [166]

---

[166] http://www.newworldencyclopedia.org/entry/Amillennialism

Literal or allegorical?

When Augustine wrote in the 5th century, 1000 years had not yet passed since the time of Christ, so he conceded that the millennial period might be literal, although he said that it could also be figurative. It was not until AD 1000 that the literal 1000 years of Augustine had to be abandoned (for obvious reasons). Gennadius writes that early Amillennialist Tyconius:

> ... explained the whole Apocalypse of John, understanding all of it in a spiritual sense, nothing carnally... He denied the idea of a kingdom of the righteous on earth lasting a thousand years after the resurrection. Nor did he admit two future resurrections of the dead in the flesh, one of the good and one of the bad, but only one of all... He showed the distinction of the resurrection really to be that we must believe that there is a revelation of the righteous now in this world, when those justified by faith rise by baptism from the death of sin to the reward of the eternal life, and the second [resurrection] to be the general one of all flesh.[167]

So it is clear that Amillennialists see prophecy and Revelation in more of a symbolic light. The Kingdom of God is strictly spiritual and heavenly. At the heart of the Premillennial versus Amillennial / Postmillennial debate is the question whether to interpret the Bible literally or allegorically, so let's address that issue first.

Origen called the belief in an earthly Millennium "superficial", a result of "refusing the labour of thinking" and of being a literalist. [168] Eusebius criticised Papias as "a man of very little intelligence" because he had interpreted apostolic accounts literally, "not realizing that they had spoken mystically and symbolically". [169]

---

[167] De Viris Illustribis ("Of Famous Men") XVIII

[168] Origen, de pricipiis, Book II chapter XI.2

[169] Papias is often criticized because of certain fantastic elements in his description of the Millennium, which may also have contributed to the low opinion Eusebius held of him.

Papias… says that there will be a Millennium after the resurrections of the dead, when the kingdom of Christ will be set up in material form on this earth. I suppose that he got these notions by a perverse reading of the apostolic accounts, not realizing that they had spoken mystically and symbolically. For he was a man of very little intelligence, as is clear from his books. [170]

Thomas Ice observes that, "Historically, allegorical interpreters have commonly looked down on literal interpreters as stupid or slow since they are unable to ascend to the deeper, spiritual insights of the allegorical approach". [171] And while critic Robert K. Whalen has stated that modern Premillennialism is "criticized roundly for naïve scholarship which confuses the poetic and inspirational prose of prophecy with fortune telling", Premillennialists "retort that they merely follow the Word of God, regardless of ridicule." [172]

We saw earlier that in Egypt, Nepos had taught "that there would be a certain millennium of bodily luxury upon this earth", by using the Revelation of John, and wrote a book on the subject, entitled Refutation of Allegorists. [173] So clearly, Nepos linked Amillennialism with an allegorical approach to interpretation. Dionysius, the opponent of Nepos, said of the Book of Revelation "that it is impossible to understand it according to the literal sense" [174] (clearly because chapter 20 teaches Premillennialism). He based his arguments against Chiliasts on the claim that the apostle John never wrote the book and that - as he personally never understood the book - it must be allegorical.

But I suppose that it is beyond my comprehension, and that there is a certain concealed and more wonderful

---

[170] Ecclesiastical History 3:39:13
[171] Literal Vs. Allegorical Interpretation - Tom's Perspectives - by Thomas Ice www.pre-trib.org/data/pdf/Ice-**LiteralvsAllegorical**.pdf
[172] Robert K. Whalen, "Premillennialism" in The Encyclopedia of Millennialism and Millennial Movements, (2000), 332.
[173] Ecclesiastical History, 7:24:1
[174] Ibid, 7:25:6

meaning in every part. For if I do not understand I suspect that a deeper sense lies beneath the words. I do not measure and judge them by my own reason, but leaving the more to faith I regard them as too high for me to grasp. And I do not reject what I cannot comprehend, but rather wonder because I do not understand it.[175]

In some of their more candid moments, even opponents of Premillennialism admit that if a literal interpretation is adapted, that it does indeed lead to Premillennial theology. Amillennialist, Floyd Hamilton, said the following:

Now we must frankly admit that a literal interpretation of the Old Testament prophecies gives us just such a picture of an earthly reign of the Messiah as the Premillennialist pictures. That was the kind of Messianic kingdom that the Jews of the time of Christ were looking for, on the basis of a literal interpretation of the Old Testament promises.[176]

And in the same vein the well-known Amillennial writer, Oswald Allis, admitted that, "the Old Testament prophecies if literally interpreted cannot be regarded as having been yet fulfilled or as being capable of fulfilment in this present age." [177]

Premillennialism is literally taught in Revelation 20. In fact, that is why we have the term "Pre---millennial"; because it speaks of the return of Christ and judgement as before (pre) the 1000 years (Millennium). The passage was so problematic for opponents of Premillennialism that Cauis had to attribute the authorship of Revelation to a heretic; Dionysius and Eusebius had to demote its author to a fictitious non-apostle called John; while Tyconius, Jerome and Augustine had to allegorise it's plain meaning - arriving at an interpretation which contradicted the literal sense. Irenaeus criticises the practice of allegorizing away the prophecies which speak of a literal earthly Millennium.

---

[175] Ibid, 7:25:4-5
[176] "The basis of Millennial faith" pp 38-39
[177] "Prophecy and the Church" pp 238

If, however, any shall endeavour to allegorize [prophecies] of this kind, they shall not be found consistent with themselves in all points, and shall be confuted (*proved to be wrong*) by the teaching of the very expressions [in question]... "And they shall build houses, and shall inhabit them themselves: and plant vineyards, and eat of them themselves." For all these and other words were unquestionably spoken in reference to the resurrection of the just, which takes place after the coming of Antichrist, and the destruction of all nations under his rule; in [the times of] which [resurrection] the righteous shall reign in the earth, waxing stronger by the sight of the Lord... [178]

Amillennialists and Postmillennialists are forced to adapt an allegorical method of interpreting prophecy in order to 'get around' the literal teaching of the Bible. Since the Bible literally teaches only a single viewpoint on this issue, surely Premillennialism is the logical prophetic view to hold?

	Literal	Allegorical
1000 (years) =	1000	Very long time
2 (resurrections) =	2 resurrections	1 resurrection
Jerusalem =	Jerusalem	Anywhere you like
On earth =	On earth	In heaven
Israel =	Israel	The Church
Jesus ruling =	Jesus ruling	Christians ruling
Terrible times in last days =	Terrible times in the last days	Golden age of Christian domination in the last days
1+ 1 =	2	Pick any number (besides 2)
Black =	Black	White, or maybe blue or red

Table 7: Literal or allegorical?

---

[178] Against Heresies 5.35.1

Kenneth Kantzer (1917-2002), Professor of Biblical and Systematic Theology and Academic Dean of Trinity Evangelical Divinity School from 1960-1978 cautioned:

> The only way to appropriate Biblical authority and to refrain from reducing the Bible to a book of mere suggestions and optional opinions is to understand the Bible in the plain, normal sense intended by the authors.[179]

Professor Bernard Ramm says that the literal method is "the only sane and safe check on the imaginations of man." [180] Otherwise you potentially have as many interpretations as you have interpreters.

Influence of Greek philosophy on Biblical interpretation:

Plato (c. 428-427 BC) was a Greek philosopher and the founder of the Academy in Athens, the first institution of higher learning in the Western world. Along with his teacher, Socrates, and his most famous student, Aristotle, Plato laid the very foundations of Western philosophy and is widely considered the most pivotal figure in its development. [181]

Platonism regarded the universe as the work of a Supreme Spirit, in which man possesses a 'spark of divinity' that would ultimately purify him and elevate him to a higher life. Virtue would accelerate and sin retard his upward progress.

The Platonic Jews of Egypt, in the 1st century, in imitation of the heathen Greeks, began to interpret the Old Testament allegorically. The Alexandrian Jew, Philo was distinguished among those who practiced this method.

One of the earliest streams of heresy that plagued the early church was the different flavours of Gnosticism. The Gnostics

---

[179] http://bereaninternetministry.org/Papers/Amillennialism%20 (Replacement%20Theology).doc
[180] The interpretation of the Bible
[181] https://en.wikipedia.org/wiki/Plato

derived their convoluted beliefs by borrowing from everything including Greek philosophy, paganism, the occult, Judaism and Christianity. Like Plato, many Gnostics presented a distinction between the highest, unknowable "alien God" and the demiurgic "creator" of the material world. In line with Greek philosophy, they rejected any idea of the resurrection of the body.

But Plato was to influence some Christian thought as well, especially those who use the allegorical approach of interpreting the Bible, and thus indirectly the Amillennial viewpoint. J. Dwight Pentecost quite aptly stated, "The allegorical method was not born, out of the study of the Scriptures, but rather out of the desire to unite Greek philosophy and the Word of God." [182]

Figure 13: The influence of Greek philosophy on
the allegorical and hence Amillennial approach

The school of Alexandria

Founded in about AD 180 by Pantaenus (a former Stoic philosopher), the theological School of Alexandria in Egypt was the first-known organized Christian institution of higher learning. Under such leaders as Clement (c. 150-215) and Origen (c. 185-254), the school fostered the restoration of relations between Christianity and Greek culture, including the Platonic philosophical tradition. It became a leading centre of the allegorical approach to interpretation of Scripture, with its devotees finding allegory in the majority of Scripture.

Although we have no record of a formal school like the one at Alexandria, the 'school' of Antioch in Syria represented a group of theologians sharing similar doctrinal characteristics. Unlike their Alexandrian counterparts, beginning with Lucian in the 3rd

---

[182] 'Things to come' - Dwight Pentecost

century, they rejected the allegorical approach in favour of a more literal interpretation of the Bible.

Clement of Alexandria

The influence of Greek philosophy on Biblical interpretation was seen mainly in the Alexandrian School. Pantaenus was succeeded as head of the school by Clement, who not only held that all Scripture must be allegorically understood, but even believed in the divine origin of Greek philosophy! In his 'Stromateis' he postulated that Christianity was really the 'true philosophy' and that while the Greeks had grasped some rudiments of truth, their knowledge was limited in contrast to the greater light that Christians possessed. According to Clement, Greek thought was in reality 'stolen' from the Old Testament. But he deduced that while Greek philosophy was inferior to Christianity's perfection, it was still extremely useful when used as groundwork for studying Christian doctrines. [183]

Origen

Origen succeeded Clement as head of the Alexandrian school at the young age of 18, and embraced a formal theory of interpretation based on the allegorical method of Philo, who in turn had borrowed this technique from Greek philosophy. Despite being a brilliant man, Origen held many heretical views, including a radical universalism which anticipated the ultimate salvation of all human beings, fallen angels and possibly even Satan.

He had many other distorted teachings far removed from Biblical Christianity, but seemingly derived from Greek philosophy. For instance, he borrowed from Greek philosophy the belief in the pre-existence of souls, surmising that there were actually two creation accounts in Genesis. The first creation consisted of spirits without bodies, but some strayed away and fell. Then followed the "second creation", of the material universe, in which some of the fallen souls became demons, while others were

---

[183] S. Lilla, Clement of Alexandria (1971), 11 - cf. Strom. 1.28.3, 1.80.5,6, and 1.28.4 for example.

made human. The reason humans were given human bodies and experience suffering is owing to our sin in the pre-existent state. Origen claimed all this was derived from the Bible, while it is actually remarkably similar to Plato's concept of souls which existed in a state of perfection, prior to taking on mortal bodies on earth. Origen also rejected the idea of a physical resurrection, this again due to the influence of Greek philosophers, who believed in the immortality of the soul only (not the body). Then he went so far as to completely spiritualize the Second Coming by stating that "Christ's return signifies his disclosure of himself and his deity to all humanity in such a way that all might partake of his glory to the degree that each individual's actions warrant".[184]

Augustine

Like Origen, Augustine had been schooled in Greek philosophy. So, this famous Bishop of Hippo also used an allegorical interpretation method, believing that Scripture had been deliberately veiled by the Lord in order to exercise those who were seeking him. Augustine popularized the views of Amillennialism, which he derived using an allegorical interpretation of prophecy. In so doing he influenced over eleven centuries of thought on the issue. There are at least three reasons why Augustine changed from a Premillennial to an Amillennial view:

1. The seeming prosperity of the church at that time.
2. The carnal views of some Premillennialists.
3. The influence of Greek philosophy (the Stanford Encyclopedia of Philosophy characterizes Augustine as a Neoplatonist [185]).

Neither Origen nor Augustine escaped the influence of Greek philosophy, despite the warning by the apostle Paul.

---

[184] Commentary on Matthew, 12.30

[185] Many of the Fathers were influenced by the Platonism and Stoicism that every educated person became acquainted with in the ancient world. Augustine was particularly influenced by Platonism, in the version modern scholars call "Neo-Platonism", i.e., the philosophy of Plotinus. – https://plato.stanford.edu/entries/medieval-political

See to it that no one takes you captive through hollow and deceptive philosophy, which depends on human tradition and the basic principles of this world rather than on Christ. (Col 2:8)

Tertullian

On the other hand, Tertullian perceptively identified Greek philosophy as "the parent of heresies" and the root cause of Gnosticism - Platonic philosophy saw the material world (flesh) as evil and believed only in a spiritual resurrection, which were the chief tenets of the Gnosticism that Tertullian opposed.

> These are "the doctrines" of men and "of demons" produced for itching ears of the spirit of this world's wisdom: this the Lord called "foolishness," and "chose the foolish things of the world" to confound even philosophy itself. For philosophy is the material of the world's wisdom, the rash interpreter of the nature and the dispensation of God. Indeed, heresies are themselves instigated by philosophy. From this source came the Aeons, and I know not what infinite forms, and the trinity of man in the system of Valentinus, who was of Plato's school. From the same source came Marcion's better god, with all his tranquillity; he came of the Stoics. Then, again, the opinion that the soul dies is held by the Epicureans; while the denial of the restoration of the body is taken from the aggregate school of all the philosophers... The same subject-matter is discussed over and over again by the heretics and the philosophers; the same arguments are involved. [186]

Tertullian then recalls Paul's warning against Greek philosophy (bracketed italicized insertions are mine, for the sake of clarity).

> From all these, when the apostle would restrain us, he expressly names philosophy as that which he would have us be on our guard against. Writing to the Colossians, he

---

[186] The Prescription against Heretics

says, "See that no one beguile (*deceive*) you through philosophy and vain deceit, after the tradition of men, and contrary to the wisdom of the Holy Ghost." He had been at Athens, and had in his interviews (with its philosophers) become acquainted with that human wisdom which pretends to know the truth, whilst it only corrupts it, and is itself divided into its own manifold heresies, by the variety of its mutually repugnant sects. What indeed has Athens to do with Jerusalem? What concord (*agreement*) is there between the Academy and the Church? what between heretics and Christians? Our instruction comes from "the porch of Solomon," who had himself taught that "the Lord should be sought in simplicity of heart." Away with all attempts to produce a mottled (*blotched*) Christianity of Stoic, Platonic, and dialectic (*the practice of arriving at the truth by the exchange of logical arguments*) composition! We want no curious disputation (*the presentation of a proposition in a public debate and the opposition to it*) after possessing Christ Jesus, no inquisition (*a rigorous interrogation*) after enjoying the gospel! With our faith, we desire no further belief. For this is our palmary (*principal*) faith, that there is nothing which we ought to believe besides.[187]

The reformation

The Reformation brought about a return to the literal approach in the interpretation of Scripture. Martin Luther noted:

> I have observed this, that all heresies and errors have originated, not from the simple words of Scripture, as is so universally accepted, but from neglecting the simple words of Scripture, and from the affection of purely subjective... tropes and inferences. [188]

---

[187] Ibid
[188] F. W. Farrar, History of Interpretation

The medieval period (5th-15th centuries) had been characterised by the belief that all Scripture had a fourfold sense: literal, typological, moral (tropological) and anagogical. [189] Following Origen, they generally regarded the literal sense as unimportant and unedifying. The argument of the allegorical translators was that theirs was the 'spiritual' way of translating. To which William Tyndale (c. 1494-1536) responded, "God is a Spirit, and all his words are spiritual. His literal sense is spiritual..." [190] This famous translator of the Bible into English, clearly favoured the literal method of interpreting, stating the following on the matter:

> The greatest cause of which captivity and the decay of the faith, and this blindness wherein we now are, sprang first of allegories. For Origen and the doctors of his time drew all the Scripture unto allegories; whose example that came after followed so long, till they at last forgot the order and process of the text, supposing that the Scripture served but to feign allegories upon; make descant upon plain song. [191]

Tyndale added somewhat disparagingly, "Then came our sophisters (an unsound reasoner) with their anagogical and 'chopological' sense, and with an antitheme of half an inch, out of which some of them drew a thread nine days long." [192] British-born Canadian Christian theologian, James I. Packer (b. 1926), notes that:

> Fanciful spiritualizing, so far from yielding God's meaning, actually obscured it. The literal sense is itself the spiritual sense, coming from God and leading to Him.[193]

We have earlier noted that Amillennialism continued to have a lingering hold on the early Magisterial Reformers, due to their uncritical acceptance of anything Augustinian. However, to their

---

[189] https://en.wikipedia.org/wiki/Allegory_in_the_Middle_Ages
[190] Tyndale, Works (Parker Society), I. 304
[191] Daniell, Tyndale's New Testament, xvi.
[192] Ibid
[193] 'Fundamentalism' and the Word of God (1958), pp. 101-114

PAGE 72

credit, the Reformers did reject the allegorical interpretation method in favour of a more literal approach, and also placed strong emphasis on the authority of the Bible over tradition. In so doing they set the stage for the future return to Premillennialism - by a future generation who applied the principle of Sola Scriptura more consistently than they did.

RULES FOR INTERPRETING SCRIPTURE

All the Old Testament prophecies concerning the First Coming of Jesus were fulfilled literally. Matthew makes frequent references to prophecies that Jesus fulfilled. No mention is made of an allegorical prophecy which was fulfilled. The Jews at the time of Christ saw no other option but literal fulfilment of the Messianic prophecies. When Herod called the chief priests and teachers of the law in order to locate the whereabouts of the Jewish king, they in unison told him that the Messiah would be born in Bethlehem (in literal fulfilment of Micah 5:2 [194]). When interpreting Scripture, we need to remember:

a) The meaning of a passage is the sense evident to any reader who allows the words their ordinary meanings and who expects the grammar and syntax to shape and combine these meanings in a normal fashion.

b) Don't spiritualize or allegorize a passage in an attempt to solve some doctrinal difficulty it presents you. If the Bible and your doctrine clash, change your doctrine - not the meaning of the text! Amillennialists use the technique of allegorisation to overcome 'problems' in Revelation 20. They spiritualize the 'first resurrection' and equate it with being 'born again'. They then relocate the Millennium's earthly rule to heaven and make the '1000 years' a synonym for 'a very long time'. Irenaeus criticizes this practice in the treatment of Rev 20, writing:

---

[194] Micah 5:2 (NASB) "But as for you, Bethlehem Ephrathah, Too little to be among the clans of Judah, From you One will go forth for Me to be ruler in Israel. His goings forth are from long ago, From the days of eternity."

For as it is God truly who raises up man, so also does man truly rise from the dead, and not allegorically, as I have shown repeatedly. And as he rises actually, so also shall he be actually disciplined beforehand for incorruption, and shall go forwards and flourish in the times of the kingdom, in order that he may be capable of receiving the glory of the Father.[195]

c) If the literal sense makes sense, don't feel obliged to seek a deeper or figurative meaning. For example, a phrase like "the trees...shall clap their hands" (Isaiah 55:12) is obviously metaphoric. However, a 1000-year Millennium with Jesus ruling on earth makes sense in the literal, so there is no need to seek another meaning. As Anglican priest and theologian, Richard Hooker (1554-1600), well noted:

I hold as an infallible rule in the exposition of sacred Scriptures, that when a literal interpretation makes sense, the furthest from the letter is usually the worst. There is nothing more dangerous than this deluding art which changes the meaning of words as alchemy does, or attempts to do, the substance of metals, making of it anything it wishes, and in the end bringing all truth to nothing". [196]

Figurative speech

Now it is true that at times the Bible may use figures of speech. A figure of speech is an expression implying an idea other than what is actually stated. Examples of figurative language are:

❖ Metaphors - A metaphor speaks of an equivalence when there is no more than a resemblance e.g. in Psalm 18:2 [197] no less than 5 metaphors occur in a single verse.

---

[195] Against Heresies 5.35.2
[196] Laws of Ecclesiastical Polity, V. lix. 2
[197] The LORD is my rock, my fortress and my deliverer; my God is my rock, in whom I take refuge. He is my shield and the horn of my salvation, my strong-hold.

God is not literally a fortress, rock, horn, shield or stronghold; He merely, in some ways, resembles them.

❖ Symbolism - Clear examples of symbolism are the mysterious women in Revelation 12 and 17.
❖ Parables - a parable uses a natural truth that we can relate to, to teach a spiritual truth.

However, if figurative language is used, then:

❖ Interpret Scripture with other Scripture.
❖ Be consistent in the interpretation.
❖ The literal sense remains valid and the primary sense. Never seek a second sense that contradicts the literal sense or primary sense, as Amillennialists attempt to do with Revelation 20.

Typology versus allegory

It is also true that, if a passage is clearly literal and employs no figurative language, that the literal meaning of the text might not always be the only possible application. At times, there may well be a secondary application, the best example being the types in the Old Testament and the corresponding antitypes in the New Testament.

Some criticise the use of typology by Premillennialists claiming that, as supposed avid literalists they are contradicting themselves, by utilising what appears to be an 'allegorical' approach, while criticising Origen for doing the same. But there is a major distinction between the use of typology and the way that Origen interpreted Scripture. When using typology:

> … Jonah, swallowed by a sea-monster and regurgitated, could be seen as a 'type' of Jesus, crucified, buried and resurrected. Jesus is the 'anti-type' of Jonah, the fulfilment of his promise. Though the story of Jonah is primarily important as a 'foreshadowing of that of Jesus, the assumption behind traditionally typological thinking is that the first episode did actually happen: what is 'figurative' or 'spiritual' is the way it is connected to the

second. Thus typology is rooted in the literal event, which then is transformed by association. [198]

By contrast, Origen actually denied the literal sense, replacing it altogether with a second sense. He sought to translate the concrete (the literal, historical actuality) into the abstract.

> Hence in discussing Genesis 19, he effectively denied the literal sense - Lot having sexual relations with his daughters - as invalid, seeing Lot as the rational human mind, his wife as the flesh, and his daughters as the sin of pride. He then saw all three as examples of the inadequacy of the Old Testament law - still bound to sin and rebellion - compared with the eternal, transcendent spirit of the New. [199]

We have already noted how Origen's system of interpretation led not only into strange beliefs, but clearly heretical ones like universalism and the pre-existence of souls. Former professor of Old Testament literature at Princeton Theological Seminary, Rev. Dr. Charles T. Fritsch (1913-89) noted that with the allegorical method of translating.

> ... the literal and historical sense of Scripture is completely ignored, and every word and event is made an allegory of some kind either to escape theological difficulties or to maintain certain peculiar religious views...[200]

Baptist theologian and apologist Bernard Ramm (1916-1992) summed up the weakness of the allegorical method of interpretation by saying:

> ... to state that the principle meaning of the Bible is a second-sense meaning, and that the principal method of

---

[198] http://www.tyndale.org/tsj02/coupe.html
[199] William W Klein, Craig L Blomberg and Robert L Hubbard, Introduction to Biblical Interpretation (1993), p 34. Also Duncan S Ferguson, Biblical Hermeneutics: an Introduction, (1986).
[200] Biblical Typology

interpretation is 'spiritualizing,' is to open the door to almost uncontrolled speculation and imagination. [201]

Ramm further writes:

> The true great curse of the allegorical method is that it obscures the true meaning of the Word of God. There are no controls on the imagination of the interpreter, so the Bible becomes putty in the hands of each interpreter. As a result, different doctrinal systems could well arise within the sanction of the allegorical method, yet no way exists for breaking the deadlock within the allegorical system. The only retreat is to the literal meaning of the Bible. [202]

Perhaps William Tyndale best summarised the issue by stating:

> You should understand, therefore, that Scripture has only one sense, which is the literal sense. And that literal sense is the root and ground of all, and the anchor that never fails; and if you cling to it, you can never go into error. However, the Scripture does at times use proverbs, similitudes, riddles or allegories, as does all other speech; but that which the proverb, similitude, riddle or allegory signifies; is over the literal sense, which you must seek out diligently. [203]

---

[201] Bernard Ramm, Protestant Biblical Interpretation pg 65
[202] Ibid pg 30
[203] William Tyndale, Doctrinal Treatises, vol. I (1848), 303

CHAPTER 4: THE RESTORATION OF ISRAEL

> *Rom 11:26-27 And so all Israel will be saved,*
> *as it is written: "The deliverer will come from*
> *Zion; he will turn godlessness away from*
> *Jacob. And this is my covenant with them*
> *when I take away their sins."*

Christians who hold to the Futurist Premillennial view see the declaration of the State of Israel in 1948, along with the retaking of the Old City of Jerusalem in the 1967 Six-Day War, as significant milestones, which will ultimately usher in the Second Coming of Jesus to establish his Millennial kingdom on earth. John Walvoord said of the return of Israel to their land in 1948:

> Of the many peculiar phenomena which characterize the present generation, few events can claim equal significance as far as Biblical prophecy is concerned with that of the return of Israel to their land. It constitutes a preparation for the end of the age, the setting for the coming of the Lord for His church, and the fulfilment of Israel's prophetic destiny.[204]

Yet amazingly, some Christians do not regard the present State of Israel as having anything to do with the fulfilment of Bible prophecy, because they subscribe to what is termed Replacement Theology.

Replacement theology

Replacement theology, also called Supersessionism or Fulfilment Theology, is the view that the church has replaced

---

[204] John F. Walvoord, Israel in Prophecy, (1964), p. 26

Israel permanently and that God's current and future plan of salvation involves only the church.

Some claim that early Premillennialists like Justin Martyr, Irenaeus and Tertullian held to some form of Replacement Theology. But this is to misunderstand the claims of Replacement Theology. Irenaeus is correctly quoted as saying, "they who boast themselves as being the house of Jacob and the people of Israel, are disinherited from the grace of God." [205] But in context, he was addressing the Ebionite heresy, which taught that Christians had to keep the Jewish Law and rites.

In speaking to Trypho the Jew, Justin is quoted as saying that the Scriptures belong to Christians, not Jews.

> They are contained in your Scriptures, or rather not yours, but ours. For we believe them; but you, though you read them, do not catch the spirit that is in them. [206]

And Tertullian writes the following, in a treatise he says was inspired by a dispute "held between a Christian and a Jewish proselyte". [207]

> Therefore, since the Jews still contend that the Christ is not yet come, whom we have in so many ways approved to be come, let the Jews recognise their own fate - a fate which they were constantly foretold as destined to incur after the advent of the Christ, on account of the impiety with which they despised and slew Him. [208]

But Justin and Tertullian and others simply pointed out, as the Scriptures teach, that in the current era the predominantly Gentile church stood in a position of favour over unbelieving Jews, because of the rejection of the gospel by the latter. They did not make the claim that the Gentiles had replaced Israel **forever** and that there would be **no restoration** of Israel, which

---

[205] Against Heresies 3.21.1 http://www.newadvent.org/fathers/0103321.htm
[206] Dialogue with Trypho, ch 29
[207] An Answer to the Jews, ch 1
[208] Ibid, ch 13

is the main idea behind Replacement Theology. In fact, Tertullian encouraged Christian to eagerly anticipate the restoration of Israel.

> For it will be fitting for the Christian to rejoice, and not to grieve, at the restoration of Israel, if it be true, (as it is), that the whole of our hope is intimately united with the remaining expectation of Israel. [209]

In reality, the apostle Paul, himself a Jew, precisely states in Rom 11:25-26 that - while there would be a later restoration ("all Israel will be saved") - that at present, Israel was indeed in a state of temporary hardness ("Israel has experienced a hardening in part until the full number of the Gentiles has come in").

Historically, Replacement Theology has always been associated with an Amillennial and Postmillennial view of eschatology and precludes any future restoration of Israel. This position is summarized well by these words of Swiss Reformed theologian Karl Barth (1886-1968):

> The first Israel, constituted on the basis of physical descent from Abraham, has fulfilled its mission now that the Saviour of the world has sprung from it and its Messiah has appeared. Its members can only accept this fact with gratitude, and in confirmation of their own deepest election and calling, attach themselves to the people of this Saviour, their own King, whose members the Gentiles are now called to be as well. Its [Israel's] mission as a natural community **has now run its course and cannot be continued or repeated.** [210]

Proponents of the Replacement Theology view consider the Church as the New Israel, teaching that the many promises made to Israel are fulfilled in the Christian Church, not in literal Israel. Prophecies in Scripture concerning the blessing and

---

[209] De Pudicitia
[210] Karl Barth, Church Dogmatics, volume III (second edition, 2010) p. 584

restoration of Israel are 'spiritualized' into promises of God's blessing for the Church. Partial Preterists Gary DeMar and Peter Leithart have said:

> In destroying Israel, Christ transferred the blessings of the kingdom from Israel to a new people, the church. [211]

Is the Church the new Israel?

The Scripture teaches that, rather than excluding Jews, the Gentiles are now included with them in the New Covenant.

> *Eph 2:11-12 Therefore, remember that formerly you who are Gentiles by birth and called "uncircumcised" … remember that at that time you were separate from Christ, excluded from citizenship in Israel and foreigners to the covenants of the promise, without hope and without God in the world.*

The New Testament doesn't teach that the Gentiles replaced the Jews, rather that both are co-heirs.

> *Gal 3:6 This mystery is that through the gospel the Gentiles are heirs together with Israel, members together of one body, and sharers together in the promise in Christ Jesus.*

A similar thought is conveyed in Gal 3:28.

> *There is neither Jew nor Gentile, neither slave nor free, nor is there male and female, for you are all one in Christ Jesus.*

The above passage doesn't mean that Paul sees no distinction between Israel and the church (Jew and Gentile), as a cursory look at Romans 11 will indicate. There is no "male or female", he also says - meaning of course that both men and women have the same status in Christ - but obviously there remains a distinction between male and female in other ways. Similarly,

---

[211] The Reduction of Christianity, Gary DeMar and Peter Leithart

Jews and Gentiles have the same status in Christ, but Paul at times differentiates between the Gentiles and Israel (i.e. unsaved Jews) referring to them as separate entities. Notice how silly meanings result, if "Israel" is consistently substituted with "Church":

> Rom 11:11 Again I ask: Did they (Israel) stumble so as to fall beyond recovery? Not at all! Rather, because of their transgression, salvation has come to the Gentiles to make Israel envious.

So, using Replacement Theology mentality (i.e. Israel = the Church), we have salvation coming to the Church (the Gentiles) to make the Church (Israel) envious. The following verse is used by proponents of Replacement Theology to teach that Christians are the 'true' Jews.

> Rom 2:28-29 A person is not a Jew who is one only outwardly, nor is circumcision merely outward and physical. No, a person is a Jew who is one inwardly; and circumcision is circumcision of the heart, by the Spirit, not by the written code.

This passage can only be used in support of Replacement Theology if it is lifted out of its context. Romans 2:17 clearly indicates that the intended audience of the passage were the Jews who received the Law ("Now you, if you call yourself a Jew; if you rely on the law...") and they are even contrasted in v24 with "the Gentiles". Paul tells them (the Jews) in v28-29 that it's not enough to be a Jew racially and to have physical circumcision; only if one has had "circumcision of the heart" - is he a true Jew. Further on, Paul is still addressing Jews, when he subsequently says that there is still advantage in being a Jew, and that their unfaithfulness will not nullify God's faithfulness.

> Rom 3:1-4 What advantage, then, is there in being a Jew, or what value is there in circumcision? Much in every way! First of all, the Jews have been entrusted with the very words of God. What if some were unfaithful? Will

their unfaithfulness nullify God's faithfulness? Not at all!
Let God be true, and every human being a liar.

The following verse has also been used in support of Replacement Theology.

Rom 9:6b For not all who are descended from Israel are Israel.

But this presents the same scenario as Rom 2:28-29 - where we saw that not all Jews belonged to God, simply by virtue of birth and circumcision. Paul is again saying that to be born a Jew, does not immediately place you in a covenant relationship with God - like Gentiles, they need a personal experience with God.

Perhaps some have forgotten that the original 12 apostles were all Jewish; the initial church was Jewish; and with the exception of Luke, [212] all the New Testament authors were Jews. A simple concordance search of the word 'Israel' in the New Testament will reveal that the writers never equated the church with the nation of Israel and that the terms are not used synonymously, the only debatable passage being Galatians 6:16 (and then, only in the NIV).

Gal 6:16 (NIV) Peace and mercy to all who follow this rule--to the Israel of God.

It is doubtful that the phrase "Israel of God" refers to the church here.

---

[212] In Col 4:10-14 after saying that Aristarchus, Mark, and Justus "are the only Jews among my fellow workers", Paul the send sends greetings from Epaphras, Luke and Demas.

STRONGS	TRANSLIT	GREEK	ENGLISH
2532	Kai	καὶ	And
3745	hosoi	ὅσοι	as many as
3588	tō	τῷ	those who
2583	kanoni	Κανόνι	rule
3778	toutō	τούτῳ	by this
4748	stoichēsousin	στοιχήσουσιν,	will walk,
1515	eirēnē	εἰρήνη	peace [be]
1909	ep'	ἐπ'	upon
846	autous	αὐτοὺς	them,
2532	kai	καὶ	and
1656	eleos	ἔλεος,	mercy;
2532	kai	καὶ	and
1909	epi	ἐπὶ	upon
3588	ton	τὸν	The
2474	Israēl	Ἰσραὴλ	Israel
3588	tou	τοῦ	-
2316	Theou	Θεοῦ.	of God.

Table 8: Gal 6:16 in Greek [213]

If we look at the original Greek, the NIV translators have not been consistent in the translation of a key word - the third "καὶ".

καὶ ὅσοι τῷ κανόνι τούτῳ στοιχήσουσιν, εἰρήνη ἐπ᾽ αὐτοὺς καὶ ἔλεος, καὶ ἐπὶ τὸν Ἰσραὴλ τοῦ θεοῦ.

The repetition of the preposition "καὶ" indicates that two groups are in view - namely "to all who follow this rule" and (also) "the Israel of God". Paul is pronouncing "peace and mercy" to both

---

[213] http://biblehub.com/text/galatians/6-16.htm

Gentile Christians and to the Jewish Christians (the Israel of God). A more accurate rendering is found in most English versions, with the exception of the NIV.

VERSION	ENGLISH RENDERING
NIV	Peace and mercy to all who follow this rule--to the Israel of God.
NASB	*And those who will walk by this rule, peace and mercy be upon them, and upon the Israel of God.*
ESV	*And as for all who walk by this rule, peace and mercy be upon them, and upon the Israel of God.*
KJV	*And* as many as walk according to this rule, peace be on them, *and* mercy, *and* upon the Israel of God.

Table 9: Gal 6:16 in English versions

While the NIV rendering (translating "καὶ" as "to") is not technically incorrect, the rendering of "καὶ" as "and" or "also" is far more commonplace (and used thus, twice in the earlier portion of the verse). Dr. S. Lewis Johnson Jr., who taught Greek at Dallas Theological Seminary for 31 years, believed that, "the least likely view among several alternatives is the view that the 'Israel of God' is the church."[214] D. Matthew Allen further notes:

> ... all the sixty-five other occurrences of the term Israel in the New Testament refer to Jews. It would thus be strange for Paul to use Israel here to mean Gentile Christians... Paul elsewhere distinguishes between two kinds of Israelites - believing Jews and unbelieving Jews (cf. Rom. 9:6). He does the same here, referring to true Israel, that is, Jews who come to Christ. [215]

---

[214] S. Lewis Johnson Jr., - "Paul and 'Israel of God', An Exegetical and Eschatological Case-Study" p. 3
[215] https://bible.org/article/theology-adrift-early-church-fathers-and-their-views-eschatology

The rise of Replacement Theology and Christian-Jewish hostility

Anti-Semitism is defined as hostility, prejudice, or discrimination against Jews. The rise of Amillennialism and the resultant Replacement Theology, strongly correlates with a rise in Anti-Semitism among Christians. And once the church obtained state backing, it produced a situation where Jews were not only frowned upon, but in cases underwent state-sanctioned harassment and persecution.

While the early church had been exclusively Jewish, after God sent Peter to preach to the Roman centurion, Cornelius - Gentiles were accepted as part of the church. The church at Antioch in Syria was a mixed Gentile and Jewish church which, under the direction of the Holy Spirit, subsequently sent Paul and Barnabas to evangelise the Gentile world. This led to a series of mission trips to predominantly Gentile areas, as well as Paul's many epistles expounding on God's acceptance of the Gentile nations (and explaining the mystery of the Church Age, when God would prepare his Gentile bride).

One of the first areas of concern that arose among Jewish Christians was how far, if at all, the Jewish Law had to be observed by Gentile converts to Christianity. This led to the Jerusalem Council, where the apostles and elders [216] ruled that Gentile converts to Christianity were not obligated to be circumcised or to be bound by Jewish Law. (The Council did, however, retain the prohibitions on abstaining "from food sacrificed to idols, from blood, from the meat of strangled animals and from sexual immorality." [217])

One of the reasons for the rise of Replacement Theology was the ever-increasing Gentile composition of the church over the subsequent centuries. But not only did the church begin to be dominated by people without Jewish roots, there was ever increasing hostility between unbelieving Jews and Christians. Even in the Book of Acts we find that Paul's major opposition in

---

[216] This included James, Peter, Paul, Barnabas-speakers recorded in Acts 15.
[217] Acts 15:28

his ministry to the Gentiles came from the Jewish quarter, at times even from Jewish converts, but in particular from those who rejected the Messianic claims of Christianity. And before this, Jesus had faced harsh opposition from the Pharisees, who were the progenitors of Rabbinic Judaism.

The destruction of Jerusalem in AD 70

Christian non-involvement in the war of AD 66-70 between the Romans and Jews served to increase their growing distance between Jewish Christians and the rest of Judaism. In his Olivet discourse, Jesus had warned the disciples:

> *Luke 21:20-24 "When you see Jerusalem being surrounded by armies, you will know that its desolation is near. Then let those who are in Judea flee to the mountains, let those in the city get out, and let those in the country not enter the city... There will be great distress in the land and wrath against this people. They will fall by the sword and will be taken as prisoners to all the nations. Jerusalem will be trampled on by the Gentiles until the times of the Gentiles are fulfilled."*

Christian natives of Jerusalem followed Jesus' advice to flee when they saw the city "surrounded by armies". An early tradition cited in the 4th century by Eusebius [218] and Epiphanius [219] relates that before the destruction of Jerusalem, the Christians fled to Pella in the region of the Decapolis across the Jordan River.

---

[218] Ecclesiastical History 3.5.3 - "The people of the Church in Jerusalem were commanded by an oracle given by revelation before the war to those in the city who were worthy of it to depart and dwell in one of the cities of Perea which they called Pella. To it those who believed on Christ travelled from Jerusalem, so that when holy men had altogether deserted the royal capital of the Jews and the whole land of Judaea..."

[219] Panarion 29,7,7-8 - "This heresy of the Nazoraeans exists in Beroea in the neighbourhood of Coele Syria and the Decapolis in the region of Pella and in Basanitis in the so-called Kokhba (Chochabe in Hebrew). From there it took its beginning after the exodus from Jerusalem when all the disciples went to live in Pella because Christ had told them to leave Jerusalem and to go away since it would undergo a siege. Because of this advice, they lived in Perea after having moved to that place, as I said."

Consequently, by heeding the warning of Jesus, these Christians escaped the devastation and resultant massacre in Jerusalem. This was an important watershed in the separation of Christianity from its Jewish roots. Jewish Christians had clearly distanced themselves from the rest of Judaism, regarding the Temple's destruction as punishment on Israel for its large-scale rejection of Jesus. But they in turn were viewed as both traitors and cowards by their fellow Jews, for having abandoned both the city and the Temple to the Romans.

After the destruction of Jerusalem, the Jewish religion was left with only two possible paths into the future; namely Christianity or the Rabbinic Judaism which arose from the sect of the Pharisees. The Sadducees had discredited themselves permanently by their political collaboration with the Romans and some believe that the Essenes had fled to Masada, thereby perishing with the final mass suicide that occurred there in AD 73/74. [220]

The first 3 centuries

In the first three centuries of Christian history, the church was persecuted, first by the Jews and then - after Nero - by pagan Rome. The Jews themselves fared no better in this period, experiencing extreme opposition at the hands of the pagan Roman Emperors, having Jerusalem destroyed and the Temple razed to the ground by Titus in the 1st century. Josephus claims that 1,100,000 people were killed during the siege, of which a majority were Jewish. 97,000 were captured and enslaved and many Jews fled the country.

Then in the 2nd century the Jews had their beloved Jerusalem secularised and renamed to Aelia Capitolina by the Emperor Hadrian, in addition to a pagan temple to Jupiter being built on the former Temple site. The failed Bar Kokhba revolt (AD 132-

---

[220] This is based on the assumptions, neither of them fully proven that either the Sicarii at Masada were Essenes, or that the Essenes fled from Qumran to Masada, after hiding the Dead Sea Scrolls. In any event, the Essenes vanish from history after this period.

136) was cruelly crushed by Hadrian. According to Cassius Dio, overall war operations in the land of Judea left some 580,000 Jews killed, and 50 fortified towns and 985 villages razed to the ground. In another act of spite and in "an effort to wipe out all memory of the bond between the Jews and the land, Hadrian changed the name of the province from Judaea to Syria-Palestina, a name that became common in non-Jewish literature".[221] The designation of the term "Palestina" for the land was, not accidentally, a reference to Israel's old enemies - the Philistines, which is of course, the origin for the modern term "Palestine".

Constantine

In the 4th century, after 250 years of Christian persecution by ten different Roman emperors, the unthinkable happened when Rome got its first Christian emperor, Constantine. While things were looking up for Christians in the Empire, the same could not be said about their former persecutors, both pagans and Jews - as the coming centuries would show. Christianity, once seen as a minority sect within Judaism, now moved into a position of power and privilege.

Because of the numerous revisionist histories and conspiracies with Constantine at the centre, all of which rely on pseudo-history and Hollywood level research, we will dismiss all the fabrications and simply look at the verifiable historical documents available. [222] Constantine instituted several legislative measures impacting on Jews and some of these actions would not have won him favour from Jewish subjects.

 ❖ AD 315 - The Jewish community could not stone a Jewish convert to Christianity. Anyone who participated

---

[221] H.H. Ben-Sasson, A History of the Jewish People (1976), page 334
[222] The primary source used is Coleman-Norton, P.R. Roman State and Christian Church, 3 volumes. London: SPCK, 1966. This work contains translations of Roman legal documents relating to the church from the years AD 113 to 534. http://fourthcentury.com/index.php/imperial-laws-and-letters-involving-religion-ad-311-364

in such an act would be burned. [223] Some allege that conversion to Judaism from Christianity was prohibited by Constantine, but in the context of this law, it was a reference to those who joined the Jews in the act of killing converts to Christianity, not those who joined Judaism.

- ❖ AD 336 - Jews were not allowed to harass Jewish converts to Christianity, and would be punished in accordance with the nature of the act. [224]
- ❖ AD 336 - If a Jew circumcised a non-Jewish slave, the slave was to be freed. [225]

Eusebius of Caesarea, a favourite of Constantine, seemingly held Jews in high regard, stating that "the Hebrew nation... is universally honoured" and highlighting Christianity's roots in Judaism. [226] According to a modern Jewish source, "Eusebius seems to have had a Jewish teacher, who instructed him in Hebrew, and through whom he became familiar with many haggadot and Jewish traditions; of these he made use in his works on Biblical exegesis." [227]

At the Council of Nicaea (AD 325) it was decided not to base the date of the celebration of the Resurrection (Pascha - later Easter) with the Jewish lunar calendar and the Feast of Passover, but to use an independent computation. This was in

---

[223] Ibid - "It is Our will that Jews and their elders and patriarchs shall be informed that if, after the issuance of this law, any of them should dare to attempt to assail with stones or with any other kind of madness—a thing which We have learned is now being done—any person who has fled their feral sect and has resorted to the worship of God, such assailant shall be immediately delivered to the flames and burned, with all his accomplices."

[224] Ibid

[225] Ibid

[226] "But although it is clear that we are new and that this new name of Christians has really but recently been known among all nations, nevertheless our life and our conduct, with our doctrines of religion, have not been lately invented by us, but from the first creation of man, so to speak, have been established by the natural understanding of divinely favoured men of old. That this is so we shall show in the following way. That the Hebrew nation is not new, but is universally honoured on account of its antiquity, is known to all. The books and writings of this people contain accounts of ancient men, rare indeed and few in number, but nevertheless distinguished for piety and righteousness and every other virtue." - Ecclesiastical History 1:4:4-5

[227] http://www.jewishencyclopedia.com/articles/5911-eusebius

part to prevent the celebration from occasionally occurring twice in the same year, but also an attempt to disassociate it from Jewish feasts. The resultant Synodal Letter of the Council issued the following pronouncement regarding the matter:

> We further proclaim to you the good news of the agreement concerning the holy Pascha, that this particular also has through your prayers been rightly settled; so that all our brethren in the East who formerly followed the custom of the Jews are henceforth to celebrate the said most sacred feast of Pascha at the same time with the Romans and yourselves and all those who have observed Pascha from the beginning.[228]

Then, in a correspondence by Constantine to the churches, he summarised the outcome of the proceedings as follows:

> And first of all, it appeared an unworthy thing that in the celebration of this most holy feast we should follow the practice of the Jews, who have impiously defiled their hands with enormous sin, and are, therefore, deservedly afflicted with blindness of soul. For we have it in our power, if we abandon their custom, to prolong the due observance of this ordinance to future ages, by a truer order, which we have preserved from the very day of the passion until the present time. Let us then have nothing in common with the detestable Jewish crowd; for we have received from our Saviour a different way. [229]

Yet despite Constantine's apparent private disdain for Jews, this didn't always translate into harsh legislation. For instance:

❖ AD 321 - Jews could be appointed to city councils. [230]

---

[228] "The Synodal Letter" - Nicene and Post-Nicene Fathers, series 2, vol. XIV
[229] Life of Constantine 3:18
[230] Law 74: To the decurions of Cologne (Dec 11, 321)

❖ AD 331 - Priests and synagogue leaders were exempt from all compulsory public service and could not be forced out of their positions. [231] [232]

Some point to the barring of Jews from Jerusalem as an act of anti-Semitism on the part of Constantine, but it was the pagan emperor Hadrian who had barred Jews from Jerusalem, after renaming the city to Aelia Capitolina. [233] Jews had also been prohibited from entering the city on pain of death but, as these measures also affected Jewish Christians, Hadrian had essentially secularized (or more precisely 'paganized') the city. But while Constantine did not instate this law barring Jews from Jerusalem, neither did he fully revoke the previous law, and allowed full exemption only to Christians. [234] He did however permit Jews to enter Jerusalem for one day each year, during the holiday of Tisha B'Av, to mourn the Temples' destruction. [235]

Yet Constantine is not viewed favourably by modern Jewish sources, [236] some alleging that after a poor response to a Christian missionary effort among Jews in Israel, he responded by imposing heavy taxes and fines, even causing some to be put to death. [237] But this may be apocryphal as I can find no primary

---

[231] Ibid

[232] http://fourthcentury.com/index.php/imperial-laws-and-letters-involving-religion-ad-311-364 "If any persons with complete devotion should dedicate themselves to the synagogues of the Jews as patriarchs and priests and should live in the aforementioned sect and preside over the administration of their law, they shall continue to be exempt from all compulsory public services that are incumbent on persons, as well as those that are due to the municipalities."

[233] https://en.wikipedia.org/wiki/History_of_the_Jews_and_Judaism_in_the_Land_of_Israel

[234] https://en.wikipedia.org/wiki/Aelia_Capitolina

[235] Larry Domnitch. "Western Wall: This remnant of the Second Temple is an important symbol in Judaism.". MyJewishLearning.com

[236] E.g. http://www.jewishhistory.org/the-roman-empire-adopts-christianity/ & http://www.jewish-history.com/palestine/period1.html

[237] "Descriptive Geography and Brief Historical Sketch of Palestine" by Rabbi Joseph Schwarz, 1850 – "At that time there lived at Rome a Jew named Joseph, who went over to Christianity, and acquired thereby much respect with Constantine, and obtained from him the permission to appear openly as converter of the people, and to build churches and monasteries. To carry out his object he travelled into Palestine as missionary, and commenced to preach publicly in order to persuade the Jews, of whom there were a great many in

source for these allegations, seemingly first made in the 19th century. It also seems out of line with the general legal religious toleration he expressed elsewhere.

The other Byzantine emperors

The following laws regarding Jews are sometimes attributed to Constantine, but were actually the work of his sons, Constantius and Constans, who succeeded him.

- ❖ AD 339 - Jews had to release all their Christian slaves. If a Jew was found to own Christian slaves, all his slaves were to be freed. Jews who circumcised non-Jewish slaves would be executed. [238]
- ❖ AD 339 - proselytising was forbidden as well as attempts to reconvert former Jews who had become Christians. [239]

Judaism was generally tolerated by Byzantine (i.e. Roman Christian) law.

- ❖ AD 341- The property rights of synagogues were protected, and assemblies gathered therein were legal.[240]

Cæsarea, Tiberias, Nazara, and Kefr Tanchum, as in fact all these towns were inhabited by Jews solely, to adopt his religion, and he already made a commencement to build churches. But the Jews regarded him not, and would not permit him to construct the like buildings in the places just named. He reported his want of success, on account of this opposition of the Jews, to Constantine, who thereupon imposed on them heavy taxes and fines, and caused a great many of them to be put to death."
http://www.jewish-history.com/palestine/period1.html

[238] http://fourthcentury.com/index.php/imperial-laws-and-letters-involving-religion-ad-311-364

[239] Constantius to Evagrius, Codex Theodosianus, - "We wish to make clear to the Jewish elders and patriarchs that if, after the enactment of this law, anyone attempts ... to reconvert a person who has given up the baleful sect of Judaism and has joined the cult of God, forthwith he and his accomplices are to be given to the flames and burned. Furthermore if anyone of the people has joined their evil sect and frequented their meeting places, he shall suffer his deserved penalty with them."

[240] "If it should appear that any places are frequented by conventides of the Jews and are called by the name of synagogues, no one shall dare to violate or to occupy and retain such places, since all persons must retain their own property in undisturbed right…"

- ❖ AD 392 - Jewish leaders could administrate their religious law. Secular judges were commanded to end the practice of forcefully reinstating Jews to the Jewish community, if they had been expelled by their own leaders. [241]
- ❖ AD 393 - No synagogues could be despoiled, and no regulation could be passed to ban Judaism, even in the name of Christianity. [242] No non-Jew could set the prices for Jewish merchants and those who did so were to be punished by local authorities. [243]
- ❖ AD 396 - Persons who made disparaging remarks about the patriarch (Jewish leader) were subject to punishment. [244]
- ❖ AD 397 - Jews who feigned a desire to join the church in order to escape debts, had to first repay their debts. [245] Jews were not to be harassed, attacked or insulted; governors were to maintain the synagogues' tranquillity.[246] Jewish clergy were allowed to retain their own laws and rituals and were exempt from service in municipal senates. They are to have the same privileges as Christian clergy. [247]
- ❖ AD 404 - Previous privileges granted to the Jewish patriarch were to be honoured. [248]

---

[241] http://fourthcentury.com/index.php/imperial-laws-364 Theodosius I, Arcadius, Honorius

[242] Ibid - Theodosius I, Arcadius, Honorius, 29 Sep 393, "It is sufficiently established that the sect of the Jews is forbidden by no law. Hence We are gravely disturbed that their assemblies have been forbidden in certain places. Your Sublime Magnitude will, therefore, after receiving this order, restrain with proper severity the excesses of those persons who, in the name of the Christian religion, presume to commit certain unlawful acts and attempt to destroy and to despoil the synagogues"

[243] Ibid - Arcadius, Honorius, 28 Feb 393

[244] http://www.mountainman.com.au/essenes/codex_theodosianus.htm

[245] Arcadius, Honorius, http://fourthcentury.com/index.php/imperial-laws-364

[246] Ibid & http://www.mountainman.com.au/essenes/codex_theodosianus.htm

[247] http://fourthcentury.com/index.php/imperial-laws-364 Arcadius, Honorius

[248] Arcadius, Honorius, 3 Feb, 404 "We order that all the privileges granted by our father, of divine memory, and by the emperors before him, to the excellent Patriarchs, and to those set by them over others, shall retain their force." http://www.ccjr.us/dialogika-resources/primary-texts-from-the-history-of-the-relationship/249-roman-laws

- ❖ AD 412 - No Jew may be compelled to fulfil a compulsory public service or to appear in court on the Sabbath or any other Jewish holiday. Likewise, Jews must not summon Christians to court on Christian holidays. [249]
- ❖ AD 412/8 - Jews may not be persecuted for their religion or have their property taken without cause. [250]
- ❖ AD 416 - False converts to Christianity from Judaism could return to Judaism e.g. if Jews had joined the church in order to avoid punishments for crimes or other duties, they were permitted to return to Judaism, but were still liable for whatever obligation they had sought to avoid.[251]
- ❖ AD 423 - Jewish synagogues and property may not be taken for church purposes or burned. If such an incident does occur, they must be compensated. [252] Jews are protected from attacks by people acting in the name of Christianity. [253] Christians may not attack or plunder Jews or pagans and must pay back three times as much as what they took from a pagan or Jew. [254]
- ❖ AD 553 - Services could be conducted in Greek and any other language, and not just in Hebrew, provided this was not used as a means of changing the meaning of Scripture. [255]

---

[249] http://fourthcentury.com/index.php/imperial-laws-364 - Honorius, Theodosius II, 29 Jul 412, "Moreover, since indeed ancient custom and practice have preserved for the aforesaid Jewish people the consecrated day of the Sabbath, We also decree that it shall be forbidden that any man of the aforesaid faith should be constrained by any summons on that day, under the pretext of public or private business, since all the remaining time appears sufficient to satisfy the public laws, and since it is most worthy of the moderation of Our time that the privileges granted should not be violated, although sufficient provision appears to have been made with reference to the aforesaid matter by general constitutions of earlier Emperors."

[250] Ibid - Honorius, Theodosius II, 6 Aug 412/8

[251] Ibid - 24 Sep 416

[252] Ibid - 15 Feb 423

[253] Ibid - 9 Apr 423

[254] Ibid - 8 Jun 423

[255] Justinian - "We decree, therefore, that it shall be permitted to those Hebrews who want it to read the Holy Books in their synagogues and, in general, in any place where there are Hebrews, in the Greek language before those assembled and comprehending, or possibly in our ancestral language (we speak of the Italian language), or simply in all the other languages, changing language and reading according to the different places; and that through this reading the

However, there were also many restrictions placed on Jews, which got progressively more severe over the course of years. Strangely a 19th century Jewish source by Rabbi Joseph Schwarz, while painting Constantine, Constantius [256] and Theodosius II [257] in a poor light, praises Valentinian, [258] Theodosius I, [259] Arcadius, [260] Justinian [261] and Maurice as being good to Jews. [262] Yet some of these 'pro-Jewish' emperors were responsible for some of the following laws (see footnotes).

---

matters read shall become clear to all those assembled and comprehending, and that they shall live and act according to them. We also order that there shall be no license to the commentators they have, who employ the Hebrew language to falsify it at their will, covering their own malignity by the ignorance of the many." http://www.ccjr.us/dialogika-resources/primary-texts-from-the-history-of-the-relationship/249-roman-laws

[256] "Descriptive Geography and Brief Historical Sketch of Palestine" (1850) http://jewish-history.com/palestine/period1.html - Constantius commenced his reign in 4099 (339). At that time there lived a large Jewish population in Zippori (Safuri), who showed themselves disobedient to the Emperor; in consequence of which, he attacked them, and out of revenge for their disobedience, he caused the city to be demolished; since that time it is but a miserable small village.

[257] Ibid - Theodosius II … was cruel and inimical to the Jews. In the eighth year of his reign he ordered all the Jews to be driven out of Alexandria in Egypt, and commanded that all the contributions and donations which were collected for the Nahssi of Palestine, for the purpose of defraying the general benevolent objects among the Jews, and the promotion of the study of the law and similar purposes, should be delivered into the imperial treasury.

[258] Ibid -Valentinian … was likewise a humane man, and especially kind to the Jews. In the twelfth year of his reign, 4140 (380), he commanded to surround Jerusalem with a new wall, and promised to make liberal expenditure for this purpose; but he died in the same year, and this project was also frustrated.

[259] Ibid - Theodosius I. commenced his reign in 4140 (380). He was a persecutor of Arian Christians, but a friend to the Jews; and he made it known in all his empire that they should have everywhere unrestricted freedom in the exercise of their religion, and that no one should place any obstacles in their way.

[260] Ibid - Arcadius commenced his reign in 4155 (395); he also was a wise ruler and a friend to the Jews.

[261] Ibid - In 4288 (528) Justinian the Great became Emperor. He was a very wise and good prince, and a friend to the Jews. In the year 4316 (556), a bloody contest arose between the Jews and the Christians residing in Cæsarea, in which very many, nearly all of the latter, were destroyed. Justinian had the matter investigated, and declared that the Jews had been in the right.

[262] Ibid - Maurice reigned in 4244 (584); he was a good and mild prince. At this time, the East was visited by many and violent earthquakes; through which means the building commenced by Julian on the temple mount, was thrown

- ❖ AD 353 - Christian converts to Judaism would have their property confiscated. [263]
- ❖ AD 388 - Jews and Christians were forbidden to intermarry; if they did, it would be considered adultery. [264]
- ❖ AD 408 - Mockery of Christianity was forbidden. Jews could not burn crosses at the feast of Purim and had to keep their customs in a way that did not offend Christians. [265]
- ❖ AD 409 - Forced conversion of Christians to Judaism was considered high treason. [266]
- ❖ AD 418 - Jews could not enter imperial service. Jews who had already taken the oath for service could remain, except those in the armed service. Jews were not prohibited from becoming advocates or decurions. [267]

---

down. The benevolent Maurice sent Jewish builders from Constantinople to Jerusalem to restore it.

[263] Emperor Constantius II, July 3, 353 - "If someone shall become Jew from Christian and shall be joined to sacrilegious assemblies, we decree that his property shall be vindicated to the fisc's [state treasury's] dominion once the accusation has been proven."

[264] Valentinian II, Theodosius I, Arcadius - "Let no Jew take a Christian woman to wife, nor any Christian seek marriage with a Jewess. For if any one admits anything of this sort, he will be charged with his crime just as if he has committed adultery, and furthermore liberty for accusations of this nature has been granted to the general public." – http://fourthcentury.com/index.php/imperial-laws-364

[265] Ibid - Honorius, Theodosius II, 29 May 408

[266] Honorius and Theodosius II, April 1, 409 "Some people... dare to transgress the Law to such an extent, that they force some to cease being Christian and adopt the abominable and vile name of the Jews. Although those that have committed this crime shall be legally condemned under the laws of the ancient emperors, still it does not bother us to admonish repeatedly, that those imbued in the Christian mysteries shall not be forced to adopt Jewish perversity, which is alien to the Roman Empire, and abjure Christianity. And if someone should believe that this be wilfully attempted, we order that the instigators of the deed with their accomplices shall suffer the punishment decreed in the former laws, for it is graver than death and crueller than massacre when someone abjures the Christian faith and becomes polluted with the Jewish incredulity... if someone shall attempt to rise against this law, let him know that he shall be punished for high treason."
http://www.ccjr.us/dialogika-resources/primary-texts-from-the-history-of-the-relationship/249-roman-laws

[267] http://fourthcentury.com/index.php/imperial-laws-364 - Honorius, Theodosius II

- ❖ AD 423 - Jews could not construct new synagogues, but old ones would not be torn down. [268] Existing synagogues could not be improved. [269] Jews still may not circumcise Christians, and will have their property confiscated and be exiled if they do. [270]
- ❖ AD 426 - Jewish parents and grandparents could not write their children out of their wills if the children converted to Christianity.[271]
- ❖ AD 527 - Jews cannot hold a place of honour in a civil office.[272]
- ❖ AD 531 - Jews cannot testify against Christians. [273]
- ❖ AD 545 - Church property cannot be sold or leased to heretics or Jews. [274]

---

[268] Ibid - Honorius, Theodosius II, 8 Jun 423

[269] http://www.mountainman.com.au/essenes/codex_theodosianus.htm

[270] http://fourthcentury.com/index.php/imperial-laws-364 - 9 Apr 423

[271] Ibid - Theodosius II, Valentinian III, 8 Apr 426

[272] Justin and Justinian, Between April and July 527 - "Indeed, we order that those who are heretics, and above all the pagans, Jews, Samaritans, and those similar to them, if they take part in any of all those we have already recalled, having obtained an honour, inscribed in the advocates' list, taken an office or put on an official belt, they shall be thrown out on the spot from participating in these. For we want all the above-mentioned to be purged from association with such as these now and forever, not only in this glorious city [Constantinople], but in practically every province and every place." http://www.ccjr.us/dialogika-resources/primary-texts-from-the-history-of-the-relationship/249-roman-laws

[273] The Emperor Anastasius to John, Praetorian Prefect, Concerning Heretics and Manichaeans and Samaritans - "We order that no testimony shall be given against orthodox litigants by a heretic, or by those who adhere to the Jewish superstition, whether one, or both parties to the suit are orthodox. We grant permission to heretics or Jews, when they have litigation with one another, to introduce witnesses qualified to testify."

[274] http://www.ccjr.us/dialogika-resources/primary-texts-from-the-history-of-the-relationship/249-roman-laws From the Code of Justinian, Chapter XIV - "If an Orthodox who possesses a property with a church in it shall alienate it forever, give it an emphyteusis, or in a lease, on in any other way of management to a Jew, Samaritan, pagan, Montanist, Arian, or any other heretic, the holiest church of that village shall vindicate the ownership of this property. If any one of the heretics ... shall dare to build a cave [derogatory term for a religious site] of his impiety, or if the Jews shall dare to build a new synagogue, the holy church of the place shall vindicate the buildings to its ownership."

- ❖ AD 553 - Prohibition against using the Mishnah (Rabbinic commentaries) in synagogues as opposed to Scripture.[275]
- ❖ AD 553 - Prohibition against propagating the former doctrine of the Sadducees (i.e. denying the resurrection and angels).[276]

John Chrysostom

Part of the reason for the ever-increasing severity of some of these laws against Jews may have been the theological justification being given from some quarters. Adversus Judaeos (Greek for "Against the Jews") was a series of 4th century homilies by John Chrysostom (349-407) directed to members of the church of Antioch of his time, who continued to observe Jewish feasts and fasts. [277] His stated motivation was for these sermons was as follows:

> Many, I know, respect the Jews and think that their present way of life is a venerable one. This is why I hasten to uproot and tear out this deadly opinion. [278]

---

[275] Ibid - Justinian - "What they call Mishnah, on the other hand, we prohibit entirely, for it is not included among the Holy Books, nor was it handed down from above by the prophets, but it is an invention of men in their chatter, exclusively of earthly origin and having in it nothing of the divine. Let them read the holy words themselves, therefore, in unfolding these Holy Books for reading, but without hiding what is said in them, on the one hand, and without accepting extraneous and unwritten nonsense they themselves had contrived to the perdition of the more simple minded, on the other hand."

[276] Justinian - "And if there are some people among them who shall attempt to introduce ungodly nonsense, denying either the resurrection or the last judgment or that the angels exist as God's work and creation, we want these people expelled from all places, and that no word of blasphemy of this kind and absolutely erring from that knowledge of God shall be spoken. We impose the harshest punishments on those attempting to utter such a nonsense, completely purifying in this way the nation of the Hebrews from the error introduced into it." http://www.ccjr.us/dialogika-resources/primary-texts-from-the-history-of-the-relationship/249-roman-laws

[277] https://en.wikipedia.org/wiki/Adversus_Judaeos

[278] John Chrysostom, Against the Jews. Homily 1, iii, (1)

He used excerpts from the Old Testament prophets to justify his reference to the synagogue as a brothel and a theatre.

> You had a harlot's brow; you became shameless before all". Where a harlot has set herself up, that place is a brothel. But the synagogue is not only a brothel and a theatre; it also is a den of robbers and a lodging for wild beasts. Jeremiah said: "Your house has become for me the den of a hyena". He does not simply say "of wild beast", but "of a filthy wild beast..." [279]

Using these denouncements by the Jewish prophets to categorise all Jewish synagogues is like applying the rebukes given to various churches in the New Testament writings as being a denouncement of all churches today. Chrysostom indicates an extreme version of Replacement Theology, saying that the Jews are beyond all hope, having been abandoned by God.

> ... and again: "I have abandoned my house, I have cast off my inheritance". But when God forsakes a people, what hope of salvation is left? When God forsakes a place, that place becomes the dwelling of demons. [280]

John Chrysostom uses very strong unchristian language to say that because the Jews claimed "that Moses and the prophets knew not Christ and said nothing about his coming" that "so it is that we must hate both them and their synagogue all the more because of their offensive treatment of those holy men". [281] Some have try to defend his actions in the following ways:

a) Chrysostom's primary targets were actually not Jews themselves, but members of his own congregation who continued to participate in Jewish festivals and took part in other Jewish observances, such as observing the Sabbath, submitting to circumcision and pilgrimage to Jewish holy places. More recent scholarly translations thus give the

---

[279] Ibid
[280] Ibid
[281] Ibid, v (4)

sermons the more sympathetic title "Against Judaizing Christians" rather than "Against the Jews".

b) According to Patristics scholars, opposition to any particular view in this period was conventionally expressed using a form of rhetoric known as the psogos, whose literary conventions were to vilify opponents in an uncompromising manner. Similar techniques were sometimes used when denouncing heretics or ever other Christians with dissenting opinions. Thus, it has been argued that to call Chrysostom anti-Semitic is to employ anachronistic terminology in a way that is incongruous with historical context and record. [282]

But our ultimate guide to the message we speak should be the Scripture and not contemporary oratory techniques. And despite the original intention, these words have been used by both enemies of the Jews to justify their mistreatment, and by enemies of Christianity to claim that this is representative of the true Christian message. And sadly, centuries later the neo-pagan Nazi Party in Germany would opportunistically quote these homilies, reprinting them frequently in an attempt to legitimize the Holocaust in the eyes of German and Austrian Christians. [283] James Parkes (1896-1981), a clergyman and social activist, called these writings by Chrysostom "the most horrible and violent denunciations of Judaism to be found in the writings of a Christian theologian". [284] In the most recent edition of John Chrysostom's works, Catholic editor Paul W. Harkins wrote that Chrysostom's "position on these points is no longer tenable… For these objectively unchristian acts he cannot be excused, even if he is the product of his times." [285]

Jerome

Unfortunately, when tracing the growth of anti-Semitism in Catholic thought, one also has to sift through a whole lot of fabricated quotations. Jerome is often cited as a classic example

---

[282] Wilken, Robert Louis. John Chrysostom and the Jews: Rhetoric and Reality in the Late Fourth Century (1983), pp. 124-126.
[283] https://en.wikipedia.org/wiki/Adversus_Judaeos
[284] James Parkes, Prelude to Dialogue (1969) p. 153; cited in Wilken, p. xv
[285] Discourses Against Judaizing Christians-The Fathers of the Church, Vol 68

of Christian anti-Semitism based on his alleged description of Jews as "serpents, wearing the image of Judas. Their psalms and prayers are the braying of donkeys... They are incapable of understanding Scripture." But although this is cited frequently, no one gives a source, and I cannot find it in any of his writings. It appears to be yet another bogus quotation.

But what Jerome does in reality say about Jews, is not much better though. Jerome, who acquired a knowledge of Hebrew by studying in Bethlehem under Baraninas, a Jewish convert to Christianity, writes:

> If it is expedient to hate any men and to loath any race, I have a strange dislike to those of the circumcision. For up to the present day they persecute our Lord Jesus Christ in the synagogues of Satan. Yet can anyone find fault with me for having had a Jew as a teacher? [286]

In the Vulgate, Jerome (AD 347-420) had chosen to translate much of the Old Testament into Latin from Hebrew (rather than using the Greek Septuagint as his basis) and so from time to time he consulted Jewish scholars as well. Jerome had moved to Bethlehem in Israel and his dislike of unconverted Jews may be due to the fact that he relates:

> What trouble and expense it cost me to get Baraninas to teach me under cover of night. For by his fear of the Jews he presented to me in his own person a second edition of Nicodemus. [287]

Jerome's reason for rejecting Premillennialism was because of the "Jewishness" of the idea and so he refers contemptuously to the Chiliasts as "our half-Jews who look for a Jerusalem of gold and precious stone from heaven, and a future kingdom of 1000 years, in which all nations shall serve Israel". [288] Premillennialism was often criticized because it seemed to favour the Jews as having a distinct, blessed future apart from Gentile Christians.

---

[286] Letter LXXXIV. To Pammachius and Oceanus
[287] Ibid
[288] Jerome, Commentary on Isaiah 60.1, 66.20

Amillennialism and Replacement theology fitted far better with the anti-Semitic tone of this age.

Gregory of Nyssa

The following quote is attributed by some to Gregory of Nyssa.

> [Jews are] murderers of the Lord, assassins of the prophets, rebels against God, God haters... advocates of the devil, race of vipers, slanderers, calumniators, dark-minded people, leaven of the Pharisees, Sanhedrin of demons, sinners, wicked men, stoners, and haters of righteousness.

However, this is from a work called "Testimonies Against The Jews" and is considered to be the work of an unknown author misidentified as Gregory of Nyssa, hence dubbed Pseudo-Gregory. As a general rule, if you cannot trace the primary source for a quote, or if there is no reference given, it is best to disregard it.

Ambrose of Milan

Despite the fact that Judaism was officially tolerated, friction often existed and manifested itself in violence between Christians and Jews. In AD 388 a bishop was accused of instigating the burning of the synagogue in Callinicum, and Emperor Theodosius was preparing to order the bishop to rebuild it. Ambrose, the Bishop of Milan (AD 340-397) wrote to the emperor discouraging him from taking this step.

> There is, then, no adequate cause for such a commotion, that the people should be so severely punished for the burning of a building, and much less since it is the burning of a synagogue, a home of unbelief, a house of

impiety, a receptacle of folly, which God Himself has condemned.[289]

Part of his argument was that Jews had caused several Christian basilicas to be burnt during the reign of Julian the Apostate, yet had never been asked to make reparation. [290] But what happened to the Biblical injunction of "do not repay anyone evil for evil" (Rom 12:17)?

Yet despite this, Ambrose does remark in one of his works, "Some Jews exhibit purity of life and much diligence and love of study." [291] The following statement is attributed by some to Ambrose, and by others to John Chrysostom, and yet by others to both.

> The Jews are the most worthless of all men. They are lecherous, greedy, rapacious. They are perfidious murderers of Christ. They worship the Devil. Their religion is a sickness. The Jews are the odious assassins of Christ, and for killing God there is no expiation possible, no indulgence or pardon. Christians may never cease vengeance, and the Jew must live in servitude forever. God always hated the Jews. It is essential that all Christians hate them.

No one supplies an actual reference and, not surprisingly, it cannot be found in any of the writings of either men.

---

[289] Council of Centers on Jewish-Christian Relations, "Ambrose of Milan, 'Letters about a Synagogue Burning' (August 388)

[290] http://ccjr.us/dialogika-resources/primary-texts-from-the-history-of-the-rel ationship/248-ambrose-of-milan-gletters-about-a-synagogue-burningq-ug388
AMBROSE OF MILAN, "Letters about a Synagogue Burning" (August, 388) - "And certainly, if I were pleading according to the law of nations, I could tell how many of the Church's basilicas the Jews burnt in the time of the Emperor Julian: two at Damascus, one of which is scarcely now repaired, and this at the cost of the Church, not of the Synagogue; the other basilica still is a rough mass of shapeless ruins. Basilicas were burnt at Gaza, Ascalon, Beirut, and in almost every place in those parts, and no one demanded punishment. And at Alexandria a basilica, which alone surpassed all the rest, was burnt by pagans and Jews. The Church was not avenged; shall the Synagogue be so?"

[291] "Enarratio in Psalmos" (i. 41, xiv. 943

Syria

At this point in history there also appears to have been a lot of religious provocation from unbelieving Jews towards Christians. Greek church historian, Socrates of Constantinople, relates the following incident in Syria in the 4th century.

> At a place named Inmestar... the Jews were amusing themselves... at length impelled by drunkenness they were guilty of scoffing at Christians and even Christ himself; and in derision of the cross ... they seized a Christian boy, and having bound him to a cross, began to laugh and sneer at him ... they scourged the child until he died under their hands. This conduct occasioned a sharp conflict between them and the Christians; and as soon as the emperors were informed of the circumstance, they issued orders to the governor of the province to find out and punish the delinquents. [292]

Augustine

The following quotation is attributed to Augustine, but also seems to be an invention.

> Judaism, since Christ, is a corruption; indeed, Judas is the image of the Jewish people: their understanding of Scripture is carnal; they bear the guilt for the death of the Saviour, for through their fathers they have killed Christ.

Again, this supposed quote by Augustine cannot be actually found in any primary source.

> The true image of the Hebrew is Judas Iscariot, who sells the Lord for silver. The Jews can never understand the scriptures, and forever bear the guilt of the death of Christ.

One author attributes it to Augustine's "Tractatus adversus Iudaeos; Patrologiae cursus completus, series latina", but this

---

[292] Ecclesiastical History 4:16

document is available online and the quotation is absent. [293] Myths aside, what was Augustine's real attitude to Jews? He clearly did not view Jews in the same light as pagans, but rather grouped them into a similar category with Christians, because of their monotheism.

> But if we divide all who have a religion into those who worship one God and those who worship many gods, the Manichaeans must be classed along with the Pagans, and we along with the Jews. [294]

The Jewish Witness

Augustine's doctrine of the "Jewish Witness" has been greatly criticized, although on closer examination it is not in any way comparable to the anti-Semitic rantings of Chrysostom. It goes something like this:

a) An analogy is drawn between Abel and Jesus; and between Cain and the Jews. In Genesis 4, Cain killed his brother and was exiled as a punishment. This is more than he can bear and he calls out to God, not for forgiveness, but to spare his life from the enemies he will come across in the world. In response God graciously grants him protection by giving him a distinctive mark, promising sevenfold retribution on anyone who harms him. Likewise the Jews are scattered among the nations because, like Cain, they killed Jesus. The mind of Cain and, by extension, the Jews is:

> ... carnal; for he thinks little of being hid from the face of God, that is, of being under the anger of God, were it not that he may be found and slain... To be carnally minded is death; but he, in ignorance of this, mourns for the loss of his earthly possession, and is in terror of bodily death.[295]

---

[293] http://www.augustinus.it/latino/contro_giudei/index.htm
[294] Contra Faustum (Answer to Faustus)
[295] Ibid

b) But the exile of the Jews, though a punishment, comes with divine protection: the mark of Cain, which prevents people from completely destroying them. No matter what one thinks of his doctrine, Augustine is also cautioning people against poor treatment of Jews, because, he says, God will apportion a sevenfold retribution on those guilty of doing this.

> But what does God reply? "Not so," He says; "but whosoever shall kill Cain, vengeance shall be taken on him sevenfold." That is, it is not as you say, not by bodily death shall the ungodly race of carnal Jews perish. For whoever destroys them in this way shall suffer sevenfold vengeance, that is, shall bring upon himself the sevenfold penalty under which the Jews lie for the crucifixion of Christ. [296]

c) This survival of the Jews and their ability to keep their identity despite being scattered among the nations, is evidence that they are under a divine order of protection. It is a "divine safeguard":

> … whereby God signals to the rest of humanity his continuing connection to and protection of the Jewish religion and thus his continuing desire that the Jews always exist as a people. [297]

d) He sees the distinguishing "mark of Cain" as being the observance of the Law. No one has been able to remove the mark - i.e. the Jews devotion to their Law.

> It is a most notable fact, that all the nations subjugated by Rome adopted the heathenish ceremonies of the Roman worship; while the Jewish nation, whether under Pagan or Christian monarchs, has never lost the sign of their law, by which they are distinguished from all other nations and peoples. No emperor or monarch who finds under his government the people with this mark kills them, that is, makes them cease to be Jews, and as Jews

---

[296] Ibid
[297] Ibid

to be separate in their observances, and unlike the rest of the world. [298]

e) Their presence and preservation in the world is a continual witness to the triumph of Christianity.

> ... no one can fail to see that in every land where the Jews are scattered they mourn for the loss of their kingdom, and are in terrified subjection to the immensely superior number of Christians. [299]

f) This state of affairs will remain until the end of time, where they remain preserved as a continuing witness to Christians regarding the consequences of disobedience to God.

> So to the end of the seven days of time, [300] the continued preservation of the Jews will be proof to believing Christians of the subjection merited by those who, in the pride of their kingdom, put the Lord to death. [301]

Thus, although Augustine sees the only function of Jews to be a constant reminder to others of the consequences of sin, he does at least caution against mistreatment of them - with the threat of divine retribution being effected against those who do so.

Magona

Based on a letter written by Bishop Severus of Minorca, [302] it is alleged that in AD 418, within a period of 8 days there was a mass conversion of most of (i.e. 540 people) the Jewish population on the island of Minorca to Christianity. At the time, Severus supposedly burned the synagogue on the island. But many scholars are sceptical of the paper's authenticity, some

---

[298] Ibid
[299] Ibid
[300] The "seven days of time" is probably being an allusion to the sexta-septamillennial view but, with an Amillennial twist, adapted to include the seventh millennial day as part of the current age.
[301] Contra Faustum
[302] Epistula Severi (Letter on the Conversion of the Jews)

claiming that the letter was a "wilful distortion or even an outright forgery".[303]

Alexandria

In 4th and 5th century Alexandria in Egypt, Christians, Jews and pagans all lived together and there were vicious clashes between these groups. The city had long been known for its violent and volatile politics; Socrates claimed that there was no people who loved a fight more than those of Alexandria. Some of the tensions were triggered by a slaughter of Christians at the hands of Jews. After instigating the public torture of the monk Hierax by the city governor, Orestes - the Jews lured Christians into the streets at night by claiming that a church was on fire.

> ... the Christians on hearing their cry came forth quite ignorant of the treachery of the Jews... the Jews arose and wickedly massacred the Christians and shed the blood of many, guiltless though they were. [304]

The Jews were supported by Orestes, so the Christians appealed to the bishop Cyril for assistance. Then a very unchristian response ensued.

> ... the Christians mustered all together and went and marched in wrath to the synagogues of the Jews and took possession of them, and purified them and converted them into churches... And as for the Jewish assassins they expelled them from the city, and pillaged all their possessions and drove them forth wholly despoiled, and Orestes the prefect was unable to render them any help.[305]

Because of the trouble in the city, 500 monks came down from Nitria to defend Cyril. In a disturbance which arose, Orestes was wounded in the head by a stone thrown by a monk named Ammonius and the prefect then had Ammonius tortured to death.

---

[303] https://en.wikipedia.org/wiki/Severus_of_Minorca
[304] John, Bishop of Nikiu, from his Chronicle 84.87-103 (c. 7th / 8th century)
[305] Ibid

Cyril attempted to make a martyr of Ammonius, but Socrates relates that he was unsuccessful because of the more sensible Christians in the city.

> But the more sober-minded, although Christians, did not accept Cyril's prejudiced estimate of him; for they well knew that he had suffered the punishment due to his rashness, and that he had not lost his life under the torture because he would not deny Christ. [306]

Jerusalem

Christian sources reveal that, in the 4th century, Jews encountered great difficulty in buying the right to pray near the Western Wall in Jerusalem, on the 9th of Av. [307] This was a day of mourning and fasting to commemorate the destruction of the two temples. In AD 438 the Empress Aelia Eudocia Augusta, wife of Theodosius II, visited Jerusalem and removed the ban on Jews entering the city to pray at the Temple Mount. Her actions encouraged the migration of several thousand Jews to Jerusalem in hope of seeing the city resurrected as a Jewish homeland, but this was met with violent opposition by the Christian population. According to De Imperatoribus Romanis, an online encyclopaedia about the Roman emperors:

> At her palace in Bethlehem and in Jerusalem, she (Eudocia) continued to receive petitions and sought to alleviate the persecution of the Jews, in spite of the unpopularity of such a stance. [308]

Gregory I

In many cases of intolerance towards Jews, it is notable that Gregory I, the bishop of Rome from AD 590 until 604, protested. In AD 591 Gregory criticized the bishops of Arles and Marseilles

---

[306] Socrates - Ecclesiastical History (Book VII)
[307] Neusner, Jacob (2001). "Judaism and the Land of Israel". Understanding Jewish Theology. pp. g. 79.
[308] http://www.roman-emperors.org/eudocia.htm

for allowing the forced baptism of Jews in Provence. After a synagogue in Caraglio, northern Italy, had been desecrated in AD 599, Gregory wrote to insist that the Jews be compensated for their loss. Writing in AD 602 to Paschasius bishop of Naples, in response to a complaint by Jews of disruption in the celebration of their religious festivals, Gregory says:

> For of what use is this, when… it avails nothing toward their faith and conversion?... One must act, therefore, in such a way that… they might desire to follow us rather than to fly from us...Rather let them enjoy their lawful liberty to observe and to celebrate their festivities, as they have enjoyed this up until now. [309]

Gregory must also be commended for grasping what the true spirit of Christianity should be towards the unconverted. Writing concerning the Jews, he says:

> For it is necessary to gather those who are at odds with the Christian religion the unity of faith by meekness, by kindness, by admonishing, by persuading, lest these… should be repelled by threats and terrors. They ought, therefore, to come together to hear from you the Word of God in a kindly frame of mind, rather than stricken with dread, result of a harshness that goes beyond due limits.[310]

Zafar and Najran

In AD 524 the Yemeni Jewish Himyar tribe, led by King Dhu Nuwas, offered Christian residents in an area in what is now Saudi Arabia, the choice between conversion to Judaism or death. As a result, more than 22,000 Christians in Zafar and Najran were massacred.[311]

---

[309] Synan, The Popes and the Jews in the Middle Ages
[310] Ibid
[311] Jacques Ryckmans,La persécution des chrétiens himyarites au sixième siè-cle, Nederlands Historisch-Archaeologisch Inst. in het Nabije Oosten, 1956 pp 1-24

The Sassanid period in Jerusalem

In AD 614, the Sassanid Empire [312] drove the Byzantines out of Jerusalem, giving the Jews control of Jerusalem for the first time in centuries. King Khosrau II of Persia (reigned AD 590-628) agreed with the head of Babylonian Jewry, that in return for supplying 30,000 Jewish soldiers to the Persian army, these soldiers would be given permission to participate in the capture of Jerusalem and a Jewish governor would be appointed to rule over the city. [313] In the Siege of Jerusalem of AD 614, after 21 days of relentless siege warfare, Jerusalem was captured.[314]

The skilled Christians were forcibly deported to Persia, the number totalling 35,000. [315] Strategos, a 7th-century monk, who lived near Jerusalem and witnessed the Persian invasion says that the surviving Christians were shut up in a reservoir, the Mamilla Pool, where many suffocated owing to the heat and to the confinement of the place. Some Jews then offered to purchase them from the Persians with silver if they would renounce Christianity. When the Christians refused the offer, these Jews still purchased them, but subsequently massacred them. The overall Christian death toll from the battle and the aftermath was 66,509. [316] Strategos writes:

> When the people were carried into Persia, and the Jews were left in Jerusalem, they began with their own hands to demolish and burn such of the holy churches as were left standing... [317]

Initially the Jews were allowed to set up a vassal state under the Sassanid Empire, called the Sassanid Jewish Commonwealth

---

[312] The Neo-Persian Empire and the last Iranian empire before the rise of Islam.
[313] http://israelbehindthenews.com/we-have-returned-to-the-temple-mount-a-survey-of-jewish-presence-on-the-jerusalem-temple-mount-from-the-destruc-tion-of-the-second-temple-70-ce-until-the-six-day-war-1967/7256
[314] https://en.wikipedia.org/wiki/Jerusalem
[315] https://en.wikipedia.org/wiki/Byzantine_Sasanian_War_of_602_-608
[316] Antiochus Strategos, The Capture of Jerusalem by the Persians in 614 AD, F.C. CONYBEARE, English Historical Review 25 (1910) pp. 502-517
http://www.tertullian.org/fathers/antiochus_strategos_capture.htm
[317] Ibid

[318] and Nehemiah ben Hushiel was appointed governor of Jerusalem. But only three years later, the Persians relieved him of the position and subsequently executed him for reasons that were never clearly stated. After thus ending the Jewish rule of the city, the Persians forbade Jews from settling within a three-mile radius of Jerusalem.[319]

The Persian control of Jerusalem, did not last long. Byzantine emperor, Heraclius (AD 575-641) waged a successful war, destroying the Persian army in AD 628 and then marched into Jerusalem at the head of his army in the following year. Unfortunately, though he had initially promised amnesty to Jerusalem's Jews, which would have been a good Christian response, he was later convinced by the clergy of Jerusalem that his promise was invalid and not binding. Subsequently the Byzantines accused the Jews of having collaborated with the Persian conquerors and massacred them.[320]

The Crusaders

The call for the First Crusade by Pope Urban II in AD 1095 sparked off persecutions of the Jews in Europe. The Rhineland massacres also known as the German Crusade of 1096 included the destruction of Jewish communities in Speyer, Worms and Mainz. These were new persecutions of the Jews in which peasant 'crusaders' from France and Germany attacked Jewish communities. [321]

The massacre of the Jews was condemned by the leaders of the Catholic Church. Although the bishops of Mainz, Speyer, and Worms had attempted to shelter the Jews of those towns within the walls of their own palaces, the peasant army broke in to slaughter them. Fifty years later when Bernard of Clairvaux was urging recruitment for the Second Crusade, he specifically

---

[318] https://en.wikipedia.org/wiki/Temple_Mount#Sassanid_period
[319] http://jewishmag.com/161mag/persian_conquest_jerusalem/persian_conquest_jerusalem.htm
[320] Ibid
[321] https://en.wikipedia.org/wiki/Rhineland_massacres

criticized the attacks on Jews which occurred in the First Crusade. [322]

In the First Crusade the Jews of Jerusalem fought with the Muslims against the Crusaders until the fall of the city. [323] A Muslim chronicler, Ibn al-Qalanisi claimed that the "Jews assembled in their synagogue, and the Franks burned it over their heads." [324] More recently some have even asserted that the Crusaders circled "the screaming, flame-tortured humanity singing 'Christ We Adore Thee!' with their Crusader crosses held high." [325] Not surprisingly, these particular accounts have been used by many to demonise the Jerusalem Crusaders. But a letter discovered among the Cairo Geniza collection in 1975 by Jewish historian Shelomo Dov Goitein, [326] which is a contemporary Jewish account of the incident, does not corroborate the report that Jews were inside of the synagogue when it was set on fire. [327] Historians believe that the letter was written just two weeks after the siege, making it "the earliest account on the conquest in any language." [328] Additional documentation from the Cairo Geniza indicates that some Jews held captive by the Crusaders were able to escape when the Ascalon Jewish community paid a ransom. [329]

In the Second Crusade (1147) the Jews in France suffered especially, while during the Third Crusade (1188) Philip II of France treated them with exceptional severity. Jews were also subjected to attacks by the Shepherds' Crusades of 1251 and 1320. [330] The attacks were opposed by the local bishops and

---

[322] Ibid

[323] Brown, Michael L. Our Hands Are Stained with Blood: The Tragic Story of the "Church" and the Jewish People. 1992

[324] Gibb, H. A. R. The Damascus Chronicle of the Crusades: Extracted and Translated from the Chronicle of Ibn Al-Qalanisi., 2003, pg. 48

[325] Rausch, David. Legacy of Hatred: Why Christians Must Not Forget the Holocaust. 1990, pg. 27

[326] Kedar, Benjamin Z. "The Jerusalem Massacre of July 1099 in the Western Historiography of the Crusades." The Crusades Vol 3 (2004) pp. 15-76, pg 63

[327] Ibid, pg. 64

[328] Ibid, pg 63

[329] https://en.wikipedia.org/wiki/Siege_of_Jerusalem_(1099)

[330] https://en.wikipedia.org/wiki/History_of_the_Jews_and_the_Crusades

widely condemned at the time as a violation of the Crusades aim, which was not directed against the Jews. [331] However, the perpetrators mostly escaped legal punishment. [332]

The issues of usury and distinctive dress

Thomas Aquinas (1225-1274) was the most important medieval Catholic theologian. Based on a letter he writes to Margaret, Countess of Flanders or to Marguerite, Duchess of Brabant, where he gives advice of certain questions raised regarding treatment of Jews, he has been accused of the following.

1) He is reputed to have said that Jews were destined to perpetual servitude.

   Actually, Aquinas simply notes that this was the position of the existing law of the day, which then entitled rulers to take things from Jews without compensation - but he wisely advises that it should be exercised with restraint, in the light of the Scriptures about Christian witness. His words, placed in context, are:

   > … it can be answered that although, as the laws say, the Jews by reason of their fault are sentenced to perpetual servitude and thus the lords of the lands in which they dwell may take things from them as though they were their own - with, nonetheless, this restraint observed that the necessary subsidies of life in no way be taken from them, because it still is necessary that we "walk honestly even in the presence of those who are outsiders (I Thes. 4:11)," "lest the name of the Lord be blasphemed (I Tim. 6:1)," and the Apostle admonishes the faithful by his example that (I Cor. 10:32-33), "they be without offense in the presence of the Jews and the Gentiles and in the Church of God"… [333]

---

[331] "The Church and the Jews in the Middle Ages". Crisismagazine.com
[332] https://en.wikipedia.org/wiki/Rhineland_massacres
[333] http://www.ccjr.us/dialogika-resources/primary-texts-from-the-history-of-the-relationship/268-aquinas Thomas Aquinas, "Letter on the Treatment of Jews" (1271), First Response

2) He says Jews should be forced to wear a distinctive badge in order to distinguish them from Christians.

> The Fourth Lateran Council headed by Pope Innocent III ruled in AD 1215 that Jews must wear distinguishable dress and a coloured badge of identification. This became common practice throughout Europe. [334] Asked for his opinion, Aquinas actually agrees with the existing statute arguing that in any event, the Jewish law is in agreement. [335] His interpretation here is somewhat questionable, as is his approval of the practice. (Later during the 17th century in Venice and in other places, Jews would be required to wear a red hat at all times in public to ensure that they were easily identified. If they did not comply with this rule, they could face the death penalty. And these practices were undoubtedly a precedent for the Nazis forcing Jews throughout occupied Europe to wear a badge in the form of a Yellow Star, as a means of singling them out.)

3) He says that Jews should be compelled to work rather than live in idleness and grow rich by usury.

> There was a papal prohibition on usury making that it was a sin to charge interest on a money loan and charging interest was viewed the same as theft. Aquinas did make

---

[334] "The Evil of Replacement Theology - The Historical Abuse of the Jews by the Church" By Dr. David R. Reagan

[335] http://www.ccjr.us/dialogika-resources/primary-texts-from-the-history-of-the-relationship/268-aquinas Thomas Aquinas, "Letter on the Treatment of Jews" (1271), Eighth Response - "Finally you ask whether it is good that Jews throughout your province are compelled to wear a sign distinguishing them from Christians. The reply to this is plain: that, according to a statute of the general Council, Jews of each sex in all Christian provinces, and all the time, should be distinguished from other people by some clothing. This is also mandated to them by their own law, namely that they make for themselves fringes on the four corners of their cloaks, through which they are distinguished from others."

this statement, but in the context of being asked if a Jew accused of usury should receive a financial penalty.[336]

While usury is defined today as the practice of making unethical or immoral monetary loans that unfairly enrich the lender because of excessive or abusive interest rates, historically in Christian societies, charging any interest at all was considered usury.[337]

Money lending became a fairly common occupation among Jews, but in many respects this was forced on them. Jews were excluded from other fields of work, most Christian kings forbade Jews to own land for farming or to serve in the government, and craft guilds often refused to admit Jews as artisans. Thus money lending was one of the few occupations still open to Jews and, as Christians were not permitted to practise usury, they typically would have to resort to lending money from Jews. [338] This led to much resentment of the Jews and the stereotyping of the Jewish money-lending villain.

In England, the departing Crusaders were joined by crowds of debtors in the massacres of Jews at London and York in 1189-1190. In 1275, Edward I of England passed the Statute of the Jewry which made usury illegal

---

[336] Ibid - Second Response – "Now, second you asked, if a Jew should sin, should this person be punished with the financial penalty, since he seems to have nothing aside from usurious money. To which question it seems the response should be, in line with what has been said before, that it is expeditious that he be punished with a financial penalty, in order that he might not accrue some benefit from his iniquity; it also seems to me that the Jew should be punished with a greater fine (or anyone else who practices usury) than anyone else in a similar case, to make the point that the money taken from him be known to be less his entitlement. ... But if it be said that the princes of countries suffer loss from this, this loss should be imputed to them as coming from their own negligence; for it would be better if they compelled Jews to work for their own living, as they do in parts of Italy, than that, living without occupation they grow rich by usury, and thus their rulers be defrauded of revenue. In the same way, and through their own fault, princes are defrauded of their proper revenues if they permit their subjects to enrich themselves by theft and robbery alone..."
[337] https://en.wikipedia.org/wiki/Usury
[338] https://en.wikipedia.org/wiki/Shylock

and linked it to blasphemy, in order to seize the assets of the violators. Scores of English Jews were arrested, 300 were hanged and their property went to the Crown. In 1290, all Jews were expelled from England, and allowed to take only what they could carry; the rest of their property became the Crown's. Usury was cited as the official reason for the Edict of Expulsion. However, not all Jews were expelled: it was easy to convert to Christianity and thereby avoid expulsion. Many other crowned heads of Europe expelled the Jews, although again converts to Christianity were no longer considered Jewish. [339]

In 1306, Philippe IV expelled the Jews from France and in 1307, he annihilated the order of the Knights Templar. He was in debt to both groups and saw them as a "state within the state". [340]

With the Jews gone, Philip appointed royal guardians to collect the loans made by the Jews, and the money was passed to the Crown. The scheme did not work well. The Jews were regarded to be good businessmen who satisfied their customers, while the king's collectors were universally unpopular. Finally, in 1315, because of the "clamour of the people", the Jews were invited back with an offer of 12 years of guaranteed residence, free from government interference. In 1322, the Jews were expelled again by the King's successor, who did not honour his commitment. [341]

In a 1523 essay entitled, "That Jesus Was Born a Jew," Martin Luther wrote of medieval anti-Semitism as follows:

Therefore, I would request and advise that one deal gently with them and instruct them from Scripture; then some of them may come along. Instead of this we are trying only to drive them by force, slandering them...So long as we thus treat them like dogs, how can we expect to work any good among them? Again, when we forbid

---

[339] https://en.wikipedia.org/wiki/Usury
[340] https://en.wikipedia.org/wiki/Philip_IV_of_France
[341] Ibid

them to labour and do business and have any human fellowship with us, thereby forcing them into usury, how is that supposed to do them any good? If we really want to help them, we must be guided in our dealings with them not by papal law but by the law of Christian love... If some of them should prove stiff-necked, what of it? After all, we ourselves are not all good Christians either.[342]

In Shakespeare's time, no Jews had been legally present in England for several hundred years (since the Edict of Expulsion in 1290). But stereotypes of Jews as money lenders remained from the Middle Ages. Shakespeare would depict the Jewish moneylender, Shylock, as a villain in "The Merchant of Venice". In the play, Shylock lends money to his Christian rival, Antonio, setting the security at a pound of Antonio's flesh from next to his heart. When a bankrupt Antonio defaults on the loan, Shylock "demands the pound of flesh", hence the idiom we use today for a particularly onerous obligation. His defeat and conversion to Christianity forms the climax of the story.[343]

The inquisition

The earlier Inquisition had targeted non-Catholic Christians or heretics, but later it turned its attention to Jews as well. Pope Innocent III had declared in AD 1199 that, as Scripture contained lessons too profound for laymen to grasp, rather than reading the Scripture themselves, Christians should rely wholly on the clergy for its interpretation. The resultant restrictions on religious literature was to be used against those attempting to reform the church, but also against Jews. [344]

In AD 1242 the Talmud (a central text of Rabbinic Judaism including the Mishna) was condemned. While years earlier in AD 553 Justinian had attempted to prohibit the use of the Mishnah

---

[342] Martin Luther, "That Jesus Was Born A Jew," translated by Walter I. Brandt in Luther's Works, 1962, pp. 200-201, 229
[343] https://en.wikipedia.org/wiki/Shylock
[344] http://jewishvirtuallibrary.org/jsource/anti-semitism/TalmudBurning.html

in synagogues, now thousands of Jewish books, including some of Maimonides' works were destroyed. [345]

In AD 1236 Nicholas Donin, a Jewish convert to Christianity in Paris, wrote to Pope Gregory IX alleging that the Talmud contained blasphemies of Jesus and Mary, attacks on the Church, pronouncements hostile to non-Jews, and foolish tales. He asserted that the Jews had elevated the Oral Law to the level of Scripture, and that this impeded their possible conversion to Christianity. In response Gregory ordered a preliminary investigation and in AD 1239 sent a circular letter to church leaders in France, ordering the confiscation and burning of certain Jewish books. Similar instructions were conveyed to the kings of France, England, Spain, and Portugal. In AD 1242, 24 wagon loads of books totalling thousands of volumes were handed over for public burning. Copies of the Talmud may also have been seized and destroyed in Rome. Subsequently the burning of the Talmud was repeatedly urged by successive popes although, outside of France, generally little action was taken in response to the papal appeals. [346] In AD 1288, the Inquisition resulted in the first mass burning of Jews at the stake in France. [347]

But the Spanish Inquisition ultimately surpassed the Medieval Inquisition, in both scope and intensity. When Pope Sixtus IV, allowed Ferdinand and Isabella to establish a special branch of the Inquisition in Spain in AD 1478, it was because of a perceived danger to the church from Jews masquerading as Christians. Such Jews were referred to as marranos ('swine'). Their conversion was the result of anti-Semitic violence during the previous century when, to escape the likelihood of death at the hands of 'Christian' mobs, many Jews had been baptised. Thomas of Torquemada came from a family of conversos (converts from Judaism) [348] and became the first Inquisitor General of Spain. Under Torquemada, Jews were given three months to become Christians or leave the country.

---

[345] Ibid
[346] Ibid
[347] Jewish Virtual Library, "Christian-Jewish Relations: The Inquisition,"
[348] http://alchetron.com/Tomas-de-Torquemada-1055980-W

Ghettos

In the 11ᵗʰ century large cities throughout Europe began to segregate Jews into designated areas within the cities called ghettos. Considering them to be 'vermin', it was decided that they should be cut off from the rest of the population. [349]

> In addition to being confined to ghettos, Jews were placed under strict regulations and disabilities in many European cities... In many instances, ghettos were places of terrible poverty and during periods of population growth, ghettos had narrow streets and small, crowded houses. [350]

Because of the ingrained Replacement Theology of Amillennialism, the Catholic Church at this stage had clearly forgotten that it claimed a Jewish fisherman as its first pope, or that its founder, Jesus, along with his apostles, were all Jewish. American historian, Will Durant, relays this official policy of the Catholic Church, which was deeply anti-Semitic.

> The Council of Vienne (1311) forbade all intercourse between Christians and Jews. The Council of Zamora (1313) ruled that they must be kept in strict subjection and servitude. The Council of Basel (1431-33) renewed canonical decrees forbidding Christians to associate with Jews, to serve them, or to use them as physicians, and instructed secular authorities to confine the Jews in separate quarters, compel them to wear a distinguishing badge, and ensure their attendance at sermons aimed to convert them. Pope Eugenius IV...added that Jews should be ineligible for any public office, could not inherit property from Christians, must build no more synagogues, and... any Italian Jew found reading Talmudic literature should suffer confiscation of his property, etc.[351]

---

[349] The Jewish Encyclopedia (1906), "Ghetto,"
[350] https://en.wikipedia.org/wiki/Jewish_ghettos_in_Europe
[351] Will Durant, The Reformation (Simon and Schuster, 1957), 729

Blood libel

"Blood libel" refers to an old false allegation that Jews murdered Christians - in particular children - to use their blood for ritual purposes, such as an ingredient in the baking of Passover matzah (unleavened bread). In medieval times this accusation was sometimes used in order to account for the otherwise unexplained deaths of children. According to Walter Laqueur:

> Altogether, there have been about 150 recorded cases of blood libel ... that resulted in the arrest and killing of Jews throughout history, most of them in the Middle Ages. In almost every case, Jews were murdered, sometimes by a mob, sometimes following torture and a trial.[352]

A notorious blood libel case occurred in AD 1493 when a two-year-old boy named Simon disappeared in Trent, Italy. His murder was blamed on the leaders of the city's Jewish community, based on his dead body being found in the cellar of a Jewish family's house. [353] 18 Jewish men and 5 Jewish women were arrested on the charge of ritual murder. In a series of interrogations involving liberal use of judicial torture, the magistrates obtained the confessions of the Jewish men and 8 were executed, with another committing suicide in jail. [354]

The Black Plague

The Black Plague in Europe peaked in the middle of the 14th century (AD 1346-1353), resulting in the deaths of an estimated 75 to 200 million people, 30-60% of Europe's total population. [355] Some sought to blame various groups for the crisis, including

---

[352] Walter Laqueur (2006): The Changing Face of Antisemitism: From Ancient Times to the Present Day, p. 56
[353] https://en.wikipedia.org/wiki/Simon_of_Trent
[354] "Toaff Controversy" - http://www.haaretz.com quoting Edwin Erle Sparks, Professor of History at The Pennsylvania State University.
[355] https://en.wikipedia.org/wiki/Black_Death

Jews, friars, foreigners, beggars, pilgrims, lepers and gypsies.[356] Because healers were at a loss to explain the cause, the poisoning of wells by Jews was proposed as one of the possible reasons for the plague's emergence. [357] One reason people may have believed this false charge was that Jews were clearly less affected, with some at the time claiming that they only died at half the rate as Gentiles. Even if this was true, it can more properly be attributed to the sanitary practices of the Jewish law.[358]

> For instance, Jewish law compels one to wash his or her hands many times throughout the day. In the general medieval world a person could go half his or her life without ever washing his hands. According to Jewish law, one could not eat food without washing one's hands, leaving the bathroom and after any sort of intimate human contact. At least once a week, a Jew bathed for the Sabbath. Furthermore, Jewish law prevents the Jew from reciting blessings and saying prayers by an open pit at latrines and at places with a foul odour. The sanitary conditions in the Jewish neighbourhood, primitive as it may be by today's standards, was always far superior to the general sanitary conditions. [359]

But the baseless allegation resulted in many attacks on Jewish communities. In 1349 the citizens of Strasbourg murdered 2,000 Jews [360] and the Jewish communities in Mainz and Cologne were exterminated. By 1351, 60 major and 150 smaller Jewish communities had been destroyed.[361]

---

[356] David Nirenberg, Communities of Violence, 1998, & R.I. Moore The Formation of a Persecuting Society, 1987.
[357] https://en.wikipedia.org/wiki/Black_Death
[358] http://www.jewishhistory.org/the-black-death
[359] Ibid
[360] Black Death, Jewishencyclopedia.com
[361] Jewish History 1340-1349 http://www.jewishhistory.org.il/history.php

Pogroms

The term 'pogrom' came from a Russian word and is used in particular of organized massacres of Jews in the Russian Empire or Eastern Europe, although it is now applied to earlier anti-Jewish massacres as well.

> The Jewish communities were targeted… in Toulon in 1348, in Barcelona and in other Catalan cities, during the Erfurt massacre (1349), the Basel massacre, massacres in Aragon, and in Flanders, as well as the "Valentine's Day" Strasbourg pogrom of 1349. Some 510 Jewish communities were destroyed in this period, extending further to the Brussels massacre of 1370. On Holy Saturday of 1389, a pogrom began in Prague that led to the burning of the Jewish quarter, the killing of many Jews, and the suicide of many Jews trapped in the main synagogue; the number of dead was estimated at 400-500 men, women, and children. [362]

Starting in 1821, there were 5 pogroms in Odessa in Tsarist Russia in the 19th century. Following the assassination of Alexander II in 1881 by Narodnaya Volya (a revolutionary political organization) - blamed on the Jews by the Russian government, this resulted in a wave of over 200 pogroms which lasted for several years. [363]

In 20th century Russia, the Kishinev pogrom of 1903 saw 47 Jews killed, hundreds wounded, 700 homes destroyed and 600 businesses pillaged. The Kiev pogrom of 1905, resulted in a massacre of about 100 Jews. When the Jewish Labour Bund began organizing armed self-defence units ready to shoot, the pogroms subsided for a number of years. Large-scale pogroms intensified during the period of the Russian Civil War and the Revolution of 1917. Professor Zvi Gitelman estimated that only in 1918-1919 over 1,200 pogroms took place in Ukraine, amounting to a greatest slaughter of Jews in Eastern Europe since 1648. The Kiev pogroms of 1919 were the first of a

---

[362] https://en.wikipedia.org/wiki/Pogrom
[363] Ibid

subsequent wave of pogroms in which between 30,000 and 70,000 Jews were massacred across Ukraine.[364] According to professor Colin Tatz, between 1881 and 1920, there were 1,326 pogroms in Ukraine which claimed the lives of 70,000 to 250,000 civilian Jews and left half a million homeless.[365]

The reformation

Unfortunately, the early Reformers still held to the Amillennial view and with it the accompanying Replacement Theology of the medieval church. With regards to Jews, John Calvin stated that "God blinded the whole people. I have never seen a drop of piety or grain of truth or common sense in any Jew." [366]

Replacement Theology is even reflected in the chapter headings of the King James Bible, published in 1611. In Isaiah 43 God addresses His promises to 'Jacob' and 'Israel,' but the chapter heading reads: "God comforteth the Church with His promises." Yet when dealing with chapters that refer to God's curses against Israel, spiritualizing the meaning of 'Israel' is not attempted and, they are readily applied to the Jews. Isaiah 59 has the heading, "The sins of the Jews", yet in the very next chapter, the promise of future glory has the heading, "Glory of the Church".

Martin Luther

Initially Martin Luther spoke out against the Church's mistreatment of the Jewish people, stating in a 1923 essay:

> If I had been a Jew and had seen such dolts and blockheads govern and teach the Christian faith, I would sooner have become a hog than a Christian. They have dealt with the Jews as if they were dogs rather than

---

[364] Ibid
[365] Ibid
[366] John Calvin, Daniel Lecture XI in Calvin's Commentaries.

human beings; they have done little else than deride them and seize their property. [367]

He believed that the Jewish people would convert to Christianity if they were treated better and presented with the true gospel.

> I hope that if one deals in a kindly way with the Jews and instructs them carefully from Holy Scripture, many of them will become genuine Christians and turn again to the faith of their fathers, the prophets and patriarchs. They will only be frightened further away from it if their Judaism is so utterly rejected that nothing is allowed to remain, and they are treated only with arrogance and scorn. If the apostles, who also were Jews, had dealt with us Gentiles as we Gentiles deal with the Jews, there would never have been a Christian among the Gentiles. Since they dealt with us Gentiles in such brotherly fashion, we in our turn ought to treat the Jews in a brotherly manner in order that we might convert some of them. [368]

But unfortunately, Luther later became disillusioned with the Jews when they continued to resist his reformed gospel, and by the 1530s he was endorsing the common medieval stereotypes of the Jews, referring to them as "iron-hearted" and "stubborn as the Devil." [369] Ultimately Luther said of the Jews, "I have no hope for them these children of the devil" [370] Concerning the possibility that Jews would return to the land of Israel, Luther took the classic Replacement Theology stance, saying:

> …all the prophecies which say that Israel and Judah shall return to their lands have been fulfilled long ago. The hopes of the Jews are utterly vain and lost. When the prophets say of Israel that it is all to come back or be

---

[367] Martin Luther, "That Jesus Was Born A Jew," translated by Walter I. Brandt in Luther's Works, 1962, pp. 200-201, 229
[368] Ibid
[369] David A. Rausch, A Legacy of Hatred: Why Christians Must Not Forget the Holocaust, 1984, p. 28
[370] Martin Luther, Lectures on the Minor Prophets

gathered, they are certainly speaking of the new covenant and the new Israel.[371]

Regrettably in his closing years, Luther had turned against the Jews with a vengeance, writing a pamphlet in 1543 entitled "Concerning the Jews and Their Lies."[372] In it, he referred to the Jews as, "a miserable and accursed people", "stupid fools", "miserable, blind and senseless", "thieves and robbers", "the great vermin of humanity", "lazy rogues" and "blind and venomous".[373] He then proceeded to make some startling proposals for dealing with them. Their synagogues and schools should be burned; their houses should be destroyed; their Talmudic writings should be confiscated; their rabbis should be forbidden to teach; their money should be taken from them; they should be compelled into forced labour.[374]

Some have tried to justify Luther's remarks attributing it to the deterioration of his health and temper in old age, or by pointing out that Luther often deliberately used "vulgarity and violence" for literary effect, not only in his writings condemning the Jews, but in his diatribes against "Turks" (Muslims) and Catholics.[375] But the fact remains that this later writing, in particular, was inexcusable. It is sad that he couldn't have been remembered instead for his earlier, softer, Christ-like approach in "That Jesus Was Born A Jew". Roland Bainton, the noted church historian and biographer of Luther, even commented, "One could wish that Luther had died before ever 'On the Jews and Their Lies' was written."[376]

---

[371] Ibid. II, 687-688
[372] The Jewish Virtual Library, "Martin Luther: The Jews and Their Lies (1543)"
[373] "The Evil of Replacement Theology - The Historical Abuse of the Jews by the Church" By Dr. David R. Reagan http://christinprophecy.org/articles/the-evil-of-replacement-theology
[374] Ibid
[375] https://en.wikipedia.org/wiki/Martin_Luther#Anti-Judaism
[376] Bainton: Here I Stand, 1983, p. 297

The Holocaust

Despite being neo-pagan and occultic in outlook, in their rise to power, the Nazis used Martin Luther's "Concerning the Jews and Their Lies" tract to their advantage in an attempt to justify their anti-Semitism to German Christians. The city of Nuremberg presented a first edition of Luther's tract to Julius Streicher, editor of the Nazi newspaper Der Stürmer, on his birthday in 1937; the newspaper described it as the most radically anti-Semitic tract ever published.[377] Hitler even referred to Luther in his book, Mein Kampf, as a "great warrior, a true statesman, and a great reformer." [378] Heinrich Himmler wrote admiringly of Luther's writings on the Jews stating "… what Luther said and wrote about the Jews. No judgment could be sharper." [379]

But while some scholars claim a direct link between Luther and the rising anti-Semitism in 20th century Germany, others disagree.

> At the heart of scholars' debate about Luther's influence is whether it is anachronistic to view his work as a precursor of the racial antisemitism of the Nazis. Some scholars see Luther's influence as limited, and the Nazis' use of his work as opportunistic. Johannes Wallmann argues that Luther's writings against the Jews were largely ignored in the 18th and 19th centuries, and that there was no continuity between Luther's thought and Nazi ideology. Uwe Siemon-Netto agreed, arguing that it was because the Nazis were already anti-Semites that they revived Luther's work. Hans J. Hillerbrand agreed that to focus on Luther was to adopt an essentially ahistorical perspective of Nazi antisemitism that ignored other contributory factors in German history. [380]

---

[377] Ellis, Marc H. Hitler and the Holocaust, Christian Anti-Semitism", (NP: Baylor University Centre for American and Jewish Studies, Spring 2004).
[378] Adolph Hitler, Mein Kampf, Volume 1 (1925), Chapter VIII
[379] https://en.wikipedia.org/wiki/Martin_Luther_and_antisemitism
[380] Ibid

Nevertheless, when speaking to thousands at a Christian gathering in Berlin in 1924, Hitler received a standing ovation when he declared: "I believe that today I am acting in accordance with the will of Almighty God as I announce the most important work that Christians could undertake - and that is to be against the Jews and get rid of them once and for all." [381] Raul Hilberg, considered to be the world's preeminent scholar of the Holocaust, who authored "The Destruction of the European Jews", made the famous quote:

> Viewing the plight of the Jews in Christian lands from the fourth century to the recent holocaust, one Jew observed, "First we were told 'You're not good enough to live among us as Jews.' Then we were told, 'You're not good enough to live among us.' Finally we were told, 'You're not good enough to live.'" [382]

Christ killers?

Jewish deicide is the belief that Jewish people as a whole were responsible for the death of Jesus. The anti-Semitic slur "Christ-killer" was often used by mobs to incite violence against Jews and contributed to many centuries of pogroms, the murder of Jews during the Crusades, the Spanish Inquisition, and even during the Holocaust. [383] With regard to the allegation that the Jews are "Christ killers," the Bible makes it clear that the culpability for the crucifixion of Jesus does not lie exclusively with the Jews.

> Acts 4:27: Indeed Herod and Pontius Pilate met together with the Gentiles and the people of Israel in this city to conspire against your holy servant Jesus, whom you anointed.

---

[381] Phyllis Petty, "Christian Hatred and Persecution of the Jews," www.therefinersfire.org/antisemitism_in_church.htm
[382] http://pre-trib.org/articles/view/hal-lindsey-dominion-theology-and-anti-semitism
[383] https://en.wikipedia.org/wiki/Jewish_deicide

Note who is listed here as responsible for the death of Jesus: the Gentiles and the Jews, along with the Roman rulers. While the Jewish authorities did instigate the execution, it was within the power of the Romans to veto the death penalty - which Pontius Pilate chose not to do. The mocking, beating and execution of Jesus was at the hand of the Gentile Roman soldiers. And it was Roman hands that placed a crown of thorns on his head, drove the nails into the cross and thrust the spear into his side. Even in our modern legal system - in a murder conspiracy trial, both those who plot the murder and those who carry out the act are equally liable. The reality is that all of us are ultimately personally responsible for Jesus' death, as it was our sins that led him down the path to the cross.

> Isaiah 53:5 But he was pierced for our transgressions, he was crushed for our iniquities; the punishment that brought us peace was on him, and by his wounds we are healed.

Modern Anti-Semitism and Anti-Zionism

Like Amillennialists, most Postmillennialists subscribe to some form of Replacement Theology. And historically, Replacement Theology has often been the theological foundation upon which anti-Semitism has been built within the confines of professing Christianity. Thomas Ice writes:

> History records that such a theology, when combined with the right social and political climate, has produced and allowed anti-Semitism to flourish. This was a point made by Hal Lindsey in The Road to Holocaust, to which Reconstructionists cried foul.[384]

But while Hal Lindsey does not claim that all Reconstructionists or Dominionists are anti-Semitic, he says that they engage in "the same sort of rhetoric that in the past formed the basis of contempt for the Jews that later developed into outright anti-

---

[384] http://pre-trib.org/articles/view/glorious-and-incomparable-promises-of-bible

Semitism." [385] He cautions Christians to "not sit idly by while a system of prophetic interpretation that historically furnished the philosophical basis for anti-Semitism infects the Church again." [386] Subsequent to and because of the Holocaust, some mainstream Christian theologians and denominations have rejected Replacement Theology. [387] Yet consider the words of Reconstructionist, James Jordan, who even denies modern Jews the claim to the land of Israel.

> Modern apostate Jews have absolutely no theological, and therefore no historical and legal right to the land of Palestine.[388]

He also bemoans the fact that many Christians support Israel.

> Christian Zionism is blasphemy. It is heresy. Christians have no theological stake whatsoever in the modern State of Israel. It is an anti-God, anti-Christ nation. [389]

Other Reconstructionists do believe that in the future individual Jews will be converted to Christ on a large scale, but almost none believe that national Israel has any future in God's dealings with mankind. Reconstructionist David Chilton (1951-1997) made a statement which stands in stark contrast to a plain reading of Scripture:

> ... ethnic Israel was excommunicated for its apostasy and will never again be God's Kingdom ... Although Israel will someday be restored to the true faith, the Bible does not tell of any future plan for Israel as a special nation. [390]

But the words of Reconstructionist, Gary North, seem more fitting to the Spanish Inquisitors, Muslims, or perhaps even the Nazis.

---

[385] The Road to Holocaust :25.
[386] Ibid
[387] R. Kendall Soulen, The God of Israel and Christian Theology, 1996)
[388] Jordan, Sociology:183. 43
[389] Ibid.:184
[390] David Chilton, Paradise Restored, 1985, p. 224

When Israel gets pushed into the sea, or converted to Christ, Scofieldism dies a fast death. Rest assured, I have a manuscript ready to go when either of these events happens.[391]

Needless to say, on the strength of God's Word, that manuscript won't ever be published!

Although in the early years of Pentecostalism, there was a strong focus on the Premillennial Dispensationalist view prophecy, in later years we have seen the rise of Dominion Theology which is taught by some Charismatic leaders. A theological anti-Semitism also exists in the Dominionist plan to replace Israel with the Church, often called the 'New Israel'. Charismatic Dominionist Earl Paulk berated those who teach that God still blesses those who bless Israel.

> ... the spirit of the antichrist is now at work in the world... through so-called Holy Spirit-filled teachers who say, 'If you bless national Israel, God will bless you.' Not only is this blatantly deceptive, it is not part of the new covenant at all! [392]

Paulk also said:

> Some of the strongest fundamental churches still preach that Christ will return to gather national Israel unto Himself, and I say that is deception and will keep the Kingdom of God from coming to pass! In almost any Christian bookstore, about 99% of the books will say that "God's time-clock is Israel" and that "God's covenant is still with Israel." ... [I say that] prophecies about Israel as a nation [are] now transferred to spiritual Israel, which is the people of God [i.e., the church].[393]

---

[391] Letter to Peter Lalonde, dated April 30, 1987

[392] The Handwriting is on the Wall

[393] Earl Paulk, The Handwriting on the Wall (booklet self-published by Paulk's Chapel Hill Harvester Church, Decatur, GA 30034), 17,19-20

But even more surprising is this statement by Rick Godwin, a popular Christian media speaker, while speaking at Edmond near Oklahoma City on 11 April 1988. He says of national Israel:

> They are not chosen, they are cursed! They are not blessed, they are cursed!... Yes, and you hear Jerry Falwell and everybody else say the reason America's great is because America's blessed Israel. They sure have. Which Israel? The Israel - the church... That's the Israel of God, not that garlic one over on the Mediterranean Sea! [394]

Preterists claim that Israel was supplanted by the Christian church at the destruction of Jerusalem in AD 70. [395] American Anglican bishop and Preterist, Ray Sutton, teaches that God has permanently divorced Israel. Explaining the parables of Matthew 21 and 22, he says:

> For the next several chapters, one section after another pronounces judgment and total discontinuity between God and Israel... total disinheritance. [396]

But while these parables do indicate the transition to an era where Gentiles would predominantly respond to the gospel, the claim that Israel was permanently rejected by God is at odds with the teaching of Paul, who makes it abundantly clear that God's calling of the Jews is 'irrevocable' (Rom 11:29) and who predicts a later restoration of Israel. When speaking of this restoration, Paul cautions Gentiles not to becoming spiritually proud or arrogant about the current position of favour of the Gentile church in God's eyes (Rom 11:17-24 [397]).

---

[394] Rick Godwin No. 2 audio tape (Sunday evening sermon at Metro Church, Edmond)

[395] Wikipedia: Preterism

[396] Sutton, That You May Prosper: Dominion By Covenant (Institute for Christian Economics, 1987)

[397] Rom 11:17-24 If some of the branches have been broken off, and you, though a wild olive shoot, have been grafted in among the others and now share in the nourishing sap from the olive root, do not boast over those branches. If you do, consider this: You do not support the root, but the root supports you. You will say then, "Branches were broken off so that I could be

16th - 18th century: growing rejection of Replacement Theology

From the 5th century, through medieval times and even to the time of the early Magisterial reformers, Amillennialism was dominant. Along with it, Replacement Theology and anti-Semitism prevailed. As the Church had supposedly permanently replaced Israel, a Millennium that had anything to do with a suggested restoration of Israel was an unpopular idea. Origen criticised Premillennialism as a Jewish view. Jerome said that Papias "is said to have perpetuated a Jewish tradition of the thousand years..." [398] The Lutherans condemned the Anabaptists "who now scatter Jewish opinions that, before the resurrection of the dead, the godly shall occupy the kingdom of the world..." [399] Heinrich Bullinger, the successor of Zwingli, stated, "We also reject the Jewish dream of a Millennium, or golden age on earth, before the last judgment." [400] Now, why would being a 'Jewish' idea be considered a derogatory statement and the basis for rejecting a viewpoint, unless someone was anti-Semitic?

Thomas Ice has pointed out that some modern historians are beginning to recognize the degree of Philo-Semitism (i.e. love of Jews) held by the Puritans. [401]

---

grafted in." Granted. But they were broken off because of unbelief, and you stand by faith. Do not be arrogant, but be afraid. For if God did not spare the natural branches, he will not spare you either. Consider therefore the kindness and sternness of God: sternness to those who fell, but kindness to you, provided that you continue in his kindness. Otherwise, you also will be cut off. And if they do not persist in unbelief, they will be grafted in, for God is able to graft them in again. After all, if you were cut out of an olive tree that is wild by nature, and contrary to nature were grafted into a cultivated olive tree, how much more readily will these, the natural branches, be grafted into their own olive tree!

[398] Jerome, Illustrious Lives 18

[399] The Augsburg Confession Art. XVII

[400] The Second Helvetic Confession

[401] http://www.pre-trib.org/articles/view/the-rise-of-philo-semitism-and-premillennialism-during-the-seventeenth-and-eighteenth-centuries#_ftnref14

According to Steven Spector, Yale PhD and professor at Stony Brook, Many Puritans no longer applied Old Testament narratives solely to themselves as re-embodied Israel. Rather, now they believed that the covenant remained in effect for the Hebrews physical descendants. And the Jews' return to Zion was, for them, the necessary prelude to the coming of the Messiah. [402]

So while hardly Premillennial Futurists yet, many Puritans started to reject Replacement Theology. Jews had not been allowed to settle in England again until the rule of the Puritan Lord Protector, Oliver Cromwell. In 1657, over 350 years after their banishment by Edward I, he encouraged Jews to return to England.

> ... Cromwell was aware of the Jewish community's involvement in the economics of the Netherlands, now England's leading commercial rival. It was this - allied to Cromwell's tolerance of the right to private worship of those who fell outside evangelical Puritanism - that led to his encouraging Jews to return ... in the hope that they would help speed up the recovery of the country after the disruption of the Civil Wars. There was a longer-term motive for Cromwell's decision to allow the Jews to return to England, and that was the hope that they would convert to Christianity and therefore hasten the Second Coming of Jesus Christ, ultimately based on Matthew 23:37-39 [403] and Romans 11. At the Whitehall conference of December 1655, he quoted from Paul's Epistle to the Romans 10:12-15 on the need to send Christian preachers to the Jews. [404]

---

[402] Stephen Spector, Evangelicals and Israel: The Story of American Christian Zionism, 2009, 17.

[403] Matt 23:37-39 "Jerusalem, Jerusalem, you who kill the prophets and stone those sent to you, how often I have longed to gather your children together, as a hen gathers her chicks under her wings, and you were not willing. Look, your house is left to you desolate. For I tell you, you will not see me again until you say, 'Blessed is he who comes in the name of the Lord.'"

[404] https://en.wikipedia.org/wiki/Oliver_Cromwell

Ice lists some 46 16th-18th century authors who were Philo-Semitic and expected the restoration of Israel, including John Milton, Joseph Mede, Philip Doddridge and Charles Wesley. [405] He writes:

> Seventeenth century Puritans took the Hebrew Bible more seriously than their Christian predecessors. This Philo-Semitism did not end when Puritanism fell out of favour in the later seventeenth century, which can be shown in the works of Isaac Newton, William Whiston, and others.

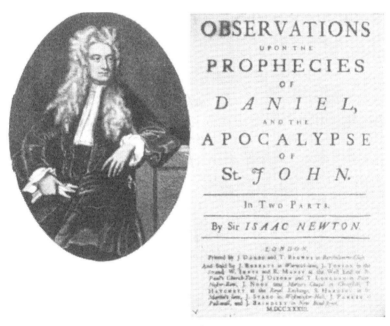

Figure 14: A writing on prophecy by renowned physicist, Isaac Newton

Isaac Newton (1642-1726/7) was a renowned English physicist and mathematician who is widely recognised as one of the most influential scientists of all time. But he was also a devout Christian and student of prophecy. Writing of the restoration of Israel, he declares that "the mystery of this restitution of all things

---

[405] http://www.pre-trib.org/articles/view/the-rise-of-philo-semitism-and-premil-lennialism-during-the-seventeenth-and-eighteenth-centuries#_ftnref14

is to be found in all the Prophets," to which he adds, "which makes me wonder with great admiration that so few Christians of our age can find it there.'" [406]

In 1708 William Whiston (1667-1752), Newton's friend and successor at Cambridge, also noted for his translation of the works of Josephus, predicts that the return of Israel to their land "is not far off".

> According to these original promises, that this land of Canaan should be to the children of Israel an everlasting possession are the prophecies all along afterwards also... And though the body of the ten tribes carried captive by Salmanasser; and the body of the two tribes by Titus are not now in the land of Canaan; yet since this is only because that period, fixed by their old prophecies for this their final restoration to their own land, is not yet come, though I believe it is not far off... And certainly, he who considers that this prediction before us has all along hitherto been exactly fulfilled in all the periods already past, will have no reason to doubt of the fulfilling of what remains yet to come in its proper season; and will not question but that then God will ultimately and completely, as he promised, give to the seed of Abraham all the land of Canaan for an everlasting possession. [407]

Dispensationalism

Just as the rise of Amillennialism and Replacement Theology saw a corresponding growth of Anti-Semitism in the church, so the rise of Dispensationalism corresponds to the growth of Philo-Semitism and what is now termed "Christian Zionism", which is not only a very pro-Jewish outlook, but also includes the active support for the modern State of Israel.

One of the fundamental tenets of Dispensationalism is the conviction that the Church and Israel are distinct peoples of God.

---

[406] In an early 18th century manuscript, under the heading "Of the Day of Judgment and World to come"
[407] "The Accomplishment of Scripture Prophecies" - William Whiston

Dispensationalists believe in a separate Dispensation of Law and a Dispensation of Grace where God focuses his attention on Israel and the Church respectively. They see Jesus' term "the time of the Gentiles" as a reference to the Church Age. But Jesus implied an end to the Church Age when Jerusalem is restored, by saying, "Jerusalem will be trampled on by the Gentiles until the times of the Gentiles are fulfilled" (Luke 21:24).

In line with the clear teaching of Romans 11, Dispensationalists believe in the spiritual restoration of Israel. This will commence in the Tribulation after the Church has been raptured, reaching its complete fulfilment in the Millennial kingdom which is centred in earthly Jerusalem. Also included in this renewal process are the promises of land restoration, in fulfilment of God's covenant with Abraham.

So most evangelical Christians today who actively support the state of Israel, do so because of the positive influence of the Dispensational Premillennial view that national Israel has a future in the plan of God. John Nelson Darby, considered to be the father of modern Dispensationalism, believed in a rigorous distinction between God's program for Israel and for the Church.

> While at Trinity College in Dublin (1819), Darby came to believe in a future salvation and restoration of a national Israel. Based on his study of Isaiah 32, Darby concluded that Israel, in a future dispensation, would enjoy earthly blessings that were different from the heavenly blessings experienced by the church. He thus saw a clear distinction between Israel and the church. Darby also came to believe in an "any moment" Rapture of the church that was followed by Daniel's Seventieth Week in which Israel would once again take centre stage in God's plan. After this period, Darby believed there would be a Millennial Kingdom in which God would fulfil His unconditional promises with Israel.[408]

---

[408] www.theologicalstudies.org/resource-library/dispensationalism/421-what-is-dispensationalism

The theology of Darby's is often claimed to be a significant awakener of American Christian Zionism. He distinguished the hopes of the Jews and that of the Church and Gentiles in a series of 11 evening lectures in Geneva in 1840. The visit of Darby to the US catalysed a new movement, which was expressed at the Niagara Bible Conference in 1878. [409] They issued a 14-point proclamation, including the following text:

> ... that the Lord Jesus will come in person to introduce the millennial age, when Israel shall be restored to their own land, and the earth shall be full of the knowledge of the Lord; and that this personal and premillennial advent is the blessed hope set before us in the Gospel for which we should be constantly looking. [410]

Romans 11

In contrast to the idea that God has permanently divorced Israel, Paul teaches in Romans 11 that Israel will be restored when "the full number of the Gentiles has come in". I encourage the reader to familiarise themselves with the full chapter 11 of the Book of Romans. Here is a brief summary of the passage:

1) God did not outright reject the Jewish people.

> *Rom 11:1-2a I ask then: Did God reject his people? By no means! I am an Israelite myself, a descendant of Abraham, from the tribe of Benjamin. God did not reject his people, whom he foreknew.*

2) Even in the Church Age, God has preserved a remnant.

> *Rom 11:2b-5 Don't you know what the Scripture says in the passage about Elijah - how he appealed to God against Israel: "Lord, they have killed your prophets and torn down your altars; I am the only one left, and they are trying to kill me"? And what was God's answer to him? "I*

---

[409] https://en.wikipedia.org/wiki/Christian_Zionism
[410] Ibid

have reserved for myself seven thousand who have not bowed the knee to Baal." So too, at the present time there is a remnant chosen by grace.

3) Israel has not stumbled beyond recovery.

Rom 11:11a Again I ask: Did they stumble so as to fall beyond recovery? Not at all!

4) God is still wooing Israel.

Rom 11:11b Rather, because of their transgression, salvation has come to the Gentiles to make Israel envious.

5) God is able to restore Israel and the predominantly Gentile church is warned not to be arrogant about their current position of favour.

Rom 11:17-18, 23 If some of the branches have been broken off, and you, though a wild olive shoot, have been grafted in among the others and now share in the nourishing sap from the olive root, do not boast over those branches... And if they do not persist in unbelief, they will be grafted in, for God is able to graft them in again...

6) Israel has experienced temporary hardening, but only until the end of the Church Age.

Rom 11:25 I do not want you to be ignorant of this mystery, brothers, so that you may not be conceited: Israel has experienced a hardening in part until the full number of the Gentiles has come in.

7) After this (the Church Age) ALL ISRAEL WILL BE SAVED.

Rom 11:26-27 And so all Israel will be saved, as it is written: "The deliverer will come from Zion; he will turn godlessness away from Jacob. And this is my covenant with them when I take away their sins."

8) In summary, God's call on Israel is irrevocable.

> *Rom 11:28-29 As far as the gospel is concerned, they are enemies on your account; but as far as election is concerned, they are loved on account of the patriarchs, for God's gifts and his call are irrevocable.*

Romans 11 is so clear on this issue, that Jonathan Edwards, despite being a Postmillennialist rejected Replacement Theology because of the passage, stating:

> Jewish infidelity shall then be overthrown. However obstinate they have been now for above seventeen hundred years in their rejection of Christ, and however rare have been the instances of individual conversions, ever since the destruction of Jerusalem … yet, when this day comes, the thick vail that blinds their eyes shall be removed, 2 Cor. iii.16. and divine grace shall melt and renew their hard hearts … And then shall the house of Israel be saved: the Jews in all their dispersions shall cast away their old infidelity, and shall have their hearts wonderfully changed, and abhor themselves for their past unbelief and obstinacy… Nothing is more certainly foretold than this national conversion of the Jews in Romans 11. [411]

The modern State of Israel

Zionist leader Chaim Weizmann met with Lord Balfour during his 1905-06 election campaign in the UK. Over a decade later the Balfour declaration was issued which stated that, "His Majesty's government view with favour the establishment in Palestine of a national home for the Jewish people, and will use their best endeavours to facilitate the achievement of this object…" [412]

---

[411] "History of Redemption" 1774
[412] "The Balfour Declaration". Israeli Ministry of Foreign Affairs. 2013

Besides geopolitical reasons, the British support under Balfour for a Jewish homeland in Palestine, was due in part to 19th century evangelical expectations and Christian feelings that England was to play a role in the Advent of the Millennium and Jesus' Second Coming. [413]

For Dispensationalists, the formation of the Jewish state in 1948 further reinforced the belief in the restoration of Israel and the folly of the general Replacement Theology found in much of Amillennialism and Postmillennialism. Dave Hunt aptly noted the following:

> If we are to believe the leaders in this "church-is-Israel" movement, then one of the greatest events in the history of the world - the return of the Jewish people to their own land and the rebirth of Israel in 1948 - is a freak accident with no significance. On the other hand, if this astonishing occurrence of undeniably great importance is, in fact, the fulfilment of biblical prophecies that the church has so long believed it to be, then here is an indisputable modern miracle of international prominence to which Christians can point - an event which gives irrefutable validity to the Word of God. "The-church-is-Israel" advocates would rob the church of the most convincing available witness to God's existence, righteous judgment and faithfulness: the remarkable history of the Jewish people, their prophecy-fulfilling odyssey and return to their historic homeland, and the prophesied climactic future events yet to occur there. [414]

Dispensationalism and Christian Zionism

According to a Wikipedia article on Christian Zionism:

> With the rise of James Frere, James Haldane Stewart and Edward Irving a major shift in the 1820s towards

---

[413] https://en.wikipedia.org/wiki/Balfour_Declaration
[414] Anti-Semitism - Aug 1988 - https://thebereancall.org/content/anti-semitism-0

Premillennialism occurred, with a similar focus on advocacy for the restoration of the Jews to Israel. [415]

Jerry Falwell, Sr. (1933-2007), an American Southern Baptist pastor and founder of Liberty University, who is identified as a Dispensationalist, said in 1981, "To stand against Israel is to stand against God. We believe that history and scripture prove that God deals with nations in relation to how they deal with Israel". [416] Falwell's statement is based on the belief that the blessing of Isaac in Gen 27:29 is still part of a valid covenant with Israel, "Those who curse you will be cursed, and those who bless you will be blessed."

The most generous segment of society to support the continuation and expansion of Israel is what is termed the 'fundamentalist' Christian movement. In his article, "Likud and the Christian Dispensationalists: A Symbiotic relationship", Prof. Colin Shindler relates that when the US based United Jewish Appeal refused to fund kibbutzim across the Green Line dividing Israeli and Palestinian land, money came in from evangelical foundations. It was estimated that two thirds of all Likud West Bank settlements received money from the Christian Right. [417] According to a Wikipedia article on Christian Zionism:

> Popular interest in Christian Zionism was given a boost around the year 2000 in the form of the Left Behind series of novels by Tim LaHaye and Jerry B. Jenkins. The novels are built around the prophetic role of Israel in the apocalyptic End Times. [418]

John Hagee (b. 1940), senior pastor of Cornerstone Church, a charismatic megachurch in San Antonio, Texas, is a renowned Dispensationalist. He is the founder and National Chairman of

---

[415] https://en.wikipedia.org/wiki/Christian_Zionism

[416] http://research.omicsgroup.org/index.php/Christian_Zionism

[417] Colin Shindler, "Likud and the Christian Dispensationalists: A Symbiotic re-lationship", Israel Studies 5, no. 1 (2000): 155-156

[418] https://en.wikipedia.org/wiki/Christian_Zionism

Christians United for Israel, an American Christian-Zionist organization which is the largest pro-Israel group in the US. [419]

While some have attempted to deny a link between Premillennial Dispensationalism and Christian Zionism, even the Reformed Church in America admits the connection, stating disapprovingly at its 2004 General Synod that it found "...the ideology of Christian Zionism and the extreme form of dispensationalism that undergirds it to be a distortion of the biblical message noting the impediment it represents to achieving a just peace in Israel/Palestine." [420]

Restoring the kingdom to Israel

Proponents of Replacement Theology are wilfully ignorant of the clear teaching of the New Testament concerning the restoration of Israel. Jesus' disciples raised this very question with him before his ascension.

> So when they met together, they asked him, "Lord, are you at this time going to restore the kingdom to Israel?" He said to them: "It is not for you to know the times or dates the Father has set by his own authority." (Acts 1:6-7)

Notice that Jesus didn't correct the disciples by saying, "The kingdom won't be restored to Israel - it has been passed on to the Church". He simply tells them that it was not for them to know the timing of the restoration of the kingdom to Israel.

Two-part restoration

Some are bothered by the fact that the Jews have returned to Israel predominantly in unbelief with regards to the ministry of Christ. Many modern Jews are not even Orthodox, "Old Covenant" religious Jews. Consequently, some assert that,

---

[419] https://en.wikipedia.org/wiki/John_Hagee & https://en.wikipedia.org/wiki/Christians_United_for_Israel
[420] https://en.wikipedia.org/wiki/Christian_Zionism

based on their present condition, Israel could not possibly fulfil the prophecies dealing with the return of a regenerated nation. But what they have overlooked is that prophecy actually speaks of a two-part restoration of Israel, notably Ezekiel's vision of the valley of dry bones. The prophet is told to prophesy to a valley filled with dry bones. Initially the bones, which speak of Israel, assemble but have no life:

> *And as I was prophesying, there was a noise, a rattling sound, and the bones came together, bone to bone. I looked, and tendons and flesh appeared on them and skin covered them, but there was no breath in them. (Ezek 37:7-8)*

But God then commands Ezekiel to prophesy again:

> *So I prophesied as he commanded me, and breath entered them; they came to life and stood up on their feet - a vast army. (Ezek 37:10)*

Figure 15: Engraving of "The Vision of The Valley of The Dry Bones" by Gustave Doré

The two phases of Israel's restoration are:

a) Land restoration (we have seen the start of this in the 20th century):

> ❖ ... *I will bring you back to the land of Israel. (Ezek 37:12)*
> ❖ *You will live in the land I gave your forefathers... (Ezek 36:28)*

b) And then spiritual restoration (this will happen in the Mid-Tribulation and Millennium):

> *I will put my Spirit in you and you will live... (Ezek 37:14)*

a) Land restoration

Firstly, there would to be a regathering - in unbelief - in preparation for judgment, the time of "Jacob's Trouble" in the Tribulation.

> *Jer 30:7 How awful that day will be! No other will be like it. It will be a time of trouble for Jacob, but he will be saved out of it.*

This is the first phase when Israel are assembled for final judgement. Israel are called to gather themselves and repent before the "day of the Lord's wrath" (i.e. the Tribulation)

> *Zeph 2:1-3 Gather together, gather yourselves together, you shameful nation, before the decree takes effect and that day passes like windblown chaff, before the Lord's fierce anger comes upon you, before the day of the Lord's wrath comes upon you. Seek the Lord, all you humble of the land, you who do what he commands. Seek righteousness, seek humility; perhaps you will be*

sheltered on the day of the Lord's anger. (Also Ezek 22:19-20, [421] Ezek 20:34-38 [422])

b) Spiritual restoration

Later there would be a restoration of faith in preparation for blessing and the promised Messianic Kingdom, after the ministry of the Two Witnesses and the consecration of the 144,000 Jews. At the spiritual restoration, the Jews will recognize Jesus as the Messiah and repent of their previous rejection of him.

> *Zech 12:10 And I will pour out on the house of David and the inhabitants of Jerusalem a spirit of grace and supplication. They will look on me, the one they have pierced, and they will mourn for him as one mourns for an only child, and grieve bitterly for him as one grieves for a firstborn son.*

Israel's relationship with God will be restored. There is genuine repentance and they will express regret for their former sin.

> *Ezek 36:31 Then you will remember your evil ways and wicked deeds, and you will loathe yourselves for your sins and detestable practices.*

They are saved from their backslidden state.

---

[421] Ezek 22:19-20 ... 'Because you have all become dross, I will gather you into Jerusalem. As silver, copper, iron, lead and tin are gathered into a furnace to be melted with a fiery blast, so will I gather you in my anger and my wrath and put you inside the city and melt you.'

[422] Ezek 20:34-38 I will bring you from the nations and gather you from the countries where you have been scattered - with a mighty hand and an outstretched arm and with outpoured wrath. I will bring you into the wilderness of the nations and there, face to face, I will execute judgment upon you. As I judged your ancestors in the wilderness of the land of Egypt, so I will judge you, declares the Sovereign Lord. I will take note of you as you pass under my rod, and I will bring you into the bond of the covenant. I will purge you of those who revolt and rebel against me.

Ezek 37:23 ... I will save them from all their sinful backsliding, and I will cleanse them. They will be my people, and I will be their God.

God's anger against them is replaced by his comfort.

Isa 12:1 In that day you will say: "I will praise you, O LORD. Although you were angry with me, your anger has turned away and you have comforted me."

God's love for Israel is ceaseless and he will build them up again. One cannot claim this is fulfilled completely in their earlier return from captivity, or how can God claim that the promise is based on him loving Israel with "an everlasting love".

Jer 31:2-4 ... "The people who survive the sword will find favour in the desert; I will come to give rest to Israel." The LORD appeared to us in the past, saying: "I have loved you with an everlasting love; I have drawn you with loving-kindness. I will build you up again and you will be rebuilt, O Virgin Israel."

God will again listen when they call on him.

Isa 65:24 "Before they call I will answer; while they are still speaking I will hear."

God will establish a new covenant with Israel.

Jer 31:31-33 "The time is coming," declares the LORD, "when I will make a new covenant with the house of Israel and with the house of Judah. It will not be like the covenant I made with their forefathers when I took them by the hand to lead them out of Egypt, because they broke my covenant, though I was a husband to them," declares the LORD. "This is the covenant I will make with the house of Israel after that time," declares the LORD. "I will put my law in their minds and write it on their hearts.

I will be their God, and they will be my people. (Also Ezek 37:26 [423])

All Israel will serve God.

Jer 31:34a No longer will a man teach his neighbour, or a man his brother, saying, 'Know the LORD,' because they will all know me, from the least of them to the greatest," declares the LORD.

Israel's sins will be forgiven and forgotten.

Jer 31:34b "For I will forgive their wickedness and will remember their sins no more."

This spiritual restoration of Israel will usher in the Millennial reign of Jesus, "the Son of David", ruling from Israel.

Ezek 37:24-25 My servant David will be king over them, and they will all have one shepherd. They will follow my laws and be careful to keep my decrees. They will live in the land I gave to my servant Jacob, the land where your ancestors lived. They and their children and their children's children will live there forever, and David my servant will be their prince forever.

As Christians, we should celebrate the future restoration of Israel, which reminds us of the same forgiveness and grace that God blessed the Gentiles with.

Rom 11:12-15 But if their transgression means riches for the world, and their loss means riches for the Gentiles, how much greater riches will their full inclusion bring! I am talking to you Gentiles... For if their rejection brought reconciliation to the world, what will their acceptance be but life from the dead?

---

[423] Ezek 37:26a I will make a covenant of peace with them; it will be an everlasting covenant

CHAPTER 5: IS SATAN BOUND NOW?

Figure 16: Gustave Dore, Paradise Lost Satan

According to Amillennialists and some Postmillennialists, Satan is bound now as he has been prevented from "deceiving the nations" by the spread of the gospel. This idea is contradicted by Scripture.

a) Satan is in control of the world system.

1 John 5:19 We know that we are children of God, and that the whole world is under the control of the evil one.

b) He leads the world astray.

> *Rev 12: 9 … that ancient serpent called the devil, or Satan, who leads the whole world astray.*

c) He is "the ruler of the kingdom of the air, the spirit who is now at work in those who are disobedient."

> *Eph 2:1-2 As for you, you were dead in your transgressions and sins, in which you used to live when you followed the ways of this world and of the ruler of the kingdom of the air, the spirit who is now at work in those who are disobedient.*

d) Unbelievers are still held captive by him

> *2 Tim 2:25-26 Opponents must be gently instructed, in the hope that God will grant them repentance leading them to a knowledge of the truth, and that they will come to their senses and escape from the trap of the devil, who has taken them captive to do his will.*

e) He has the ability to transform himself into an angel of light to deceive those on the earth.

> *2 Cor 11:14 And no wonder, for Satan himself masquerades as an angel of light.*

f) He is a ruler over kingdoms of darkness, waging war against the saints.

> *Eph 6:11-16 Put on the full armour of God so that you can take your stand against the devil's schemes. For our struggle is not against flesh and blood, but against the rulers, against the authorities, against the powers of this dark world and against the spiritual forces of evil in the*

heavenly realms… In addition to all this, take up the shield of faith, with which you can extinguish all the flaming arrows of the evil one.

g) He is walking about as a lion "seeking whom he may devour".

1 Pet 5:8 Be alert and of sober mind. Your enemy the devil prowls around like a roaring lion looking for someone to devour.

h) He instigates persecution against believers.

Rev 2:10 Do not be afraid of what you are about to suffer. I tell you, the devil will put some of you in prison to test you, and you will suffer persecution for ten days…

i) He attempts to entrap Christian leaders.

1 Tim 3:7 He must also have a good reputation with outsiders, so that he will not fall into disgrace and into the devil's trap.

j) We are instructed not to give him a foothold in our lives.

Eph 4:27 and do not give the devil a foothold.

k) We need to take care that he does not outwit us.

2 Cor 2:11 …in order that Satan might not outwit us. For we are not unaware of his schemes.

l) Paul expressed concern that the Corinthians would be deceived by him, just as he had earlier deceived Eve.

1 Cor 11:3 But I am afraid that just as Eve was deceived by the serpent's cunning, your minds may somehow be led astray from your sincere and pure devotion to Christ.

m) Satan hindered Paul from coming to Thessalonica

1 Thess 2:18 For we wanted to come to you - certainly I, Paul, did, again and again - but Satan blocked our way.

n) He filled Ananias' heart to lie to the Holy Spirit.

Acts 5:3 Then Peter said, "Ananias, how is it that Satan has so filled your heart that you have lied to the Holy Spirit and have kept for yourself some of the money you received for the land?"

o) While we are in the world, we need God's protection against him. We need to pray for strength to overcome him.

Matt 6:13 "And lead us not into temptation, but deliver us from the evil one." (Also John 17:15 [424])

p) He can be effectively resisted by those in submission to God.

Jam 4:7 Submit yourselves, then, to God. Resist the devil, and he will flee from you.

So, Satan is described as one who is very active in the world, opposing and tempting believers, leading the world astray, keeping unbelievers captive to his will, and holding the world system in his power. As Hal Lindsey aptly noted in the title of his book "Satan is alive and well on planet earth". How can Satan be both bound and yet so active at the same time? It defies common sense and the clear testimony of Scripture to affirm both of these contradictory realities. It has been well said of the Amillennialist and Postmillennialist teachings:

IF SATAN IS BOUND TODAY, THE CHAIN IS TOO LONG.

Amillennialists claim that Satan has been figuratively bound by Jesus' work on the cross and that he can no longer hinder the advance of the gospel. And Postmillennialist Keith Mathison asserts that Satan and his power have been "greatly restricted",

---

[424] John 17:15 "My prayer is not that you take them out of the world but that you protect them from the evil one."

"greatly curtailed", and "bound in some sense" in this present age. [425] He writes:

> The binding of Satan does not entail the cessation of his activity (cf. 1 Peter 5:8), but it does mean that he is no longer able to prevent the spread of the gospel to the nations. [426]

Rev 20:3 says that Satan is bound in the Abyss "to keep him from deceiving the nations anymore until the thousand years were ended." Yet the New Testament makes it clear that Satan is still deceiving the nations. He is 'the god of this age' who is currently blinding unbelievers.

> *2 Cor 4:4 The god of this age has blinded the minds of unbelievers, so that they cannot see the light of the gospel that displays the glory of Christ, who is the image of God.*

Whenever possible, he still snatches away the seed of God's Word sown in the heart of the unbeliever.

> *Matt 13:19 "When anyone hears the message about the kingdom and does not understand it, the evil one comes and snatches away what was sown in his heart."*

In spite of the numerous citations above, Amillennialists and some Postmillennialists cling to this view, which not only defies all these Scriptures, but which reduces Revelation 20 to a meaningless chronology of the resurrections and Millennium, not even getting the time period right. Short on Scriptural support, they appeal to Matthew 12:29 and Jesus' reference to the binding of the strong man, equating the "strong man" with the authority and influence of the devil in the world.

---

[425] Mathison, "Dispensationalism: Rightly Dividing the People of God?" (1995), 127
[426] Mathison, "Postmillennialism: An Eschatology of Hope" (1999), 155

> Matt 12:29 "Or again, how can anyone enter a strong man's house and carry off his possessions unless he first ties up the strong man? Then he can plunder his house."

In fact, this was the original justification Augustine gave for abandoning Premillennialism, interpreting this passage to be a binding of Satan throughout the present church age. But to interpret the verse in this fashion is to violate one of the most fundamental principles of hermeneutics - the rule of context. The verse in context has absolutely nothing to do with Jesus' death on the cross or with the atonement.

> Matt 12:22-29 Then they brought him a demon-possessed man who was blind and mute, and Jesus healed him, so that he could both talk and see ... But when the Pharisees heard this, they said, "It is only by Beelzebul, the prince of demons, that this fellow drives out demons." Jesus knew their thoughts and said to them, "Every kingdom divided against itself will be ruined, and every city or household divided against itself will not stand. If Satan drives out Satan, he is divided against himself. How then can his kingdom stand? ... Or again, how can anyone enter a strong man's house and carry off his possessions unless he first ties up the strong man? Then he can plunder his house.

The immediate contextual setting is clearly personal deliverance from demonic possession. Jesus stated these words right after driving out a demon from a man, and then subsequently being accused of doing this by the power of Beelzebul (a demonic principality). In defence, Jesus had stated that in order to deliver the possessed man from the "strong man" (the demon in question), the strong man had to be bound. He argues that if he were accomplishing this 'binding' by the power of Satan, then effectively Satan was fighting against his own kingdom i.e. the "prince of demons" is binding his own demons.

So in Revelation 20, Amillennialists have to use an allegorical interpretation that contradicts the literal sense to support their view. In this case, they resort to randomly pulling a verse out of context and making it a supposed reference to Satan being bound throughout the Church Age. And this is somehow derived from a passage where one demon is driven out of one person. Furthermore, if this bizarre application is correct, what are we to make of the subsequent words of Jesus here?

> *Matt 12:43-45 "When an impure spirit comes out of a person, it goes through arid places seeking rest and does not find it. Then it says, 'I will return to the house I left.' When it arrives, it finds the house unoccupied, swept clean and put in order. Then it goes and takes with it seven other spirits more wicked than itself, and they go in and live there. And the final condition of that person is worse than the first."*

These words make sense when talking of demonic deliverance, which is clearly what the passage is actually dealing with. Jesus implies that a person who has been delivered, needs to ensure that the "house" doesn't remain empty (i.e. a void is left which must be filled with the Holy Spirit) or they will invariably suffer a demonic counter-attack which will render them in a worse position than before. But what could it possibly mean if Matt 12:29 is teaching that Satan is bound for the church age? Who are the seven demons that return with the first and what exactly is Jesus teaching here - if you dare to employ a consistent approach with interpretation?

Destroying Satan's work

Now it is true that Jesus came to destroy Satan's work.

- ❖ *Luke 10:18 ... "I saw Satan fall like lightning from heaven."*
- ❖ *John 10:10 "The thief comes only to steal and kill and destroy; I have come that they may have life, and have it to the full."*
- ❖ *Acts 10:38 how God anointed Jesus of Nazareth with the Holy Spirit and power, and how he went around doing good and healing all who were under the power of the devil...*

And it is equally true that Satan was dealt a major blow at the cross.

- ❖ *John 12:31 "Now is the time for judgment on this world; now the prince of this world will be driven out."*
- ❖ *Col 2:15 And having disarmed the powers and authorities, he made a public spectacle of them, triumphing over them by the cross.*

But the picture of being bound in Revelation 20:3 simply does not fit, when viewing the New Testament teaching about Satan in its entirety. For instance, John tells us that the "reason the Son of God appeared was to destroy the devil's work" (1 John 3:8). While Amillennialists will use verses like these to prove that Satan is bound, the context shows that it is a work in progress. Two verses later, John goes on to say that at present there are still those who continue to be the "children of the devil".

> *1 John 3:10 This is how we know who the children of God are and who the children of the devil are: Anyone who does not do what is right is not a child of God; nor is anyone who does not love his brother.*

Likewise, Jesus became a man to break the power of the devil and to conquer death.

> *Heb 2:14-15 Since the children have flesh and blood, he too shared in their humanity so that by his death he might break the power of him who holds the power of death - that is, the devil - and free those who all their lives were held in slavery by their fear of death.*

Yet in this current age, although believers have eternal life, they still get sick and die. Although we have been freed from sin - temptation to sin, and sin itself, continues to plague our lives. Although God dwells within us - our knowledge of God at times seems quite limited. War, poverty, sickness, godlessness and death will continue until the end of the age. Because the kingdom of God is not yet here in its full expression ("as it is in heaven"), the works of this present evil age continue, though not as unlimited as it would have without the presence of the church ("you are the salt of the earth").

Jesus made it clear that Satan is here to stay until "the end of the age".

> *Matt 13:38-41 "The weeds are the sons of the evil one, and the enemy who sows them is the devil. The harvest is the end of the age, and the harvesters are angels. As the weeds are pulled up and burned in the fire, so it will be at the end of the age. The Son of Man will send out his angels, and they will weed out of his kingdom everything that causes sin and all who do evil."*

And if anyone is unsure as to when the end of the age is, Satan being crushed is viewed by Paul as a future event.

> *Rom 16:20 The God of peace will soon crush Satan under your feet.*

The future binding of Satan

Unlike Amillennialists, Premillennialists believe that binding refers to cessation - not limitation - of activity. In the true future Millennial age, Satan will indeed be prevented from deceiving the nations.

> *Rev 20:3 He threw him into the Abyss, and locked and sealed it over him, to keep him from deceiving the nations anymore until the thousand years were ended...*

The word translated 'Abyss' here is the Greek word ἄβυσσος (abussos). It is the same word used in Luke 8:31 when the demons driven out of Legion "begged Jesus repeatedly not to order them to go into the Abyss". I doubt they were imploring Jesus not to metaphorically bind them - they were concerned about a real place of torment where they were destined to go in the future.

Matt 8:29 "What do you want with us, Son of God?" they shouted. "Have you come here to torture us before the appointed time?"

In fact, we have a brief description of this Abyss earlier in Revelation, when fallen angels are released from it, in order to wreak havoc on the earth in the Tribulation period.

Rev 9:1-2 ... I saw a star that had fallen from the sky to the earth. The star was given the key to the shaft of the Abyss. When he opened the Abyss, smoke rose from it like the smoke from a gigantic furnace. The sun and sky were darkened by the smoke from the Abyss.

We are further told (Rev 9:11) that these fallen angels "had as king over them the angel of the Abyss, whose name in Hebrew is Abaddon and in Greek is Apollyon (that is, Destroyer)". So the Abyss is the current prison for the fallen Watchers (Gen 6) who fathered the Nephilim. (We examined this in detail in my previous book).

❖ *2 Pet 2:4 For if God did not spare angels when they sinned, but sent them to hell, putting them in chains of darkness to be held for judgment...*
❖ *Jude 6 And the angels who did not keep their positions of authority but abandoned their proper dwelling—these he has kept in darkness, bound with everlasting chains for judgment on the great Day.*

The well-known passage in Isaiah 14, often applied to Satan only, actually refers to this time of judgment on both Satan and his pawn, the 'king of Babylon'. While the first section (v. 1-11) of the passage declares judgment on the king of Babylon (aka the Antichrist), [427] the section that follows pronounces judgement

---

[427] Isa 14:9-11 Sheol from beneath is excited over you to meet you when you come; it arouses for you the spirits of the dead, all the leaders of the earth; it raises all the kings of the nations from their thrones. They will all respond and say to you, "Even you have been made weak as we, you have become like us." Your pomp and the music of your harps have been brought down to Sheol;

on the one who wanted to usurp God's place (Satan), by also assigning him to Sheol. This is a reference to the future binding of Satan in the Abyss.

> *Isa 14:12-15 How you have fallen from heaven, O star of the morning, son of the dawn! You have been cut down to the earth, you who have weakened the nations! But you said in your heart, "I will ascend to heaven; I will raise my throne above the stars of God, and I will sit on the mount of assembly in the recesses of the north. I will ascend above the heights of the clouds; I will make myself like the Most High." Nevertheless, you will be thrust down to Sheol, to the recesses of the pit." (NASB)*

The passage makes it clear that this binding in Sheol occurs "When the LORD will have compassion on Jacob and again choose Israel, and settle them in their own land" (14:1) and the "whole earth is at rest and is quiet" (14:7).

The bottom line is that in the real Millennium, Satan doesn't get bound with a metaphoric long chain, still free to wander the earth and seemingly do as he pleases. He is confined to the Abyss, which is a place that demons fear as a future destination of punishment (Luke 8:31), is the current abode of fallen angels (Rev 9) who sinned before the Flood (Gen 6); a place of chains and darkness (2 Pet 2:4, Jud 6), smoke (Rev 9:2) and torment (Matt 8:29).

---

maggots are spread out as your bed beneath you and worms are your covering. (NASB)

CHAPTER 6: POSTMILLENNIALISM

In Latin, the prefix 'post' indicates 'after'. Thus, Postmillennialists see Christ's Second Coming as occurring after the Millennium, which to them is a golden age of Christian prosperity and dominance. Accordingly, the forces of Satan will gradually be defeated by the expansion of the Kingdom of God throughout history up until the Second Coming of Christ.

John Walvoord observed that "Premillennialism is obviously a viewpoint quite removed from either Amillennialism or Postmillennialism" [428] because it is more consistently literal in its hermeneutical approach than the other two. Even some Postmillennialists like David Chilton have noted their closer kinship with Amillennialists, because of their common belief that the kingdom or Millennium is the current age, while Premillennialists see it as future. Although some Postmillennialists hold to a literal Millennium of 1000 years, most see the 1000 years more as a metaphor for a long period of time (as do Amillennialists). Among those holding to a non-literal Millennium, it is often understood to have already begun, which implies a less obvious and less dramatic kind of Millennium than that typically envisioned by Premillennialists.

Postmillennialists do differ, however, with the Amillennial view that good and evil will persist in the current age, leading some of them to accuse both Amillennialists (and Premillennialists) of being overly pessimistic.

> Amillennialists have countered that the parable of the wheat and weeds (Matt 24-30, 36-43) and the parable of drawing in the net (Matt 13:47-53) show that good and evil will be sorted out only at the end of the world. According to Amillennialism, therefore, although a perfect society cannot be expected to be realized during this present age, the end of the world can be optimistically hoped for. [429]

---

[428] "The Millennial Kingdom" by John F. Walvoord
[429] http://www.newworldencyclopedia.org/entry/Amillennialism

Accordingly, Amillennialists believe that they "adopt a position of sober or realistic optimism."[430] In both Premillennialism and most forms of Amillennialism there is a great apostasy immediately before the return of Christ, resulting in a time of unprecedented evil (although Amillennialists attribute this to Satan being unbound at the 'end' of the millennial age). As Postmillennialists have a very positive view of end times, some have called Postmillennialism simply a more optimistic form of Amillennialism.

But Postmillennialists also disagree with Amillennialists as to the start of the Millennial age. Amillennialists see the Millennial age as beginning at the cross and occupying the entire period of time between the First and Second Coming of Christ. While Postmillennialists also view the Millennial age commencing at some point during the present age, for them it only occurs at a point in time when the kingdom of God triumphs over the kingdoms of this world. Some see the Millennial age as entirely future, while others argue that it may have already begun to emerge. They are also divided among themselves as to whether or not the Millennial age begins abruptly or gradually.

Historic Postmillennialism

Jonathan Edwards lived at the time of the First Great Awakening. According to the Christian History Institute:

> He looked forward to a time of great holiness when "visible wickedness shall be suppressed everywhere, and true holiness shall become general, though not universal," and a time of great prosperity. He regarded Constantine's era a type of the greater reality to come, so he also expected the Millennium to be a time when

---

[430] Anthony Hoekema, "Amillennialism"

true religion would be held in great esteem and saints would rule on all fronts. [431]

Samuel Hopkins (1721-1803), a disciple of Jonathan Edwards and Congregational minister in Newport, Rhode Island, produced his own Treatise on the Millennium in 1793. Hopkins's views anticipated tendencies that would flower in the next century. He was compelled to a social activism unknown to Edwards, being an avid abolitionist advocating complete emancipation of slaves in the US. [432]

C.G. Finney regarded the Second Great Awakening in the US as a prelude to the Postmillennial golden age. Finney allegedly asserted that "if the church will do her duty, the Millennium may come in this country in three years." This led in the years before the Civil War to unprecedented social and religious reform: temperance, antislavery, peace, women's rights, education, as well as dramatic expansion in home and foreign mission work.[433] Finney did not believe that revivals were the result of miracles, but "the right use of appropriate means." Accordingly, he instituted "new measures" or techniques for instigating revivals: the anxious bench (where sinners could be singled out for counselling), informal public praying, and protracted meetings.[434]

Modern Postmillennialism

The following variants of Dominion Theology are influenced by Postmillennialism, the view which believes that godliness will eventually pervade secular society. These various flavours include Reconstructionism, The Restoration Movement, Third Wave, New Wave, Latter Rain and the Manifest Sons of God. Note that while they are often grouped together as "Dominion Theology", not all parties are in agreement on the various items

---

[431] https://www.christianhistoryinstitute.org/magazine/article/american-post-millennialism-seeing-the-glory - "American Postmillennialism: Seeing the glory", Issue 61, 1998
[432] Ibid
[433] Ibid
[434] Ibid

which might distinguish these doctrines. Yet it is true that they have much in common and so, for the sake of simplicity, we will group Dominion Theology into two main streams.

a) Kingdom Now theology - a theological belief within the Charismatic movement of Protestant Christianity.
b) Christian Reconstructionism - the Dominionism counterpart in Reformed, Calvinist theology.

Don Koenig wrltes:

> Dominion Theology transcends denominations and movements. There are Calvinist and Arminian, charismatic and non-charismatic, liberal and conservative, Preterist, Postmillennial, and Amillennial Christians who embrace Dominion Theology. Even some misguided pre-millennial Post-Tribulation rapture believers have bought into one or more Dominionist positions. [435]

Dominionism arose in religious movements reasserting aspects of Christian nationalism and it is derived from the Biblical text in Genesis 1:28-30 where God grants humanity 'dominion' over the Earth, which they believe gives a Biblical mandate for Christian control of civil governmental affairs.

> 'Dominion Theology' is invariably postmillennial and adherents believe that the Church itself will have to set up the Kingdom of God upon earth before Jesus Christ returns. It is believed that Christ's kingdom will need to be established by political, and even military means if and when that might prove necessary. A literal millennium is usually envisaged but Christianity itself, it is believed, must bring this about by Christians becoming much more political in outlook than many of them have traditionally been. So this is a highly political approach

---

[435] http://www.ukapologetics.net/09/dominionism.htm

which advocates strong, ongoing, and ultra-conservative political activism. [436]

Internationally known Dominionist-Reconstructionist George Grant says:

> But it is dominion we are after. Not just a voice. It is dominion we are after. Not just influence. It is dominion we are after. Not just equal time. It is dominion we are after. WORLD CONQUEST. That's what Christ has commissioned us to accomplish. [437]

Reconstructionists

Christian Reconstructionism was founded by R.J. Rushdoony, Gary North and Greg Bahnsen and supported by such leaders as David Chilton and Gary DeMar. It appeals mostly to conservative Reformed Calvinists. They focus on the need for economic change, social justice, peace, conservation and so forth, and believe that the Church will eventually reconstruct the world by applying and enforcing Biblical principles. These principles, or laws, must be applied to all mankind, not just believers. R. J. Rushdoony (1916-2001) writes:

> I believe that the world will see the progressive triumph of Christ's people until the whole world is Christian and a glorious material and spiritual era unfolds. [438]

---

[436] Ibid
[437] "Changing Of The Guard" - 1987
[438] R. J. Rushdoony "God's Plan for Victory: The Meaning of postmillennialism"

CHAPTER 7: THE CHURCH AND STATE

Before we look at the "Kingdom Now" variant of modern Postmillennialism, let's just consider the matter of the relationship between Church and State, which features very prominently in the minds of Reconstructionists.

One of the major areas where Amillennialism, Postmillennialism or Premillennialism affect one's overall world view is in the understanding of the relationship that should exist between spiritual and secular bodies. Should we have separation of Church and State? Neither a true Amillennialist or Postmillennialist (in particular Reconstructionists) should agree.

- ❖ If, as Amillennialists say, we are currently in the Kingdom of God, then the Church should be controlling the State (something the Catholics and Reformed Calvinists tried unsuccessfully).
- ❖ If, as Postmillennialists say, we are preparing the world for Jesus' return, then the Church should be attempting to exert jurisdiction over the State.
- ❖ But if, as Premillennialists say, we are waiting for Jesus' return and rule on earth, then the Church has no business in controlling the State, but its main focus should be on evangelising individuals. Surely there cannot be any true peace until the Prince of Peace rules?

While Postmillennial Dominionists advocate a Church takeover of State, it may be good for them to learn some lessons from history when the Amillennialists attempted the same thing. How did the belief in Amillennialism affect the relationship between Church and State? Let's consider both Catholic and Reformed Amillennialism.

Catholic Amillennialism and the State Church

Constantine

The conversion of the Roman emperor, Constantine, in the 4th century, led many to believe that the Millennial kingdom of God had indeed been realised on earth. At the time, there had been multiple contenders for leadership of the Roman Empire. On 28 October 312 AD there was a battle at the Milvian Bridge, over the Tiber River just outside Rome, between Constantine and his brother-in-law and co-emperor, Maxentius. This resulted in a victory for Constantine, in spite of overwhelming numbers - an estimated 100,000 in Maxentius' army against 20,000 in Constantine's army.

Constantine personally related the story to Eusebius of how, before this crucial battle, he was convinced that he needed divine assistance. While praying, God sent him a vision of a cross of light, bearing the inscription "in hoc signo vinces" ("in this sign you will be victorious"). [439] That night he had a dream where he was told to use the sign he'd been given as a safeguard in all of his battles. [440]

---

[439] Life of Constantine 1:28 "Accordingly he called on him with earnest prayer and supplications that he would reveal to him who he was, and stretch forth his right hand to help him in his present difficulties. And while he was thus praying with fervent entreaty, a most marvellous sign appeared to him from heaven, the account of which it might have been hard to believe had it been related by any other person. But since the victorious emperor himself long afterwards declared it to the writer of this history, when he was honoured with his acquaintance and society, and confirmed his statement by an oath, who could hesitate to accredit the relation, especially since the testimony of after-time has established its truth? He said that about noon, when the day was already beginning to decline, he saw with his own eyes the trophy of a cross of light in the heavens, above the sun, and bearing the inscription, CONQUER BY THIS. At this sight he himself was struck with amazement, and his whole army also, which followed him on this expedition, and witnessed the miracle."

[440] Ibid, ch. 29 "He said that he was unsure what this apparition could mean, but that while he continued to ponder, night suddenly came on. In his sleep, the Christ of God appeared to him with the same sign which he had seen in the heavens, and commanded him to make a likeness of that sign which he had seen in the heavens, and to use it as a safeguard in all engagements with his enemies."

Figure 17: The Chi-Rho was formed by superimposing the first two capital letters chi and rho of the Greek word "ΧΡΙΣΤΟΣ" (Christos i.e. Christ) in such a way to produce the monogram

In response Constantine ordered that the symbol of Christ's name (Chi-Rho) be used on the Standard of the Cross, called the Labarum by the Romans, which would be carried in front of his armies from that time on. [441] He related to Eusebius that he resolved "to worship no other God save Him who had appeared to him" [442] and requested and received instruction from "those who were acquainted with the mysteries of His doctrines". [443]

Constantine attributed his victory over Maxentius to the power of the God of the Christians and committed himself to reading the Scriptures from that day on, choosing to have Christians as his advisers [444] and companions. [445] Christianity had previously been decriminalized in AD 311 by an edict of toleration issued in

[441] Ibid, ch. 31 "The emperor constantly made use of this sign of salvation as a safeguard against every adverse and hostile power, and commanded that others similar to it should be carried at the head of all his armies."

[442] Ibid, ch. 32

[443] Ibid

[444] Ibid - "... he determined thenceforth to devote himself to the reading of the Inspired writings. Moreover, he made the priests of God his counsellors, and deemed it incumbent on him to honour the God who had appeared to him with all devotion."

[445] Ibid, ch 42 - "Accordingly, they were admitted to his table, though mean in their attire and outward appearance; yet not so in his estimation, since he thought he saw not the man as seen by the vulgar eye, but the God in him. He made them also his companions in travel, believing that He whose servants they were would thus help him."

the name of Galerius, Licinius and Constantine. This expressed tolerance for all religious creeds, including Christianity. Soon after the victory over Maxentius, Constantine and Licinius (Licinius was now emperor in the East and Constantine in the West) issued the Edict of Milan in AD 313, permitting citizens to accept Christianity without fear of persecution and releasing all religious prisoners. With regards to Christianity, this second edict went beyond the first edict of AD 311 and "was a decisive step from hostile neutrality to friendly neutrality and protection".[446]

Eusebius of Caesarea was an avid admirer of Constantine and viewed his reign as the Messianic banquet. In his book, "Life of Constantine", it is evident that Eusebius believed that Christianity had now triumphed over the forces of paganism and that the new Christian emperor was someone comparable to Moses, who freed Israel from slavery and brought the children of God into the "promised land". Eusebius argues as follows:

a) Like Moses, Constantine was "brought up in the very palaces and bosoms of the oppressors". [447]
b) Constantine "sought safety in flight; in this respect again keeping up his resemblance to the great prophet Moses", [448] (a comparison between the flight of Constantine to his father - because of the plots of Galerius against him - to Moses' flight to Midian).
c) As Pharaoh, the opponent of Moses, was destroyed along with his army in the waters of the Red Sea, so Maxentius, Constantine's foe, was destroyed along with his army by drowning in the Tiber river. [449]

---

[446] History of the Christian Church Vol. II - Philip Schaff
[447] Life of Constantine 1:12
[448] Ibid, Ch 20
[449] In Eusebius' words, "... the bridge began to sink, and the boats with the men in them went bodily to the bottom. And first the wretch himself, then his armed attendants and guards, even as the sacred oracles had before described, sank as lead in the mighty waters. Exodus 15:10 So that they who thus obtained victory from God might well, if not in the same words, yet in fact in the same spirit as the people of his great servant Moses, sing and speak as they did concerning the impious tyrant of old: Let us sing unto the Lord, for he has

d) And "after the example of his (God's) great servant Moses, Constantine entered the imperial city in triumph" - Eusebius thereby drawing an analogy between Constantine's entry into Rome to take power and Moses leading the children of God into the promised land. [450]

When Constantine became emperor, persecution and martyrdom of Christians became a thing of the past. With Christianity's new-found respectability in the Roman Empire, it was much easier to accept the newer Amillennial position that Satan was already bound and that people were now living in the golden age of Christ's rule over the nations through the Church. Noted church historian, Philip Schaff says of the demise of early Premillennialism:

> But the crushing blow came from the great change in the social condition and prospects of the church in the Nicene age. After Christianity, contrary to all expectation, triumphed in the Roman empire, and was embraced by the Caesars themselves, the millennial reign, instead of being anxiously waited and prayed for, began to be dated either from the first appearance of Christ, or from the conversion of Constantine and the downfall of paganism, and to be regarded as realized in the glory of the dominant imperial state-church. Augustine, who himself had formerly entertained chiliastic hopes, framed the new theory which reflected the social change, and was generally accepted. The apocalyptic millennium he understood to be the present reign of Christ in the Catholic church, and the first resurrection, the translation of the martyrs and saints to heaven, where they participate in Christ's reign. [451]

---

been glorified exceedingly: the horse and his rider has he thrown into the sea." - Life of Constantine 1:38

[450] Ibid, Ch 39

[451] History of the Christian Church, Volume II: Ante-Nicene Christianity. A.D. 100-325. - Chiliasm - http://www.ccel.org/ccel/schaff/hcc2.v.xiv.xxii.html

Figure 18: Statue of Constantine the Great outside York Minster. It was near this spot that Constantine was proclaimed Roman Emperor by his army in AD 306.

We noted earlier that Lactantius, the tutor of Constantine's son, was an avid Premillennialist. He taught that the beginning of the end would be the fall, or breakup, of the Roman Empire. [452] However, this view fell out of favour with the ever-improving lot of Christians: "Many Christians felt that any expectation of the downfall of the empire was as disloyal to God as it was to Rome." [453]

State involvement in the church

The later blurring of the lines between Church and State would never have been possible if it were not for Constantine. As the most powerful person in the world, his conversion had far reaching effects not only on the common practice of religion in his day, but also on us today. However, many have unfairly criticized Constantine without any historical evidence for their accusations. Their claims range from him deliberately corrupting Christianity by syncretism with sun god worship, to reducing him to a man motivated only by political ambitions - using the popularity of Christianity as the vehicle for his career. None of

---

[452] Froom, LeRoy (1950). "The Prophetic Faith of our Fathers", pp. 356-357.
[453] McGinn, Bernard. Visions of the End, 1998

these allegations are true. To the honest researcher, Constantine was clearly motivated by Christian values in many of his reforms.

Donatist and Arian issues

Although Constantine did dabble in Church affairs, it was always to facilitate the ruling of the existing Church leadership, seemingly recognising that he was no authority in such matters. His letters show numerous efforts to resolve factions in Christianity. He spends much time trying to resolve both the Donatist controversy and the Arian heresy. Just one example of this is his letter to Alexander the bishop and Arius the heretical presbyter in AD 323 or 324. He expresses his distress at finding that they could not agree.

> For as long as you continue to contend about these small and very insignificant questions, it is not fitting that so large a portion of God's people should be under the direction of your judgment, since you are thus divided between yourselves. I believe it indeed to be not merely unbecoming, but positively evil, that such should be the case. But I will refresh your minds by a little illustration, as follows. You know that philosophers, though they all adhere to one system, are yet frequently at issue on certain points, and differ, perhaps, in their degree of knowledge: yet they are recalled to harmony of sentiment by the uniting power of their common doctrines. If this be true, is it not far more reasonable that you, who are the ministers of the Supreme God, should be of one mind respecting the profession of the same religion? [454]

The Council of Nicaea

Although Constantine seemed determined that the church be united with a single doctrinal view, he didn't appear to try and dictate what the doctrine should be - another frivolous charge made against him. Instead he wrote to the involved parties and

---

[454] Life of Constantine 2:71

later resorted to calling councils of bishops where they could thrash out the issues and reach consensus.

The events of the Council of Nicaea have been changed beyond recognition by a few conspiracy theorists in their pseudo-documentaries and books. Contrary to popular belief, it had nothing to do with selecting which verses and gospels would be included in the Bible; and bishops did not burn books they deemed heretical there either. While this makes for a good conspiracy theory or an exciting movie story line, it is also poor history. Unfortunately, most people, including Christians, use the mass media or social media as their primary source of knowledge regarding church history.

Constantine sponsored the Council of Nicaea to get Christian bishops to negotiate a statement of orthodox Christian belief that could be recognized across the empire. The Nicene Creed continues to be used today. In his notorious novel 'The Da Vinci Code', which had been rightfully dubbed as "fiction based upon fiction", Dan Brown makes the childish allegation that Constantine was behind a 'plot' to make Jesus divine, when previously this was not commonly believed. This is a bogus claim. Firstly, in the controversy of the day, Arius did not deny Christ's deity, although he believed that Jesus was inferior to the Father. Secondly Constantine seems to have very superficial knowledge of the actual debate between Arius and Athanasius. He simply wanted unity among his Christian subjects. One gets the impression that he was not bothered which way the decision of the Christian bishops went as long as they were agreed. Subsequently Constantine exiled both Arius and Athanasius at different times, in an attempt to pressurize them to come to some agreement.

Others contend that by getting a council of bishops to settle a theological issue and reach a consensus view, Constantine brought about a shift in the way that the Church operated. They say that this was a worldly way of resolving spiritual issues. This is not true. In Acts 15 a council of the apostles convened in Jerusalem in order to settle the earliest controversial issue in the church. The issue was the question of circumcision and the conditions under which Gentiles should be allowed into the Church. After consensus was reached, the result was a letter from the attendees instructing everyone about the ruling. This was very similar to the way the Council of Nicaea was conducted.

Constantine's role in the council was to organise that travel and accommodation expenses for the delegates be covered out of public funds [455] and to facilitate the proceedings. He was present as an observer, but did not vote. [456] He organized the council along the lines of the Roman Senate with Hosius of Corduba presiding over its deliberations. In addressing the opening of the council, Constantine "exhorted the bishops to unanimity and concord" and called on them to follow the Scriptures with: "Let, then, all contentious disputation be discarded; and let us seek in the divinely-inspired word the solution of the questions at issue." [457] There's no indication that he tried to sway the decision either way though; he simply wanted consensus and a unified belief. After the debate about church doctrine "The emperor gave patient attention to the speeches of both parties" but "deferred" to the decision of the bishops. [458]

By his involvement with the council, Constantine was indirectly exercising a measure of imperial control over the church, but far from objecting, most Christians saw the participation of a Christian emperor as part of God's providence.

> Up until this time the church had not had to articulate its beliefs in a binding creed which would determine who was a Christian and who was not. The council also promulgated a number of enforceable canons to regulate church governance thus creating a disciplined institution.[459]

---

[455] The Ecclesiastical History of Theodoret, Book 1, Chapter 6
[456] http://www.newworldencyclopedia.org/entry/Constantine_I
[457] Ibid
[458] The Ecclesiastical History of Sozomen, Book 1, Chapter 20
[459] http://www.newworldencyclopedia.org/entry/Constantine_I

Was Constantine a covert pagan?

In many ways, Constantine has been unfairly vilified. De Imperatoribus Romanis, a secular online Encyclopedia of Roman Emperors, states:

> It has often been supposed that Constantine's profession of Christianity was a matter of political expediency more than of religious conviction; upon closer examination this view cannot be sustained. [460]

Similarly, the New World Encyclopedia states:

> It has been argued that he conflated the Sun God with the Christian God. His support for Christianity, however, was sincere and reflected in his policies. [461]

Although he has been blamed by some for deliberately corrupting Christianity with pagan symbolism, motivated by sinister political reasons, those making these claims are ill-informed and should carefully examine the historical record. Fortunately, Constantine was a most industrious letter-writer with over 40 letters and documents authored by him surviving, all of which are pro-Christian, anti-pagan and anti-heretic. The following contents of letters and decrees hardly indicate a compromising politician trying to endear himself to his pagan subjects.

- ❖ AD 319: He did not outlaw paganism and allowed religious freedom but, in the words of an early edict, he decreed that polytheists could "celebrate the rites of an outmoded illusion: so long as they did not force Christians to join them." [462]
- ❖ AD 324: In his edict to the people of the eastern provinces he addresses the error of polytheism. [463] He prays that all may be Christians, but compels none. [464]

---

[460] http://www.roman-emperors.org/indexxxx.htm
[461] http://www.newworldencyclopedia.org/entry/Constantine_I
[462] Codex Theodosianius 9.16.2.
[463] Life of Constantine 2:48
[464] Ibid, ch 56

- ❖ AD 330: He forbids soothsaying from being practiced in individuals' homes. [465]
- ❖ AD 332: He directed the suppression of idolatrous worship at Mamre by destroying their altars. [466]
- ❖ AD 333: In a letter to the King of Persia, he wrote how he shunned the "abominable blood and hateful odours" of pagan sacrifices, and instead worshiped the High God "on bended knee". [467]
- ❖ According to Eusebius "he forbade, by an express enactment, the setting up of any resemblance of himself in any idol temple". [468]

Sol Invictus ("Unconquered Sun") was the official sun god of the later Roman Empire and the patron of soldiers. As to the claim that Constantine was a secret admirer of the sun god, it must be noted that in Latin his official imperial title was IMPERATOR CAESAR FLAVIVS CONSTANTINVS PIVS FELIX INVICTVS AVGVSTVS. But after AD 325 he replaced INVICTUS (undefeated) with VICTOR (conqueror), as INVICTUS was reminiscent of Sol Invictus. [469] In the text of Codex of Theodosianus, Constantine finally banned outright the "madness of sacrifice". Sacrifice was the cornerstone of the pagan religion and was necessary for worship. It is not clear whether it was issued before or after his death, but it is addressed to his praetorian prefect. [470]

It cannot be denied that Constantine adapted an extremely pro-Christian course in policy-making that is totally inconsistent with someone simply seeking popularity with his many pagan,

---

[465] Law 116: To Ablavius, the praetorian prefect (Nov 29, 330)
[466] Second Letter of Constantine to Macarius (AD 332) and the rest of the bishops in Palestine
[467] Life of Constantine 4:10
[468] Ibid 4:16
[469] http://www.newworldencyclopedia.org/entry/Constantine_I
[470] http://www.mountainman.com.au/essenes/codex_theodosianus.htm
"Superstition shall cease; the madness of sacrifices shall be abolished. For if any man in violation of the law of the sainted Emperor, Our father, and in violation of this command of Our Clemency, should dare to perform sacrifices, he shall suffer the infliction of a suitable punishment and the effect of an immediate sentence (341)."

Gnostic, Jewish and even non-Orthodox Christian subjects. Besides ending the persecution of Christians, his religious reforms included:

- ❖ AD 313: Meeting places and other properties, which had been confiscated from Christians in the former persecution by pagans, were returned. [471] Christian clergy would be free from public service, that they might not be disturbed in their worship of God. [472]
- ❖ AD 316: Prohibition of simony i.e. positions in the churches were not to be claimed with money. [473]
- ❖ AD 318: Judges should let matters be settled by Christian law where possible and consider those decisions inviolable. Pending cases could be transferred from the municipal court to the episcopal court, providing both parties agreed. [474]
- ❖ AD 321: The Church was granted the right to receive property by bequest. [475]
- ❖ AD 323: Christians, who had suffered the confiscation of their private possessions in earlier persecutions, were compensated directly from the Roman treasury. [476]

Coinage

Another criticism levelled against Constantine is that he (initially) kept pagan gods on coins. From this it is 'deduced' that his

---

[471] The Edict of Milan - And since these same Christians are known to have possessed not only the places in which they had the habit of assembling but other property too which belongs by right to their body… you will order all this property… to be given back without any equivocation or dispute to all those same Christians.

[472] Second Letter of Constantine to Anulinus (AD 313)

[473] http://www.fourthcentury.com/works-of-constantine (Nov, 316?)

[474] Law 36 (23 June 318)

[475] "Every person shall have the liberty to leave at his death any property that he wishes to the most holy and venerable council of the catholic Church." Theodosian Code 16.2.4 (AD 321)

[476] The "Law of Constantine respecting piety toward God and the Christian Religion" (AD 323) is an edict, addressed to the inhabitants of Palestine, containing an exposition of the prosperity of the righteous and the adversity of the wicked, followed by edict for the restitution of confiscated property, the recall of exiles, and various other rectifications of injustices.

motivation was to maintain popularity with his pagan subjects, or that he practiced some sort of syncretism, worshipping both Christ and pagan gods. However it is extremely debatable as to whether history can be extrapolated and motives inferred from the study of old coins. Even verifiable facts - the external evidence - does not always explain the meaning of historical events or the motivations behind their occurrence.

Figure 19: Constantine's follis coin with the reverse side showing the standard planted in a serpent with head curved down, and the Chi-Rho above
[477]

The interpretation of history can be subjective, as historians often tend to provide their own understanding and interpretations based on their particular biases and prejudices. In fact, the representations of pagan gods disappear from Constantine's coinage after AD 318. In AD 315 Constantine's coins began to carry the Chi-Rho (aka Christogram), which is a Greek monogram for Christ, formed from the first two letters of his name in Greek (chi = X and rho = P).

Later coins show the emperor gazing upwards in an attitude of prayer. Contemporary historian, Eusebius, writes circa 339 AD:

---

[477] Coin from CNG Coins http://www.cngcoins.com/

How deeply his soul was impressed by the power of divine faith may be understood from the circumstance that he directed his likeness to be stamped on the golden coin of the empire with the eyes uplifted as in the posture of prayer to God: and this money became current throughout the Roman world. His portrait also at full length was placed over the entrance gates of the palaces in some cities, the eyes upraised to heaven, and the hands outspread as if in prayer.[478]

Figure 20: Coin with Constantine, head tilted back, eyes raised to heaven [479]

Military

Constantine provided for military chaplains; each legion was to have a certain number of clerics and a large tent to serve as church in the camp. [480] He prayed regularly, and before major engagements. [481] His military brilliance and devotion to God inspired his legions to repeated victories over pagan forces. He earned his title "Constantine The Great" from Christian historians after his death, but could have claimed the name on his military achievements alone, which were second only to that of Julius

---

[478] Life of Constantine 4:15
[479] https://www.google.com/culturalinstitute/beta/partner/the-british-museum
[480] https://www.religlaw.org/content/blurb/files/Chapter%209.%20Gaffney.pdf
[481] MacMullen, Ramsey; Constantine, 1969

Caesar. [482] But he directed even his pagan soldiers to join in public prayer acknowledging God as the source of their victories.[483] He also ordered that the sign of the Saviour's cross be engraved on his soldiers' shields and "commanded that his embattled forces should be preceded in their march, not by golden images, as heretofore, but only by the standard of the cross". [484]

Building projects

Throughout his reign, Constantine assisted the Church financially, building various churches, most notably the three huge churches, St. Peter's in Rome, Hagia Sophia in Constantinople and the Holy Sepulchre in Jerusalem. [485] In AD 313 he donated a royal palace, known as the Lateran, as a residence for the Bishop of Rome. A succession of Roman bishops inhabited this palace for about a thousand years. [486] Within his reign the cost of the Church became larger than the cost of the entire imperial civil service. There was a corresponding closure of pagan temples due to a lack of support. State funds were no longer allocated for the repair of pagan temples, going rather to Christian causes.

Rome's famous Arch of Constantine, which also contained the Chi-Rho Christogram was completed in time for the beginning of Constantine's decennalia (the tenth anniversary of his reign).

---

[482] He had with enormous prestige as a general, reuniting the empire under one emperor. He won major victories over the Franks and Alamanni (306-308), the Franks again (313-314), the Visigoths in 332 and the Sarmatians in 334. In fact, by 336, Constantine had actually reoccupied most of the long-lost province of Dacia, which Aurelian had been forced to abandon in 271.

[483] Life of Constantine 4:20 – Eusebius writes, "The emperor himself prescribed the prayer to be used by all his troops, commanding them, to pronounce the following words in the Latin tongue: 'We acknowledge you the only God: we own you, as our King and implore your succour. By your favour have we gotten the victory: through you are we mightier than our enemies. We render thanks for your past benefits, and trust you for future blessings. Together we pray to you, and beseech you long to preserve to us, safe and triumphant, our emperor Constantine and his pious sons.' Such was the duty to be performed on Sunday by his troops, and such the prayer they were instructed to offer up to God."

[484] Ibid, ch 21

[485] http://www.newworldencyclopedia.org/entry/Constantine_I

[486] New Catholic Encyclopedia 1908

There were all manner of festivities, but Constantine pointedly omitted the traditional sacrifices to the pagan gods. [487] Rather "he ordered the celebration of general festivals, and offered prayers of thanksgiving to God, the King of all, as sacrifices without flame or smoke." [488]

Figure 21: The Chi-Rho Christogram on Constantine's Victory Arch

Nova Roma

Constantine encountered much opposition in Rome, where the pagan party was powerful. This opposition by pagans was revealed in particular during the celebration of the twentieth anniversary of his reign and this cooled him towards the capital of the Empire. [489] As he had been born of a Greek father, in what is modern day Serbia, in his later years, between AD 324 and 330, he rebuilt the ancient Greek city, Byzantium, on the Bosporus strait, relocating the capital there in AD 330. He named the city Nova Roma (New Rome) although after his death in AD 337 it was changed to Constantinople i.e. 'City of Constantine' (modern Istanbul in Turkey).

The city became the centre of what was called the Byzantine Empire i.e. the Greek-speaking Roman Empire of late Antiquity

---

[487] http://www.roman-emperors.org/indexxxx.htm
[488] Life of Constantine 1:48
[489] http://stjohndc.work/Russian/saints/SaintsE/e_9506a.htm

and the Middle Ages. The figures of old gods were replaced and often assimilated into Christian symbolism. On the site of a temple to Aphrodite was built the new Church of the Holy Apostles. The city employed overtly Christian architecture, contained churches within the city walls and had no pagan temples. [490] In AD 333 Constantine wrote to Eusebius requesting 50 copies of the Scriptures for use in the new churches in Constantinople.[491]

The imperial court

According to J.C. Robertson, Constantine "used to attend the services of the Church very regularly" and would "stand all the time that the bishops were preaching, however long their sermons might be". He would even write discourses, something like sermons, reading them aloud in the palace to all his courtiers.[492] Eusebius relates that "he took the sacred scriptures into his hands, and devoted himself to the study of those divinely inspired oracles; after which he would offer up regular prayers with all the members of his imperial court." [493]

Christmas

Although it is alleged that Constantine made December 25th, the birthday of the pagan 'Unconquered Sun god', the official holiday it is now - the birthday of Jesus, there is no historical evidence for this. Normally those advocating this view have no primary historical support and justify their claims by quoting each other. The arguments go something like this.

1) CLAIM 1: Christians never observed Christmas until the 4th century. Therefore, (because Constantine lived in that century) it must have been him who introduced the festival as a form of honour to the sun-god (Remember he allegedly was a secret devotee of the sun cult).

---

[490] R. Gerberding and J. H. Moran Cruz, Mediaeval Worlds (2004) p. 56
[491] Fourth letter to Eusebius about the restoration of the divine books (AD 333)
[492] Sketches of Church History, from AD 33 to the Reformation - J. C. Robertson (1904) http://biblehub.com/library/roberston
[493] Life of Constantine 4:17

Actually, already in the 2nd century Theophilus, Bishop of Caesarea (AD 115-181) refers to Dec 25th as being the date of Christ's birth.[494] Trying to somehow implicate Constantine is pure speculation.

2) CLAIM 2: Constantine chose Dec 25th so that his pagan subjects could still have a holiday at Saturnalia.

   One might rightfully ask where the evidence is for this claim. In any event, the Roman feast of Saturnalia was from 17th to the 23rd December. [495] In other words, it was a week-long festival ending two days before Dec 25th.[496]

Easter

Another frivolous claim is that Constantine was responsible for creating Easter as a Christian alternative to an existing pagan festival. One recent social media post (which is of course the ultimate source for research) proclaims the following 'truth' about Easter:

> ... After Constantine decided to Christianize the Empire, Easter was changed to represent Jesus. But at its roots, Easter (which is how you pronounce Ishtar) is all about celebrating fertility and sex.

The above post appeared on the Facebook feed of notorious atheist Richard Dawkins' Foundation for Reason and Science. Regrettably similar equally ill-informed claims are made on some Christian websites.

---

[494] "We ought to celebrate the birthday of our Lord on what day soever the 25th of December shall happen." Magdeburgenses, Cent. 2. c. 6. Hospinian, de orign Festorum Chirstianorum. There was by no means any consensus on the date, because in general the Eastern church regarded Jan 6th as the date of Jesus' birth and observed it as such until the end of the 4th century, after which they joined the Western church in the observance of the Dec 25th date.
[495] http://en.wikipedia.org/wiki/Saturnalia
[496] For more detail, see our website ministry on "Should Christians celebrate Christmas?" - http://www.agfbenoni.co.za/ministry-archives.aspx?mId=787

1) Firstly, Constantine simply legalised Christianity - he did not enforce it. It was over 40 years after Constantine's death that Theodosius I made Christianity the state religion.
2) Secondly, in the late 2nd century, Roman bishop Victor weighed arguments about two competing dates for Easter.[497] How could Constantine 'invent' Easter if people were already debating about it a century before he was born?
3) Thirdly, what exactly is Constantine supposed to have changed? There was no corresponding pagan festival. The celebration date of Easter was linked to a lunar-based Jewish festival, not a solar-based Roman festival.
4) Fourthly, Constantine spoke both Greek and Latin and in those languages, the existing feast in his time was known as 'Pascha' (a word derived from the Hebrew word for Passover). The word 'Easter' is a Germanic word which was first mentioned by the Anglo-Saxon (Old English) monk Bede four centuries after Constantine (and – sorry to disappoint conspiracy theorists - has no connection either to the Babylonian goddess Ishtar.[498])
5) Finally, historic evidence, which is easily verified by any honest researcher, shows that the Council of Nicaea (where Constantine was present) only debated the day when Easter would be celebrated and actually referred to the day as "the Saviour's Passover". The feast of Pascha had already been in place for centuries, but the Eastern and Western churches had a debate about which day to celebrate it. All Constantine

---

[497] Eusebius, Ecclesiastical History 5.23.3

[498] Besides it's Germanic roots from Anglo-Saxon, English drew heavily on Latin (which in turn borrowed a lot from ancient Greek) and French. Now both the Greeks and Romans called the festival 'Pascha', the French call it 'Paques', but in English it is known as 'Easter'. So the word 'Easter' came into English not through its Latin / French / Greek roots, but through its Anglo-Saxon heritage. Old English (i.e. Anglo-Saxon) 'Eōstre' continues into modern English as Easter and derives from Proto-Germanic 'austrōn' meaning 'dawn', itself a descendent of the Proto-Indo-European root 'aus', meaning 'to shine'. This explains why these unfounded claims about Easter and Ishtar come only from English and German speakers. Ishtar is the East Semitic Akkadian, Assyrian and Babylonian goddess of fertility, love and war. So how exactly could the name of an East Semitic goddess jump all the way to England from the Middle East without stopping in Rome, Byzantium or Paris?
For more detail, see website ministry – http://www.agfbenoni.co.za/ministry-archives.aspx?mld=2769

did was to allow Pascha to be publicly celebrated, [499] while getting the church to clarify the date.

The Sunday Sabbath

It seems that no good Christian conspiracy theory is complete without Constantine and so again, he is accused by some Sabbatarians of changing the Christian day of worship from the Sabbath (i.e. the 7th day or Saturday) to Sunday. It is again claimed that he had sinister motives here because of a secret admiration for the sun god.

But Sunday is the first day of the week and was revered by New Covenant Christians because it was the day that Jesus rose from the dead. [500] Already in the book of Acts, believers were breaking bread on Sunday (Acts 20:7). [501] The church at Corinth and the province of Galatia met on Sunday (1 Cor 16:1-2). [502] We know that Christians in the 2nd century also met on Sunday, with Justin Martyr (100–165 AD) writing:

> But Sunday is the day on which we hold our common assembly...[503]

Looking at the evidence leaves no doubt as to Constantine's Christian allegiance. So, linking the choice of Sunday as the Christian day of worship to sun god worship has no historical basis. [504] In fact, this very accusation was already made by pagans at least a century earlier than Constantine and refuted by Tertullian.

---

[499] MacMullen 1969, New Catholic Encyclopedia 1908
[500] Mark 16:9 When Jesus rose early on the first day of the week, he appeared first to Mary Magdalene...
[501] Acts 20:7a On the first day of the week we came together to break bread.
[502] 1 Cor 16:1-2 Now about the collection for God's people: Do what I told the Galatian churches to do. On the first day of every week, each one of you should set aside a sum of money...
[503] First Apology of Justin, Ch 68
[504] For more detail on this, see website ministry on "Sabbath versus Lord's day". http://www.agfbenoni.co.za/ministry-archives.aspx?mld=415

Others... suppose that the sun is the god of the Christians, because it is well-known that we regard Sunday as a day of joy.[505]

Then, to say that Sunday must not be the Christian day of worship because the Romans revered the sun on that day is equally absurd. Every week day for that matter is linked to a pagan deity. You can just as well say that you can't use Saturday because Roman pagans revered Saturn on that day.

Day	Roman pagan deity	Germanic/Norse deity	Greek deity
Sunday	Sol (the sun)	Sunna / Sól	Helios
Monday	Luna (the moon)	Máni	Selene
Tuesday	Mars	Týr	Ares
Wednesday	Mercury	Wodan (Odin)	Hermes
Thursday	Jupiter	Thor	Zeus
Friday	Venus	Frigg	Aphrodite
Saturday	Saturn	Ymir	Cronus

Table 10: The 7 weekdays and how their current English names all derive from Roman or Germanic / Norse pagan gods [506]

So what did Constantine really do regarding Sunday? He did not change the Sabbath to Sunday, as neither days were Roman rest days. He merely created the first 'Sunday closure law' in AD 321, [507] legalizing the day as a time of rest for all people, even though Sunday had already been set apart for centuries as a day of worship from the time of the original apostles. [508] Markets were

---

[505] To the Nations 1:133
[506] https://en.wikipedia.org/wiki/Week
[507] "On the venerable Day of the Sun let the magistrates and people residing in cities rest, and let all workshops be closed." - Constantine's decree - Constantine, March 7, 321. Codex Justinianus lib. 3, tit. 12, 3; trans. in Philip Schaff, "History of the Christian Church", Vol. 3, p. 380, note 1
[508] Renowned church historian, Phillip Schaff, writes: "The celebration of the Lord's Day in memory of the resurrection of Christ dates undoubtedly from the apostolic age. Nothing short of apostolic precedent can account for the universal religious observance in the churches of the second century. There is no dissenting voice. This custom is confirmed by the testimonies of the earliest

banned, public offices were closed (except for the purpose of freeing slaves), [509] and work on Sunday was forbidden [510] (a big deal to the slaves). Considering that the church was struggling into existence, and that a large number of Christians were slaves of heathen masters, we cannot expect an unbroken regularity of worship and a universal cessation of labour on Sunday until the civil government in the time of Constantine came to the help of the church and legalized the observance of the Lord's Day. [511] Constantine also allowed Christian soldiers leave to attend church on Sunday. [512]

Baptism

Constantine did not receive baptism until shortly before his death in AD 337, which some have interpreted as a lack of sincerity or commitment. However, in the 4th and 5th centuries Christians often delayed their baptisms until late in life. This was because of the prevalent idea that mortal sins committed after baptism were sins against the Holy Spirit and hence unforgivable. Ancient accounts indicate that he had hoped to be baptized in the Jordan River shortly before death, but was too sick to make it. He was baptised by Eusebius of Nicomedia (not to be confused with the historian, Eusebius of Caesarea) in his imperial villa at Ankyrona.

---

post-apostolic writers." - History of the Christian Church, Volume II: Ante-Nicene Christianity. AD 100-325. by Philip Schaff (1819-1893)

[509] https://en.wikipedia.org/wiki/Constantine_the_Great_and_Christianity

[510] There were exclusions e.g. farmers. The edict continues, "In the country however persons engaged in agriculture may freely and lawfully continue their pursuits because it often happens that another day is not suitable for grain-sowing or vine planting; lest by neglecting the proper moment for such operations the bounty of heaven should be lost."

[511] History of the Christian Church, Volume II: Ante-Nicene Christianity. AD 100-325. by Philip Schaff (1819-1893)

[512] Prior to this time, the seven-day week had not been officially observed by the Roman Empire. Instead, the days of the month were denoted by counting down toward the Kalends, the Nones, and the Ides of each month. – http://orderofcenturions.net/liturgy.html

Constantine has been criticized based on the record of Roman historian Eutropius, who relates that Constantine executed his eldest and beloved son Crispus in AD 326, and shortly thereafter his second wife, Fausta. [513] For years Constantine had kept Crispus at his side and surviving sources are unanimous in declaring him a loving, trusting and protective father to his first son. [514] While the motivation for the executions are unclear and mystery surrounds the events, Zosimus (6th century) and Zonaras (12th century) both report that Crispus and his stepmother were involved in an illicit relationship. [515] The most commonly accepted version is that of Zosimus in the 6th century, who wrote that Fausta, step-mother of Crispus, was extremely jealous of him as she was reportedly afraid that Constantine would put aside the sons she bore him, so in order to get rid of Crispus, she set him up.

> Fausta allegedly told the young Caesar that she was in love with him and suggested a love affair. Crispus denied her advances leaving the palace in a state of a shock. Fausta then convinced Constantine that Crispus had no respect for his father, since he was in love with her. She claimed that she had dismissed him after his attempt to rape her. Constantine believed her and executed his son.[516]

A few months later, Constantine reportedly discovered the truth and had Fausta executed, although others claim that she committed suicide after being exposed by Constantine's mother,

---

[513] Eutropius 10.6.3 [MGH, AA II 174; (1995) 142]. NOTE: Some have questioned the historicity of these events surrounding Fausta and Crispus, as they don't even bear a mention in Eusebius' "The Life of Constantine". Others counter-claim that Eusebius was trying to portray Constantine in the best possible light, which is why he excluded it.

[514] https://en.wikipedia.org/wiki/Crispus

[515] http://www.roman-emperors.org/crispus.htm

[516] https://en.wikipedia.org/wiki/Crispus

Helena.[517] If she was indeed executed, it must be remembered that under Roman law, adultery was deemed a capital offence.

Summary of Constantine

While Constantine was not perfect by any means, he certainly was not the archvillain portrayed by many, who have treated him most unfairly, based mainly on hearsay and speculation, rather than the historical evidence that remains today. Much of what is attributed to, or rather blamed on Constantine, was actually the work of his successors. However, by establishing the framework for a State Church, he paved the way for the conditions that would cause an ultimate drop in Christian standards, compromise and power mongering. Some believe that by establishing Christianity as the preferred religion of the Roman Empire (which ultimately led to it becoming the official state religion), Constantine radically altered the church and accelerated its acceptance of heretical doctrines and syncretic pagan rituals. Church historian Walter Nigg says:

> As soon as Emperor Constantine opened the floodgates and the masses of the people poured into the Church out of sheer opportunism, the loftiness of the Christian ethos was done for.[518]

Pagan rituals and idols gradually took on Christian meanings and names and were incorporated into Christian worship. "Saints" replaced pagan gods in both worship and as patrons of cities. Mother / son statues were renamed Mary and Jesus

However, the relationship between early Christianity and the Greco-Roman world was extremely complex. Christianity was born into that world and it is true, that at times, there was some form of integration with the culture around it. Sometimes this integration may have been conscious and intentional. At other times, it may have been unconscious. When it was deliberate, it

---

[517] "Constantine: Dynasty, Religion and Power in the Later Roman Empire" By Timothy D. Barnes
[518] Walter Nigg, The Heretics (New York: Alfred A. Knopf, 1962), 102.

was sometimes a compromise with the cultures, language and rituals in order to give them new Christian meaning.

Possibly it is fairest to say that Constantine inadvertently "corrupted" the Church by legitimizing it. At first seen as a great benefit to the Christian community, entanglements with the political realm and with persons of great secular power soon burdened the Church with problems. Today there is still debate over the relationship of Church and State and concern over the use of power to enforce religious belief and practice. Bear in mind though, that there was no place in the world then, where religion and state were separated. There were no "secular states" like today.

Christianity's triumph over paganism

Undoubtedly having Christian emperors boosted the cause of Christianity and accelerated the demise of paganism. In AD 356 Constantius ordered that any persons proven to devote their attention to pagan "sacrifices or to worship images" would be subject to capital punishment. [519]

By AD 392 Theodosius promulgated a series of decrees called the "Theodosian decrees", thereby abolishing the last remaining expressions of Roman pagan religion by closing temples and disbanding the Vestal Virgins. He prohibited not only public worship through pagan sacrifices "to senseless images in any place at all or in any city," but also forbade the observance of paganism in the home, including burning lights or placing incense before statutes of the deities or suspending wreaths for them. He banned divination on pain of death, broke up some pagan associations, tolerated attacks on Roman temples and introduced the criminalization of magistrates who did not enforce laws against polytheism. He declared that those pagan feasts that had not yet been rendered Christian ones, were now to be workdays. Witchcraft and the taking of auspices (i.e. interpreting omens from the observed flight of birds) were prohibited. Ignoring the request of some non-Christian senators, he refused

---

[519] https://www.religlaw.org/content/blurb/files/Chapter%209.%20Gaffney.pdf

to restore the gold statue of the goddess Victory in the Senate House.[520] Then in AD 395:

> ... the emperors Arcadius and Honorius directed the provincial governors to enforce the decrees prohibiting access to any pagan shrine or temple throughout the empire. They revoked the privileges of the "civil priests" or ministers of the ancient pagan religion. And finally in 399 they ordered pagan temples "in the country districts" to be torn down so that "the material basis for all superstition [would] be destroyed."[521]

Hypatia (d. 415 AD) was a female Neo-Platonist philosopher of whom we have mixed reports regarding her character.[522] The Christians of Alexandria suspected her of having an adverse influence on Orestes, the city's governor, and this led to her subsequent brutal assassination by a 'Christian' mob.[523] Although there is no evidence to directly implicate the bishop Cyril in the event, the ecclesiastical historian Socrates rightfully condemns the action as unchristian.

---

[520] https://en.wikipedia.org/wiki/Theodosius_I & https://www.religlaw.org/content/blurb/files/Chapter%209.%20Gaffney.pdf
[521] https://www.religlaw.org/content/blurb/files/Chapter%209.%20Gaffney.pdf
[522] Socrates of Constantinople speaks highly of her, saying that she "made such attainments in literature and science, as to far surpass all the philosophers of her own time" and that "all men on account of her extraordinary dignity and virtue admired her the more." (Ecclesiastical History). In contrast John, Bishop of Nikiu, makes derogatory statements about her, calling her "a pagan... devoted at all times to magic" who "beguiled many people through (her) Satanic wiles." He goes on to say that Orestes, "honoured her exceedingly; for she had beguiled him through her magic. And he ceased attending church as had been his custom." (Chronicle 84.87-103)
[523] Socrates - Ecclesiastical History (Book VII) - Socrates writes the following of her brutal murder, "For as she had frequent interviews with Orestes, it was calumniously (*i.e. in a false and slanderous manner*) reported among the Christian populace, that it was she who prevented Orestes from being reconciled to the bishop. Some of them, therefore, hurried away by a fierce and bigoted zeal, whose ringleader was a reader named Peter, waylaid her returning home, and dragging her from her carriage, they took her to the church called Caesareum, where they completely stripped her, and then murdered her with tiles. After tearing her body in pieces, they took her mangled limbs to a place called Cinaron, and there burnt them."

This affair brought not the least disgrace, not only upon Cyril, but also upon the whole Alexandrian church. And surely nothing can be farther from the spirit of Christianity than the allowance of massacres, fights, and transactions of that sort. [524]

Then by the 6th century we have forced baptisms - in AD 528 the emperor Justinian commanded all pagans to receive baptism within three months. In 529 he closed the university of Athens, replacing it with a Christian university - this signalled the end of pagan Neo-Platonic philosophy. He also forbade city council funds to be used to hire pagans in education and in 530 conducted a persecution of pagans in Constantinople, confiscating the property of many of the accused. In 545 he suppressed the Manichaeans. He attempted to convert those who had been arrested, but when they remained firm in their beliefs, they were tortured and killed by burning or drowning; and their property was confiscated.

In AD 549 John of Ephesus denounced a group of senators, grammarians, sophists, lawyers and physicians - they were accused of paganism, tortured, whipped, and imprisoned. In 559 the pagans in Constantinople were ridiculed and marched in a mock procession and their books were burned. In 579 the governor of Edessa, Anatolia, was condemned to death for commissioning a portrait of Apollo (under the guise of being a portrait of Christ) to worship secretly. In the final decade of the 6th century AD, the Parthenon in Athens was converted into a Christian church.

Civil punishment of heresy

But what of the treatment of those considered to be heretics, like the Donatists for instance? The initial disagreement between Donatists and the rest of the Church was over the treatment of those who renounced their faith during the Diocletian persecution (AD 303-305). While most were more forgiving of these people, the Donatists refused to accept the authority of

---

[524] Ibid

priests and bishops who had fallen away from the faith during the persecution.

Constantine had ultimately exercised restraint in his dealings with the Donatists. In AD 321 he allowed Donatist bishops he had formerly banished to return from exile, granting them toleration and instructing the people to win them over with patience. [525] Then in AD 330, when they refused to give back to Catholics their basilicas - among which was one that Constantine himself had built for their use - he determined that the Donatists should, lest worse things befall, be left in undisturbed possession of their ill-gotten goods, and that a new church should be built, again at his expense, to provide for the religious needs of Catholics. [526] In fact, while some today have painted Constantine as a hard man, his contemporary Eusebius, writes that his administration was criticised in its own day for its frequent lenience.

> Meantime, since there was no fear of capital punishment to deter from the commission of crime, for the emperor himself was uniformly inclined to clemency, and none of the provincial governors visited offenses with their proper penalties, this state of things drew with it no small degree of blame on the general administration of the empire; whether justly or not, let every one form his own judgment: for myself, I only ask permission to record the fact.[527]

At the Council of Nicaea in 325 AD Constantine was present as both emperor and Christian. The main debate here was surrounding the orthodox doctrine of the Trinity (as championed by Athanasius) as contrasted with the ideas of Arius (that the Son of God was not eternal). Only two Egyptian bishops persistently refused to sign the resultant document produced by the council and thus were banished with Arius to Illyria.

---

[525] Letter to Verinus, vicar of Africa (5 May 321)
[526] Letter to the bishops of Numidia (Feb 5, 330)
http://www.tertullian.org/fathers/optatus_11_appendices.htm
[527] Life of Constantine 4:31

Along with the earlier exile of the Donatists, these were the first examples of the civil punishment of heresy; before excommunication had been the extreme penalty. Now banishment became a more severe penalty. The emperor was not so much concerned about punitive punishment as he was in attempting to promote unity of doctrine. Ultimately he permitted Arius and many of his adherents to return to their homes, once Arius had reformulated his Christology to mute the ideas found most objectionable by his critics. [528] And later, when some Arians accused Athanasius (the Trinitarian champion) of mistreating them, in this case Constantine sided with the Arians and exiled Athanasius. [529]

But this was a turning point in church history, because this marriage of Church and State now meant that all offences against the Church, including heresy, were regarded at the same time as crimes against the state and civil society. It was just the beginning of a long succession of civil persecutions for all departures from the Catholic faith.

Constantine initially legislated freedom of religion, but late in his reign in his "Edict against the heretics" (AD 332) he addresses Novatians (Christian dissidents), Valentinians, Marcionites, Cataphrygians, Paulians ('Christian' Gnostic sects) whom he forbids to assemble and whose houses of worship are to be given to orthodox Christians.

In AD 360 his son, Constantius II, declared Christianity the official religion of the Roman Empire. In Theodosius' Edict of 380, Christianity was made the preferred state religion and along with this came the legalization of 'retribution' against heretics.

---

[528] https://en.wikipedia.org/wiki/Arius
[529] https://en.wikipedia.org/wiki/Athanasius_of_Alexandria
Accused of mistreating Arians and Meletians, Athanasius answered those charges at a gathering of bishops in Tyre in 335. There, Eusebius of Nicomedia and other supporters of Arius deposed Athanasius. Both sides of the dispute met with Emperor Constantine I in Constantinople. At that meeting, the Arians claimed Athanasius would try to cut off essential Egyptian grain supplies to Constantinople. He was found guilty, and sent into exile to Gaul.

We command that those persons who follow this rule shall embrace the name of Catholic Christians. The rest, however, whom We adjudge demented and insane, shall sustain the infamy of heretical dogmas, their meeting places shall not receive the name of churches, and they shall be smitten first by divine vengeance and secondly by the retribution of Our own initiative... [530]

By becoming a state religion, the state could - and did - legislate and enforce religious obedience. Heretical doctrines could be believed, but not propagated. [531] Churches had to be surrendered by Arian heretics to those holding to the Nicene creed. [532]

Sadly, it was not long before the once persecuted Church turned, in part, into a persecuting Church, while seeing itself as combating heresy, false religion and evil. It is true that persecution was often initiated from the Byzantine emperors, rather than the Church itself, and there were many cases when ecclesiastical leaders protested these actions. But nevertheless, the union of Church and State had given the civil authorities a mandate to punish heretics in a far more severe fashion than the excommunication option specified by the New Testament writers. Soon the temporary banishment punishment used by Constantine was no longer the worst penalty for heresy - torture and even the death penalty was!

Around AD 380 Priscillian, Bishop of Avila in Spain, taught a Manichaean-Gnostic doctrine influenced by magic and

---

[530] Theodosius' Edict of 380

[531] "All heresies are forbidden by both divine and imperial laws and shall forever cease. If any profane man by his punishable teachings should weaken the concept of God, he shall have the right to know such noxious doctrines only for himself but shall not reveal them to others to their hurt." (379)

[532] We command that all churches shall immediately be surrendered to those bishops who confess that the Father, the Son, and the Holy Spirit are of one majesty and virtue, of the same glory... All, however, who dissent from the communion of the faith of those who have been expressly mentioned in this special enumeration shall be expelled from their churches as manifest heretics and hereafter shall be altogether denied the right and power to obtain churches, in order that the priesthood of the true Nicene faith may remain pure... (381)

astrology. He was executed by Imperial order of the Emperor Maximus, the first heretic to be executed by a Christian power. This was done at the instigation of Ithacius, the metropolitan bishop of Lusitania, whom Priscillian had attempted to oust.

It must be noted that many significant clerical leaders opposed the action of the emperor, albeit to no avail. Ambrose of Milan, Martin of Tours and Siricius, the Bishop of Rome, protested against the execution, largely on the jurisdictional grounds that an ecclesiastical case should not be decided by a civil tribunal, and worked to reduce the persecution. This was scripturally correct as the New Testament directive by Paul is that Christians should not refer church matters to a secular court, but settle them internally, the harshest punishment being temporary excommunication for the purpose of reconciliation.

> *1 Cor 6:3-6 Do you not know that we will judge angels? How much more the things of this life! Therefore, if you have disputes about such matters, appoint as judges even men of little account in the church! I say this to shame you. Is it possible that there is nobody among you wise enough to judge a dispute between believers? But instead, one brother goes to law against another - and this in front of unbelievers!*

Siricius expressed severe disapproval not only at Ithacius, but at the emperor himself. He subsequently excommunicated Ithacius and his associates. On an official visit to Trier, Ambrose refused to give any recognition to Ithacius, "not wishing to have anything to do with bishops who had sent heretics to their death". Martin of Tours had rushed to the Imperial court of Trier to remove the accused men from the secular jurisdiction of the emperor. He prevailed upon the emperor to spare the life of Priscillian. Before the trial, Martin had obtained from Maximus a promise not to apply a death penalty but on his departure, Maximus ordered that Priscillian and his followers be beheaded. Martin was so incensed that he refused to remain in communion with the emperor. He also broke off relations with Felix, bishop of Trier, and all others associated with the enquiries and the trial, and restored communion only when Maximus promised to stop the persecution of the Priscillianists. [533]

In AD 536 Paul, the patriarch of Alexandria brutalized the Monophysites. [534] He set out to remove heretical bishops and when he was opposed by the deacon Psoes, he turned him over to Rhodon, the Augustal Prefect, who had him tortured to death. When the news of this reached the Empress Theodora's ears, she rose in furious defence of the Monophysites. [535]

Besides the fact that the treatment of heretics was not acting in the spirit of Christ or according to New Testament teaching, other problems would later result from the anti-heretical laws passed in this period. Not all who were ultimately affected by these laws were even heretics. E.g.

- ❖ In AD 409, Marcellinus of Carthage, Emperor Honorius' secretary of state, decreed the Donatists heretical and demanded that they give up their churches. They were so harshly persecuted by the Roman authorities that even Augustine - their chief critic - protested.
- ❖ Justinian (AD 483-565) persecuted the Montanists, greatly reducing their numbers. Many have drawn parallels between Montanism and modern Pentecostalism. The most widely known earlier Montanist was undoubtedly Tertullian, who was a prominent Latin church writer who converted to Montanism.

Centuries later the persecution of Anabaptists was condoned by the ancient laws of Theodosius I and Justinian I, which had

---

[533] http://taylormarshall.com/2013/11/should-heretics-receive-the-death-penalty.html, Hughes, Philip (1979). History of the Church: Volume 2: The Church In The World The Church Created: Augustine To Aquinas. A&C Black. & https://en.wikipedia.org/wiki/Priscillian
[534] Monophysitism is the Christological position that Christ has only one nature (divine), as opposed to the orthodox Chalcedonian position which holds that Christ has two natures, one divine and one human.
[535] "The Power Game in Byzantium: Antonina and the Empress Theodora" - by James Allan Evans

originally been passed against the Donatists, decreeing the death penalty for any who practised rebaptism. As the medieval church went more into error, the definition of heresy shifted accordingly. Regrettably these laws would set a legal precedent for the persecution of those trying to reform the Church later in the Middle Ages. In later years, those killing the reformers were the real heretics by Biblical definition.

For instance, the Waldenses were a Christian movement originating in 12th century France, who emphasized personal Bible reading and public preaching. They opposed doctrines like purgatory, infant baptism, indulgences and prayers to and for the dead - heretical beliefs of the Catholic Church to this day. In AD 1211 more than 80 were burned as heretics at Strasbourg, beginning several centuries of persecution. Pope Innocent VIII (1484-1492) decreed their extermination. They were wiped out except for a few survivors in the Alpine Valleys southwest of Turin, who are now the leading Protestant body in Italy. In the 30 years between 1540 and 1570 no fewer than 900,000 Protestants were put to death by the Pope's war for the extermination of the Waldenses. [536]

The Hussites (i.e. followers of Jan Hus) were all but exterminated. Here is part of Pope Martin V's letter commanding the King of Poland in 1429 to exterminate the Hussites. Note the horrendous (?) crimes they stand accused of.

> Know that the interests of the Holy See, and those of your crown, make it a duty to exterminate the Hussites. Remember that these impious persons dare proclaim principles of equality... that all Christians are brethren... that Christ came on earth to abolish slavery; they call the people to liberty... While there is still time, then, turn your forces against Bohemia; burn, massacre, make deserts everywhere for nothing could be more agreeable to God or more useful to the cause of kings, than the extermination of the Hussites.[537]

---

[536] Halley's Bible Handbook
[537] Dave Hunt: Mystery Babylon Identified

Justification for Persecution of heretics

From the 1st to early 4th century, the Church was persecuted. After becoming a "State Church", sadly the tables are turned. Granted the persecutions were not on the same scale, or equal in cruelty to the pagan persecution of the Church, but this practice was in stark contrast to the teachings of Jesus and his apostles. Augustine is charged with giving the policy of heretic persecution his personal approval and for supplying the theological justification. In a letter to the Donatist priest Vincentius in AD 408, Augustine explains his reasons for changing his original more moderate view.

> For originally my opinion was, that no one should be coerced into the unity of Christ, that we must act only by words, fight only by arguments, and prevail by force of reason, lest we should have those whom we knew as avowed heretics feigning themselves to be Catholics. But this opinion of mine was overcome not by the words of those who controverted it, but by the conclusive instances to which they could point. For, in the first place, there was set over against my opinion my own town, which, although it was once wholly on the side of Donatus, was brought over to the Catholic unity by [fear of the imperial edicts... Could I therefore maintain opposition to my colleagues, and by resisting them stand in the way of such conquests of the Lord, and prevent the sheep of Christ which were wandering on your mountains and hills... from being gathered into the fold of peace, in which there is one flock and one Shepherd? [538]

Thus, for Augustine, the use of force is not wrong per se. His initial objection was that it was imprudent and might result in false Catholics. When, in practice, not only did this not occur, but whole blocks of Donatists eagerly embraced Catholicism, his objections were overcome. In effect, he argues that the ends

---

[538] Letter 93 (AD 408) http://www.newadvent.org/fathers/1102093.htm

justify the means. He also endorses state legislation against heretics by saying:

> ... let the kings of the earth serve Christ by making laws for Him and for His cause." [539]

In the same letter, Augustine offers this theological defence to Vincentius' objections.

> You are of opinion that no one should be compelled to follow righteousness; and yet you read that the householder said to his servants, "Whomsoever ye shall find, Compel Them To Come In." ... Whatever therefore the true and rightful Mother does, even when something severe and bitter is felt by her children at her hands, she is not rendering evil for evil, but is applying the benefit of discipline to counteract the evil of sin, not with the hatred which seeks to harm, but with the love which seeks to heal. When good and bad do the same actions and suffer the same afflictions, they are to be distinguished not by what they do or suffer, but by the causes of each: e.g. Pharaoh oppressed the people of God by hard bondage; Moses afflicted the same people by severe correction when they were guilty of impiety: their actions were alike; but they were not alike in the motive of regard to the people's welfare - the one being inflated by the lust of power, the other inflamed by love. [540]

So, Augustine appeals to Jesus' word in Luke 14:23. The phrase "Compel them to come in" is amazingly generous in the context of Jesus' parable and amazingly dangerous used out of context by Augustine, to justify persecution of heretics.

In fairness to Augustine, the following facts bear mention, which seem to indicate that he may have underestimated the severity of the state response. Two years later, Augustine wrote to Donatus, a Roman proconsul responsible for enforcing imperial

---

[539] Ibid
[540] Ibid

edicts against the Donatists. Firstly, Augustine explicitly rejects execution of heretics; in fact, he would rather risk death himself than expose one of his opponents to the risk of execution. Secondly, he recognizes that no good is done when a man is compelled by force to join the Church. In AD 412, Augustine continues to call for leniency in sentencing against the Donatists, as seen in this letter to Marcellinus:

> As to the punishment of these men, I beseech you to make it something less severe than sentence of death, although they have, by their own confession, been guilty of such grievous crimes. [541]

But killing of heretics had the full support of Thomas Aquinas (1225-1274), who is considered to be the most influential Catholic theologian in the medieval period. He was a Dominican, who from their inception were dedicated to eliminating heresy, namely that of the Albigenses. He writes:

> Therefore if forgers of money and other evil-doers are forthwith condemned to death by the secular authority, much more reason is there for heretics, as soon as they are convicted of heresy, to be not only excommunicated but even put to death.[542]

Aquinas believed that in accord with the Old Testament and the New Testament (Romans 13), that the death penalty is a present reality and a right of the secular prince. Murderers kill the body and they get the death penalty. Heretical teachers kill the soul and that is much worse. Therefore, heretics should receive the death penalty.[543]

Forced conversion and baptism

Charlemagne (AD 742/747/748-814), the Christian king of the Franks and first Holy Roman Emperor, was staunchly anti-

---

[541] Letter 139 (AD 412) http://www.newadvent.org/fathers/1102139.htm
[542] Summa theologiae II-II, q. 11. a. 3
[543] http://taylormarshall.com/2013/11/should-heretics-receive-the-death-penalty.html

pagan. On conquering the Saxons, he had insisted that they convert to Christianity. Einhard, the courtier and biographer of Charlemagne writes:

> The war lasted thirty-three years with great fury, and the Saxons came off worse than the Franks. It would have ended sooner, had it not been for the duplicity of the Saxons. They were conquered repeatedly and humbly submitted to the King, promising to do follow his commands. Sometimes they were so weakened that they promised to renounce their worship of devils, and to adopt Christianity, but they were as quick to violate these terms as they were to accept them...This long war finally ended with the Saxons submitting on Charlemagne's terms, renouncing their national religious customs and the worship of devils, accepting the sacraments of the Christian faith and religion, and uniting with the Franks to form one people. [544]

The Capitulatio de partibus Saxoniae was a law imposed by Charlemagne on conquered Saxons that prescribed death to those who refused to convert to Christianity. [545]

In AD 1201 Pope Innocent III pronounced that if someone had agreed to be baptized to avoid torture and intimidation, they could be compelled to outwardly observe Christianity:

> Those who are immersed even though reluctant, do belong to ecclesiastical jurisdiction at least by reason of the sacrament, and might therefore be reasonably compelled to observe the rules of the Christian Faith... Thus one who is drawn to Christianity by violence, through fear and through torture, and receives the sacrament of Baptism in order to avoid loss, he (like one who comes to Baptism in dissimulation) does receive the impress of Christianity, and may be forced to observe the Christian Faith as one who expressed a conditional

---

[544] "The Life of Charlemagne" by Einhard
[545] https://en.wikipedia.org/wiki/Forced_conversion#Medieval_era

willingness though, absolutely speaking, he was unwilling... [546]

He does admit at least that, "It is, to be sure, contrary to the Christian Faith that anyone who is unwilling and wholly opposed to it should be compelled to adopt and observe Christianity." [547]

Temporal power

As indicated earlier, Constantine had relocated the Roman Empire's capital from Rome to Nova Roma (Constantinople) in AD 330. With Rome no longer the centre of power for the empire, the Church began to fill in the gap at Rome. As the later Emperor's power declined, the Bishop of Rome's increased.

While Ambrose, the Bishop of Milan, is to be commended for his treatment of the Emperor Theodosius because of the Massacre of Thessalonica in AD 390, it still indicates how powerful the Christian clergy had become at this stage. On hearing of the slaughter that had resulted in Thessalonica because of Theodosius' orders, Ambrose left Milan (the residence of Theodosius at that time) and refused to celebrate a mass in the emperor's presence, until he repented. [548] According to Theodoret, when the emperor tried to enter a Milanese church, where Ambrose was about to celebrate a mass, the bishop stopped him and rebuked him for what he had done. [549]

The Gelasian doctrine

In the Roman Catholic Church, canon law is ecclesiastical law laid down by papal pronouncements. In a letter written in AD 494 by the Bishop of Rome, Gelasius I, to Byzantine Emperor Anastasius I Dicorus, he expressed what became known as the Gelasian doctrine; referred to as the canon "Duo Sunt". [550]

---

[546] Ibid
[547] Ibid
[548] https://en.wikipedia.org/wiki/Massacre_of_Thessalonica
[549] Theodoret, Historia ecclesiastica 5.17
[550] The letter is referred to as Famuli Vestrae Pietatis, also known by the Latin mnemonic Duo Sunt ("there are two").

According to commentary in the Enchiridion Symbolorum, [551] the letter is "the most celebrated document of the ancient Church concerning the two powers on earth."

> The Gelasian doctrine articulates a Christian theology about division of authority and power. All Medieval theories about division of power between priestly spiritual authority and secular temporal authority were versions of the Gelasian doctrine. According to the Gelasian doctrine, secular temporal authority is inferior to priestly spiritual authority since a priestly spiritual authority is responsible for the eternal condition of both a secular temporal authority and the subjects of that secular temporal authority but "implies that the priestly authority is inferior to the secular authority in the secular domain".[552]

Another canon which bears mention is "Cum ad verum", also based on a letter of Gelasius, as quoted by Pope Nicholas I. According to the Stanford Encyclopedia of Philosophy:

> A distinction between Church and State - more exactly, between the priesthood and the power of the emperor, each independent in its own sphere, though the priesthood has the higher function. The classic place for this doctrine is the canon Duo sunt. Another canon, Cum ad verum, gave reasons for the separation: mutual limitation of their powers would restrain the pride of priest and emperor, and those on God's service (the clergy) should be kept free of worldly entanglements. [553]

Increasing secular power of the Popes

When Christians and Jews clashed in 4th and 5th century Alexandria (Egypt), the Jews were supported by the city governor, Orestes, so the Christians appealed to the bishop Cyril

---

[551] Enchiridion Symbolorum is a compendium of all basic texts of Catholic dogma and morality since the apostles, commissioned by Pope Pius IX,
[552] https://en.wikipedia.org/wiki/Famuli_vestrae_pietatis
[553] https://plato.stanford.edu/entries/medieval-political

for assistance. The contemporary 5th century Greek church historian, Socrates of Constantinople, notes that the source of the friction between Orestes and Cyril was due to the increasing power the bishops exercised.

> Now Orestes had long regarded with jealousy the growing power of the bishops, because they encroached on the jurisdiction of the authorities appointed by the emperor... [554]

Then in AD 452, the Bishop of Rome, Leo I, allegedly negotiated and saved Rome from Attila the Hun. One would have expected that this was the work of the imperial staff (as the emperor was based in Constantinople).

In the Middle Ages the Catholic Church believed that they were the inheritors of Israel's promises including the 'Kingdom' which had been promised to Israel. It followed therefore that the Church should assume authority over the secular and political powers of the world, ultimately arriving at the policy of "temporal power" (i.e. control of state and governmental activity).

The Donation of Pepin

Pepin (AD 714-768), the King of the Franks, defended the papacy against the Lombards and issued the Donation of Pepin, in which he gave the land around Rome to the Pope, thereby elevating the Pope from being a subject of the Byzantine Empire to a head of state, with temporal power over the newly constituted Papal States. This formed the legal basis for the Papal States in the Middle Ages. [555]

The Holy Roman Empire

When the Lombard king, Desiderius, took over certain papal cities and headed for Rome, Pope Adrian sent ambassadors to Pepin's son Charlemagne (i.e. Charles the Great) requesting

---

[554] Socrates - Ecclesiastical History (Book VII)
[555] https://en.wikipedia.org/wiki/Religious_views_of_Isaac_Newton, https://en.wikipedia.org/wiki/Pope_Leo_III & https://en.wikipedia.org/wiki/Pepin_the_Short

him to enforce the policies of his father. [556] Charlemagne successfully intervened militarily and confirmed Pepin's grants of land to the Pope. Out of gratitude for Charlemagne's protection of the popes, he was formally crowned as "Holy Roman Emperor" by Pope Leo III in AD 800. The resultant "Holy Roman Empire" would remain in continuous existence for around 1000 years until Napoleon brought it to an end in 1806. This was perhaps the first moment in which the Pope was generally granted a power of control of the imperial dignity, thus demonstrating a sort of power of international veto.

After Charlemagne's death for centuries during the period of the Holy Roman Empire, there was ceaseless struggle between popes and German and French kings for supremacy. [557] While the kings had the military power and the pope relied on them for protection, if the kings did not cooperate the popes threatened them and their subjects with excommunication. This was a very real threat because, even if the kings didn't care, their subjects certainly didn't want to be excommunicated from the Church and face potential damnation. The kings often got around this by appointing an alternative puppet pope, so you have periods when there were two or three popes at the same time (each normally taking turns in excommunicating each other).

But there was open conflict between Pope Boniface VIII (1230-1303) and King Philippe IV (1268-1314) of France. Philippe IV was convinced that the wealth of the Catholic Church in France should be used in part to support the state and in particular his war against England. With the clergy beginning to be taxed in both France and England to finance their ongoing wars against each other, Boniface took a hard stand against it. Viewing the taxation as an assault on traditional clerical rights, in 1296 he ordered the bull Clericis laicos, forbidding lay taxation of the clergy without prior papal approval. [558] But Philippe retaliated by denying the exportation of money from France to Rome, funds that the Church required to operate. He also decreed laws

---

[556] https://en.wikipedia.org/wiki/Charlemagne
[557] Halley's Bible Handbook
[558] https://en.wikipedia.org/wiki/Pope_Boniface_VIII

prohibiting the export of gold, silver, precious stones, or food from France to the Papal States.[559]

In the bull Ausculta Fili in 1301 Boniface appealed to Philippe to listen to the Vicar of Christ as the spiritual monarch over all earthly kings. He protested against the trial of clergymen in the royal courts and the continued use of church funds for state purposes, threatening to summon the bishops and abbots of France to take measures "for the preservation of the liberties of the Church". But when the bull was presented to Philippe; Robert II, Count of Artois, reportedly snatched it from the hands of Boniface's emissary and flung it into the fire. [560]

In 1302 Boniface VIII issued another papal bull (Unam Sanctam) setting forth a doctrine called the "two swords". Rather than the Church and State being separate kingdoms, he declares that there is only one Kingdom, the Church (meaning the Catholic Church), and it controls the spiritual sword, while the temporal sword is controlled by the State. The temporal sword is hierarchically lower than the spiritual sword, allowing for Church influence in politics and society at large. [561]

In a bull dated 1303, King Philippe was excommunicated. Boniface was subsequently attacked at his palace in Anagni and the French Chancellor and the Colonnas (a powerful family in papal Rome) demanded his resignation. When he responded that he would "sooner die", Sciarra Colonna allegedly slapped him. According to a modern interpreter, Boniface was probably beaten and nearly executed, but was released from captivity after three days, dying shortly after.

So Philippe ultimately brought the papacy under his yoke and laid the foundations of the national monarchy of France. [562] He also carried out the destruction of the powerful order of the Knights Templar, his motivation being to get out of paying back the money he owed them. Philippe used forced confessions

---

[559] Ibid

[560] Ibid

[561] https://en.wikipedia.org/wiki/Two_kingdoms_doctrine

[562] http://www.nndb.com/people/986/000093707/

admitting to heresy, to have many Templars burned at the stake.[563]

A few years after the death of Boniface, the Papal Palace was removed from Rome to Avignon on the south border of France and for 70 years (AD 1305-1377) the papacy was the mere tool of the French Court. This became known as the "Babylonian Captivity" of the popes. [564] Then Pope Gregory XI abandoned Avignon and moved the Papal Court back to Rome in AD 1377, but following his death in AD 1378, a second line of Avignon popes was started (now known as antipopes). [565] Subsequently for the next 40 years (until AD 1417), in what is called the "Western Schism", there were two sets of popes, one at Rome and the other at Avignon, each claiming to be the sole "Vicar of Christ," hurling anathemas and curses at each other. [566] Then in the latter part of the "Western Schism" period there were three popes at once; in Avignon, Rome and Pisa.

The Papal States remained under the sovereign direct rule of the Pope until 1870. They were considered to be a manifestation of the temporal power of the Pope, as opposed to his ecclesiastical primacy. By 1861, most of the territory had been conquered by the Kingdom of Italy. Only Lazio, including Rome, remained under the Pope's control. But in 1870, the Pope lost Lazio and Rome and was left with no physical territory at all, not even the Vatican. Benito Mussolini solved the crisis by signing the Lateran Treaty in 1929, granting the Vatican City State sovereignty.[567]

The Donation of Constantine

Years earlier Gregory I, the Bishop of Rome from AD 590 to 604, had reproached the Patriarch of Constantinople for taking the title "universal bishop":

---

[563] https://en.wikipedia.org/wiki/Philip_IV_of_France
[564] Halley's Bible Handbook
[565] https://en.wikipedia.org/wiki/Avignon_Papacy
[566] Halley's Bible Handbook
[567] https://en.wikipedia.org/wiki/Papal_States

I say it without the least hesitation, whoever calls himself the universal bishop, or desires this title, is, by his pride, the precursor of Antichrist, because he thus attempts to raise himself above the others. The error into which he falls springs from pride equal to that of Antichrist; for as that Wicked One wished to be regarded as exalted above other men, like a god, so likewise whoever would be called sole bishop exalteth himself above others. [568]

In humility, Gregory preferred to be called "the servant of the servants of God". In stark contrast, Nicholas 1 (AD 858-867) became the first pope to wear a crown, [569] known as the papal tiara. He asserted that the Pope should have suzerain authority over all Christians, even royalty, in matters of faith and morals. [570] To promote his claim of universal authority he used with great effect the Pseudo-Isidorian Decretals, a set of extensive, influential medieval forgeries that appeared about AD 857, containing documents that purported to be letters and decrees of bishops and councils of the 2nd and 3rd centuries, all tending to exalt the power of the Pope. All of these were deliberate forgeries and corruptions of ancient historical documents, but their spurious character was not discovered till some centuries later. [571] While it is possible that Nicholas never knew that they were fake, opinion is divided as to whether he lied in claiming that they had been kept in the archives of the Roman Church from ancient times.

But they served their purpose, in "stamping the claims of the medieval priesthood with the authority of antiquity." The Papacy, which had evolved over a period of several centuries, was made to appear as something complete and unchangeable from the very beginning. The object was to antedate by five centuries the Pope's temporal power. [572] This is undoubtedly the most colossal

---

[568] "The Papacy" by Rene-Francois Guette, Book VII, Ep. 33.
[569] Halley's Bible Handbook
[570] https://en.wikipedia.org/wiki/Pope_Nicholas_I
[571] Although Catholic theologians initially tried to defend the authenticity of at least some of the material, since the 19th century Protestants and Catholics alike regard them as forgeries.
[572] Halley's Bible Handbook

literary fraud in history. But the most infamous forgery to be used by the medieval popes, to support their claims in their political conflicts with the secular powers, was the "Donation of Constantine". This manuscript was an alleged proclamation made by Constantine in AD 324 where he purportedly demonstrated his gratitude for being baptized by the Bishop of Rome, Sylvester, by granting him and his successors the tiara and imperial insignia, besides transferring to them authority over Rome and the western part of the Roman Empire. [573] The 'discovery' of this document helped firmly establish the control of the Pope in these areas.

During the Middle Ages, the Donation was widely accepted as authentic, although the Emperor Otto III did possibly raise suspicions of the document as a forgery. Cardinal Nicholas of Cusa declared it to be fraudulent. [574] Then in AD 1440, a scholar named Lorenzo Valla questioned the authenticity of the document e.g. Constantine was not baptized by Sylvester of Rome, but by Eusebius of Nicomedia. Another glaring error in the document was the fact that it quoted from Jerome's translation of the Bible, despite the fact that Jerome was born 26 years after the alleged date of its writing. In 1453, five years before becoming pope, Pius II wrote an unpublished tract, admitting the Donation was a forgery. [575] Although the Catholic Church has now openly admitted to the falseness of this document, it gave them great power for centuries, deceiving many into accepting their authority for a great part of the Middle Ages.

The sad result
In later years, some would purchase the position of bishop in the Church with money, as it came to be seen as a position of political influence. To give an idea of the type of power wielded by popes in this period, in AD 860 Pope Nicholas I 'ordered' the king of Bulgaria to destroy another king, writing:

---

[573] https://en.wikipedia.org/wiki/Donation_of_Constantine
[574] Ibid
[575] Ibid

A king need not fear to command massacres, when these will retain his subjects in obedience, or cause them to submit to the faith of Christ; and God will reward him in this world, and in eternal life, for these murders… We order you, in the name of religion, to invade his states, burn his cities, and massacre his people. [576]

Pope Innocent III (AD 1198-1216) claimed to be "Supreme Sovereign over the Church and the World" and asserted that "all things on earth and in heaven and in hell are subject to the Vicar of Christ." The kings of Germany, France, England, and practically all the monarchs in Europe obeyed his will, including those in the Byzantine Empire. [577] Pope Gregory VII (c. AD 1020-1085) was a prominent champion of papal supremacy, claiming the following powers for the Pope: [578]

- ❖ All princes were obliged to kneel before the Pope.
- ❖ The Pope could be judged by no one on earth.
- ❖ He could depose and reinstate emperors.

This deposing power was the most powerful tool in the political arsenal of the papacy whereby they could declare a king heretical and thus powerless to rule. [579] Catholic doctrine was that the Pope, as the Vicar of Christ on earth, had the ultimate authority not only over the Church, but indirectly over the State. Throughout the Middle Ages the Pope claimed the right to depose the Catholic kings of Western Europe and exercised it, at times successfully, sometimes not [580] (as was the case with Henry VIII of England and Philippe IV of France).

Sadly, this was one of the most oppressive periods in Christian history, towards both non-Christians and Christians alike. While

---

[576] Cormenin: "History of the Popes"
[577] Halley's Bible Handbook
[578] https://en.wikipedia.org/wiki/Dictatus_papae
[579] De Rosa: Vicars of Christ & https://en.wikipedia.org/wiki/Papal_deposing_power
[580] https://en.wikipedia.org/wiki/Separation_of_church_and_state

the Papal Church held this Amillennial mindset that it was the Kingdom of God on earth, the following things resulted.

a) Crusades

- ❖ There were numerous crusades in which the use of force was endorsed by the Pope in order to retake the Holy Land from the Muslims.
- ❖ The Albigenses, or Cathari, in southern France, northern Spain and northern Italy allegedly held beliefs similar to 2nd and 3rd century Gnostic heretics. They also spoke out against the immoralities of the priesthood and the veneration of saints and images. In AD 1208 Pope Innocent III ordered a crusade of extermination which wiped out town after town. The inhabitants were murdered without discrimination until all of the Albigenses were obliterated. In the Albigensian Crusade (1208-1249) an estimated 1 million Frenchmen suspected of being Albigensians were slain. [581] Among the cities wiped out was Beziers, where 60,000 were massacred, including women and children, which Pope Innocent III called "the crowning achievement" of his papacy. [582] The Albigenses may well have been heretics, but their torture and murder sanctioned by the pope was not the way of Christ.

b) 'Holy'-wars

The following wars were started by Catholic kings, who were actively encouraged by the popes and Jesuits with the explicit purpose of destroying Protestantism in a "Counter-Reformation".

- ❖ The war on the German Protestants (1566-1609)
- ❖ War on the Protestants of the Netherlands (1566-1609)
- ❖ Huguenot Wars in France (1572 1598)
- ❖ Philip's attempt against England (1588)
- ❖ Thirty Years War (1618-1648)

---

[581] Max Dimont (Jews, God, and History), Helen Ellerbe (The Dark Side of Christian History)
[582] Dave Hunt: Mystery Babylon Identified

c) The Inquisition

In the 6th century, Pope Pelagius defined a heretic as being anyone who did not submit to the Roman Church. In AD 1184, the Inquisition was made official at the Synod of Verona by Pope Lucius III, in agreement with the Holy Roman Emperor Frederick I Barbarossa.

> Under it everyone was required to inform against heretics. Anyone suspect was liable to torture, without knowing the name of his accuser. The proceedings were secret. The Inquisitor pronounced sentence and the victim was turned over to civil authorities to be imprisoned for life or to be burned. The victim's property was confiscated and divided between the church and the state. [583]

The Inquisition claimed vast multitudes of victims in Spain, Italy, Germany and the Netherlands. It is generally divided into 3 major phases, each one authorized by the presiding pope.

1. The Medieval Inquisition, authorized by Pope Gregory IX in 1231. It was initially directed against some of the Christian sects of that day such as the Cathari, Albigenses, and Waldenses. Each of these sects actively opposed the corrupt popish clergy of the day. And while the belief system of the Cathari and of the Albigenses may have been heretical (there is not enough of a record remaining for us to know for sure), the beliefs of the Waldenses were orthodox - in fact, more orthodox than those of papal Rome.
2. The Spanish Inquisition, commencing in 1478, added to the objects of papal wrath Jewish and Muslim converts to Christianity, who conversions were mostly insincere, having been the result of coercion and/or social pressure. Also, suspected Protestants were targeted at this time. Innocent VIII appointed the brutal Thomas of Torquemada Inquisitor General of Spain, and ordered all rulers to deliver up heretics

---

[583] Halley's Bible Handbook

to him. Between 8,800 [584] to 10,220 [585] were burnt in the 18 years of Torquemada.

3. The Roman Inquisition, instituted by Pope Paul III in 1542 focused papal terror upon the Protestants.

J. H. Ignaz Von Döllinger, a leading 19th century Catholic professor of Church History, writes:

> The view of the Church had been... [that] every departure from the teaching of the Church must be punished with death, and the most cruel of deaths, by fire... Both the initiation and carrying out of this... must be ascribed to the Popes alone... who compelled bishops and priests to condemn heretics to torture, confiscation of their goods, imprisonment, and death, and to enforce the execution of this sentence on the civil authorities, under pain of excommunication. [586]

In 1233, Pope Gregory IX assigned the duty of carrying out inquisitions to the Dominican Order. Inquisitors acted in the name of the Pope and with his full authority. Innocent IV (1241-1254), gave papal sanction to the use of torture in extracting confessions from suspected heretics. [587] A Romanist writer, who deplored the persecuting policy of his church, Professor Gabriele Rossetti (1783-1854) writes:

> It makes the heart of a true Christian bleed to think of this fatal error of the Latin Church, which by persecuting others laid the foundation of her own irreparable ruin. That the opinions held by these so-called heretics were most injurious to the Church of Rome cannot be denied, but the means taken to destroy them were, of all others, the most likely to strengthen them, and render them more deeply rooted. Daniel and St. John foretold that Satan's delegate would use horrid cruelties, and inundate Babylon with the blood of Christ's martyrs; and the pope,

---

[584] Philip Schaff, History of the Christian Church
[585] Motley, Rise of the Dutch Republic
[586] The Pope and the Council (London, 1869) 190-193
[587] Halley's Bible Handbook

to prove that he was not that delegate, did use horrid cruelties, and caused Rome to overflow with the purest of Christian blood! [588]

The Spanish Inquisition was first abolished during the domination of Napoleon and the reign of Joseph Bonaparte (1808–1812). [589] Peter De Rosa, a former Jesuit, writes:

> When Napoleon conquered Spain in 1808, a Polish officer in his army, Colonel Lemanouski, reported that the Dominicans blockaded themselves in their monastery in Madrid. When Lemanouski's troops forced an entry, the inquisitors denied the existence of any torture chambers. The soldiers searched the monastery and discovered them under the floors. The chambers were full of prisoners, all naked, many insane. The French troops, used to cruelty and blood, could not stomach the sight. They emptied the torture-chambers, laid gunpowder to the monastery and blew the place up. [590]

Canon Juan Antonio Llorente (1756-1823) was General Secretary of the Inquisition from 1789 to 1801 and had access to the archives of all the tribunals. In his "Critical History of the Spanish Inquisition" he estimated that the number of victims in the Spanish Inquisition alone was 341,021 with about 31,912 being executed between 1480 and 1808. [591]

Was this the promised Amillennial
"kingdom of God" on earth ushered
in by Jesus' First Coming? Clearly not!

---

[588] Rossetti - Disquisitions on the Antipapal Spirit Which Produced the Reformation
[589] https://en.wikipedia.org/wiki/Spanish_Inquisition
[590] Vicars of Christ: The Dark Side of the Papacy
[591] In contrast to this high estimate, Will Durant in 'The Reformation' (1957) supported the following lower estimates from Catholic sources: - Hernando de Pulgar, secretary to Queen Isabella, estimated 2,000 burned before 1490. - An unnamed "Catholic historian" estimated 2,000 burned, 1480-1504, and 2,000 burned, 1504-1758.

Conversion by Coercion?

Does the New Testament teach that we should spread the gospel through force? No! In the New Testament, there is no record of religiously condoned physical violence by Christians against non-Christians or Christians, which could be used as a precedent for Christian persecution of other groups.

Treatment of unbelievers

When the rich young ruler turned his back on Jesus and rejected his message, Jesus didn't dispatch a hit squad of disciples to punish him. Rather we are told that "Jesus looked at him and loved him" (Mark 10:21). In John 6 we see that, on hearing a difficult teaching from Jesus, "many of his disciples turned back and no longer followed him" (John 6:66). Again Jesus takes no punitive action against them, but instead simply asks the other disciples, "You do not want to leave too, do you?" (John 6:67). After healing the demoniac, "the people of the region of the Gerasenes asked Jesus to leave them". Rather than forcing himself on them, "he got into the boat and left" (Luke 8:37). When the Samaritans refused Jesus passage through their city and his disciples suggested that he destroy the village by fire, we read:

> But He turned and rebuked them, and said, "You do not know what kind of spirit you are of, for the Son of Man did not come to destroy men's lives, but to save them." (Luke 9:55-56 NASB)

So Jesus never forced his message on those who were unreceptive. The enemies of Christianity are reached when:

a) We love them (our enemies) and show mercy.

> Luke 6:35-36 But love your enemies, do good to them... (Then) you will be sons of the Most High, because he is kind to the ungrateful and wicked. Be merciful, just as your Father is merciful.

b) They see the love Christians have for other Christians.

> *John 13:35 By this all men will know that you are my disciples, if you love one another.*

c) We live exemplary lives, despite being slandered.

> *1 Pet 2:12 Live such good lives among the pagans that, though they accuse you of doing wrong, they may see your good deeds and glorify God on the day he visits us.*

d) We share our faith with "gentleness and respect" (not torture and coercion).

> *1 Pet 3:15 Always be prepared to give an answer to everyone who asks you to give the reason for the hope that you have. But do this with gentleness and respect...*

Bona fide Christians do not convert by the sword, and Christianity should not be embraced for political or social advantage. Jesus should be sought for his own sake. The message of the early Christian church was spread by love and example.

Despite the prevailing spirit of his age, the Bishop of Rome, Gregory I (d. 604 AD), must be commended for grasping what the true spirit of Christianity should be towards the unconverted.

> Those who, with sincere intent, desire to lead people outside the Christian religion to the correct faith, ought to make the effort by means of what is pleasant, not with what is harsh, lest opposition drive afar the mind of men whom reasoning... could have attracted. Those who act otherwise... demonstrate that they are concerned with their own enterprises, rather than with those of God! [592]

---

[592] The Apostolic See and the Jews, Documents: 492-1404; Simonsohn, Shlomo

Disputes between Christians

Christians are not even to take other professing Christians to court, but to settle these matters in the church.

> *1 Cor 6:1 If any of you has a dispute with another, do you dare to take it before the ungodly for judgment instead of before the Lord's people?*

Paul states unequivocally the true Christian attitude in matters of disputes between fellow Christians.

> *1 Cor 6:7-8 The very fact that you have lawsuits among you means you have been completely defeated already. Why not rather be wronged? Why not rather be cheated? Instead, you yourselves cheat and do wrong, and you do this to your brothers.*

Church discipline

Church discipline in the New Testament comprises of admonishing in the church, or expelling people from the church, but never persecution or killing. Jesus taught us to break fellowship (i.e. excommunication) with those who sin against us. This is after failed attempts to settle the matter privately, then with witnesses, then publicly.

> *Matt 18:15-17 "If your brother sins against you, go and show him his fault, just between the two of you. If he listens to you, you have won your brother over. But if he will not listen, take one or two others along, so that 'every matter may be established by the testimony of two or three witnesses.' If he refuses to listen to them, tell it to the church; and if he refuses to listen even to the church, treat him as you would a pagan or a tax collector."*

Paul also taught excommunication for the unrepentant Christian (the goal being restorative, not punitive):

> *1 Cor 5:1-5 It is actually reported that there is sexual immorality among you, and of a kind that does not occur*

even among pagans: A man has his father's wife. And you are proud! Shouldn't you rather have been filled with grief and have put out of your fellowship the man who did this? ... When you are assembled in the name of our Lord Jesus... hand this man over to Satan, so that the sinful nature may be destroyed and his spirit saved on the day of the Lord.

Excommunication (or disfellowship) is not just for the sexually immoral, but includes the following:

1 Cor 5:9-11 I have written you in my letter not to associate with sexually immoral people—not at all meaning the people of this world who are immoral, or the greedy and swindlers, or idolaters. In that case you would have to leave this world. But now I am writing you that you must not associate with anyone who calls himself a brother but is sexually immoral or greedy, an idolater or a slanderer, a drunkard or a swindler. With such a man do not even eat.

The intention of disfellowship is restoration. In the case of the Corinthians, Paul instructs them in his second epistle regarding the man who had been disfellowshipped earlier:

2 Cor 2:6-11 The punishment inflicted on him by the majority is sufficient for him. Now instead, you ought to forgive and comfort him, so that he will not be overwhelmed by excessive sorrow. I urge you, therefore, to reaffirm your love for him. The reason I wrote you was to see if you would stand the test and be obedient in everything. If you forgive anyone, I also forgive him. And what I have forgiven—if there was anything to forgive—I have forgiven in the sight of Christ for your sake, in order that Satan might not outwit us. For we are not unaware of his schemes.

Reformed Amillennialism and the State Church

Now the previous criticism against the State-Church model cannot only be levelled at government under the influence of Catholic Amillennialists. Were the Church-sanctioned governments under the influence of the later Amillennial Magisterial Reformers much better?

One of the Five Solas of the Reformation was "Sola Scriptura" i.e. Scripture Alone. But for the Magisterial Reformers clearly it was not Scripture alone. It was Scripture plus some baggage from the Roman Catholic Church - like infant baptism and Amillennialism. For instance, John Calvin wrote that Premillennialism is a 'fiction' that is "too childish either to need or to be worth a refutation." [593]

Along with Amillennialism came other associated medieval leftovers - the idea of a State Church with the active involvement of the Church in State affairs and vice versa - along with persecution of those who disagree with you doctrinally. This has led to the term "Magisterial Reformers" because they relied on the authority of the civil magistrates to enforce and further their agenda by enforcing discipline or suppressing heresy. In contrast, many of those termed "Radical Reformers" were Anabaptists, who had no State sponsorship and believed that the Church should have no official ties to the secular government.

Zwingli

Both Calvin and Zwingli are considered Magisterial Reformers, because their reform movements were supported by the city councils in Geneva and Zürich respectively. Zwingli (1484-1531) had initially condemned Romish intolerance and defended the principle of liberty of conscience. Later he agreed to a union of the Church with the State, which meant the abandonment of the principle of religious liberty. Zürich became a theocracy ruled by Zwingli and a Christian magistrate.

---

[593] Calvin's "Institutes"   .

Ironically the Anabaptists began as an offshoot of the Church reforms instigated by Zwingli, when he began to question or criticize Catholic practices such as the mass and infant baptism. But some of Zwingli's more radical disciples felt that he was not moving fast enough in his reforms in Zurich. Zwingli was content to let the reforms go as fast as the city council allowed them. But to the radicals, the council had no right to make these decisions, as they saw the Scripture as being the final authority on Church reform. While studying the Scriptures, as Zwingli had taught them to, some of his followers concluded that infant baptism isn't a valid practice, because a child cannot commit to a religious faith, and the Scriptures clearly teach "believer's baptism".

Figure 22: Portrait of Ulrich Zwingli [594]

Frustrated with the slow pace of reform by the civil government, Zwingli's radical students began to refuse baptism of their infants. They were then banned from assembling and discussing their views by the Zurich city council, [595] who further ordered that all unbaptized infants be baptized, under threat of banishment.[596] (In many cases, citizens of a nation at that time

---

[594] Portarit of Zwingli after his death 1531 - by Hans Asper

[595] George H. Williams, The Radical Reformation (1962), 99

[596] "...those therefore who have hitherto allowed their children to remain un-baptised, must have them baptized within the next week: and whosoever will not do this, must with wife and child, goods and chattels, leave our city, juris-diction, and dominions, or await what will be done with him." - Carter Lindberg, The European Reformations (1996), 214

were required under penalty of law to belong to the State Church. Infant baptism marked the infant as a citizen of the nation and a loyal subject as much as it marked the infant as a Christian. [597])

In response, the radicals met at the home of Felix Manz on 17th January 1524, where Conrad Grebel baptized George Blaurock, and Blaurock in turn baptized the others, to demonstrate their support for believer's baptism. This completed the break with Zwingli and the council, and the resultant formation of the first church of the Radical Reformation. The movement spread rapidly and Manz was very active in it. [598] Despite calling themselves the Swiss Brethren, they were labelled 'Anabaptist', a derogatory term meaning "again-baptized" (referring to the practice of baptizing persons when they converted even if they had been 'baptized' as infants).

Zwingli believed that Felix Manz was creating too great a division within society by pressing for a Church completely separate from State interference. Ultimately, in a desperate attempt to stop the new movement, Zwingli and the council decreed that Manz be executed by drowning in the Limmat river and that his property be confiscated. After his martyrdom; three more were to follow, after which all others either fled or were expelled from Zurich. [599] The punishment by drowning was seen as appropriate - as "against the waters of baptism he sinned... so by the water shall he die". [600]

Luther

Although Luther is also considered to be a Magisterial Reformer, he was far less concerned with the reform of civil society than either Calvin or Zwingli. While many of his writings affected German society and politics, his primary aim still remained the salvation of the individual, not the establishment of a Christian government on earth.

---

[597] https://en.wikipedia.org/wiki/Believer's_baptism
[598] https://en.wikipedia.org/wiki/Felix_Manz
[599] https://en.wikipedia.org/wiki/Huldrych_Zwingli
[600] Christian History Institute

The Peasants' War was a widespread popular revolt in the German areas of Central Europe from 1524 to 1525. On this issue, Luther took a middle course, criticizing both the injustices imposed on the peasants and the rashness of the peasants in fighting back. He did not support the revolt because it broke the peace, an evil he thought greater than the evils the peasants were rebelling against. Luther made a tour of southern Saxony in an attempt to dissuade the rebels from action, although in some of these places he was roundly heckled. [601] Thereafter, he encouraged the nobility to take severe action, but then later criticized them for their merciless suppression of the insurrection.[602]

Figure 23: Luther in 1533 by Lucas Cranach the Elder

The Münster Rebellion which followed the Peasants' War was an attempt by radical Anabaptists to establish a communal sectarian government in the city of Münster. [603] While the Lutheran states again cruelly crushed the rebellion, one cannot draw a direct analogy between this event and the persecution of Anabaptists elsewhere in Europe. The Anabaptists here were

---

[601] https://en.wikipedia.org/wiki/Thomas_M%C3%BCntzer
[602] https://en.wikipedia.org/wiki/German_Peasants%27_War#Luther_and_M.C3.BCntzer
[603] https://en.wikipedia.org/wiki/M%C3%BCnster_Rebellion

not pacifists as they were in other areas. Indeed some scholars do not even group them together with other "true Anabaptists", [604] due to their use of violence and their attempt to gain political control. (Most Anabaptists refused to even take civil oaths and retreated from any involvement in secular affairs.)

While Luther has been criticised by some for his role in these events, firstly - unlike Zwingli and Calvin - he was not actively involved in politics. Secondly, he clearly regarded those who were revolting not so much as religious dissidents, but similar to how we would view modern terrorists - he considered these people to be disturbers of the peace, not just heretics. Thirdly, while he supported the suppression of civil uprising by the state, he clearly didn't condone execution as a means of punishment for holding and propagating heretical beliefs. With regards to the treatment of heretics, in the Ninety-Five Theses (1517) Martin Luther had earlier written, "The burning of heretics is contrary to the will of the Holy Spirit." He wrote in his "To the Christian Nobility" (1520), "If it were scholarly to conquer heretics with fire, then the henchmen would be the most learned doctors on earth".

Writing to the princes of Saxony in 1524 before the Peasants' War, Luther stated that Andreas Karlstadt and Thomas Münster were both dangerous sectarians with revolutionary tendencies.[605] Yet he argued that these men should be allowed to preach as much as they wished; the Word of God must go to battle; some will no doubt be led astray, but this is what happens in the real course of war. Then when the Anabaptists in Switzerland were drowned in 1525, Luther did not approve of

---

[604] The monogenesis theory of Anabaptist origins usually rejects the Münster-ites and other radicals from the category of true Anabaptists. E.g. William Estep claims that in order to understand Anabaptism, one must "distinguish between the Anabaptists, inspirationists, and rationalists." He classes the likes of Blaurock, Grebel, Balthasar Hubmaier, Manz, Marpeck, and Simons as Ana-baptists. He groups Müntzer, Storch, et al. as inspirationists, and anti-trinitari-ans such as Michael Servetus, Juan de Valdés, Sebastian Castellio, and Faustus Socinus as rationalists.
https://en.wikipedia.org/wiki/Anabaptism
[605] https://en.wikipedia.org/wiki/Andreas_Karlstadt

these measures. [606] Commenting on the Parable of the Tares (1525) Luther aptly applied this parable of Jesus' to the treatment of heretics (as did Tyndale):

> As to heretics and false doctors, we must not pluck them out or destroy them. Christ tells us plainly to allow them to grow. The Word of God is our only resource, for in this field whoever is bad today may become good tomorrow. Who knows whether his heart will not be touched by the Word of God? But if he is burnt or eliminated, his conversion has become impossible. He is cut off from the Word of God, and he who otherwise might have been saved is of necessity lost. That is why the Lord said that the good grain might be uprooted with the tares. This is abominable in the eyes of the Lord and absolutely indefensible.

He also argued that in instances, heresy has a good side effect in that it causes the truth to be defended more vigorously.

> Heretics admonish to alertness and thus cause the faith and doctrine of the church to be practiced... If Cerinthus had not been, the John the Evangelist would never have written his gospel.

The two kingdoms doctrine

In principle Luther's doctrine of the "two governments" (or "two kingdoms") effectively taught separation between Church and State. He held that the Church should not exercise worldly government. Likewise, princes should not rule the Church or have anything to do with the salvation of souls, as the temporal kingdom has no authority to coerce in matters pertaining to the spiritual kingdom. No doubt Luther had in mind the way in which the Catholic Church had involved itself in secular affairs, as well as the princes' involvement in religious matters, in particular their ban on his German translation of the New Testament. [607]

---

[606] "Luther and the Radicals: Another Look at Some Aspects of the Struggle between Luther and the Radical Reformers" - by Harry Loewen
[607] https://en.wikipedia.org/wiki/Two_kingdoms_doctrine

God has ordained the two governments: the spiritual, which by the Holy Spirit under Christ makes Christians and pious people; and the secular, which restrains the unchristian and wicked so that they are obliged to keep the peace outwardly... The laws of worldly government extend no farther than to life and property and what is external upon earth. For over the soul God can and will let no one rule but himself. Therefore, where temporal power presumes to prescribe laws for the soul, it encroaches upon God's government and only misleads and destroys souls. We desire to make this so clear that every one shall grasp it, and that the princes and bishops may see what fools they are when they seek to coerce the people with their laws and commandments into believing one thing or another. [608]

Luther's teaching in this regard follows the exact Scriptural directive found in the New Testament. Christians, he says, should not allow temporal rulers to meddle with their hearts in matters of belief, warning that "if you give into him and let him take away your faith and books, you have truly denied God". Yet, in all temporal matters, he declares that subjects must obey civil rulers. [609]

We are to be subject to governmental power and do what it bids, as long as it does not bind our conscience but legislates only concerning outward matters... But if it invades the spiritual domain and constrains the conscience, over which God only must preside and rule, we should not obey it at all but rather lose our necks. Temporal authority and government extend no further than to matters which are external and corporeal. [610]

James Madison was probably one of the most important modern proponents of the separation of Church and State, which is enshrined in the First Amendment to the US Constitution, of

[608] Martin Luther, "On Secular Authority"
[609] https://en.wikipedia.org/wiki/Two_kingdoms_doctrine
[610] Martin Luther, "On Secular Authority"

which he was the principal author. Madison explicitly credited Luther as the one who "led the way" in providing the proper distinction between the civil and the ecclesiastical spheres. [611]

Calvin

John Calvin (1509-1564), despite his somewhat poor reputation in this regard, claimed to believe in the separate jurisdictions of Church and State.

> Some...are led astray, by not observing the distinction and dissimilarity between ecclesiastical and civil power. For the Church has not the right of the sword to punish or restrain, has no power to coerce, no prison nor other punishments which the magistrate is wont to inflict. Then the object in view is not to punish the sinner against his will, but to obtain a profession of penitence by voluntary chastisement. The two things, the fore, are widely different because neither does the Church assume anything to herself which is proper to the magistrate, nor is the magistrate competent to what is done by the Church. [612]

Yet his later actions in Geneva seem to indicate that he was in favour of a theocracy, in which the Church and State were intertwined. Like Zwingli he continued to endorse the idea of State Church, which had prevailed since the time of the Emperor Theodosius. Although he did not hold office in the government, Calvin had immense influence in Geneva. He drafted the new ordinances that the government modified and adopted as a constitution for Geneva governing both secular and sacred matters. [613] Under his influence the city became the model centre of Calvinism and was dubbed the "Protestant Rome" and Calvin nicknamed "the Pope of the Reformation".

---

[611] Ibid
[612] Institutes of the Christian Religion
[613] 1996 Grolier Multimedia Encyclopedia, Microsoft Encarta 98 Encyclopedia

Figure 24: John Calvin

A 'model' Calvinist city

While in Geneva, Calvin insisted that the city ordinances comply with his religious teaching and that they rigorously enforce morality. Card playing, drunkenness, gambling and swearing were outlawed. Absence from sermons, criticism of ministers, family quarrels, laughing during a sermon, having one's fortune told, or praising the Pope, were all punishable by law. [614] Seemingly anything that remotely resembled pleasure was viewed with suspicion. Calvin allowed neither dancing nor theatre-going, no art other than music - and even that could not involve instruments. [615] According to Stanford Rives [616] even so innocent a sport as skating stirred Calvin's bile. The only tolerated attire was sober and almost monkish. The tailors, therefore, were forbidden, unless they had special permission from the town authorities, to cut in accordance with new fashions. Lace, gloves, frills and slashed shoes were forbidden. Married folk were not allowed to give one another presents at the wedding, or for six months afterwards. They measured the

---

[614] http://www.historydoctor.net/Advanced%20Placement%20European%20 History/Notes/zwingli_Anabaptism_and_Calvinism.htm
[615] http://www.biography.com/people/john-calvin-9235788#death-and-legacy
[616] Did Calvin Murder Servetus? (2008)

hairstyle of women to see if it was too high or too low, counted the rings on their fingers, and the pairs of shoes in their closets. They enforced dietary regulations to prevent one from indulging with too much meat, and to ensure that jams and sweets were not hidden in the kitchen. In addition, Calvin suppressed the celebration of Christmas, New Year's Day, the Annunciation and the Ascension.

Michael Servetus

Many critics of Calvin have condemned him in particular for the very active role he played in the trial and execution of Michael Servetus. Servetus was a Spanish physician, who questioned the conventional view of the Trinity [617] and as such was considered a heretic by Catholics and Protestants alike. He also rightfully opposed the practice of infant baptism as well as Calvin's doctrine of predestination. When he sent certain of his manuscripts to Calvin stating his own ideas, in an attempt to correct him Calvin had sent him a copy of his own book "Institutes of the Christian Religion". Servetus responded by returning the book with a lot of critical marginal comments, which had incensed Calvin.

At the time, Servetus was living under an assumed name in Vienne, France. Due to some manipulation behind the scenes, Calvin ensured that the Catholic Inquisition in France was made aware of Servetus' real identity and his teachings, resulting in his arrest in 1553 on charges of heresy. He was initially released due to lack of evidence, but was subsequently rearrested, thanks to Calvin who furnished the Catholic authorities with some incriminating letters and writings which had been sent to him by Servetus. Servetus managed to escape, but was sentenced to be burned with his books in absentia. His property and possessions were confiscated to pay for the legal costs.

Intending to flee to Italy, he inexplicably stopped in Geneva, where his teachings had already been denounced by Calvin. He attended a sermon by Calvin, where he was recognised and - at

---

[617] Servetus believed that Jesus became the Son of God at his incarnation, but was not the eternal Son of God.

Calvin's instigation - arrested. Calvin supplied the charge list and furnished the evidence used in the subsequent trial. Servetus' reasonable request for a lawyer acquainted with the laws and customs of the country was refused by the General Prosecutor, the reason given that - being able to lie so well - he didn't need one.

At his trial, Servetus was convicted on two counts - for propagating Non-trinitarianism and anti-paedobaptism (opposing infant baptism). The city's governing council determined that he be burnt at the stake as a heretic. Some try to downplay Calvin's role in his death by saying that it was the state, not Calvin, who executed him. However, it's notable that in his following denunciation of Anabaptists, Calvin takes personal responsibility for Servetus' death. In 1561 he writes in a letter regarding the Anabaptists that, "Such monsters should be exterminated, as I have exterminated Michael Servetus the Spaniard." In fact, 7 years prior to Servetus' execution, Calvin already wrote to his friend, William Farel:

> Servetus has just sent me a long volume of his ravings. If I consent he will come here, but I will not give my word; for if he comes here, if my authority is worth anything, I will never permit him to depart alive.

Again Calvin admitted his culpability in the death of Servetus when he writes in 1554, "Many people have accused me of such ferocious cruelty that I would like to kill again the man I have destroyed." Then he wrote to Bullinger, "... there are others who assail me harshly as a master in cruelty and atrocity, for attacking with my pen not only a dead man, but one who perished by my hands." It was at Calvin's instigation that Servetus was arrested. Calvin compiled the list of 38 charges surrounding the nature of God, infant baptism, and the attacks on his own teaching. He also supplied the evidence that was used to bring about a successful conviction. Writing to Sultzerus, he observes:

> When at last he was driven here by his evil destiny, one of the syndics, at my instigation, ordered him to be

committed to prison: for I do not dissemble that I deemed it my duty to restrain as much as lay in my power a man who was worse than obstinate and ungovernable, lest the infection should spread more widely.

While the charges against Servetus were submitted by Calvin's secretary Nicholas de la Fontaine, both Calvin and Theodore Beza admitted that it originated from Calvin himself. Calvin possibly used de la Fontaine as his proxy because the laws regulating criminal actions in Geneva required that in certain grave cases the complainant himself should also be incarcerated pending the trial. Calvin candidly admits the role he played:

> All the proceedings of our senate are ascribed to me: and indeed I do not dissemble that he was thrown into prison through my interference and advice. As it was necessary according to the laws of the state that he should be charged with some crime, I admit that I was thus far the author of the transaction. [618]

And so, Phillip Schaff, the renowned Church historian, writes of Calvin, "He is responsible, on his own frank confession, for the arrest and trial of Servetus, and he fully assented to his condemnation and death 'for heresy and blasphemy'..." [619] In typical Catholic Inquisition style, Calvin believed that the punishment of heretics by death was deserved, because they refused to listen to admonition. He writes:

> To these irreligious characters and despisers of the heavenly doctrines... And at length matters had come to such a state, that an end could be put to their machinations in no other way than cutting them off by an ignominious death; which was indeed a painful and pitiable spectacle to me. They no doubt deserved the severest punishment, but I always rather desired that they might live in prosperity, and continue safe and untouched; which would have been the case had they

---

[618] Fidel. Expos. Serve ti Errorum
[619] The History of the Christian Church

not been altogether incorrigible, and obstinately refused to listen to wholesome admonition. [620]

In his Prefatory Address in his Institutes to Francis, King of the French in 1536, Calvin outlays his views on the treatment of heretics.

> For I fear not to declare, that what I have here given may be regarded as a summary of the very doctrine which, they vociferate, ought to be punished with confiscation, exile, imprisonment, and flames, as well as exterminated by land and sea. This, I allow, is a fearful punishment which God sends on the earth; but if the wickedness of men so deserves, why do we strive to oppose the just vengeance of God? [621]

In contrast his foe, Michael Servetus, had written:

> It seems to me a grave error to kill a man only because he might be in error interpreting some question of the Scripture when we know that even the most learned are not without error. [622]

Actually, in his early years, Calvin had also written that the death penalty for heresy was entirely unjust. In the first edition of his Institutes of the Christian Religion published in 1536, he talked about kindness and persuasion against the excommunicated, expressing convictions that heretics should not be punished with harshness. After quoting from Calvin's earlier version of the Institutes, Richard Stevenson writes, "This and other passages are altered in later editions. What changed the man?" [623] The answer, no doubt, is – the gaining of political influence. At the beginning of his own career, when he was persecuted himself, Calvin, in theory supported toleration, advocated clemency against vengeance, and opposed any violence such as "prison, exile, proscription and fire." In his Commentary on Acts, he

---

[620] Preface to Commentaries, July 22, 1557
[621] http://www.a-voice.org/tidbits/calvinp.htm
[622] Letter to Oecolampadius in Calvini, Opera, op. cit., Vol. IX, 861-862
[623] John Calvin the Statesman (1907) pg 159

wrote: "Wisdom is driven from among us, and the holy harmony of Christ's kingdom is compromised, when violence is pressed into the service of religion." [624] But as soon as he gained political power, his behaviour was no different from that of the Catholic Church he condemned.

Servetus correctly maintained in his trial defence that there had been no criminal prosecution for doctrinal disagreement in the early church and that during Constantine's days, heresy deserved no more than banishment. (Remember Arius, also Nontrinitarian, was temporarily banished by Constantine after his defeat at the Council of Nicæa.) Schaff writes:

> Calvin should have contented himself with banishing his fugitive rival from the territory of Geneva, or allowing him quietly to proceed on his contemplated journey to Italy, where he might have resumed his practice of medicine in which he excelled. [625]

But just briefly consider why the State was even involved in a question on heresy. The answer lies in the differences between the Magisterial and Radical Reformation, and ultimately to the differences between Amillennialism and Premillennialism.

An isolated incident?

Some defend Calvin by saying that this was an isolated incident. E.g. Alister McGrath claims that "Servetus was the only individual put to death for his religious opinions in Geneva during Calvin's lifetime, at a time when executions of this nature were a commonplace elsewhere". [626] But sadly, Servetus' death was not an isolated incident. In the first five years of Calvin's "rule" in Geneva, 58 people were executed and 76 exiled for their religious beliefs. [627] There was an earlier case with the libertine Jacques Gruet. Gruet was indeed an obstinate and disagreeable

---

[624] Calvin's dedicatory epistle to the king of Denmark, Christian III - The Christian Disciple and Theological Review, Volume 3 - by Noah Worcester
[625] The History of the Christian Church
[626] A Life of John Calvin, pg 116
[627] http://www.biography.com/people/john-calvin-9235788#leading-figure-of-reformation

person, as well as an infidel. [628] He attached a note to Calvin's pulpit calling him a hypocrite [629] and was also heard uttering threats against Calvin, also being implicated in state treason. He was arrested, tortured every day for a month, then beheaded in 1547.

The Libertine Pierre Ameaux hated Calvin's theology and discipline. At a supper party in his own house he freely indulged in drink and roundly abused Calvin. [630] Part of what he said included, "And this foreigner from Picardy, this liar and seducer of the people, who wants to make himself bishop - it's a laugh, were it not so tragic! No one in the Council any longer dares to speak his frank opinion, without having first inquired about his views." [631] For this offence, he was imprisoned by the Council for 2 months and condemned to a fine of 60 dollars. [632] He made an apology and retracted his words. But Calvin was not satisfied, and demanded a second trial. The Council condemned him to a degrading punishment called the "amende honorable", namely, to parade through the streets in his shirt, with bare head, and a lighted torch in his hand, and to ask on bended knees the pardon of God, of the Council, and of Calvin. This harsh judgment provoked a popular outbreak in the quarter of St. Gervais. [633] Two preachers, Henri de la Mare and Aimé Maigret, who had taken part in the drinking scene, were deposed. The former had said before the Council that Calvin was, a good and virtuous man, and of great intellect, but sometimes governed by his passions, impatient, full of hatred, and vindictive." [634]

---

[628] (Subsequent to his execution) In his house were found a copy of Calvin's work against the Libertines with a marginal note, Toutes folies, and several papers and letters filled with abuse of Calvin as a haughty, ambitious, and obstinate hypocrite who wished to be adored, and to rob the pope of his honour. There were also found two Latin pages in Gruet's handwriting, in which the Scriptures were ridiculed, Christ blasphcmed, and the immortality of the soul called a dream and a fable.- History of the Christian Church, Volume VIII: Modern Christianity. The Swiss Reformation by Philip Schaff

[629] Ibid

[630] Ibid

[631] http://albatrus.org/english/potpourri/historical/burning_of_servetus.htm

[632] http://www.ccel.org/ccel/schaff/hcc8.iv.xiii.xii.html

[633] Ibid

[634] Ibid

Jerome Bolsec was a French Carmelite theologian and physician, who became a Protestant and subsequently settled at Veigy, near Geneva. He deemed Calvin's doctrine of predestination to be an absurdity. In 1551, at one of the public discussions held at Geneva every Friday, he interrupted the orator, who was speaking on predestination, and argued against him. Unaware that Calvin was present, Bolsec was surprised when Calvin himself subsequently stood up and refuted his argument point by point. [635] The city magistrates arrested Bolsec and he was placed on trial by the city. To demonstrate the correctness of the Genevan doctrine and the unity of Swiss Protestants, the magistrates in Geneva sent a letter to get advice from Basel, Zurich and Bern. The responses were extremely disappointing to Calvin: the support of the doctrine of predestination was tepid at best and the counsel of the cities was to be lenient with Bolsec. Nevertheless, he was charged with attacking the religious establishment of Geneva and banished permanently from the city. [636] Bolsec subsequently published a vicious and extremely slanderous biography of Calvin, which modern scholarship has deemed to be of questionable historical merit. Later in his life he reconciled with the Catholic Church.

The following persecutions at Geneva were also mentioned in "The Minutes Book of the Geneva City Council", 1541-59.

- ❖ A book printer who, while drinking, had railed at Calvin, was sentenced to have his tongue perforated with a red-hot iron before being expelled from the city. [637]
- ❖ A man who publicly protested against Calvin's doctrine of predestination was flogged at all the crossways of the city and then expelled. [638]

Calvin also considered Anabaptists (who correctly opposed the unbiblical practice of infant baptism) to be heretics and labelled them as "poor fools", "scatterbrains", "ignoramuses" and

---

[635] https://en.wikipedia.org/wiki/Jérôme-Hermès_Bolsec
[636] http://wscal.edu/resource-center/resource/calvin-bolsec-and-the-refor-mation
[637] "Erasmus: The Right to Heresy" by Stefan Zweig
[638] Ibid

"enemies of government" [639] He actively persecuted them and encouraged others to do the same. In a letter to Farel, Calvin writes of a man in Geneva called Belot:

> In these days an Anabaptist, when he was laying out foolish
> writings publicly for sale, was at my instigation arrested... he was expelled from the city. Two days later, when he was again seized in the city, he was beaten, his books publicly burned, and he himself was told not to come again, on penalty of the gallows. This is a man or rather a beast of desperate wickedness. [640]

Treatment of heretics

Some contend that killing people for differences of opinion in religious matters was common practice and considered acceptable in Calvin's time. David Bennett notes:

> Using that logic is like saying the Apostles should have converted people by the sword and crucifixion because that was the way things were done at the time. The "everybody else is doing it" argument never worked on my parents when I was growing up. The Bible tells us we are to be in the world, not of the world. [641]

But despite these attempts to sanitize Calvin's actions or to rationalize his heavy-handed tactics, no one defends the Catholic Inquisitors with this line of argument. To this day, they are justifiably criticized for killing both Protestants and Jews over religious matters. But Calvin and the Papal church acted in the same way with 'heretics' - it was just the definition of heresy that varied. Lutheran author Juergen Neve writes:

---

[639] Benjamin Wirt Farley, ed. John Calvin: Treatises against the Anabaptists and against the Libertines (1982). 16.
[640] Global Anabaptist Mennonite Encyclopedia Online
http://www.gameo.org/index.php?title=Calvin,_John_(1509-1564)
[641] http://www.freewill-predestination.com/the_golden_rule

Calvin's mistake was his refusal to recognize the freedom of conscience. In his dealing with teachers of false doctrine within the Church, Christ speaks of excommunication after previous brotherly admonition; but neither He nor the apostles have commanded that they are to be put to death. Calvin's practice was a return to medieval methods which Luther had characterized ironically with the remark: "With a death sentence they solve all argumentation." [642]

Neve continues:

Luther admitted that there might be cases where in the interest of tranquillity troublesome persons may be banished from the country. But he was opposed to bodily punishment for heresy. These were his words: 'Heresy can never be restrained with force. It must be grasped in another way. This is not the sort of battle that can be settled with the sword. The weapon here to be used is God's Word. If that does not decide, the decision will not be effected by worldly force, though it should drench the whole world with blood. Heresy is a thing of the soul; no steel can cut it out, no waters can drown it." [643]

New Testament treatment of heretics

In the New Testament, the principle of disfellowship was applied to false teachers.

2 John 9-11 Anyone who ... does not continue in the teaching of Christ does not have God... If anyone comes to you and does not bring this teaching, do not take him into your house or welcome him. Anyone who welcomes him shares in his wicked work.

False teachers should be silenced, not by torture or death, but by rebuke and by refuting them with sound doctrine.

---

[642] A History of Christian Thought, vol. I, pg 285
[643] Ibid

❖ *Titus 1:9-11 He must hold firmly to the trustworthy message as it has been taught, so that he can encourage others by sound doctrine and refute those who oppose it. For there are many rebellious people, full of meaningless talk and deception, especially those of the circumcision group. They must be silenced, because they are disrupting whole households by teaching things they ought not to teach—and that for the sake of dishonest gain.*

❖ *1 Tim 1:3 ... stay there in Ephesus so that you may command certain men not to teach false doctrines any longer...*

Naturally judging matters of doctrine and heresy in the church precludes a death sentence for anything. But having a State Church complicates matters, because the state courts are presumably deemed to be Christian courts - and the State has the power to prescribe a far more severe sentence. Biblical church discipline comprises of admonishing in the church, or expelling people from the church - not persecution or killing. The New Testament teaches us that divisive people are to be avoided after the failure of repeated warnings.

❖ *Rom 16:17 I urge you, brothers, to watch out for those who cause divisions and put obstacles in your way that are contrary to the teaching you have learned. Keep away from them.*

❖ *Titus 3:10 Warn a divisive person once, and then warn them a second time. After that, have nothing to do with them.*

If Calvin considered men to be divisive, this was the approach he should have followed - "keep away from them" or "have nothing to do with them" - not contrive to have them publicly humiliated (like Pierre Ameaux) or executed (like Servetus). And the same can be said of Zwingli's treatment of the Anabaptists.

Summary

The Radical reformers thought that the Magisterial reformers were still captive to a political marriage of Church and State. Anabaptists insisted that the Church be separate, govern itself, and have no official ties to the State. While this sounds acceptable to many today, then it was revolutionary. Ever since the 4th century when Constantius II made Christianity the official religion - and Theodosius I subsequently made it the preferred state religion - Christianity and government had always been linked together. Some claim that the tension between the Church and the Roman Empire in the first three centuries of Christianity was normal, that the Church is not to be allied with government, that a true Church is always inviting persecution; and that the conversion of Constantine was therefore the great apostasy that marked the end of pure Christianity.

❏ Catholic view
➢ The Pope is the head of the Church and answerable only to God. As Church members, kings are subject to the Pope.

❏ Magisterial reformers view
➢ Church heads are subject to the king or government who in turn are answerable only to God.

❏ Radical reformers view
➢ Separation of Church and State. Church leaders are answerable only to God as are leaders of State.

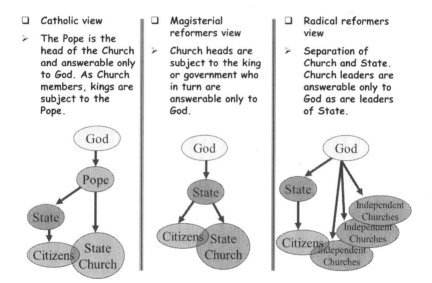

Figure 25: State Church and Church-State relationship

Authority	Treatment of perceived heretics
New Testament	After failed dialogue, excommunication (until restitution was effected)
Emperor Constantine	After failed dialogue, temporary exile (until restitution was effected)
Augustine	Recommended preventative legislation and prosecution - but not execution
Ambrose, Martin of Tours, Siricius	Recommended matters of doctrine to be settled by the Church, not the State - but not execution
Emperor Maximus	Execution (beheading)
Emperor Justinian	Torture, confiscation of property, execution (burning or drowning)
Aquinas	Endorsed execution of heretics
The Inquisition	Torture, forced confessions, confiscation of property, life imprisonment, execution (burning)
Luther	Toleration or exile (in extreme cases)
Zwingli	Exile or execution (drowning)
Calvin	Exile or execution (burning)
Anabaptists	Excommunication

Table 11: Progressive treatment of heretics resulting from the introduction of the Amillennial State-Church model

They believe that the Church should not be supported by the State, neither by taxes, nor by the use of the sword; Christianity is a matter of individual conviction, which should not be forced on anyone, but rather requires a personal decision by the individual. [644]

When the Catholic Church was state-supported, this became an impediment to reform in the Church. Whenever this system was simply replaced with a Protestant State Church, we still have cases of state-sanctioned religious persecution, rather than freedom of religion.

---

[644] Gonzalez, A History of Christian Thought

Postmillennialism

But while the events we have just considered should have served as a warning to Postmillennialists and Dominionists, their proposed treatment of heretics simply seems to resonate with what we have already seen in the history of Amillennialist state control. Rushdoony's vision of a reconstructed 'Christian' society proposed a death sentence for idolatry, apostasy, public blasphemy and false prophesying. [645] And Bahnsen listed Sabbath-breaking, apostasy and blasphemy as crimes that deserve capital punishment in the reconstructed society. [646] So how does the belief in Postmillennialism (including Dominion Theology) affect the relationship between Church and State?

Reconstructionists

Reconstructionists believe that the Old Testament laws, even apparently minor ones, are by no means obsolete, and should be adhered to today. Some Reconstructionists have designed entire political, economic, financial and legal agendas solely on the basis of Mosaic law, although allowing for certain modifications in the light of the New Testament. [647] Considered the founder of Reconstructionism, R. J. Rushdoony, laid out a vision for the reconstruction of society based on Christian principles, proposing that there should be a Christian theonomy with the reinstatement of the Mosaic law's penal sanctions. Crimes carrying a death sentence would include homosexuality, adultery, incest, lying about one's virginity, bestiality, witchcraft, kidnapping, rape, and bearing false witness in a capital case. [648]

Rushdoony was also active in the home-schooling movement, appearing as an expert witness in order to defend the rights of home schoolers. He saw home-schooling as a way to combat

---

[645] https://en.wikipedia.org/wiki/Rousas_Rushdoony
[646] www.ukapologetics.net
[647] Ibid
[648] https://en.wikipedia.org/wiki/Rousas_Rushdoony

the intentionally secular nature of the US public school system, vigorously attacked school reformers such as Horace Mann and John Dewey and argued for the dismantling of the state's influence on education. [649]

Most Reconstructionists are critical of democracy, viewing it as a heretical concept. Rushdoony taught that in the reconstructed society there would be no democracy because "the heresy of democracy has ... worked havoc in Church and State... Christianity and democracy are inevitably enemies." He stated elsewhere that "Christianity is completely and radically anti-democratic; it is committed to spiritual aristocracy," and characterized democracy as "the great love of the failures and cowards of life." [650] Although he supported the separation of Church and State at the national level, Rushdoony also believed that both institutions were under the rule of God, and thus he conceived secularism as posing endless false dichotomies... [651] An article on the "UK Apologetics" website lists some other key teachings of Reconstructionists:

> Rushdoony envisaged a society in which the Bible would be the only charter and constitutional document. He also denied that women could rightfully claim "priority or even equality" with men... 'Reconstructionists' will quote the Old Testament laws condemning usury, and usually argue that a thirty-year mortgage on a home is an unbiblical practice (citing Deuteronomy 15). They often suggest debts being limited to no more than six years... The Reconstructed society would have no property tax, since taxes supposedly imply that the state, not God, owns the Earth, and the practice of tithing would replace all income tax...[652]

The late Dr. Greg L. Bahnsen (1948-1995) was an American minister in the Orthodox Presbyterian Church. A Calvinist

---

[649] Ibid
[650] "In Extremis - Rousas Rushdoony and his connections". British Centre for Science Education. Nov 4, 2007.
[651] https://en.wikipedia.org/wiki/Rousas_Rushdoony
[652] www.ukapologetics.net

apologist and debater, he was also a major advocate of Reconstructionism. Besides apostasy and blasphemy, other crimes he believed deserve capital punishment were murder, rape, homosexuality, witchcraft, and incorrigibility in children.

> The envisaged 'Reconstructed society' will have no prisons. Under biblical law, "men either died as criminals or made restitution." Career criminals would be executed and occasional lawbreakers would pay for the damages of their actions as slaves. [653]

Fortunately, this theology is not widely-accepted and only enjoys a minority following.

The enigma of Francis Schaeffer

The well-known Francis Schaeffer read the works of Rushdoony in the 1960s and was impressed by them. But Schaeffer later lost this fervour because Rushdoony was a Postmillennialist, while he was a Historic Premillennialist. He also thought that Rushdoony's system required a merger of Church and State, which he opposed, holding rather that the principles, not the actual details, of Old Testament civil law were applicable under the New Covenant. [654] Thus, he wrote in 1981:

> The moral law [of the Old Testament], of course, is constant, but the civil law only was operative for the Old Testament theocracy... I do not think there is any indication of a theocracy in the New Testament until Christ returns as king. [655]

Yet interestingly, many see Francis Schaeffer as one of the major influences, not only on Dominionists (despite criticism of his work by Christian Reconstructionists Gary North and David Chilton), but on many Christians seeking to avoid a life of retreat from political involvement. American sociologist, attorney and

---

[653] Ibid
[654] https://en.wikipedia.org/wiki/Francis_Schaeffer
[655] Hankins, Barry (2008). Francis Schaeffer and the Shaping of Evangelical America. Eerdmans

author, Dr. Sara Rose Diamond writes about Schaeffer's impact on the Christian Right:

> The idea of taking dominion over secular society gained widespread currency with the 1981 publication of... Schaeffer's book A Christian Manifesto. The book sold 290,000 copies in its first year, and it remains one of the movement's most frequently cited texts. [656]

Diamond summarizes the book and its importance to the Christian Right in the US as follows:

> In A Christian Manifesto, Schaeffer's argument is simple. The United States began as a nation rooted in Biblical principles. But as society became more pluralistic, with each new wave of immigrants, proponents of a new philosophy of secular humanism gradually came to dominate debate on policy issues. Since humanists place human progress, not God, at the centre of their considerations, they pushed American culture in all manner of ungodly directions, the most visible results of which included legalized abortion and the secularization of the public schools. At the end of -- A Christian Manifesto, Schaeffer calls for Christians to use civil disobedience to restore Biblical morality, which explains Schaeffer's popularity with groups like Operation Rescue. Randall Terry has credited Schaeffer as a major influence in his life. [657]

Kingdom Now Charismatics

Within some Charismatic circles, the propagation of Dominion Theology has marked a transition from an initial passive theology, in which believers are waiting to be raptured to escape the imminent judgment, to a politicized theology in which

---

[656] Diamond, Sara (1994). "Dominion Theology: The Truth About the Christian Right's Bid for Power", Z Magazine (column) February 1995.
http://www.publiceye.org/diamond/sd_domin.html
[657] Ibid

believers take control over society and government (similar to Reconstructionism).

Since Dominionists teach that the mission of the Church goes beyond the spiritual transformation of individuals to a mandate to change society, they must change the laws of the land, elect Christians to office, and seek to take dominion over our world and bring it under the Mosaic Law. For example, Dominionists made much of Reagan's open confession of Christianity as well as that of George W. Bush. They place much focus on Christians being elected to public office. While this in itself may be a commendable practice, the intended end goal (Christian-Dominionist-rule) is not sanctioned in the Scripture. (Even Augustine, in The City of God, does not suggest that only good Christians can be rulers, although he believes that Christian virtue makes for better government. [658])

Like their Postmillennial theological relatives, Kingdom Now adherents see the last days as the time of great progress and revival. Paul Cain prophesied that a new breed of elite endtime Christians would be revered by the enemies of the gospel and would have world leaders seeking their counsel:

> There's going to be an awesome, reverential fear and respect for the church because the church is going to regain her power, lose her restrictions, lose her weakness... you're going to be called upon by presidents and kings of nations, heads of state... God is going to have his army and they are going to be a fearful bunch and they are going to go to every place on the face of the earth... [659]

But in the last days predicted by John in his Apocalypse, the world leaders are not consulting Christians, but rather swearing allegiance to the Antichrist.

---

[658] https://plato.stanford.edu/entries/medieval-political/
[659] Clifford Hill and Peter Fenwick, David Forbes, David Noakes; Blessing the Church?; Eagle; p.130

Rev 17:12-13 "The ten horns you saw are ten kings who have not yet received a kingdom, but who for one hour will receive authority as kings along with the beast. They have one purpose and will give their power and authority to the beast."

So, two unlikely alliance partners, 'Reconstructionist' Calvinists and 'Kingdom Now' Charismatics have formed somewhat of a loose unity - and in this aspect, at least, they both have the same world view and goal. They are not looking for Christ to return and set up his Kingdom; they are attempting to set it up for him. But nowhere in the New Testament are we instructed to infiltrate the government in order to affect a covert Christian takeover.

Postmillennialists are attempting to do what Amillennialists have already done - and failed at! As we have observed, there was already a period when the state was controlled by the Catholic and Reformed Amillennialists and this resulted (at least ultimately) in the darkest periods of Christian history and abuse of power.

Now does this mean that Christians should go to the other extreme and ignore politics altogether and never vote or get involved in government? We then have to consider the alternative as stated by the Plato, "The price good men pay for indifference to public affairs is to be ruled by evil men".

Premillennialism and separation of Church and State

How does the belief in Premillennialism affect the relationship between Church and State? Thomas Ice writes:

> Evangelical Postmillennialism is to be distinguished from the liberal form. However, one cannot overlook the role that Postmillennialism, in all its guises, has played in the rise and development of the 'social gospel'. Postmillenarians blame Premillennial Dispensationalism

for creating a climate of retreat from social and political issues. [660]

Roger Williams

Roger Williams (c.1603-1683), the co-founder of the First Baptist Church of America, was a Premillennialist [661] who argued for a "wall of separation" between Church and State in his 1644 book "The Bloudy Tenent". He advocated for state toleration, not only of various Christian denominations including Catholicism, but also "paganish, Jewish, Turkish or anti-Christian consciences and worships." Using the Bible, he contended that Christianity required the existence of a separate civil authority that may not generally infringe upon liberty of conscience, which he interpreted to be a God-given right. [662]

Williams rejected any attempt by State to enforce the "first Table" of the Ten Commandments i.e. those commandments dealing with the relationship between God and individuals. Instead, he believed that the State must confine itself to the commandments which deal with the relations between people: murder, theft, adultery, lying, honouring parents, and so forth. When the Puritan leaders expelled him from the colony of Massachusetts for spreading "new and dangerous ideas", he began the colony of Providence Plantation in 1636 which provided a refuge for religious minorities. [663] This colony in present-day Rhode Island had the first government in which Church and State were fully separated, well before any similar secular case was made for this.

God's true mandate regarding our civic duty to the State

The Church should not control all and the civil government should not control all - each has their own domain. Even in the

---

[660] http://www.pre-trib.org/data/pdf/Ice-TheUnscripturalTheolo.pdf Thomas Ice: "The unscriptural theologies of Amillennialism and Postmillennialism"
[661] http://www.newworldencyclopedia.org/entry/Millennialism
[662] https://en.wikipedia.org/wiki/The_Bloudy_Tenent_of_Persecution_for_Cause_of_Conscience
[663] https://en.wikipedia.org/wiki/Roger_Williams

Old Testament there were separate offices for priest and king. Jehoshaphat appointed one man to administer matters "concerning the LORD" and another man to matters "concerning the king".

> *2 Chron 19:11 "Amariah the chief priest will be over you in any matter concerning the Lord, and Zebadiah son of Ishmael, the leader of the tribe of Judah, will be over you in any matter concerning the king..."*

When kings like Saul (1 Sam 13:8-14) or Uzziah (2 Chron 26:16-20) tried to usurp the priest's authority, God judged them. And the prophets were not involved in governing, despite often bringing rebuke to the kings – they functioned as an independent cross-check.

One of the primary Biblical arguments for the separation of Church and State comes from Jesus's statement that we must "Render therefore unto Caesar the things which are Caesar's; and unto God the things that are God's" (Matt 22:21 KJV). Jesus warned his disciples not only against the yeast (or leaven) of the Pharisees, but also against the yeast of the Sadducees.

> *Matt 16:11-12... But be on your guard against the yeast of the Pharisees and Sadducees. Then they understood that he was not telling them to guard against the yeast used in bread, but against the teaching of the Pharisees and Sadducees.*

Leaven always has a negative connotation in the Bible. It is always used to represent evil, sin and false doctrine. It was used by both Jesus and Paul (1 Cor 5:1-8) to symbolize the doctrine of men being mixed with the doctrine of God, thereby corrupting it. The yeast of the Pharisees was hypocrisy, legalism and tradition, while the yeast of the Sadducees was liberalism and political entanglement. The Sadducees were the rich and sophisticated Jews in the time of Jesus. They were politically driven and in control of the Sanhedrin, which was the supreme judicial council of Judaism. The equivalent today, which we are cautioned to avoid, is the belief that politics and social reform, rather than preaching the gospel, is the primary work of the Christian.

God has given his people a mandate regarding our civic duty toward the state, but it is not civil disobedience. Jesus, Paul and Peter all taught people to obey the pagan Roman government and to conform to the tax laws. Yet when Paul and Peter wrote these letters, Nero had already become Emperor. Nero undertook a massive persecution of Christians throughout the Empire and was ultimately responsible for the execution of both of these apostles. But the apostolic teaching is that:

a) All governments are established by God (even bad ones).

   ❖ *Rom 13:1b-2 … for there is no authority except that which God has established. The authorities that exist have been established by God. Consequently, he who rebels against the authority is rebelling against what God has instituted, and those who do so will bring judgment on themselves.*

b) Governments act on God's behalf and will be accountable to God for the way they governed.

   ❖ *Rom 13:6 … the authorities are God's servants, who give their full time to governing.*
   ❖ *Rom 13:4 For he is God's servant to do you good. But if you do wrong, be afraid, for he does not bear the sword for nothing. He is God's servant, an agent of wrath to bring punishment on the wrongdoer.*
   ❖ *1 Pet 2:13-14 … the king… governors, who are sent by him (God) to punish those who do wrong and to commend those who do right.*

c) We must submit to and obey the civil authorities

   ❖ *Rom 13:5 Therefore, it is necessary to submit to the authorities, not only because of possible punishment but also because of conscience.*

❖ *Rom 13:3 For rulers hold no terror for those who do right, but for those who do wrong. Do you want to be free from fear of the one in authority? Then do what is right and he will commend you.*

❖ *1 Pet 2:13 Submit yourselves for the Lord's sake to every human authority: whether to the emperor, as the supreme authority, or to governors...*

Note that this applies to bad governments as well. In 1 Pet 2:18-19 slaves were told to obey their masters, "not only to those who are good and considerate, but also to those who are harsh"; [664] this despite the fact that slavery is frowned upon [665] and Christians were told to obtain their freedom if possible. [666]

❖ *1 Pet 2:17-19 Show proper respect to everyone... fear God, honour the emperor. Slaves, in reverent fear of God submit yourselves to your masters, not only to those who are good and considerate, but also to those who are harsh. For it is commendable if someone bears up under the pain of unjust suffering because they are conscious of God.*

d) The only exception is when the civil authorities instruct us to do something that is forbidden by God, who is a higher authority (or they instruct us not to do something God has instructed us to do).

❖ *Acts 5:27-29 (NASB) When they had brought them, they stood them before the Council. The high priest questioned them, saying, "We gave you strict orders not*

---

[664] 1 Pet 2:18-19 Slaves, in reverent fear of God submit yourselves to your masters, not only to those who are good and considerate, but also to those who are harsh. For it is commendable if someone bears up under the pain of unjust suffering because they are conscious of God.

[665] 1 Tim 1:9 We also know that law is made not for the righteous but for law-breakers and rebels, the ungodly and sinful, the unholy and irreligious... for slave traders and liars... and for whatever else is contrary to the sound doctrine...

[666] 1 Cor 7:21 Were you a slave when you were called? Don't let it trouble you—although if you can gain your freedom, do so.

to continue teaching in this name, and yet, you have filled Jerusalem with your teaching and intend to bring this man's blood upon us." But Peter and the apostles answered, "We must obey God rather than men. (See also Acts 5:27-29 [667]*)*

e) We are to pay our taxes. Paul instructs the Christian citizens living in Rome to do this and to respect the civil ruling authorities.

    ❖ *Rom 13:6-7 This is also why you pay taxes, for the authorities are God's servants, who give their full time to governing. Give everyone what you owe him: If you owe taxes, pay taxes; if revenue, then revenue; if respect, then respect; if honour, then honour.*

    And then one can hardly forget the passage regarding Jesus' attitude to Roman taxation:

    ❖ *Luke 20:22-25 "Is it right for us to pay taxes to Caesar or not?" He saw through their duplicity and said to them, "Show me a denarius. Whose portrait and inscription are on it?" "Caesar's," they replied. He said to them, "Then give to Caesar what is Caesar's, and to God what is God's."*

f) We must respect our leaders.

    ❖ *1 Pet 2:17 Show proper respect to everyone... honour the emperor.*

g) We must pray for government.

    ❖ *1 Tim 2:1-2 I urge, then, first of all, that requests, prayers, intercession and thanksgiving be made for everyone - for*

---

[667] Acts 5:27-29 Having brought the apostles, they made them appear before the Sanhedrin to be questioned by the high priest. "We gave you strict orders not to teach in this name," he said. Yet you have filled Jerusalem with your teaching and are determined to make us guilty of this man's blood." Peter and the other apostles replied: "We must obey God rather than men!"

kings and all those in authority, that we may live peaceful and quiet lives in all godliness and holiness.

h) The Church is explicitly told that it has no mandate from God to judge those outside the Church.

   ❖ *1 Cor 5:12-13 What business is it of mine to judge those outside the church? Are you not to judge those inside? God will judge those outside.*

These instructions are not the teachings presented by Dominionists, in particular Reconstructionists. To actually seek to overthrow a pagan or secular government, to deal in the affairs of state, to take the world politically by force for Christ is something quite different entirely! God has NOT given any mandate for any such action. In New Testament times, despite the extreme paganism of the state, the Roman Empire served as "God's servant to do you good" (Rom 13:4).

As Premillennialists, we believe that Jesus' control of the state is only promised in a future millennial kingdom.

> *Luke 22:25-26 Jesus said to them, "The kings of the Gentiles lord it over them; and those who exercise authority over them call themselves Benefactors. But you are not to be like that. Instead, the greatest among you should be like the youngest, and the one who rules like the one who serves."*

Note that Jesus says with regards to the secular authority that was seated in the pagan governmental institutions that "you are not to be like that". The Kingdom of God in its present form is "not of this world" and thus Jesus said his servants were non-combative pacifists.

> *John 18:36 Jesus said, "My kingdom is not of this world. If it were, my servants would fight to prevent my arrest by the Jews..."*

Rather the kingdom of God is within us.

Luke 17:20-21 Once, having been asked by the Pharisees when the kingdom of God would come, Jesus replied, "The kingdom of God does not come with your careful observation, nor will people say, 'Here it is,' or 'There it is,' because the kingdom of God is within you."

Incidentally this in no way implies that Christians do not speak out against sins and social ills. Both Elijah and John the Baptist rebuked wicked rulers for their public sin. Many of the Old Testament prophets acted as a cross-check on the Judean and Israelite kings by bringing a rebuke or pronouncing judgement on their actions. But they did this, without being active participants in the civil governing process.

CHAPTER 8: KINGDOM NOW

The Charismatic equivalent of the Reformed Dominion Theology (Reconstructionism) is Kingdom Now Theology. But while various strains of Dominion Theology are taught by some within the Charismatic movement, some of its most ardent critics are also from within the Pentecostal and Charismatic movements.

Basic beliefs

Charismatic Dominion theology is predicated upon some basic beliefs:

a) God gave man dominion over the earth. This is derived from the Biblical text in Genesis 1:28-30.
b) This gives Christians a mandate for control of civil governmental affairs. (Many Christians simply interpret this passage to mean that God gave mankind responsibility to take care of the earth - both animals and vegetation.)
c) This dominion (according to the lunatic fringe) also meant that whatever the animals could do, man could do, e.g. Benny Hinn made the ludicrous claim of Adam being able to fly because he had dominion over the birds. He further claimed that Adam was even able to go to the moon, because he had dominion over all that God made. These are arguments from silence, which are hopefully embarrassing for most other Charismatic Dominionists.
d) Satan usurped man's dominion over the earth. This is true – when Satan offered the kingdoms of the world to Jesus (Matt 4), he didn't dispute his ownership of them.
e) The Church is God's instrument to take dominion back from Satan. This is not true - Jesus does this through his work on the cross and ultimately through his Millennial rule after the Second Coming.
f) Jesus cannot or will not return until the Church has taken dominion by gaining control of the earth's governmental and social institutions. Again incorrect - there will be "terrible times in the last days" (2 Tim 3:1).

g) As we are in the Kingdom of God now, health and wealth is the right of every believer today. False - we are expressly told to avoid the love of money, and to be content, whatever our financial circumstance - 1 Tim 6:6-10 [668].

The Latter Rain Movement

The Latter Rain teachings appear in many guises and under many different names, including: the Manchild Company, the Sonship, the Melchizedek Priesthood, the Shulamites, Joel Company, Elijah Company, the Many-membered Christ, the New Order, Overcomers, God's Army, the Corporate Body, Feast of Tabernacles, Tabernacle of David, etc.

William Branham was an American minister, generally acknowledged as initiating the post-World War II healing revival. While initially getting a favourable response from most mainstream Pentecostals, he later became the centre of a Pentecostal personality cult. [669] After his death in a car crash in 1965 Branham faded into obscurity, beside a few who still follow him as their prophet. Over 60 years ago, in the late 1940's, some admirers of Branham in Western Canada (not Branham himself as some erroneously believe) started what would become known as the Latter Rain Movement. Developing out of events at Sharon Orphanage and Schools at North Battleford, Saskatchewan (Canada) between 1947 and 1948, the founders thought that this "new wave" of the Spirit was the "latter rain" referred to in Joel 2:23.

---

[668] 1 Tim 6:6-10 But godliness with contentment is great gain. For we brought nothing into the world, and we can take nothing out of it. But if we have food and clothing, we will be content with that. Those who want to get rich fall into temptation and a trap and into many foolish and harmful desires that plunge people into ruin and destruction. For the love of money is a root of all kinds of evil. Some people, eager for money, have wandered from the faith and pierced themselves with many griefs.

[669] Branham eventually came to believe that he was the angel of the seventh church mentioned in Revelation. He rejected the doctrine of the Trinity in favour of Modalism, taught Annihilationism, as well as the Serpent Seed doctrine (claiming that Eve was seduced by the serpent in the garden of Eden and the offspring was Cain). He ultimately claimed to be one of the end-time 2 witnesses (aka the prophet Elijah).

*Be glad then, you children of Zion, and rejoice in the LORD your God: for he has given you the former rain faithfully, and he will cause to come down for you the rain, **the former rain**, **and the latter rain** in the first month.* [670]

Using a very allegorical approach, unusual for their background of literalism with Pentecostal Premillennialism, they interpreted the "rain" as an end-times outpouring of the Holy Spirit which would be greater than the "former rain." Not even the original apostles, they believed, had witnessed such a movement of the Holy Spirit. Other key verses used (KJV rendering) included:

- ❖ *Jer 3:3 Therefore the showers have been withheld, and there has been no **latter rain**; and you had a harlot's forehead, you refused to be ashamed.* [671]
- ❖ *Hos 6:3 Let us know, let us press on to know the LORD: his going forth is prepared as the morning; and he shall come unto us as the rain, as the **latter and former rain** unto the earth.* [672]
- ❖ *Zech 10:1 Ask of the LORD rain **in the time of the latter rain**; so the LORD shall make bright clouds, and give them showers of rain, to everyone grass in the field.* [673]
- ❖ *James 5:7 Be patient therefore, brethren, unto the coming of the Lord. Behold, the farmer waits for the precious fruit of the earth, and has long patience for it, until he **receives the early and latter rain**.* [674]

Apostles

The movement had no clear leader as they emphasized relational networks over organizational structure. They taught that there would be a restoration of the five ministerial roles mentioned in Ephesians 4:11 (apostle, prophet, evangelist,

---

[670] King James 2000 Bible
[671] Ibid
[672] Ibid
[673] Ibid
[674] Ibid

pastor and teacher). The roles of apostle and prophet were considered foundational, but were said to have been lost after the time of the very first apostles. However, they believed that God was restoring the ministries of apostle and prophet in the present day. These ideas form part of what is called the "prophetic movement" and "New Apostolic Reformation". [675] They deemed these restored ministries to be greater than those of the "former rain" in the New Testament period. They held that the Church should be divided on geographical, not denominational, lines. Their expectation was that in the coming "last days" the various Christian denominations would dissolve; and the true Church would coalesce into city-wide churches under the leadership of these newly restored apostles and prophets. [676]

The view of classical Pentecostals on apostles

Belief in the restoration of the offices of apostle and prophet distinguished the Latter Rain Movement from the rest of Pentecostalism. Classical Pentecostals understood the fivefold ministry mentioned in Ephesians 4:11-12 not as offices or authority designated to any particular person, but as functions available to the entire Spirit-filled congregation, been giving at the discretion of the Holy Spirit. [677]

> *Eph 4:11-12 So Christ himself gave the apostles, the prophets, the evangelists, the pastors and teachers, **to equip his people for works of service**, so that the body of Christ may be built up.*

W.F. (Fred) Mullan (1903-81) was for years the general chairman of the Assemblies of God in South Africa. He believed that church government should reside solely with the local oversight of elders and deacons, rather than having any accountability to an apostolic founder of the church. [678] Mullan

---

[675] https://en.wikipedia.org/wiki/Latter_Rain_(post–World_War_II_movement)
[676] Ibid
[677] Shane Jack Clifton, An Analysis of the Developing Ecclesiology of the Assemblies of God in Australia, 2005, p. 150. & https://en.wikipedia.org/wiki/Latter_Rain_(post–World_War_II_movement)
[678] http://www.agfbrakpan.co.za/aog-in-sa.aspx

held that the ministry of apostles and prophets ceased to exist after the first generation of New Testament believers. In support, he cited Eph 2:20 which spoke of "the foundation of the apostles and prophets", taking this to mean that they were foundational ministries only. This objection arose out of a reaction to certain groups overseas (presumably the Latter Rain movement) whose views on apostles and prophets had become extreme. [679]

Even to those Pentecostals who accept that apostles are still part of the fivefold ministry, it should be noted that the term "apostle" designates function rather than status. The Greek word "apostolos" denoted an envoy, ambassador, or messenger commissioned to carry out the instructions of the commissioning agent. We are instructed that those claiming to be apostles need to be tested:

- ❖ *Rev 2:2b I know that you cannot tolerate wicked men, that you have tested those who claim to be apostles but are not, and have found them false.*
- ❖ *1 Cor 11:13-15 For such men are false apostles, deceitful workmen, masquerading as apostles of Christ. And no wonder, for Satan himself masquerades as an angel of light. It is not surprising, then, if his servants masquerade as servants of righteousness. Their end will be what their actions deserve.*

What is the Biblical criteria to test an apostle?

a) These are signs that mark a true apostle: Signs, wonders and miracles.

- ❖ *2 Cor 12:12 The things that mark an apostle - signs, wonders and miracles - were done among you with great perseverance.*

b) Church-planting

---

[679] http://www.agfbrakpan.co.za/aog-in-sa.aspx & "From Africa's Soil" - Peter Watt

- ❖ *Acts 14:21-23 They preached the gospel in that city and won a large number of disciples. Then they returned to Lystra, Iconium and Antioch, strengthening the disciples and encouraging them to remain true to the faith... Paul and Barnabas appointed elders for them in each church and, with prayer and fasting, committed them to the Lord, in whom they had put their trust.*

c) Persecution

- ❖ *2 Tim 1:11-12 And of this gospel I was appointed a herald and an apostle and a teacher. That is why I am suffering as I am.*

d) A physical eyewitness of the resurrected Christ

- ❖ *Acts 1:21-22 "Therefore it is necessary to choose one of the men who have been with us the whole time the Lord Jesus was living among us, beginning from John's baptism to the time when Jesus was taken up from us. For one of these must become a witness with us of his resurrection."*
- ❖ *1 Cor 9:1 Am I not free? Am I not an apostle? Have I not seen Jesus our Lord? Are you not the result of my work in the Lord?*
- ❖ *1 Cor 15:4-8 ... that he was raised on the third day according to the Scriptures... Then he appeared to James, then to all the apostles, and last of all he appeared to me also, as to one abnormally born.*

Some like James Mullan, [680] in support of his belief that the apostolic ministry was still valid today, claimed that this last qualification was only required for the "12 apostles of the Lamb" and not "apostles of the ascended Christ".

---

[680] James Mullan was the brother of Fred Mullan and the leader of the "Group" assemblies in South Africa.

Neo-prophets

Some of those who shaped the current Apostolic-Prophetic Movement in the US were based in Kansas City, Missouri and thus became known to detractors and supporters alike as the "Kansas City Prophets". Members of this group included Bob Jones, Bill Hamon, Rick Joyner, Larry Randolph, Paul Cain, Mike Bickle, James Goll, John Paul Jackson and Lou Engle. [681] Bob Jones claimed to be a prophet personally commissioned by Gabriel. Not to be confused with his namesake/s at the Bob Jones University) Jones had a background, which by normal Christian standards, is bizarre to say the least. According to his website:

> When only seven years old and walking on a dirt road in Arkansas; the Arch Angel Gabriel appeared to Bob Jones on a white horse and blew a double silver trumpet in his face. He then threw an old bull skin mantle at Bob's feet. Although fearful at the time he ran, however, many years later he returned to pick up that old mantle which is that of a Seer Prophet. [682]

Then when he was 13, God reaffirmed the calling by speaking his name while he was walking past a cane field. After years of spiritual rebellion, brawling and alcoholism, he was admitted to hospital where he was told he would remain the rest of his life. According to Jones, nine days later a demon appeared to him with a list of 12 people responsible for his mistreatment and instructed him to kill them. (It's unclear how a bedridden person would accomplish this?) God then audibly spoke to him telling him to forgive them. The next day he was miraculously healed and released from the hospital. [683]

> He went from seeing demons regularly ("... I didn't have trouble seeing the devils at all... I knew the devils real good when I drank - used to party with 'em out in the beer

---

[681] https://en.wikipedia.org/wiki/Apostolic-Prophetic_Movement#Kansas_City_Prophets & https://en.wikipedia.org/wiki/Mike_Bickle_(minister)
[682] http://www.bobjones.org/
[683] http://www.worldviewweekend.com/news/article/vineyard-and-kansas-city-prophets-report-1991-worth-reading-2011

joints...") to suddenly seeing angels regularly and having strange nightly visions and out-of-body experiences. Both Jones and Bickle estimate that "Bob normally gets 5 to 10 visions a night, maybe sees angels 10 to 15 times a week," and has done so since 1974. [684]

Jones allegedly saw blue lights singling out people that God would heal. When filled with the Spirit, he claimed to be able to see and taste spiritual states and sins in others with all his five senses. His hands turned purple when he got his best revelations and he felt a tingling in his fingers indicating those who were prophets, evangelists or pastors. [685] Jesus warned that in the last days:

> "For false messiahs and false prophets will appear and perform great signs and wonders to deceive, if possible, even the elect." (Matt 24:24)

Despite the Latter Rain prophets supposedly being greater than their Early Rain prophets, their admitted success rate at prophesying accurately is a lot lower than the Biblical counterparts, which was 100%. In a taped interview between Bob Jones and Mike Bickle, principal leader of Kansas City Fellowship (now Metro Vineyard Fellowship), we learn that: [686]

1) Unlike Old Testament prophets, New Testament prophets are often wrong. They may be 90% wrong. 60% accuracy is about the best they can expect - the Neo-Prophetic Movement prophecies have never been more than 60% accurate.
2) Bob Jones himself expected to be only about two-thirds accurate.
3) We can only know a prophet is telling the truth when "three or four of us bring the same word."
4) Even when God "loads the gun" of the rhema revelations, some of his bullets are blanks.

---

[684] Ibid
[685] http://www.dtl.org/shield/latter-rain-1.htm
[686] Ibid

Surely if 90% of prophecies may be incorrect, you might as well be guessing then, rather than relying on their revelations? In the same interview, we are told:

1) The Kansas City Fellowship will eventually become twelve city churches each with its own personal prophet, while the children of the Kansas City Fellowship leaders will become Melchizedekian priests.
2) 1000 religious leaders would die in 1990 for misusing "the anointing".
3) The Reorganized Mormon Church will join the Neo-Prophetic Movement.

These prophecies clearly fall in the 40-90% section allocated to failed prophecies. As with apostles, the Bible tells us to test prophets.

> *1 John 4:1 Dear friends, do not believe every spirit, but test the spirits to see whether they are from God, because many false prophets have gone out into the world.*

Here are the tests:

a) Do their prophecies come true?

> *Deut 18:21-22 (ESV) And if you say in your heart, 'How may we know the word that the Lord has not spoken?' - when a prophet speaks in the name of the Lord, if the word does not come to pass or come true, that is a word that the Lord has not spoken; the prophet has spoken it presumptuously. You need not be afraid of him.*

b) The fruit i.e. the lifestyle of the prophet.

> *Matt 7:15-16 "Watch out for false prophets. They come to you in sheep's clothing, but inwardly they are ferocious wolves. By their fruit you will recognize them."*

c) Do their prophecies line up with Scripture? Peter cautions us not to open ourselves to heresy.

> *2 Peter 2:1 But there were also false prophets among the people, just as there will be false teachers among you. They will secretly introduce destructive heresies, even denying the sovereign Lord who bought them--bringing swift destruction on themselves.*

Regarding those who claim what they have received is a 'new' revelation, superior to that of the Apostolic Age, bear in mind the following caution:

> *Rom 16:17-18 I urge you, brothers and sisters, to watch out for those who cause divisions and put obstacles in your way that are contrary to the teaching you have learned. Keep away from them. For such people are not serving our Lord Christ, but their own appetites. By smooth talk and flattery they deceive the minds of naive people.*

Paul warns us that the gospel that they preached in the 1st century (and embodied in the New Testament) shouldn't change.

> *Gal 1:8 But even if we or an angel from heaven should preach a gospel other than the one we preached to you, let them be under God's curse!*

The unknown prophet who rebuked Jeroboam, took bad advice from a fellow prophet, who claimed to have received a message from an angel, but was lying. The unknown prophet lost his life as a result of listening to him (1 Kings 13). So be careful who you listen to! Not everyone who claims to have heard from God is telling the truth. Remember Ahab's false prophets who purported to bring advice from God, but it was bad advice which led to his death. Just because it is attributed to God, it does not necessarily follow that it is of God.

Ezek 13:3,6 ... Woe to the foolish prophets who follow their own spirit and have seen nothing! ... Their visions are false and their divinations a lie. They say, "The LORD declares," when the LORD has not sent them; yet they expect their words to be fulfilled. (Also Jer 14:14 [687])

The "Manifest Sons of God" and "Joel's army"

Like classic Postmillennialism, the Charismatic brand of Dominionism also proclaims that the church is responsible for taking over the world in the name and power of Christ. Proponents believe that God lost control over the world to Satan when Adam and Eve sinned. Since then God has been trying to re-establish control over the world by seeking a special group of believers. Some taught that as the end of the age approached, a select group of "overcomers" would arise within the Church called these "Manifest Sons of God" who would complete the Great Commission, spreading the gospel throughout the world. They would take dominion of the earth under the leadership guidance of the latter-day prophets and apostles. Through these people - known as "Manifest Sons of God", "Joel's army" or the "Manchild Company", depending on the source - social institutions, including governments and laws, would be brought under God's authority.

> Paul Cain's version of the Manifested Sons doctrine goes under the label "Joel's Army" and the "New Breed"... This super-naturally-endowed future body will be manifested to unite and perfect the Church, judge the world, and conquer the earth for Christ. These prophetic paragons will lead millions to Christ, heal people and raise the dead, etc. [688]

Bob Jones taught that God was preparing a "special breed" or an army of "dread champions" which was composed of young

---

[687] Jer 14:14 "The prophets are prophesying lies in my name. I have not sent them or appointed them or spoken to them. They are prophesying to you false visions, divinations, idolatries and the delusions of their own minds.

[688] http://www.dtl.org/shield/latter-rain-1.htm "The Latter Rain Movement: Its Continuing Influence" by R. K. McGregor Wright, Th.M., Ph.D

people (at the time). This generation of children born since 1973 would form the final generation of believers whom God was preparing as the Bride of Christ to take control of the world and present the kingdom to Christ on his return. [689] Rick Joyner heads MorningStar Ministries, which he co-founded in 1983 in Jackson, Mississippi with his wife, Julie. Rick Joyner taught:

> What is about to come upon the earth is not just a revival, or another awakening; it is a veritable revolution. The vision was given in order to begin to awaken those who are destined to radically change the course, and even the very definition of Christianity. The dismantling of organizations and disbanding of some works will be a positive and exhilarating experience for the Lord's faithful servants...the Lord will raise up a great company of prophets, teachers, pastors and apostles that will be of the spirit of Phinehas ... this 'ministry of Phinehas' will save congregations, and at times, even whole nations. ...Nations will tremble at the mention of their name... [690]

As with most false doctrine this doctrine of Joel's army is based on arbitrary use of passages out of context. In its primary fulfilment, the army in Joel 2:1-11 was an ungodly Babylonian army that destroyed Jerusalem in 586 BC. Like much prophecy, the passage from Joel has a dual fulfilment in that it also points to the Antichrist's army that will attack Israel at the end of the age. As such, this passage is reminiscent and associated by some with the army of locusts (aka fallen angels) released from the Abyss in Revelation 9. Those who have come under Latter Rain influence mistakenly identify Joel's army as an elite band of end time prophets and apostles who will lead the church, but we noted in my former book, [691] that the army of locusts Joel is describing has some striking parallels with the Revelation passage.

---

[689] Clifford Hill and Peter Fenwick, David Forbes, David Noakes; Blessing the Church?; Eagle; p.130
[690] The Harvest
[691] The Profile of the Antichrist (Part 1) - Gavin Paynter
https://www.amazon.com/Profile-Antichrist-Part-1-ebook/dp/B014854DKK

Joel 1-2	Revelation 9
1:4 What the locust swarm has left the great **locusts** have eaten…	9:3 And out of the smoke **locusts** came down upon the earth…
1:6 A nation has invaded my land… it has the **teeth of a lion**, the fangs of a lioness.	9:8 … **their teeth were like lions' teeth**.
2:4 They have the **appearance of horses**; they gallop along like cavalry.	9:7 The locusts **looked like horses** prepared for battle.
2:5 With a **noise like that of chariots** … like a mighty army drawn up for **battle**	9:9 … **the sound** of their wings **was like** the thundering of many horses and **chariots rushing into battle**.

Table 12: Comparison of the 'locusts' in Joel and Revelation 9

In addition, the following verse is particularly interesting:

> *Joel 2:7 They run like mighty men (Heb: gibborim), They climb the wall like soldiers; And they each march in line, Nor do they deviate from their paths. (NASB)*

Because of its use in Genesis 6:4 'gibborim' is often associated with the Nephilim [692] who were the giant offspring of the angels (elsewhere known as Watchers) and human women.

> *Gen 6:4 The Nephilim were on the earth in those days, and also afterward, when the sons of God came in to the daughters of men, and they bore children to them. Those were the mighty men (gibborim) who were of old, men of renown. (NASB)*

---

[692] That being said, we must remember that 'gibborim' is not used exclusively of the Nephilim, but many times of humans as well (e.g. of David's "mighty men" in 2 Sam 10:7).

The chorus "Blow the Trumpet in Zion" encapsulates the faulty theology of the Manifest Sons of God and Joel's army.

> They rush on the city; they run on the wall.
> Great is the army that carries out His Word…
> Blow the trumpet in Zion, Zion.
> Sound the alarm on My holy mountain...

Rather than being a triumphant blast, the trumpet in the passage sounds the warning of a watchman upon the approach of an enemy army. This song would seemingly have Christians celebrate their implied participation in the troops depicted in Joel 2, which are actually 'locusts' (aka fallen angels released from the Abyss) coming to attack God's people on his holy mountain. A statement issued by the US Assemblies of God in 2000 has the following rebuttal to the doctrines of the Manifest Sons of God and Joel's Army.

> Manifest Sons of God and Joel's Army. These are some of the names used to describe those who have caught the vision of the Kingdom Now and are actively at work seeking to overcome the opposition and declaring Christians who hold a biblical understanding of Christ's imminent return at any time to be cowardly for not joining the "anointed," as they sometimes call themselves. Without question, the Old Testament Book of Joel includes many endtime references. But the great and powerful army in Joel 2 is one of terrible locusts, an instrument of judgment on Israel. After Israel's repentance, the army of locusts is destroyed by the Lord.[693]

The 144,000

Former associate professor of Old Testament at Dallas Theological Seminary, Jack Deere, abandoned his former theological positions and became a charismatic pastor in the late

---

[693] "Assemblies of God Position Paper on End Time revival" http://ag.org/top/Beliefs/Position_Papers/pp_downloads/pp_endtime_revival.pdf

1980s. [694] Speaking of Joel's army, Jack Deere links them to the 144,000 of Revelation 7.

> … This army, there's never been one like it and there never will be one like it in ages to come… What's going to happen now will transcend what Paul did, what David did… what Moses did… there'll be a numerous company… Revelation hints at this when it talks about the 144,000 that follow the Lamb wherever He goes and no one, no one can harm that 144,000. See, that's a multiple of 12. What's 12? Twelve is the number of the Apostles, 12 is Apostolic government. And when you take an important number in the Bible and you multiply it, it means you intensify it. So 12,000 times 12,000 = 144,000 [*Bad maths here*]. That is the ultimate in Apostolic government. Revelation talks about that. Well, here Joel is talking about it now in different words, a powerful, a mighty army with many Pauls, many Moses', many Davids. [695]

But the literal interpretation of the 144,000 is that they are restored Jews - 12,000 from each of the 12 tribes of Israel.

> *Rev 7:4 Then I heard the number of those who were sealed: 144,000 from all the tribes of Israel.*

Again we see the danger of allegorically interpreting something that makes perfect sense literally. And in this case, Kingdom Now proponents borrow from the Replacement Theology of Amillennialists and Postmillennialists, making Israel equal to the church.

The manchild

The "Manifest Sons of God" teachers believe that, prior to Christ's physical return, he comes again spiritually to a select

---

[694] https://en.wikipedia.org/wiki/Jack_Deere
[695] Joel's Army, Vineyard Ministries International, 1990

group of endtime believers. God's glory re-inhabits his temple, referring again to this new breed of elite Christians. [696]

> *Rev 12:5 (NASB) And she gave birth to a son, a male child, who is to rule all the nations with a rod of iron; and her child was caught up to God and to His throne.*

According to Paul Cain, these Manifest Sons of God are really the "male child" or "manchild" (KJV) of Revelation 12, who will rule the nations with a rod of iron. They will receive divine gifts, including the ability to change their physical location, to speak in any language, and be able to perform miracles such as divine healing and the raising of the dead. [697]

Who is the manchild? According to Premillennialists, as the offspring of Israel (the woman), the manchild is Jesus. We are also told that the manchild "will rule all the nations with an iron sceptre" (Rev 12:5) which seems to be a reference to Jesus' Millennial rule. Others say it represents the 144,000 Israelites, as in Rev 2:26-27 ruling the nations with an iron sceptre is also applied to overcomers and, like Jesus, they too are the offspring of the woman (Israel).

Immortality

The perfected believers of the "Manifest Sons of God" group apparently also qualify for immortality upon the earth, prior to Jesus' return.

> Taking childish cues from Paul's teaching in Romans eight and misunderstanding them, they suggested that a company of overcoming believers "the sons of God" will be manifested upon the earth with never dying spiritual bodies before the return of Christ. This would have to be the ultimate in dominion teaching.[698]

Paul Cain said:

---

[696] http://www.deceptioninthechurch.com
[697] Ibid
[698] http://so4j.com/new-apostolic-reformation-latter-rain

If you're really in the vine and you're the branch, then the life sap from the Son of the living God keeps you from cancer, keeps you from dying, keeps you from death... Not only will they not have diseases, they will also not die. They will have the kind of imperishable bodies that are talked about in the 15th chapter of Corinthians... this army is invincible. If you have intimacy with God, they can't kill you. they just can't. There's something about you; you're connected to that vine; you're just so close to him. oh, my friends, they can't kill you.[699]

In an interview between Bob Jones and Mike Bickle, principal leader of Kansas City Fellowship we are told that the Manifested Sons of God would appear within 30 years to glorify the Church on earth. This new generation will put death under their feet and they'll bring forth the glorious Church and reveal the manchild. [700] In a similar vein, Earl Paulk stated:

Jesus Christ, as the first-fruit of the Kingdom, began the work of conquering death on an individual basis, but we, as His church, will be the ones to complete the task. Jesus said (Matthew 28:18), 'all power is given unto me in heaven and in earth,' and the church today has that same power. Death will not be conquered by Jesus returning to earth. It will be conquered when the church stands up boldly and says, "We have dominion over the earth'. [701]

Ernie Gruen released a report in 1990 highlighting aberrant teachings of the Kansas City Fellowship, which we will consider shortly. Suffice to say at this stage that:

... in the wake of the Gruen controversy, Paul Cain has claimed (both through John Wimber, and in printed

---

[699] Paul Cain, "Joel's Army," cited in Documentation of the Aberrant Practices and Teachings of Kansas City Fellowship (Shawnee, KS: Full Faith Church of Love, 1990, p. 218)
[700] http://www.dtl.org/shield/latter-rain-1.htm
[701] Earl Paulk, The Proper Function of the Church

articles) that "He does not hold to the doctrine of the Manifested Sons, but totally denies ever having believed in that teaching"… In his own statements he has said that "There are several significant errors in this doctrine." He then repudiates the notion that "some Christians will have fully glorified bodies this side of heaven, or attain physical immortality this side of heaven. [702]

Little gods

Earl Paulk (1927-2009) was the founder of the Cathedral at Chapel Hill, a charismatic megachurch in Decatur, Georgia, a suburb of Atlanta. [703] Perhaps the most controversial and objectionable aspect of his flavour of the "Manifest Sons of God" doctrine, is the teaching of the ongoing incarnation of God in believers, who are "little gods" exercising autonomous sovereignty within their spheres of dominion. Here are some snippets of his teaching.

- ❖ We are on earth as extensions of God to finish the work He began. We are the essence of God, His on-going incarnation in the world. [704]
- ❖ The completion of the incarnation of God in the world must be in His Church... Jesus Christ is the firstfruit, but without the ongoing harvest, the incarnation will never be complete.[705]
- ❖ The Word became flesh in the God man, Jesus Christ (John 1:1). Likewise, the Word of God must be made flesh in the Church in order for us to bear witness to the Kingdom which God has called us to demonstrate. [706]

---

[702] http://www.dtl.org/shield/latter-rain-1.htm "The Latter Rain Movement: Its Continuing Influence"
by R. K. McGregor Wright, Th.M., Ph.D
[703] https://en.wikipedia.org/wiki/Earl_Paulk
[704] Thrust in the Sickle and Reap (1986), 132
[705] Held in the Heavens Until (1985), 60-61
[706] Earl Paulk, The Proper Function of the Church

The occult

John Robert Stevens was dismissed by both the Foursquare Gospel
Churches and the Assemblies of God, the latter because of his involvement in the Latter Rain teachings. In 1951 he organized "The Walk", undoubtedly one of the most heretical tributaries of the Latter Rain movement. Claiming to be an apostle and prophet, he taught that regular denominations were of the Old Order, Babylonish, worldly and largely apostate and so God was using The Walk to establish a New Order, which would eventually birth the Manifested Sons, of whom Stevens would be the first. [707]

But Stevens' worst heresy by far was that the spiritual practices and forces of the occult are 'neutral' and that the methods of the occult should also be used by Christians to help them achieve a similar or even better spirituality. Satan, he said, originally stole these methods from the righteous, so believers should reclaim their use for God by studying the occult and appropriating their techniques. [708] The Scripture comes to mind:

> *1 Tim 4:1 (NASB) But the Spirit explicitly says that in later times some will fall away from the faith, paying attention to deceitful spirits and doctrines of demons…*

Stevens further claimed that communication with angels and deceased believers had already become possible and that he had communication with the "great cloud of witnesses" [709] mentioned in Hebrews 12:1. He taught that God will bless this syncretism and the Latter Rain fire will fall at last, birthing the perfected Church. The Walk will be glorified into the Manifested Sons, thereby becoming themselves the Parousia (the Second Coming) of Christ. [710]

---

[707] http://www.dtl.org/shield/latter-rain-1.htm
[708] Ibid
[709] Ibid
[710] Ibid

By their fruit

Jesus said that one of the tests of a false prophet is "their fruit" i.e. their lifestyle:

> *Matt 7:15-17 "**Watch out for false prophets**. They come to you in sheep's clothing, but inwardly they are ferocious wolves. **By their fruit you will recognize them.** Do people pick grapes from thornbushes, or figs from thistles? Likewise, every good tree bears good fruit, but a bad tree bears bad fruit."*

So, let's look at some of the 'fruit' of the Latter Rain prophets. Despite having had close ties to the Reconstructionist movement (who advocate the death penalty for homosexuals), in his later years Paulk became one of the few mainstream Charismatic leaders to welcome openly gay and lesbian members. He was also involved in multiple sex scandals spanning several decades. [711] Then in 2004, Paul Cain admitted to being an alcoholic and being involved in homosexual activity, yet refused to submit to discipline. [712]

The American hippie preacher, Lonnie Frisbee (1949-1993) was a key figure in the Jesus movement and a notable evangelist in the signs and wonders movement of the 1970s and 1980s, [713] who contended that Joel's prophecy (namely the great end-days outpouring of the Holy Spirit) was being fulfilled by the Jesus People of the 1960s and 70s. [714] Frisbee has been credited by many as one of the main reasons for the initial explosive growth

---

[711] https://en.wikipedia.org/wiki/Earl_Paulk

[712] The following was released on Rick Joyner's website: "In February 2004, we were made aware that Paul had become an alcoholic. In April 2004, we confronted Paul with evidence that he had recently been involved in homosexual activity. Paul admitted to these sinful practices and was placed under discipline, agreeing to a process of restoration, which the three of us would oversee. However, Paul has resisted this process and has continued in his sin... With our deepest regrets and sincerity, Rick Joyner, Jack Deere, Mike Bickle" http://morrnnsstrarministries.ore/oages/special~bulleu.ns/Oct_19.html

[713] https://en.wikipedia.org/wiki/Lonnie_Frisbee

[714] Enroth, Ronald M., Edpiano covers E. Ericson, Jr., and C. Breckenridge Peters.; The Jesus People: Old Time Religion in the Age of Aquarius; p.12; Grand Rapids, MI: William B. Eerdmans, 1972

of both Chuck Smith's "Calvary Chapel" and John Wimber's "Vineyard Movement", two worldwide denominations and among the largest evangelical denominations to emerge in the last thirty years. [715] But according to his own report Frisbee struggled with homosexuality. Both churches later disowned him because of his active sexual life, removing him first from leadership positions, then ultimately, firing him. [716] In an article chronicling Frisbee's life titled "The First Jesus Freak", Matt Coker writes:

> Chuck Smith Jr. says he was having lunch with Wimber one day when he asked how the pastor reconciled working with a known homosexual like Frisbee. Wimber asked how the younger Smith knew this. Smith said he'd received a call from a pastor who'd just heard a young man confess to having been in a six-month relationship with Frisbee. Wimber called Smith the next day to say he'd confronted Frisbee, who openly admitted to the affair and agreed to leave. [717]

According to a documentary movie on Frisbee in 2001, he "privately socialized as a gay man before and during his evangelism career".[718] However, in interviews he admitted that both denominations prohibited gay sexual behaviour and stated that he never believed homosexuality was anything other than a sin in the eyes of God. Ultimately Lonnie Frisbee died from complications related to AIDS in 1993. [719]

Todd Bentley was a key figure of the Lakeland Revival. He sponsored an internship program called "Joel's Army," in addition to having the words "Joel's Army" tattooed across his sternum, demonstrating a level of commitment to the doctrine of the Manifest Sons of God. [720] On 9 July 2008, ABC News' Nightline broadcast an investigative report on Bentley, focusing

---

[715] https://en.wikipedia.org/wiki/Lonnie_Frisbee
[716] David di Sabatino (2001). Frisbee: The Life and Death of a Hippie Preacher (Documentary movie) US
[717] Matt Coker, "The First Jesus Freak" - Orange County Weekly, 3 Mar 2005
[718] David di Sabatino (2001). Frisbee: The Life and Death of a Hippie Preacher
[719] https://en.wikipedia.org/wiki/Lonnie_Frisbee
[720] https://en.wikipedia.org/wiki/Todd_Bentley

on his faith healing claims, finances, and criminal past. Following the report, Bentley took time off from the revival, but returned on 18 July 2008. [721] Five days later, it was announced that Bentley would be leaving the revival permanently. He announced his separation from his wife in August 2008, and resigned from the board of Fresh Fire. A statement released by the remaining board members said, "Todd Bentley has entered into an unhealthy relationship on an emotional level with a female member of his staff," and that he would "refrain from all public ministry for a season to receive counsel in his personal life." A committee was formed to oversee the process of spiritually restoring Bentley's family, but in Nov 2008, the board announced that Bentley was not submitting to the process. On March 9, 2009, Rick Joyner announced that Bentley had remarried. [722]

Figure 26: Todd Bentley in April 2008

We again recall the words of our Lord Jesus:

> *"A good tree cannot bear bad fruit, and a bad tree cannot bear good fruit. Every tree that does not bear good fruit is cut down and thrown into the fire. Thus, by their fruit you will recognize them." (Matt 7:18-20)*

---

[721] Ibid
[722] Ibid

John Robert Stevens' "The Walk" movement was clearly the most extreme lunatic fringe of the Latter Rain movement. A former member writes:

> I soon found out that being in the Walk was going to be a whole lot more fun than traditional church life. Walk people took the doctrine of "salvation by faith alone" into interesting new levels. It didn't matter a whole lot how you lived as long as "your heart was right" and you believed the right things. I didn't smoke, drink, or visit bars when I joined the Walk, but that all changed. Many Walk members would often frequent bars and strip clubs, drink excessively and generally whoop it up, and I was soon going along with them. This was considered to be a healthy development for me since I was coming from a "religious" background… one of the biggest hindrances to true spirituality was to have what we termed a "religious spirit". Being religious was 'old order' and would hinder the ability to receive the new revelation coming from JRS. It was believed that one of the best ways to break a religious spirit was to let it all hang out and indulge your fleshly cravings. Indulging and expressing "the flesh" was considered more honest and "being real", and therefore closer to God than phony, restrictive, "religious" behaviour. So in the topsy-turvy world of the Walk, carnality and sinful indulgence was an accepted route to spirituality. Many of those regarded to be the most spiritually mature were also often the wildest drinkers and party goers. But it was generally agreed that this was perfectly fine, because they were considered spiritually strong enough to handle it. [723]

This practice is best summarized by the apostle John's words.

> *1 John 3:7-10 Dear children, do not let anyone lead you astray. He who does what is right is righteous, just as he is righteous. He who does what is sinful is of the devil, because the devil has been sinning from the beginning.*

---

[723] http://www.deceptioninthechurch.com/cultsandcharismatic.html

The reason the Son of God appeared was to destroy the devil's work. No one who is born of God will continue to sin, because God's seed remains in him; he cannot go on sinning, because he has been born of God. This is how we know who the children of God are and who the children of the devil are: Anyone who does not do what is right is not a child of God; nor is anyone who does not love his brother.

Rejection by Pentecostals

The Latter Rain key emphases are still some of the most noticeable difference between Pentecostals and Charismatics. So, while these teachings gained inroads into Charismatic circles, the US Assemblies of God deemed the movement to contain heresy from the very outset, as delineated by their 2000 position paper on End Time Revival.

> Kingdom Now or Dominion theology. The thought that God's kingdom can come on earth with a little help from humankind is intriguing to those who advocate this approach to impacting society... this errant theology says that Jesus will not return until the Church takes dominion of the earth back from Satan and his followers. By taking control, through whatever means possible, of political, ecclesiastical, educational, economic, and other structures, Christians supposedly can make the world a worthy place for Christ to return and rule over. This unscriptural triumphalism generates other related variant teachings. [724]

In fact, as early as 1949 the General Council of the Assemblies of God, in Seattle, Washington, adopted a resolution disapproving the doctrines of the New Order of the Latter Rain. The minutes of that Council record that after brief debate the resolution was adopted with an overwhelming majority. [725] The

---

[724] "Assemblies of God Position Paper on End Time revival" - http://ag.org/top/Beliefs/Position_Papers/pp_downloads/pp_endtime_revival.pdf
[725] Ibid

teachings were also rejected by other classical Pentecostal denominations. [726]

Ultimate Rejection by the Vineyard

After a series of disagreements and meetings between a Kansas City Charismatic pastor, Ernie Gruen, and the Kansas City Fellowship, a 233-page report was published by Gruen in May 1990, entitled "Documentation of the Aberrant Practices and Teaching of the Kansas City Fellowship (Grace Ministries)".[727] The charges included:

- ❖ Promoting their own ministry and influencing other churches to come under the KCF (Kansas City Fellowship) umbrella.
- ❖ Strange teachings i.e. Bob Jones' use of the Shepherd's Rod ceremony.
- ❖ The idea that New Testament prophets are fallible.
- ❖ Documentation of occult type activities such as the promotion of out-of-body experiences.
- ❖ Various false doctrines that are documented include an "elected seed generation" theology to promote their uniqueness.
- ❖ A doctrine teaching that the "new order" following the pattern of Samuel will replace the old order after the pattern of Eli.
- ❖ Teaching Dominion theology.
- ❖ Doctrine about seeking new revelation from God including seeking dreams, visions, communication with angels, the dead, and out-of-body experiences.
- ❖ Doctrine about the restoration of Apostles and Prophets, while claiming that hundreds of these will be trained at KCF.

---

[726] Riss, Richard (1982), "The Latter Rain Movement of 1948", Pneuma: The Journal of the Society for Pentecostal Studies, **4** (1): 35

[727] http://www.worldviewweekend.com/news/article/vineyard-and-kansas-city-prophets-report-1991-worth-reading-2011

- ❖ Inconsistency in Bickles' support of Bob Jones, depending on how the groups he is addressing view Bob Jones. [728]

In June 1990, when Ernie Gruen and members of his staff met with Mike Bickle, Paul Cain and John Wimber, a truce was called.

> It is important to recognize that it was not a reconciliation. Paraphrasing Wimber, most of the key issues were not resolved… However, Gruen and his staff were willing to remove themselves from the controversy and turn the problems over to the leadership of the Vineyard churches. [729]

Subsequently, Bickle announced that he was submitting to Wimber's oversight and joining the Association of Vineyard Churches in part to address the issues raised by his critics. [730] On 28 June 1990, Bickle received public correction from Wimber for exaggerating some prophecies and for allowing too much latitude with some prophetic ministers, in particular Bob Jones. Bickle read a prepared statement repenting from a few of the things pointed out by Gruen as well as admitting to and repenting of the errors brought to light by the Vineyard. These included:

- ❖ KCF was guilty of exalting the prophetic ministry.
- ❖ They had issued a number of inaccurate prophecies.
- ❖ There was a lack of accountability for prophecies that didn't come true or bear the witness of the person receiving it.
- ❖ The attempt by some prophetic ministries to establish doctrine or to establish practice by revelation alone, apart from clear Biblical support.
- ❖ The use of prophetic gifting for controlling purposes.
- ❖ The releasing of men to minister publicly in a teaching format, who were not qualified as teachers.

---

[728] Ibid
[729] Ibid
[730] https://en.wikipedia.org/wiki/Mike_Bickle_(minister)

- ❖ Unnecessarily provoking other Kansas City churches with the "city church" doctrine i.e. that God only intended one church per city and for Kansas City it was KCF. Bickle admitted that making these statements was an act of pride and inadvertently developed an attitude of elitism among some of the people.
- ❖ Teaching or implying that KCF and the Vineyard were leaders of a new elite group about to be revealed by God.
- ❖ Using jargon reflecting the teaching of groups they didn't want to be aligned with i.e. Manifest Sons of God or Latter Rain.
- ❖ Calling John Wimber or others apostles or prophets, instead of apostolic leadership or prophetic ministry. (John Wimber was adamant about not being called an apostle.)

Bickle later noted that, "We were tempted to say that the attacks were all of the devil. In retrospect, we see that God's hand (*was*) in all of this - even using the things that came from Satan's hand as well. Some of the criticisms were valid, especially concerning our pride; others were not." [731] Ernie Gruen still believes that Bob Jones operated based on occultic power, similar to the slave girl Paul encountered at Philippi "who had a spirit by which she predicted the future" (Acts 16:16).

Latter Rain resurgence under the guise of Dominionism

As the term "Latter Rain" became somewhat of a pejorative label, many ministers who were influenced by it were reluctant to acknowledge the connection. Over the years much of the movement simply dissolved into parts of the larger Charismatic movement. [732] But of late, the Dominionist worldview seems to have subtly made it its way back into much of mainstream Christian thinking through the mass media, in particular Christian television.

---

[731] Ibid
[732] https://en.wikipedia.org/wiki/Latter_Rain_(post–World_War_II_movement)

Dominion Theology has been popularized in modern times mostly through "Word of Faith" media preachers preaching a hard form of Dominionism and popular Evangelical leaders preaching a softer form of Dominionism...[733]

Yet the situation is complicated by the fact that, due to the generally negative connotations of the term "Dominion Theology", some who teach aspects of Dominionism, will at the same time vehemently deny being Dominionists. In fact, those labelled "Dominionists" by others rarely use the term for self-description. They often do not seem to understand what Dominion Theology is, but know it is controversial and so deny any association.

Inconsistent views

Some Dominionists have seemingly contradictory eschatological views, believing on the one hand in a Premillennial Pre-Tribulation Rapture, but on the other hand espousing a Dominionist world takeover by Christians (implying an opposing Postmillennial view). One wonders why Christians would need to be raptured from a predominantly Christian culture, or why God would pour out his wrath on such a reformed world. Perhaps the Charismatic 'Kingdom Now' theology has been rightly criticised by some - as being largely undeveloped and inconsistent.

> So it would be fair to say that this brand of theology, while being rooted within a branch of Presbyterian Reconstructionism, is much more naive and less well-ordered. It is a bite out of the cake and an admiration of the flavour rather than being a fully consistent approach. The political aspect excites, the worldliness excites, the power excites but few Charismatics truly understand, nor even want to understand, the precise recipe or baking routine of this particular Dominionist cake... This

---

[733] http://www.thepropheticyears.com Web article "The Woman On The Beast In End Time Prophecy Has Dominion Theology" By Don Koenig - 2006

unquestionably more naive branch of Dominion Theology (that is, 'Kingdom Now') has developed a much wider following than its parent - but only among Charismatics whose grasp of theological essentials might be said to be often very uncultivated. [734]

Rapture denial

Other adherents of the Charismatic Dominionist teaching have followed it to its logical conclusion by denying a Rapture in the classical sense, this quote by Rick Joyner (one of the "Kansas City Prophets") being representative of the teaching:

> ... the doctrine of the Rapture was a great and effective ruse of the enemy to implant in the Church a retreat mentality ... already this yoke has been cast off by the majority in the advancing church, and it will soon be cast off by all. [735]

According to proponents of this Manifest Sons of God theology we are not to look for Jesus to come back physically but rather to come to his body corporately and invisibly through the glorification of these elite group of overcomers who will be perfected here on earth. [736]

---

[734] Ibid
[735] Rick Joyner, THE HARVEST 1989 /1990 revised booklet on pg.121
[736] http://www.deceptioninthechurch.com

CHAPTER 9: THE SOCIAL GOSPEL

South African Postmillennialist, Peter Hammond, aptly notes the following regarding the Church's impact on our civilisation:

> The Christian Church has made more positive changes on earth than any other force or movement in history. Most of the languages of the world were first codified and put into writing by Christian missionaries. More schools and universities have been started by Christians than by any other group. The elevation of women (from the second-class status they were assigned to by other religions) was a Christian achievement; as was the abolition of slavery, cannibalism, child sacrifice and widow burning. Those countries which enjoy the most civil liberties are generally those lands where the Gospel of Christ has penetrated the most... It is the secular humanists who have a heritage of oppression. The 44 secular or atheistic states have caused the deaths of over 160 million people in the 20th century alone. The abuses of human rights, atrocities and massacres in the Soviet Union, Nazi Germany, Red China, North Korea, Eastern Europe, Vietnam, Laos, Cambodia, Ethiopia, Angola, Mozambique and Cuba were the inevitable results of rejecting God's Law. [737]

Postmillennialists argue that, as Christianity had a positive impact on pagan culture in the past, it is quite possible do so in the present and future.

Christianity's Impact on the Roman empire

Before the conversion of Constantine, Christianity was a persecuted religion which, although it impacted many common people, played no major role in the affairs and policies of the state. But that all changed quite dramatically in the early 4th century, just after the tenth and worst Roman persecution of

---

[737] "Our Christian heritage" - by Dr. Peter Hammond

Christians by Diocletian. The Edict of Milan in AD 313 permitted citizens to accept Christianity without fear of persecution and guaranteed freedom of religion for all men. [738] Constantine went on to become the sole emperor (AD 323-337) of the Roman Empire, effecting many improvements in Roman law. While not all his legislation might meet our approval today or go far enough; judged by the standards of his day, he brought about many progressive and commendable civil reforms, including:

For slaves

- ❖ AD 313: Freeborn children could not become slaves. [739]
- ❖ AD 321: Slaves could be freed without the previously difficult process in the civil courts. He approved the freeing of slaves in the church by the clergy. [740]
- ❖ AD 326: He created a middle state between slave and free for the children of such mixed marriages. [741]
- ❖ AD 334: Slaves were not to be separated from their families as masters divided up inheritance. [742] [743]

For women

- ❖ AD 320: Those who abducted girls could face execution. [744] This may actually refer to elopements, which were

---

[738] Edict of Milan - "We grant both to Christians and to all men freedom to follow whatever religion each one wishes, in order that whatever divinity there is in the seat of heaven may be appeased and made propitious towards us and towards all who have been set under our power."

[739] Law 10

[740] Law 31: To Maximus, prefect of the city (June 8, 316) & Law 68: To Maximus, prefect of the city.

[741] Law 104: To Menander (Aug 27, 326)

[742] Law 125: To Gerulus, accountant of three provinces (Apr 29, 334?)

[743] Some articles on Constantine claim that slave nurses or chaperons caught allowing the girls they were responsible for to be seduced, were to have molten lead poured down their throats. But I can find no primary source for any such law, and it appears to be yet another fabrication. And yet another claim is that slave masters could beat slaves to death, again something for which no primary source appears to exist. This in fact contradicts the actual Law as related to Bassus on 11 May 319, whereby masters could still physically discipline their slaves but were not allowed to kill them or to treat them barbarically. (Law 45: To Bassus - May 11, 319)

[744] Law 58: To the people (Apr 1, 320)

considered kidnapping because girls could not legally consent to the elopement.

- ❖ AD 322: A woman had a right to prosecute in court. [745]
- ❖ AD 326: No man could have a concubine in his home while his marriage still continued. [746]
- ❖ AD 330: Widows would inherit their husband's property even if a will did not specify this. [747]

For children

- ❖ AD 315: Hammond writes that in the Roman pagan culture, "A father had the legal right to kill his children, to marry them to whomsoever he pleased, or to sell them as slaves." [748] But Constantine prohibited parents from killing their children, an action permissible under pagan rule. [749]
- ❖ AD 322: Parents too poor to raise children should not sell them but instead be supported by the state. [750]

For animals

- ❖ AD 316: Those abusing animals were threatened with demotion or deportation. [751]

For criminals

- ❖ AD 314: The death penalty could only be used for adultery, murder and sorcery - in cases of confession or certain evidence. [752]
- ❖ AD 320: Strict provisions were made for the ethical treatment of people awaiting trial. [753] A prisoner could no

---

[745] Law 75: To Agricolanus (Feb 9, 322)
[746] Law 101: To the people (June 14, 326)
[747] Law 113: To Valerianus, the acting prefect (Apr 29, 330)
[748] "Our Christian heritage" - by Dr. Peter Hammond
[749] Law 24: To Ablavius (May 13, 315)
[750] Law 76: To Menander (July 6, 322)
[751] Law 30: To Titianus (May 14, 316)
[752] Law 19: To Catalinus (Nov 3, 314?)
[753] Law 59: To the accountant Florentius (Jun 30, 320)

longer be kept in total darkness, but had to be given the outdoors and daylight. [754]

❖ AD 337: Crucifixion was abolished out of respect for Christ and replaced with the more humane hanging. [755]

The games

❖ AD 315: People condemned to the games or the mines could be branded in the hands or calves, but not the face, as it was formed in the image of the heavenly Son. [756]
❖ Later under Constantine's sole rule, in AD 325 gladiatorial games were ordered to be eliminated altogether, with mine work replacing it as a more humane punishment. [757] At these games in the day of pagan rule, men had previously fought to the death and Christians were fed to the lions, both done for the 'amusement' of the crowd.

General

❖ AD 314: In all things justice and fairness had to take priority over the letter of the law. [758]
❖ AD 320: Wills could not be invalidated because of poor form. [759] Proper will form was not necessary as long as its intent is apparent. [760]
❖ AD 321: Citizens were protected from tax officials who threatened them with death or perpetual exile. [761]
❖ AD 328: Anonymous accusations endangering people's lives were forbidden. [762]
❖ AD 337: There was a prohibition against deceptive selling practices. [763]

---

[754] MacMullen 1969, New Catholic Encyclopedia 1908
[755] http://www.bible-archaeology.info/crucifixion.htm
[756] Law 22: To Eumelius (March 21, 315)
[757] Law 89: To Maximus, the praetorian prefect (Oct 1, 325)
[758] Law 17: To Dionysius (May 15, 314)
[759] Law 54: To the people (Jan 31, 320)
[760] Law 56 (Feb 1, 320)
[761] Law 70 (1 July 1, 13 July and 1 Aug, 321)
[762] Law 42: To Dionysius (Oct 21, 328)
[763] Law 7: To Rufinus, the praetorian prefect (Aug 29, 313 and Feb 4, 337)

Thus there is no doubt that by having a Christian emperor, there was genuine reform in the Roman Empire and change for the better. Julian 'the Apostate', in his brief reign (AD 361-363), sought to undo much that Constantine had done, by again elevating paganism at the expense of Christianity. However even Julian grudgingly admitted a challenge because of the social involvement of Christians (whom he called Galileans) with regards to their treatment of the poor (both Christian and non-Christian alike).

> These impious Galileans not only feed their own poor, but ours also; welcoming them into their agapae (*love-feasts* [764]), they attract them, as children are attracted, with cakes. [765]

And in another place, he rants:

> Whilst the pagan priests neglect the poor, the hated Galileans devote themselves to works of charity, and by a display of false compassion have established and given effect to their pernicious errors. See their love-feasts, and their tables spread for the impoverished. Such practice is common among them, and causes a contempt for our gods.[766]

After a brief stint of paganism under Julian, Theodosius I (AD 378-395) made Christianity the state religion in his Edict of 380. [767] After the Massacre of Thessalonica in AD 390, where

---

[764] The agapae referred to were "love feasts"; not only the love for God, but the love of Christians for each other as being members of a divinely inspired communion. The agapae were meetings for prayer, song, reading, exhortation, exchange of news, and ended with the brotherly kiss.

[765] Charles Schmidt. The Social Results of Early Christianity, (1889), 328

[766] Gaetano Baluffi and Denis Gargan. The Charity of the Church, a Proof of Her Divinity. (1885), 16

[767] Excerpt from Theodosius' Edict of 380 - "It is our will that all the peoples who are ruled by the administration of Our Clemency shall practice that religion which the divine Peter the Apostle transmitted to the Romans, as the religion which he introduced makes clear even unto this day. It is evident that this is the religion that is followed by the Pontiff Damascus and by Peter, Bishop of Alexandria, a man of apostolic sanctity; that is, according to the apostolic discipline and the evangelic doctrine, we shall believe in the single Deity of the

Theodosius' knee-jerk reaction resulted in the slaughter of 7,000 people, Ambrose of Milan refused to celebrate a mass in the Emperor's presence, until Theodosius repented. Guilty and innocent people had been killed without trial in crushing a civil unrest in Thessalonica. In a letter to the emperor, Ambrose explained his position:

> Should I remain silent? But then the worst thing would happen as my conscience would be bound and my words taken away. And where would they be then? When a priest does not talk to a sinner, then the sinner will die in his sin, and the priest will be guilty because he failed to correct him.[768]

When the emperor tried to enter a Milanese church, where Ambrose was about to celebrate a mass, the bishop stopped him and rebuked him for what he had done. [769] And because, in Theodoret's words, the emperor "had been brought up according to divine words and understood well that some affairs are handled by priests, others by emperors", [770] he never took any action against Ambrose. Ambrose only restored relations with Theodosius, when the latter promised to promulgate a law, which in cases of death sentences would introduce a thirty-day lag before the execution. [771]

Paradoxically, despite his severe treatment of heretics and pagans, in other aspects many of Justinian's laws were actually quite revisionary and humane, especially with regards to women e.g. He protected prostitutes from exploitation and women from being forced into prostitution. Further, his policies dictated severe treatment of rapists. Women charged with crimes had to be guarded by other women to prevent sexual abuse; if a woman was widowed, her dowry had to be returned to her; and a husband could not take on major debt without his wife giving her

---

Father, the Son, and the Holy Spirit, under the concept of equal majesty and of the Holy Trinity."

[768] https://en.wikipedia.org/wiki/Massacre_of_Thessalonica
[769] Ibid
[770] Theodoret, Historia ecclesiastica 5.17
[771] https://en.wikipedia.org/wiki/Massacre_of_Thessalonica

consent twice. [772] In AD 535, at the insistence of the empress Theodora (the wife of Justinian), an edict was issued that banished pimps and keepers of brothels from all major cities of the empire.

Protestant social reform

Skipping forward a couple of centuries, let's briefly look at some of the civil and social reform that was prompted by the rise of Protestantism. Historian Robert Fogel identifies numerous reforms in the period of the 3rd Great Awakening, especially the battles involving child labour, compulsory elementary education and the protection of women from exploitation in factories. In addition, there was a major crusade for the prohibition of alcohol. [773] Christian based reform was also responsible for addressing the issues of feeding the poor, the abolition of slavery, and the establishment of orphanages, schools, hospitals and prisons.

Opium trade

Primarily because of the China Inland Mission's campaign against the Opium trade, Hudson Taylor (1832-1905) has been referred to as one of the most significant Europeans to visit China in the 19th Century. [774]

Abolition of slavery

John Newton (1725-1807) was a former slave trader, who after his conversion to Christianity became a Church of England pastor. While best remembered for writing the words to 'Amazing Grace', Newton influenced William Wilberforce (1759-1833), a young British politician who was the chief instrument in banning slavery from the British Empire.

When General Charles Gordon went to Sudan, 7 out of every 8 black people there were slaves. Gordon was a dedicated

---

[772] https://en.wikipedia.org/wiki/Justinian_I
[773] https://en.wikipedia.org/wiki/Third_Great_Awakening
[774] https://en.wikipedia.org/wiki/Hudson_Taylor

evangelical Christian who succeeded in setting many slaves free and eradicating the slave trade in Sudan. [775]

Figure 27: William Wilberforce [776]

David Livingstone raised in Europe so powerful a feeling against the slave trade in Africa, that it is through him that slavery may be considered as having received its death blow. [777] In the US, Samuel Hopkins was a Congregational minister in Newport, Rhode Island, which was at the centre of the triangular trade, involving the exchange of rum for African slaves. Hopkins launched a crusade against the trade, advocated complete emancipation, ministered to more blacks than any other New England minister, and predicted God's judgment on the nation as long as it denied freedom to Africans. [778]

Schooling

Robert Raikes (1736-1811) was an Anglican layman who initiated the Sunday School Movement. He had inherited a business from his father and initially covered most of the costs

---

[775] www.higherpraise.com

[776] By Karl Anton Hickel, c. 1794

[777] www.christian-action.org.za

[778] https://christianhistoryinstitute.org/magazine/article/american-postmillenni-alism-seeing-the-glory

himself. The movement started in 1780 with a school for boys (and later girls too) in the slums. Raikes had been involved with those incarcerated at the county Poor Law (part of the jail at that time) and saw that crime would be better prevented than cured. He saw schooling as the best intervention. The best available time was Sunday as the boys were often working in the factories the other 6 days. The best available teachers, were lay people, the textbook was the Bible, and the curriculum included learning to read. [779] By 1831, Sunday School in Great Britain was ministering weekly to 1,250,000 children, approximately 25% of the population. As these schools preceded the first state funding of schools for the common public, they are sometimes seen as a forerunner to the current English school system. [780]

Figure 28: Robert Raikes

The Young Men's Christian Association

The YMCA began among evangelicals and was founded in London in 1844, by a young man named George Williams. At the time, the organization was dedicated to putting Christian principles into practice. Young men who came to London for work were often living in squalid and unsafe conditions, and the

---

[779] SOURCES: (1) "Robert Raikes, 1736-1811, Sunday School Movement". Believer's Web. (2) John Carroll (1863). The Rise and Progress of Sunday Schools: A Biography of Robert Raikes and William Fox. New York: Sheldon & Company. (3) https://en.wikipedia.org/wiki/Robert_Raikes
[780] https://en.wikipedia.org/wiki/Robert_Raikes

YMCA was dedicated to replacing life on the streets with prayer and Bible study. The organisation became a force in many cities, as did denominational youth groups such as the Epworth League (Methodist) and the Walther League (Lutheran). [781]

Figure 29: George Müller

Orphanages

Prussian-born George Müller, who initially came to England as a missionary, moved to Bristol in 1832. The work of Müller and his wife with orphans began in 1836 with the preparation of their own home in Bristol for the accommodation of 30 girls. Soon after, 3 more houses were furnished, growing the total of children to 130. In 1845, as growth continued, Müller decided that a separate building designed to house 300 children was necessary, and in 1849, at Ashley Down, Bristol, that home opened. By 1870, more than 2,000 children were being accommodated in 5 homes. Every morning after breakfast there was a time of Bible reading and prayer, and every child was given a Bible upon leaving the orphanage. [782]

---

[781] https://en.wikipedia.org/wiki/Third_Great_Awakening & https://en.wikipedia.org/wiki/YMCA

[782] https://en.wikipedia.org/wiki/George_Müller

William Booth was a British Methodist preacher who founded the Salvation Army in 1865 and became the first General. This Christian movement, with a quasi-military structure and government - but with no physical weaponry, has spread from London, England, to many parts of the world and is known for being one of the largest distributors of humanitarian aid. Booth described the organizations approach: "The three S's best expressed the way in which the Army administered to the 'down and outs': first, soup; second, soap; and finally, salvation." William preached to the poor, and Catherine Booth spoke to the wealthy, gaining financial support for their work. The Salvation Army's main converts were at first alcoholics, drug addicts, prostitutes and other 'undesirables' of society. These 'undesirables' were not welcome in polite Christian society, which prompted the Booths to start their own church. [783]

Figure 30: William Booth

The social impact of Christian Missions

To those secular anthropologists who have tried to vilify Christian missionaries, by complaining that they eradicated

---

[783] https://en.wikipedia.org/wiki/The_Salvation_Army

ancient cultural practices and that the world is somehow poorer, Dr. Peter Hammond relates this anecdote:

> During a recent visit to a museum I saw a similar display of reverence for paganism. Part of the exhibit included the cover of an old Time magazine cover "Lost Tribes - Lost Knowledge". The cover picture was of a primitive tribesman from Papua New Guinea with a bone through his nose. The sub title read: "Treasure troves of scientific knowledge are being lost by tribes going extinct." I wondered what scientific knowledge would be possessed by tribes without a written language, but closer examination revealed that these tribes were "going extinct" because of the work of Christian missionaries! As these tribes are evangelized and come to Christ they abandoned their old tribal religions of head hunting, cannibalism, spirit worship and polygamy. To the "scientist" the tribes were "going extinct" because they no longer walked around naked and no longer engaged in body scarification, tattooing and body piercing! Now they wore clothes and glasses, went to the doctor instead of the witchdoctor, had schools, were learning to read, only married once and worshipped in Church! [784]

Hammond then sums up the situation rather sarcastically, but very aptly, with this response:

> Being somewhat ignorant of the science of anthropology I would have thought that ending inter-tribal warfare, cannibalism, polygamy and occultism was good. I would have also assumed that giving people the gift of literacy, medicines to improve their health and extend life expectancy, improving people's sight with glasses and bringing them the life transforming Gospel of Jesus Christ was all preferable to allow them to languish in superstition, ignorance and animistic fear. But NO! As National Geographic articles bemoaning the "cultural

---

[784] "Our Christian heritage" - by Dr. Peter Hammond

genocide" of New Tribes Mission, and other pioneer missions in the Amazon jungle, have pointed out, these missionaries are destroying "the cultural distinctives" of unique tribal cultures. Apparently, it is preferable to have illiteracy, polygamy, incessant tribal warfare, cannibalism, human sacrifices, slavery, high infant mortality and low life expectancies - not to mention people dying without the knowledge of Christ - just so that journalists and anthropologists can have the more interesting, and financially lucrative, photo ops of naked savages engaging in body scarification and the eating of their neighbours. [785]

Figure 31: Mary Slessor

Women Christian missionaries like Anna Bowden, Mary Slessor, Amy Carmichael and Gladys Aylward saved thousands of abandoned children, raising them in their own homes or orphanages. Mary Slessor (1848-1915) was a Scottish missionary to Calabar in southern Nigeria, who is credited with having stopped the practice of the killing of new-born twins among the Efik, a particular ethnic group in Nigeria. The birth of twins was considered a particularly evil curse. Locals believed

---

[785] Ibid

that the father of one of the infants was an evil spirit. Unable to determine which twin was fathered by the evil spirit, they often abandoned both babies in the bush. Slessor adopted every child she found abandoned, and sent out "twins missioners" to find, protect and care for them at the Mission House.[786]

Sati was a Hindu funeral custom whereby a widow was burnt on her husband's pyre, or had to commit suicide in another fashion shortly after her husband's death. In the 19th century, Anna Bowden, a British missionary to India battled, not only against sati, but also the practices of female infanticide and cultic abortifacient (i.e. causing abortion) procedures.

> Anna established a ministry among the town's children and outcast untouchables. It wasn't long before she was confronted with the culture's ritualistic killing of women and children... British colonial policy dictated a practice of "non-interference"... Anna could not comply. She established a rescue network which worked to help widows escape being put to death. Anna was ordered by the British administrator to cease all activities not directly related to her missionary outpost but she refused to quit, stating that rescuing humans was, indeed, directly related to her mission work. Local opposition finally organized a mob which attacked the compound, burned the buildings, and raped the women. Anna was tortured and killed... Bowden's journal was published after her death and her example ignited a revival among missionaries in India. Her story had such a great impact back in England that the policy of non-interference was significantly altered which paved the way for the eradication of barbaric practices such as the ones Anna struggled against. [787]

Attempts to limit or ban the practice of sati had been made by individual British officers in the 18th century, but without the

---

[786] https://en.wikipedia.org/wiki/Mary_Slessor
[787] "Lost Causes" - George and Karen Grant & "Fighting For A Lost Cause — When Is It Worth It?" Jeff Wright Jr. http://clashdaily.com/2013/09/fighting-lost-cause-worth/ (28 Sep 2013)

backing of the British East India Company. In the beginning of the 19th century, the evangelical church in Britain, and its members in India, started campaigns against sati. Leaders of these campaigns included Baptist missionary William Carey (1761-1834) and the Christian statesman William Wilberforce. These movements put pressure on the British East India Company to ban the act. [788] In 1813, in a speech to the House of Commons, William Wilberforce, with particular reference to the statistics on sati collected by William Carey and the other Serampore missionaries, forced through a bill that made Christian missionary preaching in British India legal, to combat such perceived social evils like sati. [789] This was instrumental in the ultimate total outlawing of sati in 1829.

Figure 32: Amy Carmichael with children

Amy Carmichael (1867-1951) was an Irish Protestant Christian missionary in India. Carmichael's most notable work was with girls and young women, some of whom were saved from customs that amounted to forced prostitution. Hindu temple children were primarily young girls dedicated to the gods, then usually forced into prostitution to earn money for the priests. Her ministry of rescuing temple children started with a girl named Preena, who had become a temple servant against her wishes,

---

[788] https://en.wikipedia.org/wiki/Sati_(practice)
[789] Mangalwadi, Vishal; Stetson, Chuck (ed.) (2007). "India: Peril & Promise". Creating the Better Hour: Lessons from William Wilberforce. Macon, pp. 140-141.

but managed to escape. Amy provided her shelter and withstood the threats of those who insisted that the girl be returned to continue her sexual assignments. The number of such incidents soon grew, thus beginning Amy's new ministry.[790]

Gladys Aylward (1902-1970) was a British evangelical Christian missionary to China, who assisted the local Chinese authorities in banning the gruesome practice of foot-binding young girls in the Yangcheng area. She also intervened and ended a volatile prison riot, subsequently advocating and achieving much-needed prison reform to improve the plight of prisoners. In 1938, when the region was invaded by Japanese forces, Aylward led over 100 orphans to safety over the mountains, despite being sick. [791]

Should we retreat from social involvement?

Has Christianity positively impacted culture in the past? We would totally agree with Postmillennialists that it has. But this in no way vindicates a belief in a great end time revival, which we shall see is contrary to what Scripture teaches. We also take issue with any insinuation that a Postmillennial outlook is a prerequisite to be able to make any impact on society. While many of the people we have just cited as having impacted their culture were Postmillennialists (at least by virtue of their denominational affiliation), some too were Premillennialists (e.g. George Müller and Hudson Taylor were Plymouth Brethren, the noted Dispensationalist movement). So, contrary to what some would have us believe, Premillennialists do not all have a policy of retreatism and social inactivity. Gavin Hopps and Trevor Hart note:

> Marsden, after making the argument that early dispensational premillennialists were much more fully involved in social work than has usually been acknowledged by scholarship, acknowledges that a shift occurred in the nature of Christian social efforts. Between

---

[790] https://en.wikipedia.org/wiki/Amy_Carmichael
[791] "The Small Woman" by Alan Burgess

1865 and 1900, revivalist evangelicals began to lose interest in promoting the welfare of society through political action, but they often continued to care for the needs of the poor and oppressed through acts of private charity. This decreased political involvement represented a change from a 'Calvinistic' understanding of politics as a means to advance the kingdom of God to a 'pietistic' view of it primarily as a way to restrain evil. [792]

The accusation made against the apostles in Thessalonica was "These men who have turned the world upside down have come here also". [793] Could the same accusation be made against us? Are we still turning our world upside down? Yet the reference was surely not made regarding social work conducted by the apostles, but to their evangelistic efforts. Paul was inadvertently responsible for a major civil unrest in Ephesus. His preaching was so effective that the trade of making shrines for the pagan goddess Artemis entered a recession, inciting the affected silversmiths to riot (Acts 19). While Jesus kept a bag for the poor, one could hardly argue that feeding the poor was the main impetus of his ministry. Rather he said, "The Spirit of the Lord is on me, because he has anointed me to **preach good news** to the poor" (Luke 4:18).

However, on the other hand, the apostle John says:

> *1 John 3:17-18 If anyone has material possessions and sees his brother in need but has no pity on him, how can the love of God be in him? Dear children, let us not love with words or tongue but with actions and in truth.*

And James reminds us of the need to be practical:

> *Jam 2:15-16 Suppose a brother or sister is without clothes and daily food. If one of you says to him, "Go, I wish you well; keep warm and well fed," but does nothing about his physical needs, what good is it?*

---

[792] Art, Imagination and Christian Hope: Patterns of Promise (Routledge Studies in Theology, Imagination and the Arts) 19 Dec 2012
[793] Acts 17:6 ESV

Any Christian, of whom the charge is true regarding a retreatist attitude, needs to remember that as Christians, we are called to be the salt and light of the world.

> *Matt 5:13-16 You are the salt of the earth. But if the salt loses its saltiness, how can it be made salty again? It is no longer good for anything, except to be thrown out and trampled by men. You are the light of the world. A city on a hill cannot be hidden. Neither do people light a lamp and put it under a bowl. Instead they put it on its stand, and it gives light to everyone in the house. In the same way, let your light shine before men, that they may see your good deeds and praise your Father in heaven.*

If we have a problem with the world we live in, John Stott has said that we should not ask, "What is wrong with the world?" for that diagnosis has already been given. Rather, we should ask, "What has happened to the salt and light?"

CHAPTER 10: IS IT THE MILLENNIUM NOW?

Micah 4:1-4 In the last days the mountain of the Lord's temple will be established as the highest of the mountains; it will be exalted above the hills, and peoples will stream to it. Many nations will come and say, "Come, let us go up to the mountain of the Lord, to the temple of the God of Jacob. He will teach us his ways, so that we may walk in his paths." The law will go out from Zion, the word of the Lord from Jerusalem. He will judge between many peoples and will settle disputes for strong nations far and wide. They will beat their swords into plowshares and their spears into pruning hooks. Nation will not take up sword against nation, nor will they train for war anymore. Everyone will sit under their own vine and under their own fig tree, and no one will make them afraid, for the Lord Almighty has spoken.

While it is undoubtedly true that Christianity had a positive impact on pagan culture, Premillennialists will argue that in many ways our world (or rather the Western world) has entered a post-Christian era and cannot be fairly compared to the golden age of Christian missions. Is our modern society still improving as Postmillennialists say, or as Dominionists hope? Are we getting better and better every day in every way?

Many of the reforms introduced by Constantine, which undid the evils of paganism, are being reversed in our modern world. For instance, with regards to divorce, our new laws in the West have regressed away from pro-Christian ideals and back to pagan values. Constantine rendered divorce more difficult - no changes were made where the divorce was agreed to by both parties, but severe conditions were imposed when the demand for separation came from one side only. [794] But our culture has made divorce much easier, certainly not an indication of a society that is progressing morally.

Are we becoming more Christian or are we returning to neo-pagan values? In this chapter let us examine briefly whether, as some would have us believe, we are in the Millennium now, based on the character of our age. Are the moral trends we are seeing in our modern world showing improvement or decline?

1) Justice

Justice in our age

Let's reflect on the moral progression (or regression) in the ages from a Western civilisation perspective. As the morality and justice of a society can be measured by how it treats the most weak and vulnerable, consider just the treatment of children in the ages.

- ❖ **The 'Pagan era'** - In this culture, children were sacrificed on altars to pagan 'gods', aborted and abandoned to die in infancy.
- ❖ **The Christian era (Post-pagan)** - Children were cherished and protected. Not surprisingly this ultimately led to the rise of views like Postmillennialism where it was believed that the progress would continue until the whole world was converted before Jesus returned.
- ❖ **The Current era (Neo-Paganism)** - Now despite the moral advancement brought by Christianity, we are reverting to neo-pagan values and to what some are calling a post-Christian era. Once again, with the plague of state-approved abortion, children are being sacrificed to the gods of selfishness and convenience.

---

[794] Law 120: To Ablavius, the praetorian prefect (331) limited lawful grounds for divorcing a man to murder, witchcraft, and graverobbing and divorcing a woman to adultery, witchcraft, and prostitution.

❖ **The Millennium** - Eventually in the Millennial age, Jesus will institute true justice and establish a golden age of peace, where again children will be cherished and protected.

Rather than advancing, in many ways we are turning our backs on Christian values and returning to the evils of paganism, but this time in the form of secular humanism.

Abortion and infanticide

Just take abortion for example, a moral evil that was once removed from Western civilization through Christian influence. Promiscuity and immorality in the Roman Empire resulted in widespread infanticide and abortion, as well as a slave trade in child prostitutes who were treated, in Justin Martyr's words, "like herds of oxen, goats, or sheep."

> The Greek philosophers Plato, Aristotle and Socrates lived in, and accepted, a culture which practiced slavery and human sacrifice and glorified paedophilia (sexual abuse of children). And it was the persistent work of Christians which outlawed abortion, abandonment and infanticide, first in the Roman Empire, then throughout Europe and America. [795]

In some periods of Roman history, it was traditional (and legal) for a new-born to be brought to the pater familias (the family patriarch), who would then decide whether the child was to be kept and raised, or to be abandoned outside the city walls to die of starvation or exposure or from wild animals. The Twelve Tables of Roman law obliged him to put to death a child that was visibly deformed. [796] A letter from a Roman citizen to his pregnant wife, dating from 1 BC, demonstrates the casual nature with which infanticide was often viewed:

> I am still in Alexandria... I beg and plead with you to take care of our little child, and as soon as we receive wages,

---

[795] "Our Christian heritage" - by Dr. Peter Hammond
[796] https://en.wikipedia.org/wiki/Infanticide

I will send them to you. In the meantime, if (good fortune to you!) you give birth, if it is a boy, let it live; if it is a girl, expose it...[797]

But Christians regarded exposure of children as equal to murder and often got possession of such abandoned foundlings and adopted them. We have already noted that Constantine prohibited parents from killing their children. Yet our modern culture has reverted to neo-pagan values, by promoting abortion on demand and hence the large-scale slaughter of unborn children. In a 2012 article in the Journal of Medical Ethics, a philosopher and a bioethicist jointly proposed that infanticide be legalized, calling it "after-birth abortion" and claiming that both "the foetus and the new-born are potential persons". Euthanasia applied to children that are gravely ill or that suffer from significant birth defects is already legal in the Netherlands. [798]

Chinese abortion policies

The People's Republic of China, influenced by atheistic Communism, has reverted to barbaric practices similar to those practiced by the pagans of old. They have adopted a one-child policy which is enforced with compulsory abortions, sometimes even late-term. In an article by Yuan Ren in the Telegraph, it is related how an eight months' pregnant woman in southwest China was being pressured into a late-term abortion so that her husband would not lose his job. The woman in question already had a daughter and was legally obliged to abort the baby. If their second child were born, the woman's police officer husband would be sacked, in line with rules that specifically apply to public servants as upholders of Chinese law. [799]

Not only pregnancy with a second child, but even first pregnancies without a birth permit are considered illegal in China. Family Planning officials, tasked with ensuring "out-of-plan" children are never born, track down pregnant women and

---

[797] Ibid
[798] Ibid
[799] http://www.telegraph.co.uk/women/womens-life/11858723/China-Forced-abortion-late-term-to-avoid-one-child-policy.html

forcibly terminate pregnancies. [800] 25th Sept 2014 marked the 34th year since China's enforcement of the one-child Policy which at that point had resulted in the abortion of 400 million babies, [801] more babies than the entire combined population of the US [802] and the UK. [803] There have also been some allegations that infanticide occurs in China due to the one-child policy. [804]

US abortion

Here is a comparison of US Abortion Deaths compared to US War Deaths - Each ♦ symbol represents 10,000 people (or fraction) killed. [805]

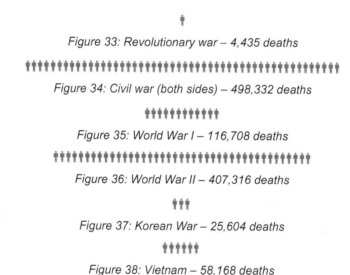

Figure 33: Revolutionary war – 4,435 deaths

Figure 34: Civil war (both sides) – 498,332 deaths

Figure 35: World War I – 116,708 deaths

Figure 36: World War II – 407,316 deaths

Figure 37: Korean War – 25,604 deaths

Figure 38: Vietnam – 58,168 deaths

On the same scale following is the total children killed by abortion from 1973 until 2008 - 35,000,000 deaths (or

[800] http://www.allgirlsallowed.org/forced-abortion-statisticsl
[801] http://www.lifenews.com/2014/09/25/34-years-of-chinas-one-child-policy-400-million-abortions-37-million-sex-selection-abortions
[802] 319 million in 2014
[803] 64.1 million in 2013
[804] https://en.wikipedia.org/wiki/Infanticide
[805] http://www.htmlbible.com/abortstats.htm

approximately equivalent to the entire population of Canada in 2016).

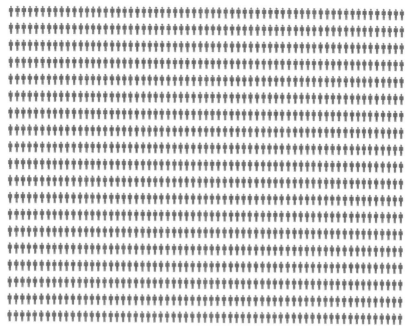

Figure 39: Children killed by abortion in the US 1973-2008 – 35,000,000 deaths

In reality, those promoting abortion and euthanasia are not offering us progress, but only a return to primitive, barbaric, pre-Christian paganism. In our Western society, you can watch all kinds of medical operations on television, but you won't be shown an abortion procedure. If you look at pictures of aborted babies, you'll understand why. Then ask yourself:

1. Is our world really improving?
2. Are we in a Christian golden age?
3. Will we escape God's judgment?

Corruption in our age

In his famous 'gangster-state' analogy Augustine of Hippo wrote, "What is a state without justice, but a band of robbers!" [806] 'State capture' is a type of systemic political corruption in which private

---

[806] Augustine - 'City of God'

interests significantly influence a state's decision-making processes to their own advantage through unobvious channels, that may not be illegal. [807] Indeed, in my own country of residence (South Africa) we currently (2016) have many leading government officials being implicated by the former public protector of being complicit in state capture.

One of the measures of justice in a country is determined by the level of state corruption. The CPI (Corruption Perceptions Index) generally defines corruption as "the misuse of public power for private benefit." Since 1995 Transparency International has published the CPI, annually ranking countries "by their perceived levels of corruption, as determined by expert assessments and opinion surveys." The diagram below is a world map of the 2015 CPI which measures "the degree to which corruption is perceived to exist among public officials and politicians". High numbers (blue) indicate less perception of corruption, whereas lower numbers (red) indicate higher perception of corruption. [808] The resultant picture certainly doesn't indicate that people perceive a very just society in our world today.

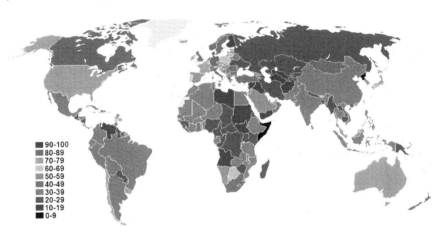

Figure 40: A world map of the 2015 Corruption Perceptions Index [809]

---

[807] http://siteresources.worldbank.org/INTWBIGOVANTCOR/Resources/Legal_Corruption.pdf
[808] https://en.wikipedia.org/wiki/Corruption_Perceptions_Index
[809] Attribution: https://commons.wikimedia.org/wiki/User:Turnless

Justice in the Millennium

But in the Millennium, we will finally have true justice and a righteous government.

> *Isa 11:1-4 A shoot will come up from the stump of Jesse... with righteousness he will judge the needy, with justice he will give decisions for the poor of the earth.*

He will protect the weak and the vulnerable.

> *Isa 42:1-4 Here is my servant, whom I uphold, my chosen one in whom I delight; I will put my Spirit on him and he will bring justice to the nations... A bruised reed he will not break, and a smouldering wick he will not snuff out. In faithfulness he will bring forth justice; he will not falter or be discouraged till he establishes justice on earth. In his law the islands will put their hope.*

Corrupt scoundrels will no longer hold positions of authority.

> *Isa 32:1,5 See, a king will reign in righteousness and rulers will rule with justice... No longer will the fool be called noble nor the scoundrel be highly respected.* (Also Isa 65:22-23, [810] Jer 23:5, [811] Isa 9:7 [812])

Jesus Christ will rule the nations "with an iron sceptre" (Ps 2:6,9). This points to a strong central rule which will deliver prompt justice to nations and individuals who revolt against God. No sin or rebellion will be allowed, because the Lord will withhold rain and send plagues on any who would rebel.

---

[810] Isa 65:22-23 No longer will they build houses and others live in them, or plant and others eat... They will not toil in vain or bear children doomed to misfortune; for they will be a people blessed by the LORD, they and their descendants with them.

[811] Jer 23:5 "The days are coming... when I will raise up to David a righteous Branch, a King who will reign wisely and do what is just and right in the land."

[812] Isa 9:7 ... He will reign on David's throne ... establishing and upholding it with justice and righteousness from that time on and forever.

Zech 14:17-18 If any of the peoples of the earth do not go up to Jerusalem to worship the King, the LORD Almighty, they will have no rain… The LORD will bring on them the plague he inflicts on the nations that do not go up to celebrate the Feast of Tabernacles.

2) War and peace

War in our age

For those Postmillennialists and secular humanists who still believe that man is continually improving (the moral equivalent of evolution) note the following. Although there have been armed conflicts throughout the history of nations, the 'enlightened' 20th century saw more wars than any previous period. Wikipedia lists 355 major wars, revolutions and conflicts in that century. [813] The International Red Cross estimated that over 100 million people were killed in 20th century wars. Four of the ten most costly wars, in terms of loss of life, were waged in the last century. These are of course the two World Wars, followed by the Second Sino-Japanese War and the Russian Civil War. The death toll of World War II, being 60 million plus, surpasses all other war-death-tolls by a factor of two. [814]

Worldwide, an estimated 1.6 million people lost their lives to violence in AD 2000. About half were suicides, one-third were homicides, and one-fifth were casualties of armed conflict. [815] Homicide was the second leading cause of death for people aged 10 to 24 (2001). Suicide was the third leading cause of death for people aged 10 to 24 (2002). [816] In AD 2007, approximately 14,000 terrorist incidents occurred worldwide, and deaths caused increased to 22,000 persons. [817] 2013 saw a

---

[813] http://en.wikipedia.org/wiki/Lists_of_wars
[814] http://en.wikipedia.org/wiki/War
[815] World Report on Violence and Health, WHO, 2002
[816] Web-based Injury Statistics Query and Reporting System - 2002, Centres for Disease Control and Prevention
[817] Report on Terrorist Incidents, 2007, National Counterterrorism Centre

61% increase in the number of people killed in terrorist attacks.[818]

More Americans died in gun homicides and suicides every 6 months than have died in the last 25 years in every terrorist attack and the wars in Afghanistan and Iraq combined. [819] What of the numerous wars, public shootings and other acts of public terror we see and read of daily in the news media? In just the most recent civil war in Syria, we have the worst humanitarian crisis of our time where half the country's pre-war population - more than 11 million people - have been killed or forced to flee their homes.

Peace in the Millennial age

In contrast, the rule by the "Prince of Peace" will be characterized by both national and individual peace and "of the increase of his government and peace there will be no end" (Isa 9:6-7).

> *Isa 14:7 All the lands are at rest and at peace; they break into singing.* (Isa 55:12, [820] Isa 54:13, [821] Isa 66:12 [822])

Unlike their plight today, the people in Israel will live in peace.

> *Jer 30:8-10 'In that day... I will break the yoke off their necks and will tear off their bonds; no longer will foreigners enslave them... Jacob will again have peace and security, and no one will make him afraid.'*

Domestically, there will be no more need for "anti-gun" lobbying and internationally there will be global disarmament, with weapons and war being abolished.

---

[818] 2014 Global Terrorism Index
[819] Nicholas Kristoff, New York Times & www.icasualties.org
[820] Isa 55:12 You will go out in joy and be led forth in peace...
[821] Isa 54:13 ... great will be your children's peace.
[822] Isa 66:12 I will extend peace to her like a river...

Hos 2:18 Bow and sword and battle I will abolish from the land, so that all may lie down in safety. (Also Zech 9: 10, [823] Joel 3:17 [824])

Besides the loss of lives, the financial cost of World War II is estimated at about a trillion US dollars worldwide, making it the costliest war in capital as well as lives. By the end of the war, the European economy had collapsed with 70% of the industrial infrastructure destroyed. Property damage in the Soviet Union inflicted by the Axis invasion was estimated to a value of 679 billion roubles. The combined damage consisted of complete or partial destruction of 1,710 cities and towns, 70,000 villages/hamlets, 2,508 church buildings, 31,850 industrial establishments, 40,000 miles of railroad, 4,100 railroad stations, 40,000 hospitals, 84,000 schools, and 43,000 public libraries. [825]

The cessation of war in the Millennium will result in economic prosperity as there will no longer be a need to spend vast amounts on armaments and defence, nor will there be the vast destruction of life and property caused by war.

> *Isa 2:4 They will beat their swords into ploughshares and their spears into pruning hooks. Nation will not take up sword against nation, nor will they train for war anymore.*[826]

This is certainly not a description of our present world!

3) *Safety*

Safety in our age
Here is some data regarding the state of safety in our present age. It demonstrates the point that we are far from any Millennial age ideal.

---

[823] Zech 9:10 I will take away the chariots from Ephraim and the war-horses from Jerusalem, and the battle bow will be broken. He will proclaim peace to the nations.
[824] Joel 3:17 Jerusalem will be holy; never again will foreigners invade her.
[825] http://en.wikipedia.org/wiki/War
[826] Also Micah 4:4

Homicide

According to UNODC [827] half a million people were intentionally murdered in 2012. The top ten countries with highest murder rates are listed below, from highest to lowest.

Rank	Country	Homicide rate (per 100,000)
1	Honduras	90.4
2	Venezuela	53.7
3	Belize	44.7
4	El Salvador	41.2
5	Guatemala	39.9
6	Jamaica	39.3
7	Swaziland	33.8
8	Saint Kitts and Nevis	33.6
9	South Africa	31
10	Colombia	30.8

Table 13: Homicide rates by country or territory (2012 or latest year) [828]

Treatment of women

What of the plight of women? A 2005 UN report compiled from government sources showed that more than 250,000 cases of rape or attempted rape were recorded by police annually. The reported data covered 65 countries. While the number of recorded rapes is relatively small, it is because it is a severely under-reported crime with surveys showing figures of up to 91.6%. [829]

The 2009 report by the World Economic Forum listed predominantly Islamic nations in the bottom of their annual

---

[827] UN Office on Drugs and Crime
[828] UNODC (United Nations Office on Drugs and Crime)
[829] https://en.wikipedia.org/wiki/Rape_statistics

Global Gender Gap (GGG) index. In fact, the only nation not predominantly Islamic was Benin. [830]

Nation	GGG rank	Population
Pakistan	132	176,242,949
Saudi Arabia	130	28,686,633
Iran	128	66,429,284
Egypt	126	83,082,869
Turkey	129	76,805,524
Qatar	125	833,285
Yemen	134	23,822,783
Mali	127	12,666,987
Chad	133	10,329,208
Morocco	124	34,859,364

Table 14: Global Gender Gap Rank

The Thompson Reuters Foundation reports the following regarding the dilemma of women in 2011. In the DRC 1,150 women are raped every day. In Afghanistan, there is a 1 in 11 chance of dying in childbirth, 87% of women are illiterate, 70 to 80% face forced marriages. In Pakistan 1,000 women and girls are victims of honour killings every year; 90% experience domestic violence. In India 50 million women are 'missing' over the past century due to infanticide and foeticide; 100 million are estimated to be involved in trafficking. In Somalia 95% of girls (mostly ages 4-11) face genital mutilation. [831] These few statistics provide a snapshot of the situation many women face in the world - certainly no Millennial golden age.

---

[830] http://wikiislam.net/wiki/Muslim_Statistics_-_Women - The analysis also excluded other predominantly Islamic nations like Somalia, Sudan, Afghanistan and Iraq.
[831] Ibid

Based on the UNODC 2012 report, here are the top ten countries with the highest robbery rates in the world.

Rank	Country	Rate per 100,000	Robberies
1	Belgium	1,728.1	191,126
2	Spain	1,074.9	502,546
3	Mexico	618.0	746,894
4	Costa Rica	521.6	25,066
5	Brazil	493.1	979,571
6	Chile	467.6	81,664
7	Uruguay	454.0	15,414
8	Trinidad and Tobago	331.7	4,436
9	Panama	264.0	10,038
10	Honduras	226.6	17,980

Table 15: Highest robbery rates in the world (2012) [832]

Millennial safety

Contrast the previous statistics with the safety experienced by the people in the Millennium.

> Ezek 34:28b They will live in safety, and no one will make them afraid. (Ezek 35:27, [833] Isa 60:18, [834] Isa 32:18 [835])

.

Could we honestly apply these verses to our present situation in the world?

---

[832] UNODC (United Nations Office on Drugs and Crime)

[833] Ezek 35:27 ... the people will be secure in their land...

[834] Isa 60:18 No longer will violence be heard in your land, nor ruin or destruction within your borders...

[835] Isa 32:18 My people will live in peaceful dwelling places, in secure homes, in undisturbed places of rest.

4) Joy and depression

Depression in our age

Major depression is the number one psychological disorder in the Western world. It is growing in all age groups, in virtually every community, and the growth is seen mostly in the young, especially teens. [836] In the US, depression is occurring more frequently and at earlier ages than in years past, with the depression rate doubling every 20 years. According to a Harvard Medical Centre study the rate of childhood depression is increasing by 23% a year.

Up to 20% of people experience symptoms of depression. There is 10 times more major depression in people born after 1945 than in those born before. This clearly shows that the root cause of most depression is not a chemical imbalance as human genes do not change that quickly. [837] According to the World Health Organization, at the rate of increase, depression will be the second largest killer after heart disease by 2020. Studies are increasingly linking illness to depression, including osteoporosis, diabetes, heart disease, some forms of cancer, eye disease and back pain. [838] Suicide is the third leading cause of death in 15 to 24 year olds and the fourth leading cause of death in 10 to 14 year olds. [839]

Joy in the Millennial age

The Millennium will be characterized by joy and singing.

> *Isa 35:11 They will enter Zion with singing; everlasting joy will crown their heads. Gladness and joy will overtake them, and sorrow and sighing will flee away.* (See also

---

[836] http://clinical-depression.co.uk/dlp/depression-information/major-depression-facts
[837] Ibid
[838] http://www.holistichealthtools.com/depression_overview.html
[839] American Association of Suicidology, 1996

Isa 55:12, [840] Isa 12:3, [841] Isa 61:2-3, [842] Isa 25:8, [843] Jer 30:18-19, [844] Jer 31:4,13, [845] Zeph 3:14 [846])

The King will personally comfort his people in that day.

Isa 40:1-2 Comfort, comfort my people, says your God. Speak tenderly to Jerusalem, and proclaim to her that her hard service has been completed, that her sin has been paid for, that she has received from the LORD's hand double for all her sins. (Also Isa 49:13-16, [847] Isa 12:1 [848])

5) *Hunger*

Hunger in our age

The WHO (World Health Organization) estimates that about four million people a year die of starvation, or about thirty people every minute. "Some 40,000 hunger-related deaths occur every day, mostly in rural regions," according to World Bank vice president Ismail Serageldin. It is estimated that one third of the world is well-fed, one third is under-fed, and one third is starving. More than 800 million people are chronically undernourished.

---

[840] Isa 55:12 You will go out in joy... the mountains and hills will burst into song before you, and all the trees of the field will clap their hands.

[841] Isa 12:3 With joy you will draw water from the wells of salvation.

[842] Isa 61:2-3 ... to bestow on them... the oil of gladness instead of mourning, and a garment of praise instead of a spirit of despair.

[843] Isa 25:8 The Sovereign LORD will wipe away the tears from all faces...

[844] Jer 30:18-19 "From them (Jerusalem and the palace) will come songs of thanksgiving and the sound of rejoicing."

[845] Jer 31:4,13 ... Again you will take up your tambourines and go out to dance with the joyful ... They will come and shout for joy on the heights of Zion... Then maidens will dance and be glad, young men and old as well. I will turn their mourning into gladness; I will give them comfort and joy instead of sorrow.

[846] Zeph 3:14 Sing, O Daughter of Zion; shout aloud, O Israel! Be glad and rejoice with all your heart, O Daughter of Jerusalem!

[847] Isa 49:13-16 Shout for joy, O heavens; rejoice, O earth; burst into song, O mountains! For the LORD comforts his people and will have compassion on his afflicted ones... "Can a mother forget the baby at her breast and have no compassion on the child she has borne? Though she may forget, I will not forget you! See, I have engraved you on the palms of my hands..."

[848] Isa 12:1 In that day you will say: "I will praise you, O LORD. Although you were angry with me, your anger has turned away and you have comforted me."

According to the World Bank, water shortages in parts of the world in the next 25 years will pose the single greatest threat to food production and human health. 1,3 billion people worldwide have no access to clean water. The terrible irony is that the world can produce enough food to feed its expanding population. While some famines are caused by drought or other natural disasters, most starvation in the world today could be avoided were it not for man's selfishness and inhumanity. War, embargoes, government corruption and economic oppression are all factors of the real problem. While innocent children starve, some rich nations destroy millions of tons of food in order to keep prices artificially high.

The curse removed

In Rev 21:1 we learn that the earth will not be destroyed until after the 1000 years. [849] The existing earth is simply restored during the Millennial period. Irenaeus writes:

> For neither is the substance nor the essence of the creation annihilated (for faithful and true is He who has established it), but the fashion of the world passes away; 1 Corinthians 7:31 that is, those things among which transgression has occurred, since man has grown old in them. [850]

There will be a removal of the curse upon the earth, which began with Adam's fall, and a restoration of the earth's ecology. Previously God told man that because of his sin in Eden:

> *"Cursed is the ground because of you; through painful toil you will eat of it all the days of your life. It will produce thorns and thistles for you…" (Gen 3:17-18)*

But in the Millennium the Edenic state is restored:

---

[849] Rev 21:1 Then I saw a new heaven and a new earth, for the first heaven and the first earth had passed away…
[850] Against Heresies 5.36.1

Ezek 36:34-35 The desolate land will be cultivated instead of lying desolate in the sight of all who pass through it. They will say, 'This land that was laid waste has become like the garden of Eden...'

Irenaeus believed that Paul referred to the restoration of the earth in the Millennium, when he spoke of the creation being "liberated from its bondage to decay and brought into the freedom and glory of the children of God" (Rom 8:21).

It is fitting, therefore, that the creation itself, being restored to its primeval condition, should without restraint be under the dominion of the righteous; and the apostle has made this plain in the Epistle to the Romans, when he thus speaks..." *(he then quotes Rom 8:19-21)* [851]

In the light of Irenaeus' comments, the said passage does appear to be highly relevant to the idea of an earthly millennial kingdom.

Rom 8:19-21 For the creation waits in eager expectation for the children of God to be revealed. For the creation was subjected to frustration, not by its own choice, but by the will of the one who subjected it, in hope that the creation itself will be liberated from its bondage to decay and brought into the freedom and glory of the children of God.

The Earth, and especially the Land of Israel, will become extremely fruitful.

Ezek 34:29 I will provide for them a land renowned for its crops, and they will no longer be victims of famine in the

---

[851] Ibid 5.32.1

land or bear the scorn of the nations. (Also Zech 8:12, [852] Isa 4:2, [853] Jer 31:12, [854] Ezek 35:26-27, [855] Joel 3:18 [856])

The desert will become "a fertile field" (Isa 32:15, [857] also Isa 35:1-2,6-7, [858] Isa 55:13 [859]).

6) *Economy of the Millennial age*

Unemployment and labour in our age

In a 2011 news story, BusinessWeek reported:

> More than 200 million people globally are out of work, a record high, as almost two-thirds of advanced economies and half of developing countries are experiencing a slowdown in employment growth, the group said. [860]

---

[852] Zech 8:12 The seed will grow well, the vine will yield its fruit, the ground will produce its crops, and the heavens will drop their dew.

[853] Isa 4:2 ... the fruit of the land will be the pride and glory of the survivors in Israel.

[854] Jer 31:12 ... they will rejoice in the bounty of the LORD - the grain, the new wine and the oil, the young of the flocks and herds. They will be like a well-watered garden...

[855] Ezek 35:26-27 I will bless them and the places surrounding my hill. I will send down showers in season; there will be showers of blessing. The trees of the field will yield their fruit and the ground will yield its crops...

[856] Joel 3:18 In that day the mountains will drip new wine, and the hills will flow with milk; all the ravines of Judah will run with water. A fountain will flow out of the LORD's house and will water the valley of acacias.

[857] Isa 32:15 till the Spirit is poured on us from on high, and the desert becomes a fertile field, and the fertile field seems like a forest.

[858] Isa 35:1-2,6-7 The desert and the parched land will be glad; the wilderness will rejoice and blossom. Like the crocus, it will burst into bloom; it will rejoice greatly and shout for joy. The glory of Lebanon will be given to it, the splendour of Carmel and Sharon ... Water will gush forth in the wilderness and streams in the desert. The burning sand will become a pool, the thirsty ground bubbling springs. In the haunts where jackals once lay, grass and reeds and papyrus will grow.

[859] Isa 55:13 Instead of the thornbush will grow the pine tree, and instead of briers the myrtle will grow.

[860] http://en.wikipedia.org/wiki/Unemployment

But the Millennial age will not be characterized by any want or need. and there is no hint of idleness. Agriculture as well as construction will provide employment.

> *Isa 65:21 They will build houses and dwell in them; they will plant vineyards and eat their fruit.*

Rather than depicting a period of carnal idleness, the Bible speaks of industrious labour, the abundance being a result of both this and the ideal conditions. Amos speaks of coming days "when the reaper will be overtaken by the ploughman and the planter by the one treading grapes" (Amos 9:13).

> *Ezek. 48:18-19 Its produce will supply food for the workers of the city. The workers from the city who farm it will come from all the tribes of Israel.*

While our current age undergoes cycles of recessions and booms in the world economy, this future perfect labour situation will produce economic abundance, so that there will be no want.

> *Joel 2:22-26 … The trees are bearing their fruit; the fig tree and the vine yield their riches… He sends you abundant showers, both autumn and spring rains, as before. The threshing floors will be filled with grain; the vats will overflow with new wine and oil. 'I will repay you for the years the locusts have eaten… You will have plenty to eat, until you are full…* (Also Isa 30:23-24 [861])

And while Papias may have exaggerated the quantities or misread a metaphor, Ezekiel does in fact foretell an increase in the fruitfulness of individual plants.

> *Ezek 36:29-30 … I will call for the grain and make it plentiful and will not bring famine upon you. I will increase the fruit of the trees and the crops of the field …*

---

[861] Isa 30:23-24 He will also send you rain for the seed you sow in the ground, and the food that comes from the land will be rich and plentiful. In that day your cattle will graze in broad meadows. The oxen and donkeys that work the soil will eat fodder and mash, spread out with fork and shovel.

7) *Health and sickness*

Sickness in our age

In the 1980's some in the medical profession were claiming victory over a wide array of bacterial and viral killers. But instead the cases of infectious diseases actually increased dramatically throughout the 90's. The Associated Press reported:

> The emergence of bacteria strains that cannot be killed by current antibiotics could become a public health threat worse than AIDS. Diseases recently considered conquered are becoming unstoppable... Scientists expect nothing short of a medical disaster. [862]

According to the WHO (World Health Organization) in a 1996 report:

> Drug-resistant strains of microbes are having a deadly impact on the fight against tuberculosis, malaria, cholera, diarrhoea and pneumonia - major diseases which together killed more than 10 million people last year... Many of the most powerful antibiotics have been rendered impotent. The two most common bacteria which are the major cause of death in children through acute respiratory infections, particularly pneumonia, are becoming more and more resistant to drugs. [863]

And the situation is clearly not improving as an updated 2016 report by the WHO indicates:

> Without effective antibiotics, the success of major surgery and cancer chemotherapy would be compromised... Globally, 480 000 people develop multi-drug resistant TB each year, and drug resistance is starting to complicate the fight against HIV and malaria,

---

[862] AP, 26 Mar 95
[863] http://www.who.int/whr/1996/media_centre/press_release/en/index4.html

as well... Antimicrobial resistance happens when microorganisms (such as bacteria, fungi, viruses, and parasites) change when they are exposed to antimicrobial drugs (such as antibiotics, antifungals, antivirals, antimalarials, and anthelmintics). Microorganisms that develop antimicrobial resistance are sometimes referred to as "superbugs". As a result, the medicines become ineffective and infections persist in the body, increasing the risk of spread to others... In 2010, an estimated 7% of people starting antiretroviral therapy (ART) in developing countries had drug-resistant HIV. In developed countries, the same figure was 10–20%. Some countries have recently reported levels at or above 15% amongst those starting HIV treatment, and up to 40% among people re-starting treatment. This requires urgent attention. [864]

Infectious diseases are a leading cause of death, accounting for a quarter to a third of the estimated 54 million deaths worldwide in 1998. [865] The rate of infectious diseases in the US increased 58% between 1980 and 1992, according to JAMA (Journal of American Medical Association). [866] According to a CIA study:

- ❖ Twenty well-known infectious diseases such as tuberculosis, malaria, and cholera have re-emerged or spread since 1973, some appearing in "deadlier, drug-resistant forms".
- ❖ At least 30 previously unknown disease agents have been identified since 1973, including human immunodeficiency virus (HIV), Ebola, hepatitis C, and Nipah virus, for which no cures are available.
- ❖ Of the seven biggest killers worldwide, TB, malaria, hepatitis, and, in particular, HIV/AIDS continue to surge, with HIV/AIDS and TB likely to account for the overwhelming majority of deaths from infectious diseases in developing countries by 2020.

---

[864] http://www.who.int/mediacentre/factsheets/fs194/en/
[865] National Intelligence Estimate 99-17D: The Global Infectious Disease Threat and Its Implications for the United States, January 2000
[866] http://jama.ama-assn.org/content/275/3/189.abstract

❖ Acute lower respiratory infections--including pneumonia and influenza--as well as diarrheal diseases and measles, appear to have peaked at high incidence levels. There is, however, always the possibility of an influenza pandemic such as "Spanish flu" of 1918-1920, which actually appears to have originated in the US. By whatever name, that virus, of serotype H1N1 (i.e., different than the H5N1 "bird flu") killed between 40 and 50 million people. Its genome has been sequenced, there is a much better understanding of why it was so lethal, and there are some meaningful treatments. Those treatments, however, require, at the least, a robust pharmaceutical industry with appropriately fast drug distribution, and, at the higher levels of care, respiratory intensive care. Not even the most developed nations have adequate ICUs to handle a major epidemic; SARS was a warning in a city with the excellent medical facilities of Toronto. [867]

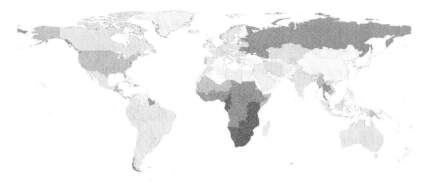

Figure 41: A global view of HIV infection (Source: WHO) in 2009. The darkest areas indicate 15 - 28% prevalence in adults.

According to the WHO and UNAIDS (the Joint UN Programme on HIV/AIDS) at the end of 1999, an estimated 34.3 million people were living with HIV/AIDS. By 2009, worldwide 33.3 million people were living with HIV. Besides these infectious

---

[867] http://en.wikipedia.org/wiki/CIA_transnational_health_and_economic_activities

diseases, there is also cancer, which is non-infectious. According to the WHO, in 2008 alone 7.6 million people worldwide died from cancer. [868]

Health in the Millennial age

When Jesus rules on earth, sickness will no longer be a problem because, "the sun of righteousness shall arise with healing in its wings" (Malachi 4:2). The ministry of our King as a healer will be seen throughout the age, so that sickness will be removed and "no one living in Zion will say, 'I am ill'" (Isa 33:24).

> Isa 35:5-6 Then will the eyes of the blind be opened and the ears of the deaf unstopped. Then will the lame leap like a deer, and the mute tongue shout for joy. (Also Isa 29:18 [869])

Even stuttering and feeble-mindedness will be healed.

> Isa 32:4 The mind of the rash will know and understand, and the stammering tongue will be fluent and clear.

8) Life expectancy

In our age

In our age life expectancy in 2010 was estimated at 77-90 years (in developed countries) and 32-80 years (in developing countries).[870] While life expectancies around the world are on the gradual increase, they are nothing close to the lifespans we saw in the antediluvians (i.e. pre-Flood) world, or to what Isaiah predicted would occur in the Millennial era.

---

[868] http://www.who.int/cancer/en/
[869] Isa 29:18 In that day the deaf will hear the words of the scroll, and out of gloom and darkness the eyes of the blind will see.
[870] https://en.wikipedia.org/wiki/Longevity

In the Millennial age

While a person who lives to 100 will be considered exceptional in terms of longevity in our age, in the Millennium, they will be considered a child, since, presumably, a person could live throughout the entire 1000 years in the restored environment. So longevity will be restored to that experienced by the antediluvians.

> *Isa 65:20 Never again will there be in it an infant who lives but a few days, or an old man who does not live out his years; he who dies at a hundred will be thought a mere youth; he who fails to reach a hundred will be considered accursed.*

The oldest tree now living is a 4600+ year old bristlecone called 'Methuselah' in the White Mountains of California. And Isaiah writes of the Millennial age:

> *For as the days of a tree, so will be the days of my people; my chosen ones will long enjoy the works of their hands. (Isa 65:22)*

9) *Population in the Millennial age*

Those who go into the Millennium in their natural bodies will have children throughout the age and the earth will be repopulated. The resurrected and formerly raptured saints will be immortal and rule with Christ. Without war, famine, disease and pestilence, in addition to the increased longevity, the earth's population should explode. The Jewish population will also boom.

> *Ezek 37:26 I will establish them and increase their numbers ...* (Also Ezek 36:37-38 [871])

---

[871] Ezek 36:37-38 Once again I will yield to the plea of the house of Israel and do this for them: I will make their people as numerous as sheep, as numerous as the flocks for offerings at Jerusalem during her appointed feasts. So will the ruined cities be filled with flocks of people...

Those born in this age will still have a sinful nature, so salvation will still be required, but there will be no more curse and no more original (inherited) sin.

> *Jer 31:29-30 In those days people will no longer say, 'The fathers have eaten sour grapes, and the children's teeth are set on edge.' Instead, everyone will die for his own sin; whoever eats sour grapes - his own teeth will be set on edge.*

10) Education and knowledge

Knowledge in our age

Despite the situation being far from ideal, literacy seems to be one of the few areas where we are making movement in the right direction. The relative literacy rate has improved astonishingly in the last 2 centuries. This is partly due to the fact that in the last century, school enrolment and attendance increased dramatically, as did the years of schooling, along with reductions in the gender inequalities of the educated.

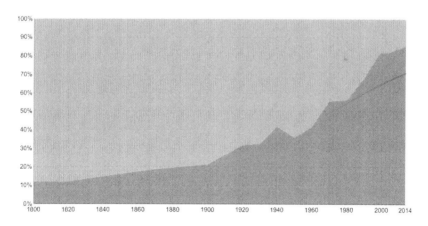

Figure 42: Relative literate and illiterate world population, 1800 to 2014 [872]

---

[872] Literate World Population (Our World In Data based on OECD and UNESCO)

However, it is also clear that the delivery of education in the world (in the West and Communist countries in particular) has become increasingly secularised. While the levels in education have risen, much of the material taught is based on a humanist anti-religious worldview. E.g. in the US:

> Courts have ruled that public schools must conduct secular programs of study that keep religious espousal, guidance, and practice out of the public schools' curriculum and instruction. Schools also are required to serve all the youngsters—both religious and nonreligious—fairly and equitably. [873]

While this is supposed to mean that education should be "religiously neutral", more often this equates to an anti-religious or in particular anti-Christian bias in the material taught, or the manner in which it is presented. The ideas of American psychologist and educational reformer John Dewey (1859-1952) have probably had more impact on American education than anyone else. Yet he has been referred to by critics as a "totalitarian socialist who envisioned total government control over all education through the agency of public schools." [874]

> Dewey was especially influential as the philosopher of "progressive education." He sought the reconstruction of society through education in which children discovered knowledge for themselves rather than repeat rote learning. Dewey was one of the main intellectual forces behind American liberalism… [875]

Along with Charles Darwin, Karl Marx, Julius Wellhausen, Sigmund Freud, John Maynard Keynes and Soren Kierkegaard; John Dewey was listed by Dave Breese as one of "7 Men Who Rule the World from the Grave" in the book with the same title. But according to the scholar Steven C. Rockefeller, Dewey was keenly interested in gutting what he saw as Christianity's "false" and "harmful" supernatural characteristics. Initially Dewey

---

[873] http://worldvieweducation.org/untyingtangle.html
[874] http://www.conservapedia.com/John_Dewey
[875] Ibid

believed he possessed a deep philosophical understanding of Christianity, but he rejected the Incarnation and all other biblical miracles. [876] But as an atheist and a secular humanist in his later life, he participated with a variety of humanistic activities from the 1930s into the 1950s, which included sitting on the advisory board of Charles Francis Potter's First Humanist Society of New York (1929); being one of the original 34 signatories of the first Humanist Manifesto (1933) and being elected an honorary member of the Humanist Press Association (1936). [877] According to Will Durant, "What distinguished Dewey was the undisguised completeness with which he accepted the evolution theory... His starting point in every field was Darwinian." [878]

Dewey viewed conservative Christianity (i.e. Protestant fundamentalism and mainline Catholicism) as a dark, evil lair harbouring political enemies if not intellectual rivals of his own philosophy. This can be seen in part in a 1924 essay titled "Fundamentals" written for the New Republic. [879]

> Those traditionalists and literalists who have arrogated to themselves the title of fundamentalists recognize of course no mean between their dogmas and blank, dark, hopeless uncertainty and unsettlement. Until they have been reborn into the life of intelligence, they will not be aware that there are a steadily increasing number of persons who find security in methods of inquiry, of observation, experiment, of forming and following working hypotheses.

Historian Edward A. White proposed that it was Dewey's work that had led to the rift between science and religion in the 20th century. [880] Dewey wrote a book entitled "A Common Faith" which proposes a religion of humanity to replace biblical religion

---

[876] "John Dewey: Religious Faith and Democratic Humanism", Rockefeller, p.442
[877] https://en.wikipedia.org/wiki/John_Dewey
[878] Will Durant, The Story of Philosophy (1961), 522.
[879] "John Dewey: Religious Faith and Democratic Humanism", Rockefeller, p.442
[880] Science and Religion in American Thought (1952)

and to redirect the religious impulse from heavenly things to earthly things. [881] His book, "Democracy and Education", was listed by Human Events magazine as fifth in a list of the ten most harmful books of the 19th and 20th centuries behind The Communist Manifesto by Karl Marx, Mein Kampf by Adolf Hitler, Quotations from Chairman Mao by Mao Zedong, and the Kinsey Report by Alfred Kinsey. [882] Yet this is the man with the greatest influence on Western secular education.

Knowledge in the Millennial age

In the Millennium, knowledge will abound "for the earth will be full of the knowledge of the LORD as the waters cover the sea" (Isa 11:9). But the King will lead the subjects of his kingdom into godly understanding and knowledge, untainted by the secular humanism of our age.

❖ *Isa 54:13 All your sons will be taught by the LORD…*

11) *Animals in the Millennial age*

Animal creation will be changed so as to lose their venom and ferocity. They will be friendly to one another and to humans.

> *Isa 11:6-9 The wolf will live with the lamb, the leopard will lie down with the goat, the calf and the lion and the yearling together; and a little child will lead them. The cow will feed with the bear, their young will lie down together, and the lion will eat straw like the ox. The infant will play near the hole of the cobra, and the young child put his hand into the viper's nest. They will neither harm nor destroy on all my holy mountain…*

Incidentally the "lion lying down with the lamb" symbolism is a misquote. It's the wolf living with the lamb and the leopard lying

---

[881] http://creationmoments.com/resources/articles/education/educationtext books/evolving-child-john-deweys-impact-modern-education--0
[882] http://www.conservapedia.com/John_Dewey

down with the goat. (Also Isa 65:25, [883] Ezek 34:28, [884] Ezek 35:25. [885]) For those in any doubt as to whether or not we're in the Millennium now, you can perform a simple experiment to test the thesis. Put a wolf and a lamb together and see what happens. The only way a wolf lies down with a lamb today - is when the lamb is in its stomach! Irenaeus writes of these Scriptures:

> I am quite aware that some persons endeavour to refer these words to the case of savage men, both of different nations and various habits, who come to believe, and when they have believed, act in harmony with the righteous. But although this is [true] now with regard to some men coming from various nations to the harmony of the faith, nevertheless in the resurrection of the just [the words shall also apply] to those animals mentioned. For God is rich in all things. And it is right that when the creation is restored, all the animals should obey and be in subjection to man, and revert to the food originally given by God (for they had been originally subjected in obedience to Adam), that is, the productions of the earth.[886]

John Walvoord notes how these passages, if interpreted literally, undoubtedly refer to an earthly Millennium.

> Isaiah 11 paints the graphic picture of the reign of Christ on earth, a scene which cannot be confused with the present age, the intermediate state, or the eternal state if interpreted in any normal literal sense. As presented it describes the millennial earth... The description... describes animals such as wolves, lambs, leopards, kids, calves, young lions, all of which are creatures of earth

---

[883] Isa 65:25 The wolf and the lamb will feed together, and the lion will eat straw like the ox, but dust will be the serpent's food. They will neither harm nor destroy on all my holy mountain...
[884] Ezek 34:28 ... nor will wild animals devour them.
[885] Ezek 35:25 I will ... rid the land of wild beasts so that they may live in the desert and sleep in the forests in safety.
[886] Against Heresies 5.33.4

and not of heaven, and further pictures them in a time of tranquillity such as only can apply to the millennial earth.[887]

12) *Geographical changes*

The Mount of Olives will be split at Jesus Second Coming (Zech 14:4 [888]) and there will be a river stretching from the Mediterranean to the Dead Sea, flowing through Jerusalem (*Zech 14:8* [889]). There will be changes to the Red Sea and Euphrates River.

> *Isa 11:15 The LORD will dry up the gulf of the Egyptian sea; with a scorching wind he will sweep his hand over the Euphrates River. He will break it up into seven streams so that men can cross over in sandals.*

13) *Increase of light in the Millennial age*

There will be a radical increase of both solar and lunar light. While many feel compelled to interpret this passage allegorically, there is no reason why there should not be a literal fulfilment of this prophecy.

> *Isa 30:26 The moon will shine like the sun, and the sunlight will be seven times brighter, like the light of seven full days, when the LORD binds up the bruises of his people and heals the wounds he inflicted.*

---

[887] http://walvoord.com/article/73 - The Doctrine of the Millennium—Part I: The Righteous Government of the Millennium.

[888] Zech 14:4 On that day his feet will stand on the Mount of Olives, east of Jerusalem, and the Mount of Olives will be split in two from east to west, forming a great valley, with half of the mountain moving north and half moving south.

[889] Zech 14:8 On that day living water will flow out from Jerusalem, half to the eastern sea and half to the western sea, in summer and in winter.

To those who object on the basis of an associated increase in heat, it seems that God will protect people from this occurrence (Isa 4:5-6 [890]).

14) Israel restored

Jews will no longer be despised - in stark contrast to the anti-Semitism of our present age (Zech 8:13 [891]). Jews will be held in high esteem and treated accordingly.

> *Zech 8:23... In those days ten men from all languages and nations will take firm hold of one Jew by the hem of his robe and say, 'Let us go with you, because we have heard that God is with you.'*

Figure 43: 'Brave' Nazi soldiers brutalizing a Jew in Poland - Are we in the kingdom of God now?

---

[890] Isa 4:5-6 Then the Lord will create over all of Mount Zion and over those who assemble there a cloud of smoke by day and a glow of flaming fire by night; over everything the glory will be a canopy. It will be a shelter and shade from the heat of the day, and a refuge and hiding place from the storm and rain.

[891] Zech 8:13 "As you have been an object of cursing among the nations, O Judah and Israel, so will I save you, and you will be a blessing. Do not be afraid, but let your hands be strong."

The previous picture shows four men taking hold of one Jew in our age, hardly a fulfilment of Millennial promises!

Israel restored territorially

The Jews will return to Israel. The fulfilment of this has already started in our age, but at present still fewer than a third of the Jews in the world are in Israel.

> *Isa 14:1 The LORD will have compassion on Jacob; once again he will choose Israel and will settle them in their own land.* (Also Ezek 36:21, [892] Ezek 37:21-22 [893])

After the time of Jacob's Trouble in the Tribulation, we know that one third of the population of Israel will enter the Millennium (Zech 13:8-9 [894]).

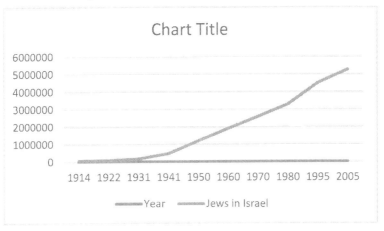

Figure 44: Jews in Israel 1914-2005

---

[892] Ezek 36:21 For I will take you out of the nations; I will gather you from all the countries and bring you back into your own land.

[893] Ezek 37:21-22 … I will take the Israelites out of the nations where they have gone. I will gather them from all around and bring them back into their own land. I will make them one nation in the land, on the mountains of Israel.

[894] Zech 13:8-9 "In the whole land… two-thirds will be struck down and perish; yet one-third will be left in it. This third I will bring into the fire; I will refine them like silver and test them like gold. They will call on my name and I will answer them; I will say, 'They are my people,' and they will say, 'The LORD is our God.'"

Irenaeus was probably the first to argue that a future earthly Millennial kingdom is necessary because of the land promises to Abraham.

> Now God made promise of the earth to Abraham and his seed; yet neither Abraham nor his seed... do now receive any inheritance in it; but they shall receive it at the resurrection of the just. [895]

He holds that the words of Jesus in Matt 5:5, ("Blessed are the meek, for they shall inherit the earth") will have a literal fulfilment in the Millennium. [896] In another place, he explains that the blessing to Jacob:

> ... belongs unquestionably to the times of the kingdom when the righteous will bear rule, after their rising from the dead. It is also the time when the creation will bear fruit with an abundance of all kinds of food, having been renovated and set free... And all of the animals will feed on the vegetation of the earth... and they will be in perfect submission to man.[897]

The full territory promised by God to Abraham will belong to Israel i.e. from the River Euphrates to the Nile River.

> *Gen 15:18 (NASB) On that day the LORD made a covenant with Abram, saying, "To your descendants I have given this land, From the river of Egypt as far as the great river, the river Euphrates..."*

This promised area comprises all of modern Israel, the Palestinian Territories, Lebanon, Syria, Jordan, part of Iraq, Saudi Arabia and Turkey. While there is debate over the exact size of the area, depending on the interpretation of the shape of

---

[895] Against Heresies 5.32.2
[896] Ibid 5.32.2
[897] Ibid 5.33.3

the area between the Euphrates and the Nile, there can be no question that it included the Sinai Peninsula and the part of Egypt east of the Nile river. Like Irenaeus, Premillennialists today assert that Israel has never held all this territory specified in Gen 15:18; therefore in order for God to fulfil his promise to Abraham - this necessitates a complete fulfilment in the Millennium.

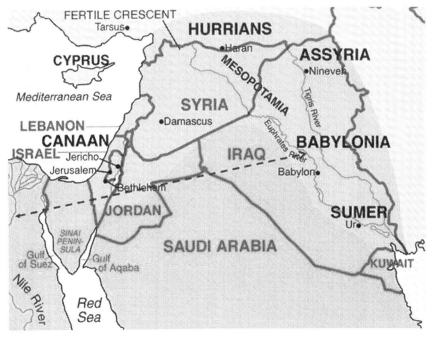

Figure 45: The territory promised to Abraham extended from the Euphrates to the Nile River, including the Sinai Peninsula and Egypt east of the Nile.

But some Amillennialists use the following Scripture to assert that in Solomon's reign, Israel actually did hold this territory.

> *2 Chron 9:26 He ruled over all the kings from the Euphrates River to the land of the Philistines, as far as the border of Egypt.*

As a result, combined with their views on Replacement Theology, they summarily dismiss the future fulfilment of this land claim as being a valid argument for an earthly Millennial kingdom. Hence Wayne Jackson writes:

> *There is no land promise awaiting the Jewish people in the future. The Hebrew people lost their deed to material territory as a result of their spiritual rebellion, which was consummated by their murder of the Messiah. (see Joshua 23:15-16). The only hope now for those of Jewish background is in the gospel of Jesus Christ (Romans 1:16-17).* [898]

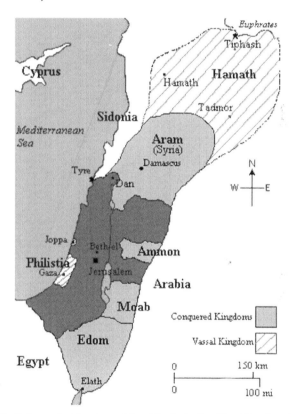

Figure 46: Solomon's kingdom did not include the Sinai Peninsula and the border was still far from reaching the eastern tributaries of the Nile

---

[898] https://www.christiancourier.com/articles/402-genesis-15-18-will-israel-once-again-possess-the-promised-land - Genesis 15:18 - Will Israel Once Again Possess the Promised Land?

But 2 Chron 9:26 indicated that Solomon's territory only extended to the "border of Egypt", not to the Nile. Hence to support their claim, Amillennialists argue that the term "river of Egypt" actually refers to the Wadi Al Arish on the Sinai Peninsula, and not to the Nile River. However one can hardly argue that to use the term "river of Egypt" without further qualification, could refer to anything but the Nile. Church of England commentator Charles Ellicott (1819-1905) writes of Gen 15:18:

> The river of Egypt - That is, the Nile. In the Hebrew the Wadi-el-Arish, on the southern border of Simeon, is always distinguished from the Nile, though the distinction is neglected in our version. Thus in Numbers 34:5; Joshua 15:4; Isaiah 27:12 (where alone an attempt is made at accuracy by translating stream), the Hebrew has, the torrent of Egypt, that is, a stream full after the rains, but dry during the rest of the year… The word used here signifies a river that flows constantly; and Abram's posterity are to found a kingdom conterminous with the Nile and the Euphrates, that is, with Egypt and Babylonia.[899]

Whenever a wadi is meant, the Hebrew word is 'nahal', a feminine noun meaning a stream bed that is sometimes dry and sometimes has water flowing through it, depending on the amount of rain in the area at any given time. But the word used in Gen 15:18 is 'nahar', a masculine noun meaning a large, flowing river e.g. every Biblical reference to the Euphrates River uses this word exclusively. But, perhaps influenced by this Amillennial sidestep, NIV translators render the promise to Abraham as follows:

> Gen 15:18 (NIV) …"To your descendants I give this land, from the Wadi of Egypt to the great river, the Euphrates…"

---

[899] http://biblehub.com/commentaries/genesis/15-18.htm

We have already noted that the NASB provides a more literal translation, without applying any eschatological bias. So do most English versions, including the ESV and KJV.

- ❖ *Gen 15:18 (ESV) "... from the river of Egypt to the great river, the river Euphrates"*
- ❖ *Gen 15:18 (KJV) ... from the river of Egypt unto the great river, the river Euphrates*

The Hebrew word translated "river" remains the same in both instances, giving no justification for substituting the word for 'wadi' in the same verse, unless perhaps an attempt is being made to move the border back to the opposite side of the Sinai Peninsula to imply an earlier fulfilment of the covenant.

STRONGS	TRANSLIT	HEBREW	ENGLISH
776	hā-'ā-reṣ	הָאָרֶץ	Land
2063	haz-zōṯ,	הַזֹּאת	This
5104	min-nə-har	מִנְּהַר	From the river
4714	miṣ-ra-yim,	מִצְרַיִם	Of Egypt
5704	'aḏ-	עַד-	To
5104	han-nā-hār	הַנָּהָר	the river
1419	hag-gā-ḏōl	הַגָּדֹל	Great
5104	nə-har-	נְהַר-	the river
6578	pə-rāṯ.	פְּרָת׃	Euphrates

Table 16: Gen 15:18 in Hebrew [900]

Consequently if "the river of Egypt" refers to the easternmost branch of the Nile (or more precisely the Pelusian arm - a no longer extant branch of the Nile), the promise to Abraham would include what is called the Sinai Peninsula, which historically has always belonged to Egypt. Thus "the border of Egypt" in Solomon's time would have been east of the Sinai Peninsula, while the Nile is further west.

---

[900] http://biblehub.com/text/genesis/15-18.htm

Furthermore, to assign the fulfilment of this remarkable prophecy to a period less than 40 years in duration is somewhat of an anticlimactic fulfilment. In the context of discussing Israel's covenant, Paul speak of "God's gifts" as being "irrevocable". Thus in light of the promised restoration of Israel spoken of in Romans 11, it seems reasonable that this promise to Abraham points to a more complete Millennial fulfilment, coinciding with Israel's spiritual restoration.

Israel restored spiritually

We saw earlier how Ezekiel's vision of the valley of dry bones points to a two-phase restoration of Israel, namely land restoration (Ezek 37:12) and then spiritual restoration (Ezek 37:14). We noted how the Jews will recognize Jesus as the Messiah and repent over their previous rejection of him (Zech 12:10-11) and that they will express regret for their former sin (Ezek 36:28-31). There will be no spiritual deception. Satan's activity in the world will cease after he is bound and thus unable to deceive the world's inhabitants. (See Zech 14:9, [901] Isa 11:10 [902]).

Figure 47: Sharing your recent trip to Egypt with an Amillennialist

---

[901] Zech 14:9 On that day there will be one LORD, and his name the only name.
[902] Isa 11:10 In that day the Root of Jesse will stand as a banner for the peoples; the nations will rally to him, and his place of rest will be glorious.

CHAPTER 11: THE GREAT APOSTASY

> *1 Tim 3:1-5 But mark this: There will be terrible times in the last days. People will be lovers of themselves, lovers of money, boastful, proud, abusive, disobedient to their parents, ungrateful, unholy, without love, unforgiving, slanderous, without self-control, brutal, not lovers of the good, treacherous, rash, conceited, lovers of pleasure rather than lovers of God - having a form of godliness but denying its power.*

In stark contrast to Premillennialists, most Postmillennialists do not believe in an end-time apostasy, and some like B. B. Warfield, believe that the apostasy refers to the Jews' rejection of Christianity either during the 1st century, or possibly until the return of Christ at the end of the 'Millennium'. [903] Modern adherents of Dominion theologies like "Kingdom Now" theology and Reconstructionism still hold that in the End Times godliness will eventually pervade secular society.

> This dominion mentality is conceived as a gigantic end-time revival that will sweep the whole earth in its wake. Some even refer to a billion souls being swept in to the kingdom. An elite company of overcomers from out of the larger church will subdue all things and will be so endued with supernatural power that the first church apostles will be envious of the latter day apostles. [904]

---

[903] https://en.wikipedia.org/wiki/Postmillennialism
[904] http://so4j.com/new-apostolic-reformation-latter-rain#latter_rain_early_pentecostals

So, while Paul tells Timothy, "there will be terrible times in the last days" some are trying to 'correct' Paul by saying, "there will be great times in the last days." And who can forget the sobering words spoken by Jesus, "However, when the Son of Man comes, will he find faith on the earth?" (Luke 18:8).

Figure 48: Terrible times or great times?

Jesus cautions his disciples against an end time apostasy:

> *"At that time many will turn away from the faith and will betray and hate each other, and many false prophets will appear and deceive many people. Because of the increase of wickedness, the love of most will grow cold, but he who stands firm to the end will be saved." (Matt 24:10-13)*

Paul seemingly speaks of this very same apostasy, telling the Thessalonians that the Lord has not come yet (as some were teaching) because this apostasy hadn't yet occurred.

> *2 Thess 2:3 Let no one in any way deceive you, for it will not come unless the apostasy comes first, and the man of lawlessness is revealed, the son of destruction…*

Paul speaks not of a Christian reformed society, but of an endtime world that is deluded by the Antichrist and people who believe a lie.

> *2 Thess 2:10-12... They perish because they refused to love the truth and so be saved. For this reason God sends them a powerful delusion so that they will believe the lie and so that all will be condemned who have not believed the truth but have delighted in wickedness.*

When studying the Book of Revelation chapters 2 to 3, we read the letters of Jesus to the seven churches. Although these were seven literal churches in Asia Minor, they are also typical of seven periods of Church history. The last church mentioned was in Laodicea, which presented a state of lukewarmness, indifference, materialism and apostasy characteristic of much of the Western Church today. Of the 7 churches listed, this is the only church which receives no praise from Jesus.

No	Church	+/- Period	Church Age
1	Ephesus	30 - 100	Apostolic Church
2	Smyrna	100 - 300	Persecuted Church
3	Pergamum	300 - 600	State Church
4	Thyatira	600 - 1500	Papal Church
5	Sardis	1500 - 1700	Reformation Church
6	Philadelphia	1700 - 1900	Missionary Church
7	Laodicea	1900 -	Apostate Church

Table 17: The 7 church ages

In contrast to the optimistic view held by Postmillennialists regarding the conversion of the world, in a lecture given in Geneva in 1840, John Nelson Darby insisted:

> What we are about to consider will tend to show that, instead of permitting ourselves to hope for a continued progress of good, we must expect a progress of evil; and that the hope of the earth being filled with the knowledge of the Lord before the exercise of His judgement, and the

consummation of this judgement on the earth, is delusive. We are to expect evil, until it becomes so flagrant that it will be necessary for the Lord to judge it... I am afraid than many a cherished feeling, dear to the children of God, has been shocked this evening; I mean, their hope that the gospel will spread by itself over the whole earth during the actual dispensation. [905]

Unfinished work

But isn't this attitude of Darby's a hindrance to evangelism and missions and an impediment to Christians fulfilling the Great Commission? After all, didn't Jesus himself say, "And this gospel of the kingdom will be preached in the whole world as a testimony to all nations, and then the end will come" (Matt 24:14)? The gospel must indeed be preached to all nations, but not all will respond positively. While it is true that one third of the world has never heard the gospel, it is also true that another third has heard it and rejected it. The duty of Christians in order to accomplish the Great Commission and fulfil the above prophecy by Jesus is to ensure that all who have not heard, get an opportunity to have the gospel presented to them.

In 2007 researchers David B. Barrett and Todd M. Johnson estimated the number of unreached people to be 1.8 billion people. [906] The term "unreached" does not apply to those who have rejected Jesus – but to those who have never heard of Jesus! Despite Jesus' command to evangelize, one third of all humans have never even heard of his name. And while we all look forward to the return of Jesus, we have unfinished work! Oswald J. Smith (1889-1986), a Canadian pastor, author and missions advocate, said, "We talk of the Second Coming; half the world has never heard of the first".

While some seemingly insinuate that Postmillennialism is the only motivator for all evangelism and mission work and almost

---

[905] J. N. Darby, 'Progress of Evil on the Earth' Collected Writings., Prophetic, Vol. 1, pp. 471, 483
[906] World Christian Trends AD 30-AD 2000

imply that this said movement was solely responsible for all the great missionary endeavours, it is simply not true. In fact, it wasn't even true of Darby himself. Darby was a zealous missionary and personally founded Plymouth Brethren churches as far away as Germany, Switzerland, France and the US. [907] The churches Darby planted in turn sent missionaries to Africa, the West Indies, Australia and New Zealand, so that by the time of his death in 1885, around 1500 Plymouth Brethren churches had already been founded world-wide. [908]

Hudson Taylor, the renowned missionary to inland China and founder of China Inland Mission (now OMF International) is just one example of a mission zealot who traced his roots to the Plymouth Brethren. Other missionaries and evangelists linked in some way to the Brethren were: [909]

- ❖ James George Deck - evangelist and missionary to New Zealand.
- ❖ Anthony Norris Groves - missionary to Baghdad and India.
- ❖ George Müller - missionary, evangelist and founder of the Bristol Orphanage.
- ❖ Watchman Nee - the leader in the "Little Flock" movement in China, was originally inspired by books from Plymouth Brethren teachers like Darby, William Kelly and C.H. Mackintosh.
- ❖ John Parnell - missionary to Mesopotamia. [910]

What of revival?

But what about Joel's prophecy which features so prominently in Latter Rain teaching and which seems to indicate an end-time revival?

---

[907] http://www.thebiblicalworldview.org/john-nelson-darby-father-of-di/
[908] Joseph Canfield, The Incredible Scofield and his Book (1988), pp. 122 ff.
[909] https://en.wikipedia.org/wiki/Plymouth_Brethren
[910] Incidentally other notable Brethren include Joseph M. Scriven - writer of the words to the hymn "What a friend we have in Jesus" and William Edwy Vine - author of Vine's Expository Dictionary of Old and New Testament Words and numerous commentaries.

> *Joel 2:28 "And afterward, I will pour out my Spirit on all people. Your sons and daughters will prophesy, your old men will dream dreams, your young men will see visions."*

Firstly, Peter quoted this as being fulfilled on Pentecost (Acts 2:15-18 [911]). Secondly, while it is true that the context of Joel seems to indicate a later more complete fulfilment, it points to an ultimate fulfilment in the Millennial reign of Christ i.e. to "the survivors whom the Lord calls" after the events of the sun turning to darkness and the moon to blood, which happens during the Tribulation.

> *Joel 2:29-33 "Even on my servants, both men and women, I will pour out my Spirit in those days. I will show wonders in the heavens and on the earth, blood and fire and billows of smoke. The sun will be turned to darkness and the moon to blood before the coming of the great and dreadful day of the Lord. And everyone who calls on the name of the Lord will be saved; for on Mount Zion and in Jerusalem there will be deliverance, as the Lord has said, even among the survivors whom the Lord calls."*

A statement issued by the US Assemblies of God in 2000 explains:

> Only after this destruction of the instrument of judgment does the promised revival come. "And afterward, I will pour out my Spirit on all people" (Joel 2:28). It is a complete misinterpretation of Scripture to find in Joel's army of locusts a militant, victorious force attacking society and a non-cooperating Church to prepare the earth for Christ's millennial reign. [912]

---

[911] Acts 2:15-18 These people are not drunk, as you suppose. It's only nine in the morning! No, this is what was spoken by the prophet Joel: "'In the last days, God says, I will pour out my Spirit on all people. Your sons and daughters will prophesy, your young men will see visions, your old men will dream dreams...'"

[912] "Assemblies of God Position Paper on End Time revival" http://ag.org/top/ Beliefs/Position_Papers/pp_downloads/pp_endtime_revival.pdf

After "Joel's army of locusts" judgement, God promises restoration to Israel:

> *Joel 2:25 "I will repay you for the years the locusts have eaten - the great locust and the young locust, the other locusts and the locust swarm - my great army that I sent among you."*

Consequently, while Joel 2:25 is used to further bolster the teachings of the current Restoration Movement, it actually refers a future Millennial period.

Should we retreat?

Premillennialists are often accused by Postmillennialists of retreatism and isolationism - and in certain cases, this is a fair accusation. Some Christians are so shocked by the evil in the world that they are just waiting for Jesus' return, without doing anything in terms of completing the Great Commission. They simply want to gather in a 'laager' [913] and "hold out" till Jesus comes back. So, should we, like Jesus' disciples did after his death, be hiding behind closed doors from the world? Those who would despair at the thought of a world growing more increasingly wicked, need to remember that it is possible for the Church to experience revival in areas, while in other areas the world is seemingly getting more wicked and dark - the two can happen together. When Peter quoted the passage from Joel on the day of Pentecost, there was a mighty revival in Jerusalem, but not all were saved. There were still those who opposed the gospel and later a persecution of Christians even broke out in Jerusalem. The great move of God that Paul initiated in many areas, all over the known world, was frequently accompanied by persecution from a wicked pagan society or even by established religion.

---

[913] The word 'laager' is Afrikaans in origin and refers to an improvised mobile military formation used by the Voortrekkers, whereby they would arrange ox-wagons into a circle as a form of defence for themselves and their animals.

While the Scriptures do not speak of a Postmillennial world, where godliness pervades society, the church can still experience revival -despite being surrounded by increasing darkness and evil in the world. Indeed, that is exactly what we are seeing today. While the Western church is in decline, the Third World (Asia, Africa and South America) church is experiencing revival. Christianity, which a century ago was overwhelmingly the religion of Europe and the Americas, has made a historic advance into Africa and Asia.

Year	% Christians in Europe & N. America	% Christians in Latin America, Africa & Asia
1800	99%	1%
1900	90%	10%
1985	50%	50%
2010	31%	69%

Table 18: Source: Joshua Project

54% of evangelical Christians are non-whites. [914] True Christianity has grown by more than 300 million believers in the past 10 years. 10 million (3%) from North America and Europe while 290 million (97%) from developing countries like Nigeria, Brazil, India and China. [915] Converts daily are estimated at:

❖ 28,000-37,000 Chinese
❖ 34,000 South American
❖ 23,000-25,000 African [916]

So interestingly the Western church - that has spawned both the prosperity doctrine and the ideas of Postmillennial glory - is in decline, while the poor and persecuted church of Asia and Africa is experiencing growth and revival.

---

[914] World Evangelization Research Centre
[915] Joshua Project
[916] David Barrett

Figure 49: The new faces of true Christianity

When Jesus spoke of a nobleman (representing himself), who first went to a faraway country (heaven) to receive a kingdom, and then returned later (the Second Coming) - his servants were told to, "Occupy till I come." (Luke 19:12-13) So as Christians we are not to sit and idly wait for Jesus' return; he said the gospel must first be preached to "all nations" before the end comes (Matt 24:14). However, the call is for evangelism; not political, secular or financial dominion.

Is Postmillennialism a prerequisite for effective evangelism?

The 18th and 19th century Postmillennialists believed that the Great Awakenings were the start of a great sustainable end-time revival. Jonathan Edwards believed that the Postmillennial vision was a necessary incentive in order to sustain the best efforts of the church:

> Indeed, the keeping alive such hopes in the church has a tendency to enliven all piety and religion in the general amongst God's people, that it should be carried on with greater earnestness and cheerfulness and faith. [917]

---

[917] Edwards - "Miscellaneous observations on important theological subjects", Part 1, ch 5

Samuel Hopkins believed that ultimately the vast majority of human beings would be saved, with the saved outnumbering the unsaved by 1,000:1. [918]

> Even as Hopkins speculated about ratios, revival surged again. This wave - the Second Great Awakening in the first half of the nineteenth century - swelled the tide of millennial anticipation. So numerous and regular were the awakenings that it raised the possibility of a "perpetual revival of religion - a revival without a consequent decline." [919]

Likewise, renowned evangelist and Postmillennialist, Charles Finney, felt that the revival of his day (the Second Great Awakening) would be jeopardized, if Christians succumbed to a belief in Premillennialism. [920]

Incidentally, while we acknowledge and applaud the work done by the many great Postmillennialist men of God, the assertion, still used by some today - that it is a prerequisite to be a Postmillennialist in order to be an effective missionary or evangelist - is hardly true. Without radio or television, the famous 19th century evangelist, D.L. Moody, preached to an estimated 100 million people and his work was dubbed by some as a "third Great Awakening." Yet Moody was clearly a Premillennialist, who was also sympathetic to Dispensationalism. [921] Billy Sunday, who by 1917 "was considered by many to be the greatest revivalist in American history, perhaps the greatest since the days of the apostles," [922] was a Premillennialist.

---

[918] https://www.christianhistoryinstitute.org/magazine/article/american-post-millennialism-seeing-the-glory - "American Postmillennialism: Seeing the glory", Issue 61, 1998
[919] Ibid
[920] Ibid
[921] Moody met the famous dispensationalist, C.I. Scofield, in St. Louis and invited him to speak at Northfield and the Niagara Conferences. In 1895 he invited Scofield to come and pastor his home church in East Northfield, Massachusetts, where he subsequently laboured for 7 years. - (The Company of the Preachers: Volume 2)
[922] William G. McLoughlin, Jr., Billy Sunday Was His Real Name (1955), xvii

And yet another Premillennialist, namely Billy Graham, through his crusades, has preached the gospel to more people in person than anyone in the history of Christianity. He is estimated to have had more than 3.2 million people respond to the invitation at his crusades to "accept Jesus Christ as their personal Saviour". As of 2008, Graham's estimated lifetime audience, including radio and television broadcasts, topped 2.2 billion. [923]

St. Petersburg Times writer Sharon Tubbs stated in an article (9 Nov 2003) [924] that Pentecostalism is currently the world's fastest-growing Christian movement. It is, after Roman Catholicism, the largest Christian tradition. Yet most Pentecostals are predominantly Dispensational in outlook. In fact, Premillennialists might argue that belief in an imminent coming of Jesus should give a greater sense of urgency in reaching the world before he returns.

---

[923] https://en.wikipedia.org/wiki/Billy_Graham
[924] Article: "Fiery Pentecostal Spirit Spreads into Mainstream Christianity"

CHAPTER 12: PREMILLENNIALISM

Premillennialism is the belief that:

a) Christ himself will
b) literally reign
c) on the earth
d) from Jerusalem
e) with his saints
f) for a literal 1000 years
g) after his Second Coming
h) with a renewed covenant with a restored Israel (in Dispensationalism).

It is distinct from the other forms of Christian eschatology such as Amillennialism or Postmillennialism, which view the Millennium occurring prior to the Second Coming, Christians ruling in place of Christ, the Church replacing Israel, and the Millennium length as (optionally) figurative. Premillennialism views the future Millennial age as a time of fulfilment for the prophetic hope of God's people as given in the Old Testament. It adapts the approach that the covenant with Israel is distinct and irrevocable, rather than replaced by the New Covenant. The chronology of Premillennialism is largely based upon a literal interpretation of Revelation 20, which describes Christ's coming to the earth and subsequent reign occurring at the end of an apocalyptic period of tribulation and Armageddon.

Sexta-septamillennial tradition

This view holds that there are 6 millennial days before the Second Advent, followed by a 7th millennial day of rest. In explaining God's perspective on time, the apostle Peter wrote:

> ... *With the Lord a day is like a thousand years, and a thousand years are like a day (2 Pet 3:8).*

The early Church Fathers expressed their belief in Premillennialism through their acceptance of the sexta-septamillennial tradition. Irenaeus believed that the first 6 days of creation week were typical of the first 6000 years of human history, with the Antichrist manifesting himself in the sixth period. He expected the Millennial kingdom to begin with the Second Coming of Christ, who would inaugurate the reign of the kingdom of God during the seventh thousand-year period - the millennial Sabbath - as signified by the Sabbath of creation week. Irenaeus writes that current age will end after the 6,000[th] year.

> For in as many days as this world was made, in so many thousand years shall it be concluded. And for this reason the Scripture says: "Thus the heaven and the earth were finished, and all their adornment. And God brought to a conclusion upon the sixth day the works that He had made; and God rested upon the seventh day from all His works." This is an account of the things formerly created, as also it is a prophecy of what is to come. For the day of the Lord is as a thousand years; and in six days created things were completed: it is evident, therefore, that they will come to an end at the sixth thousand year. [925]

Day	Age	Start - Finish	Period
1	Age of	Adam - Enoch	~4000 - ~3000 BC
2	Conscience	Enoch - Abraham	~3000 - ~2000 BC
3	Age of Law	Abraham - Solomon	~2000 - ~1000 BC
4		Solomon - Christ	~1000 - 1 AD
5	Age of	Christ - Antichrist	1 AD - ~1000 AD
6	Grace		~1000 - ~2000 AD
7	Millennium	Antichrist - Satan's second and final demise	~2000 - ~3000 AD
8	The new heaven and earth		~3000 AD →

Table 19: The sexta-septamillennial view

---

[925] Against Heresies 5.28.3

Clarence Larkin illustrated the sexta-septamillennial view as follows, with the first and second day (2000 years) being the Age of Conscience, the third and fourth day (2000 years) being the Age of Law, the fifth and sixth day (2000 years) being the Age of Grace and the seventh Sabbatical day (1000 years) being the Millennium.

If this view is correct, the appearance of the Antichrist is eminent. The 6000th year is the 6th millennial 'day' and Antichrist has the number 666 (number of man, who was created on the 6th day). Even Augustine, who originally held the Premillennial viewpoint described the belief in the context of the sexta-septamillennial tradition:

> Those who, on the strength of this passage, have suspected that the first resurrection is future and bodily, have been moved, among other things, specially by the number of a thousand years, as if it were a fit thing that the saints should thus enjoy a kind of Sabbath-rest during that period, a holy leisure after the labours of the six thousand years since man was created, and was on account of his great sin dismissed from the blessedness of paradise into the woes of this mortal life, so that thus, as it is written, One day is with the Lord as a thousand years, and a thousand years as one day, 2 Peter 3:8 there should follow on the completion of six thousand years, as of six days, a kind of seventh-day Sabbath in the succeeding thousand years; and that it is for this purpose the saints rise, viz., to celebrate this Sabbath. [926]

The sexta-septamillennial idea was not unique to Irenaeus, but was held by the author of the Epistle of Barnabas, Hippolytus of Rome, Cyprian and Victorinus of Pettau in the 3rd century, and Methodius of Olympus in the early 4th century. The author of the Epistle of Barnabas (probably written between AD 70 - 131) writes:

---

[926] The City of God (Book XX), chapter 7
http://www.newadvent.org/fathers/120120.htm

The Sabbath is mentioned at the beginning of the creation [thus]: And God made in six days the works of His hands, and made an end on the seventh day, and rested on it, and sanctified it. Attend, my children, to the meaning of this expression, He finished in six days. This implies that the Lord will finish all things in six thousand years, for a day is with Him a thousand years. And He Himself testifies, saying, Behold, today will be as a thousand years. Therefore, my children, in six days, that is, in six thousand years, all things will be finished. And He rested on the seventh day. This means: when His Son, coming [again], shall destroy the time of the wicked man, and judge the ungodly, and change the-sun, and the moon, and the stars, then shall He truly rest on the seventh day. [927]

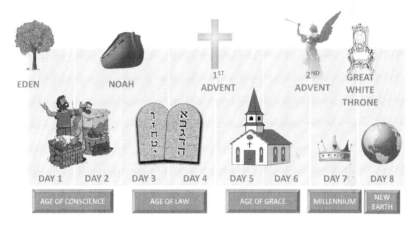

Figure 50: The 7 millennial days of human history -
The sexta-septamillennial view with a Dispensational understanding

Hippolytus (AD 170-236), in his Commentary of Daniel, echoes this sexta-septamillennial view:

For the first appearance of our Lord in the flesh took place in Bethlehem, under Augustus, in the year 5500; and He suffered in the thirty-third year. And 6,000 years

---

[927] The Epistle of Barnabas, Chapter 15

must needs be accomplished, in order that the Sabbath may come, the rest, the holy day "on which God rested from all His works." For the Sabbath is the type and emblem of the future kingdom of the saints, when they "shall reign with Christ," when He comes from heaven, as John says in his Apocalypse: for "a day with the Lord is as a thousand years." Since, then, in six days God made all things, it follows that 6,000 years must be fulfilled. [928]

Writing on the significance of the number seven in Scripture, Cyprian (AD 200-258) alludes to this same scheme:

As the first seven days in the divine arrangement containing seven thousand of years, as the seven spirits and seven angels which stand and go in and out before the face of God, and the seven-branched lamp in the tabernacle of witness, and the seven golden candlesticks in the Apocalypse...[929]

Commodianus (c. 240 AD) also describes the Millennial period in the framework of the sexta-septamillennial timing.

This has pleased Christ, that the dead should rise again, yea, with their bodies; and those, too, whom in this world the fire has burned, when six thousand years are completed, and the world has come to an end.... Those who are more worthy, and who are begotten of an illustrious stem, and the men of nobility under the conquered Antichrist, according to God's command living again in the world for a thousand years, indeed, that they may serve the saints, and the High One, under a servile yoke, that they may bear victuals on their neck. [930]

Victorinus of Pettau (died c. 303 AD) writes:

---

[928] Commentary on Daniel 2.4; The Ante-Nicene Fathers, vol 5, 179
[929] Treatise 11, 11
[930] On Christian Discipline (Commodianus)

And in Matthew we read, that it is written Isaiah also and the rest of his colleagues broke the Sabbath Matthew 12:5 - that that true and just Sabbath should be observed in the seventh millenary of years. Wherefore to those seven days the Lord attributed to each a thousand years; for thus went the warning: In Your eyes, O Lord, a thousand years are as one day. Therefore in the eyes of the Lord each thousand of years is ordained, for I find that the Lord's eyes are seven. Zechariah 4:10 Wherefore, as I have narrated, that true Sabbath will be in the seventh millenary of years, when Christ with His elect shall reign. [931]

Feast of Tabernacles

Methodius of Olympus (martyred c. 311 AD) accepted the sexta-septamillennial and raised an interesting point relating to the fulfilment of the Feast of Tabernacles in the New Covenant. He noted that the said feast was celebrated in the 7th month, hence a correlation with the 7th millennium.

> For since in six days God made the heaven and the earth, and finished the whole world, and rested on the seventh day from all His works which He had made, and blessed the seventh day and sanctified it, Genesis 2:1 so by a figure in the seventh month, when the fruits of the earth have been gathered in, we are commanded to keep the feast to the Lord, which signifies that, when this world shall be terminated at the seventh thousand years, when God shall have completed the world, He shall rejoice in us...Then, when the appointed times shall have been accomplished, and God shall have ceased to form this creation, in the seventh month, the great resurrection-day, it is commanded that the Feast of our Tabernacles shall be celebrated to the Lord, of which the things said in Leviticus are symbols and figures... [932]

---

[931] On the Creation of the World
[932] Banquet of the Ten Virgins (Discourse 9), Ch 1

Consequently Methodius saw the Millennium as the fulfilment of the Feast of Tabernacles.

- ❖ … in the seventh thousand of years, resuming again immortal, we shall celebrate the great feast of true tabernacles in the new and indissoluble creation, the fruits of the earth having been gathered in, and men no longer begetting and begotten, but God resting from the works of creation. [933]
- ❖ For like as the Israelites, having left the borders of Egypt, first came to the Tabernacles, and from hence, having again set forth, came into the land of promise, so also do we. For I also, taking my journey, and going forth from the Egypt of this life, came first to the resurrection, which is the true Feast of the Tabernacles, and there having set up my tabernacle, adorned with the fruits of virtue, on the first day of the resurrection, which is the day of judgment, celebrate with Christ the millennium of rest, which is called the seventh day, even the true Sabbath.[934]

The first 4 of the 7 Jewish feasts occur during springtime (Passover, Unleavened Bread, First Fruits, and Pentecost), and they all have already been fulfilled by Jesus at his First Coming. The final 3 (Trumpets, the Day of Atonement, and Tabernacles) occur during the Autumn, and are yet to be fulfilled at the Second Coming. This is how Jesus fulfilled the first 4 feasts.

Along with the other prophets, Micah saw the day when God would dwell or "tabernacle" among his people (Micah 4:1-4 [935]). After the creation of the new heavens and earth, we again read of the continued fulfilment of the Feast of Tabernacles when "the tabernacle of God is among men, and He will dwell among them" (Rev 21:3).

---

[933] Ibid

[934] Ibid, Chapter 5

[935] Micah 4:2 Many nations will come and say, "Come, let us go up to the mountain of the Lord, to the temple of the God of Jacob. He will teach us his ways, so that we may walk in his paths."

No	Old Covenant Feast	New Covenant fulfilment
1	Passover (Lev 23:5)	Pointed to Jesus as our Passover lamb (1 Cor 5:7) whose blood would be shed for our sins.
2	Unleavened Bread (Lev 23:6)	Pointed to the Jesus' sinless life (leaven is a picture of sin in the Bible), making him the perfect sacrifice for our sins (Heb 4:15).
3	First Fruits (Lev 23:10)	Pointed to Jesus' resurrection, Paul refers to him as the "first fruits from the dead" (1 Cor 15:20).
4	Pentecost (Lev 23:16)	Pointed to the pouring out of the Holy Spirit (Acts 2).
5	Trumpets (Lev 23:24)	Points to the Rapture of the church when Jesus will return with the sound of a loud trumpet (1 Thess 4:13-18 and 1 Cor 15:52).
6	Day of Atonement (Lev 23:27)	Points to the day of the Second Advent when Jesus returns at the end of the Tribulation. This will be the Day of Atonement for the Jewish remnant when they will "look upon him whom they have pierced," repent and accept Jesus as their Messiah (Zech 12:10).
7	Tabernacles (Lev 23:34)	Points to God's promise that he will "tabernacle" with his people when he rules in the Millennium and later in the new earth (Micah 4:1-4).

Table 20: The Old Testament feasts fulfilled in the New Covenant

Jewish Antecedents to Premillennialism

As noted earlier, many critics of Premillennialism like Origen, Jerome, Heinrich Bullinger and Cranmer recognized and objected to the perceived 'Jewishness' of Premillennialism. We have already seen how Premillennialism dominated the first three centuries of the Church. However, the concept of a temporary earthly messianic kingdom at the coming of the

Messiah was not new to Christianity, but was predated by views expressed in the Old Testament and intertestamental Judaism (i.e. covering the 400-year period between the Old and New Testaments).

Many of the doctrines regarding the Millennium come from the writings of Isaiah, David, Ezekiel, Zechariah and Malachi. In intertestamental Judaism, there was a distinction between the current age and the 'age to come.' The age to come was commonly viewed as a nationalistic golden age in which the hopes of the prophets would become a reality for the nation of Israel.

While on the Mount of Olives just outside Jerusalem, before his ascension, probably prompted by the location, the disciples question Jesus about the timing of the Messianic kingdom (which they knew would be in Jerusalem). In line with the thinking of their day and unaware of the coming 'Church Age' with the gospel going to the Gentiles, they expected the Messianic reign to come immediately. We have already noted that in response, Jesus doesn't reprimand the disciples for believing in a Jerusalem-based Kingdom Age, but simply tells them that it's not for them to know the timing. [936]

Jesus and Premillennialism

The people of Jesus' day were very aware of the Old Testament prophecies about the Messiah ruling from Jerusalem.

> While they were listening to this, he went on to tell them a parable, because he was near Jerusalem and the people thought that the kingdom of God was going to appear at once. (Luke 19:11)

Again, we see that the proximity of Jesus to Jerusalem led the people to think that he was going to set up the earthly Messianic

---

[936] Acts 1:6-7 So when they met together, they asked him, "Lord, are you at this time going to restore the kingdom to Israel?" He said to them: "It is not for you to know the times or dates the Father has set by his own authority."

kingdom that they were expecting. Luke informs us that it was this that prompted Jesus to tell the 'Parable of the Ten Minas'. Here, for the first time, Jesus hints that the Kingdom Age will not follow immediately but that the king-to-be would go away (to a distant country) first. He tells a story about a king rejected by his subjects while he was away (fulfilled in the predominant Jewish rejection of Jesus).

> *He said: "A man of noble birth went to a distant country to have himself appointed king and then to return. So he called ten of his servants and gave them ten minas. 'Put this money to work,' he said, 'until I come back.' But his subjects hated him and sent a delegation after him to say, 'We don't want this man to be our king.' He was made king, however, and returned home." (Luke 19:12-15a)*

Notice that on returning (Second Coming) the king rewards his faithful followers by allowing them to rule over cities (we will reign with Christ in the Millennium).

> *"Then he sent for the servants to whom he had given the money, in order to find out what they had gained with it. The first one came and said, 'Sir, your mina has earned ten more.' 'Well done, my good servant!' his master replied. 'Because you have been trustworthy in a very small matter, take charge of ten cities.' The second came and said, 'Sir, your mina has earned five more.' His master answered, 'You take charge of five cities.'..." (Luke 19:15b-19)*

Did Jesus say anything else about him ruling on earth? Yes, Jesus taught his disciples to pray, "Our Father in heaven … your kingdom come, your will be done on earth as it is in heaven" (Matt 6:9-10). Jesus explicitly confers a kingdom on his disciples which involves "judging the twelve tribes of Israel" (Matt 19:27-29 [937]). Jesus' Jewish followers expected the Messiah to set up

---

[937] Matt 19:27-29 Peter answered him, "We have left everything to follow you! What then will there be for us?" Jesus said to them, "I tell you the truth, at the renewal of all things, when the Son of Man sits on his glorious throne, you who

an earthly kingdom and as a result, after Jesus fed the 5000, they wanted to forcefully make him king (John 6:14-15 [938]). His disciples not only expected an immediate Messianic rule on earth; James and John's mother wanted to reserve preferential positions for her sons in the kingdom (Matt 20:20-21 [939]). In line with the Jewish understanding of the Old Testament prophecies, Satan expected the Messiah to immediately try and take back the kingdoms of this world, which he had usurped. He offered Jesus an easy solution to get these kingdoms.

> Matt 4:8-10 Again, the devil took him to a very high mountain and showed him all the kingdoms of the world and their splendour. "All this I will give you," he said, "if you will bow down and worship me." Jesus said to him, "Away from me, Satan! For it is written: 'Worship the Lord your God, and serve him only.'"

Dispensationalism

Israel and the church

Dispensationalists believe that Israel and the church are distinct peoples of God. They oppose Replacement Theology and, in line with Romans 11, believe in the future restoration of Israel. This restoration is both spiritual and national, in terms of the covenant to Abraham which included very specific promises regarding the land of Israel.

---

have followed me will also sit on twelve thrones, judging the twelve tribes of Israel. And everyone who has left houses or brothers or sisters or father or mother or children or fields for my sake will receive a hundred times as much and will inherit eternal life."

[938] John 6:14-15 After the people saw the miraculous sign that Jesus did, they began to say, "Surely this is the Prophet who is to come into the world." Jesus, knowing that they intended to come and make him king by force, withdrew again to a mountain by himself.

[939] Matt 20:20-21 Then the mother of Zebedee's sons came to Jesus with her sons and, kneeling down, asked a favour of him. "What is it you want?" he asked. She said, "Grant that one of these two sons of mine may sit at your right and the other at your left in your kingdom."

Darby	Ryrie	Scofield	Larkin
	Paradisaical state	Innocence	Edenic
		Conscience	Antediluvian
Noah (Government)	Noah	Human Government	Postdiluvian
	Abraham	Promise	Patriarchal
Moses (Law)	Israel: under Law	Law	Legal
Aaron (Priesthood)	Israel: under priests		
Kingly (Manasseh)	Israel: under kings		
Spirit (Gentile)	Gentiles	Grace	Ecclesiastical
	Spirit		
	Millennium	Kingdom	Messianic
			Fullness of times

Table 21: Dispensational covenants of Darby, Ryrie, Scofield and Larkin

What is a dispensation?

A dispensation can be defined as a period during which God deals with his people in a particular manner. Here are the views of Darby, Ryrie, Scofield and Larkin, although similar, using varying terminology.

Here is my Dispensational view, most closely aligned to that of Scofield and Larkin, where each dispensation is ushered in by a distinct covenant and terminated by a judgement.

No	Dispensation	Covenant started with	Judgement ended with
1	Innocence	Edenic covenant	Judgement of serpent and man
2	Conscience	Adamic covenant	The flood
3	Human Government	Noachic covenant	The tower of Babel
4	Patriarchal	Abrahamic covenant	The 10 plagues
5	The Law	Mosaic covenant	The crucifixion
6	Grace	New covenant in Christ	The Tribulation and the judgement of the nations
7	Millennium	New covenant with Israel	The Great White Throne

Table 22: Dispensational covenants and judgements

These 7 dispensational covenants are as follows:

1. The Age of Innocence was ushered in by the Edenic covenant and ended with the judgement of man and the serpent.
2. The Age of Conscience commenced with the Adamic covenant and ended with the judgement of the Deluge (flood).
3. The Age of Human Government commenced with the Noachic covenant and ended with the judgement at Babel.
4. The Age of Patriarchal Rule started with the Abrahamic covenant and ended with the judgement of the 10 plagues in Egypt. While normally the covenant also ended with the dispensation, in this case Scripture teaches that the Abrahamic covenant didn't cease when the newer Mosaic covenant was put in place.
5. The Age of Law began with the Mosaic covenant and ended with the judgement of man's sin through Jesus' crucifixion.
6. The present Age of Grace began with the New Covenant in Christ and will end with the judgement of the Tribulation, followed by the Judgement of the Nations on their fitness to enter the Millennium.

7. The Millennium will begin with a new covenant with Israel and ends with the Great White Throne judgement.

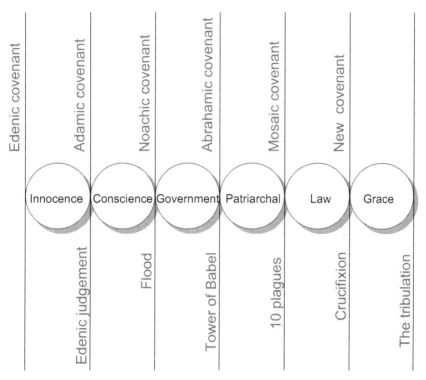

Figure 51: Dispensational ages, covenants and judgements

Resurrection of the righteous

The Millennium is preceded by the following events - the Rapture, then a 7-year tribulation, Armageddon, the Second Coming of Jesus and the last phase (there are 3) of the First Resurrection (i.e. the 'gleanings' or resurrection of the Tribulation saints).

> *Rev 20:5 ... This is the first resurrection. Blessed and holy are those who have part in the first resurrection.*

Those who go into the Millennium in their natural bodies will repopulate the earth. Irenaeus writes:

… and [with respect to] those whom the Lord shall find in the flesh, awaiting Him from heaven, and who have suffered tribulation, as well as escaped the hands of the Wicked one. For it is in reference to them that the prophet says: And those that are left shall multiply upon the earth, And Jeremiah the prophet has pointed out, that as many believers as God has prepared for this purpose, to multiply those left upon earth, should both be under the rule of the saints to minister to this Jerusalem, and that [His] kingdom shall be in it, saying, Look around Jerusalem towards the east, and behold the joy which comes to you from God Himself. [940]

The resurrected and formerly raptured saints will be immortal and rule with Christ (Rev 20:5-6). That those who partake of the first resurrection are distinct from those survivors of the Tribulation - who still marry and repopulate the earth - is indicated by Jesus' words.

> "The people of this age marry and are given in marriage. But **those who are considered worthy of taking part in that age and in the resurrection from the dead** will neither marry nor be given in marriage, and they can no longer die; for they are like the angels. They are God's children, since they are children of the resurrection. (Luke 20:34-36)

The creation shall be free from the bondage of corruption and the curse and those who partake in the first resurrection will not only rule with Christ, but have fellowship with him. Irenaeus says:

> John, therefore, did distinctly foresee the first resurrection of the just, Luke 14:14 and the inheritance in the kingdom of the earth; and what the prophets have prophesied concerning it harmonize [with his vision]. For the Lord also taught these things, when He promised that He would have the mixed cup new with His disciples in

---

[940] Against Heresies 5.35.1

the kingdom. The apostle, too, has confessed that the creation shall be free from the bondage of corruption, [so as to pass] into the liberty of the sons of God. Romans 8:21 [941]

Judgement

After Armageddon, the survivors of the Tribulation will be judged on their fitness to enter the Millennium. The Valley of Jehoshaphat is only mentioned in the Book of Joel. There, after the northern army is repelled, God will gather all the heathen nations and sit in judgment on their misdeeds to Israel.

> Joel 3:2,12 "I will gather all the nations and bring them down to the valley of Jehoshaphat. Then I will enter into judgment with them there on behalf of my people and my inheritance, Israel, whom they have scattered among the nations; and they have divided up my land... Let the nations be roused; let them advance into the Valley of Jehoshaphat, for there I will sit to judge all the nations on every side." (NASB)

The significance of the name Jehoshaphat is 'Yahweh judges'. Some believe that this valley may be the Kidron Valley outside Jerusalem.

> Zech 14:16 Then the survivors from all the nations that have attacked Jerusalem will go up year after year to worship the King, the LORD Almighty, and to celebrate the Feast of Tabernacles.

These "survivors from all the nations that have attacked Jerusalem" are the same as the 'sheep' of Matthew 25 and the 'wheat' and 'good fish' of Matthew 13. The parable of the 'Wheat and Tares' is about this judgment and not about the Rapture. The angels gather the wicked at 'the end of the age' to weed them 'out of his kingdom', while at the Rapture the righteous are

---

[941] Ibid 5.36.3

removed with no need for angelic assistance (because we shall be equal to angels).

> *Matt 13:37-43 He answered, "The one who sowed the good seed is the Son of Man. The field is the world, and the good seed stands for the sons of the kingdom. The weeds are the sons of the evil one, and the enemy who sows them is the devil. The harvest is the end of the age, and the harvesters are angels. As the weeds are pulled up and burned in the fire, so it will be at the end of the age. The Son of Man will send out his angels, and they will weed out of his kingdom everything that causes sin and all who do evil. They will throw them into the fiery furnace, where there will be weeping and gnashing of teeth. Then the righteous will shine like the sun in the kingdom of their Father. He who has ears, let him hear."*

Likewise, the parable of the net. Note the key phrases again, 'end of the age', the wicked are separated and the angels are involved.

> *Matt 13:47-50 "Once again, the kingdom of heaven is like a net that was let down into the lake and caught all kinds of fish. When it was full, the fishermen pulled it up on the shore. Then they sat down and collected the good fish in baskets, but threw the bad away. This is how it will be at the end of the age. The angels will come and separate the wicked from the righteous and throw them into the fiery furnace, where there will be weeping and gnashing of teeth."*

We'll look at this in more detail when we consider the Pre-Tribulation Rapture.

> *Daniel 12:11-12 "From the time that the daily sacrifice is abolished and the abomination that causes desolation is set up, there will be 1,290 days. Blessed is the one who waits for and reaches the end of the 1,335 days."*

As the 'Abomination that causes desolation' is set up in the middle of the Tribulation and the second half of the Tribulation is 1260 (Rev 12:6) days, the phrase "Blessed is the one who … reaches the end of the 1,335 days" has led some to believe that the Sheep-Goat Nation Judgment may last 75 days (1335 - 1260 = 75). In the 'Sheep-Goat' Judgment of the Nations that Jesus described in Matt 25:31-46, the criteria are how the nations have treated the people of Israel i.e. the 'brothers' of Jesus. Bear in mind that during the Tribulation, the Antichrist will persecute the Jews in a similar way that the Nazis persecuted them during the Holocaust. This judgment determines who is allowed to enter into the Millennial Earth. It is not the same as the Great White Throne judgment at the end of the Millennium (Matt 25:31-43).

> Matt 25:31-43 "When the Son of Man comes in his glory, and all the angels with him, he will sit on his throne in heavenly glory. All the nations will be gathered before him, and he will separate the people one from another as a shepherd separates the sheep from the goats. He will put the sheep on his right and the goats on his left. Then the King will say to those on his right, 'Come, you who are blessed by my Father; take your inheritance, the kingdom prepared for you since the creation of the world. For I was hungry and you gave me something to eat, I was thirsty and you gave me something to drink, I was a stranger and you invited me in, I needed clothes and you clothed me, I was sick and you looked after me, I was in prison and you came to visit me.' "Then the righteous will answer him, 'Lord, when did we see you hungry and feed you, or thirsty and give you something to drink? When did we see you a stranger and invite you in, or needing clothes and clothe you? When did we see you sick or in prison and go to visit you?' "The King will reply, 'I tell you the truth, whatever you did for one of the least of these brothers of mine, you did for me.' "Then he will say to those on his left, 'Depart from me, you who are cursed, into the eternal fire prepared for the devil and his angels. For I was hungry and you gave me nothing to eat, I was thirsty and you gave me nothing to drink, I was a stranger and you did not invite me in, I needed clothes and you

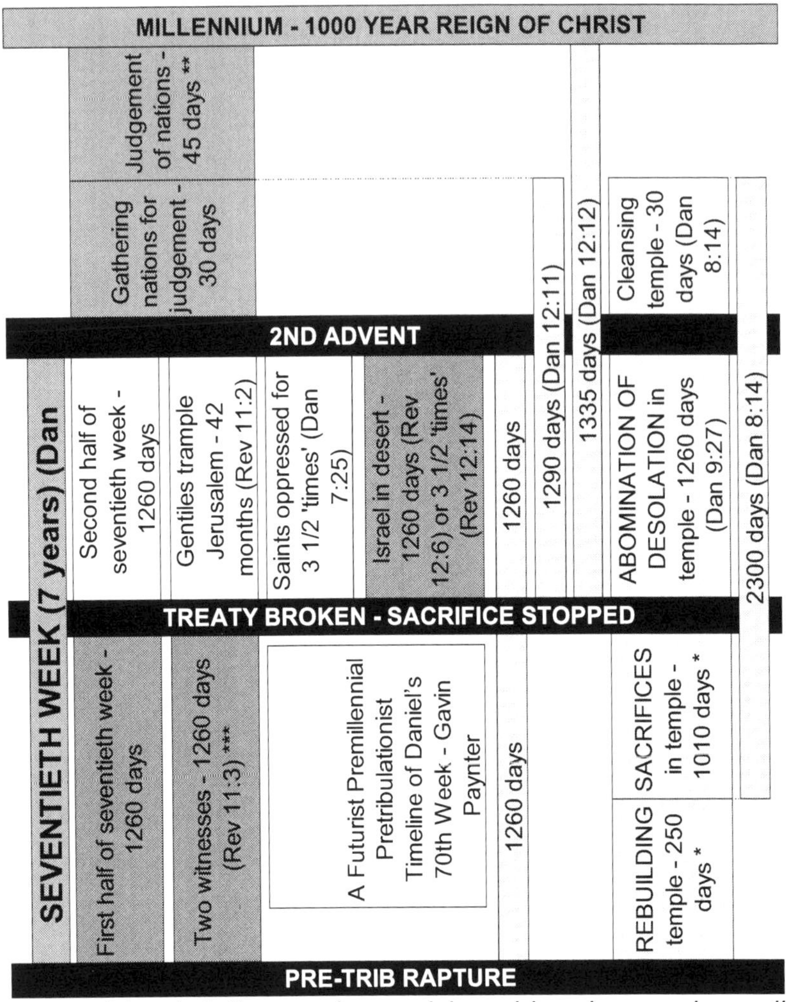

MILLENNIUM - 1000 YEAR REIGN OF CHRIST

SEVENTIETH WEEK (7 years) (Dan

Judgement of nations - 45 days **

Gathering nations for judgement - 30 days

2ND ADVENT

Second half of seventieth week - 1260 days

Gentiles trample Jerusalem - 42 months (Rev 11:2)

Saints oppressed for 3 1/2 'times' (Dan 7:25)

Israel in desert - 1260 days (Rev 12:6) or 3 1/2 'times' (Rev 12:14)

1260 days

1290 days (Dan 12:11)

1335 days (Dan 12:12)

Cleansing temple - 30 days (Dan 8:14)

ABOMINATION OF DESOLATION in temple - 1260 days (Dan 9:27)

2300 days (Dan 8:14)

TREATY BROKEN - SACRIFICE STOPPED

First half of seventieth week - 1260 days

Two witnesses - 1260 days (Rev 11:3) ***

A Futurist Premillennial Pretribulationist Timeline of Daniel's 70th Week - Gavin Paynter

1260 days

REBUILDING temple - 250 days *

SACRIFICES in temple - 1010 days *

PRE-TRIB RAPTURE

did not clothe me, I was sick and in prison and you did not look after me.'

Figure 52: Typical Premillennial Pre-Tribulationist timeline of Daniel's 70th Week (* Time period inferred from the 2300-day period ** Judgement inferred by statement regarding 1335 days in Dan 12:12)

CHAPTER 13: THE INTERIM CHURCH AGE

Eph 3:8-11 ... this grace was given me: to preach to the Gentiles the unsearchable riches of Christ, and to make plain to everyone the administration of this mystery, which for ages past was kept hidden in God, who created all things. His intent was that now, through the church (ecclesia), the manifold wisdom of God should be made known to the rulers and authorities in the heavenly realms, according to his eternal purpose which he accomplished in Christ Jesus our Lord.

The kingdom in its two forms

The Kingdom of God is the domain over which God is spiritually sovereign. Dispensationalists view the Kingdom of God as consisting of an earthly theocratic kingdom promised to Israel in the Old Testament. It is the 1000-year reign of Christ on earth. Jesus offered the kingdom to the Jews, but they rejected the offer, and so, instead of establishing the kingdom, he postponed it until the Second Coming. In the interim, he established the 'mystery form' of the kingdom during the inter-advent age, in which Christ rules spiritually in the hearts of believers, without fulfilling the prophecies of the kingdom on earth. This provisional kingdom is what we call 'the Church Age'. Paul explains to the Ephesians how the Church Age and the preaching of the gospel to the Gentiles was a 'mystery' that had been hidden in ages past (Eph 3:8-11).

This Church Age was not foreseen by the Old Testament prophets. They sometimes refer to both the First and Second Coming in the same passage. Clarence Larkin used an apt analogy called "The Mountain Peaks of Prophecy" to illustrate this. The First and Second Coming are depicted as mountains and both can be seen by the Old Testament prophets, although they appear as one mountain. The Church Age is a valley that cannot be seen by the Old Testament prophets. From their perspective those in the valley can see the valley and both mountain peaks of the First and Second coming.

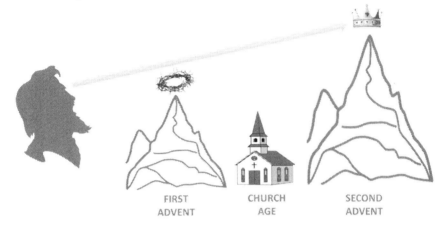

FIRST
ADVENT

CHURCH
AGE

SECOND
ADVENT

Figure 53: A simplified depiction of "The Mountain Peaks of Prophecy", the Church Age unseen by the prophets, and the First and Second Advent appearing as one event.

Following are two references to both the First and Second Coming in an Old Testament passage where the distinction between the two comings is not apparent.

1) This well-known prophecy of the promised child (referring to Jesus' at his First Coming) also speaks of him reigning on David's throne, which will only be fulfilled at his Second Coming.

> *Isa 9:6-7 For to us a child is born, to us a son is given, and the government will be on his shoulders. And he will be called Wonderful Counsellor, Mighty God, Everlasting Father, Prince of Peace.* (FIRST COMING) *Of the increase of his government and peace there will be no end. He will reign on David's throne and over his kingdom…* (SECOND COMING)

2) The following passage which was quoted by Jesus refers predominantly to his ministry of his First Coming but the latter part, the "day of vengeance of our God", refers to his Second Coming.

> *Isa 61:1-2 The Spirit of the Sovereign LORD is on me, because the LORD has anointed me to preach good news to the poor. He has sent me to bind up the brokenhearted, to proclaim freedom for the captives and release from darkness for the prisoners, to proclaim the year of the LORD's favour* (FIRST COMING) *and the day of vengeance of our God...* (SECOND COMING)

Note that when Jesus quotes Isaiah 61:1-2 in the synagogue in Nazareth, saying that he has fulfilled it, he leaves out the portion that refers to the Second Coming.

> *Luke 4:16-21 The scroll of the prophet Isaiah was handed to him. Unrolling it, he found the place where it is written: The Spirit of the Lord is on me, because he has anointed me to preach good news to the poor. He has sent me to proclaim freedom for the prisoners and recovery of sight for the blind, to release the oppressed, to proclaim the year of the Lord's favour." Then he rolled up the scroll, gave it back to the attendant and sat down. The eyes of everyone in the synagogue were fastened on him, and he began by saying to them, "Today this scripture is fulfilled in your hearing."*

By omitting the last part of the Scripture "the day of vengeance of our God", Jesus was showing that this part was not fulfilled by his First Coming. The earlier part ending with "to proclaim the year of the LORD's favour" applied to the declaration of the gospel and Jesus coming as Saviour at his first appearance. The latter part refers to the Second Advent where Jesus returns as judge. In between the two events is the Church Age or "the time of the Gentiles".

An interim kingdom - the Church age

The various teachings on the kingdom of God found throughout the New Testament, speak of the coming of the kingdom of God as a future event in some places (the Millennium), but in other places as an ongoing event (the Church age). The present day is caught between these two ages: Jesus Christ has established the kingdom of God on earth, but will not abolish this present evil age until he returns.

Dispensationalists see the Church Age as an interim kingdom before the literal kingdom on earth. This a period when Jesus has a kingdom 'not of this world', but Jesus' use of the word 'now' when speaking to Pilate indicates that this is a temporary situation.

> John 18:36 Jesus said, "My kingdom is not of this world… But now my kingdom is from another place."

In John's Apocalypse, he sees the day when the "kingdom of the world has become the kingdom of our Lord and of his Christ, and he will reign for ever and ever" (Rev 11:15). This however will happen after the Tribulation when Jesus defeats his enemies at the Battle of Armageddon and enters Jerusalem to establish his Millennial kingdom.

Jesus had implied to the Pharisees that, before the earthly kingdom they were expecting would come, there would be a kingdom (the Church Age) that would be "within you". [942] But both Amillennialists and Postmillennialists confuse the future Millennium with the current Church Age, which is an interim kingdom.

This Church Age kingdom would be established by Jesus. He told his disciples, "I will build my church" (Matt 16:18). This said kingdom is "not of this world" because its authority and mandate

---

[942] Luke 17:20-21 Once, having been asked by the Pharisees when the kingdom of God would come, Jesus replied, "The kingdom of God does not come with your careful observation, nor will people say, 'Here it is,' or 'There it is,' because the kingdom of God is within you."

does not come from man, but from God. [943] Yet it exists within the kingdom of the world, comprising of an assembly of "called out ones". The term 'church', as we understand it, was unknown in Jesus' time. [The word translated 'church' (Greek - εκκλησια / ecclesia) in Matt 16:18 means 'assembly' in Greek or "called out ones". The English word 'church' derives from the Greek κυριακή (kyriake) and means "Lord's house". This refers to a building and is not the word used in Matthew 16.] Thus, this kingdom is non-physical, but exists "within you". A kingdom implies a king; the king is Jesus. If we are part of this kingdom of the true Church, we should obey the king. [944] Entrance into this kingdom is by a new birth, [945] repentance, [946] and the divine call. [947] We are told to seek this kingdom first [948] above all other things. But we are also told to pray for the ultimate arrival of God's kingdom "on earth as it is in heaven" (Matt 6:10).

Does God ever postpone?

Some, in particular Calvinists with their ideas of determinism, reject the Dispensational idea that the kingdom could have been offered to the Jews, who subsequently rejected it, because they think it implies that somehow God is not in control or that he gets taken by surprise and has to come up with a "Plan B". But contrary to what some believe, the concept of postponement by God is not foreign to Scripture.

a) The wicked king Ahab had God's judgment pronounced on him by the prophet Elijah. But on hearing the pronouncement he humbled himself before God and his judgement was postponed. God told Elijah "Have you noticed how Ahab has

---

[943] Luke 22:29 And I confer on you a kingdom, just as my Father conferred one on me.
[944] Matt 7:46 "Why do you call me, 'Lord, Lord,' and do not do what I say?
[945] John 3:3 In reply Jesus declared, "I tell you the truth, no one can see the kingdom of God unless he is born again."
[946] Matt 4:17 From that time on Jesus began to preach, "Repent, for the kingdom of heaven is near."
[947] 1 Thess 2:12 encouraging, comforting and urging you to live lives worthy of God, who calls you into his kingdom and glory.
[948] Matt 6:33 "But seek first his kingdom and his righteousness, and all these things will be given to you as well."

humbled himself before me? Because he has humbled himself, I will not bring this disaster in his day, but I will bring it on his house in the days of his son." (1 Kings 21:29)

b) The message Jonah preached was, "Forty more days and Nineveh will be overthrown" (Jonah 3:4), a message he had received from God. But when the people repented at his preaching (Matt 12:41) this prophesied judgement did not happen - it too was postponed. Decades later the people of Nineveh returned to their wicked ways and the entire book of Nahum is dedicated to prophesying the latter destruction of the city. The time lapse between Jonah's preaching (somewhere between 786-746 BC [949]) and the ultimate destruction of Nineveh in 612 BC by the Median army was about a century and a half.

c) Then Hezekiah had his date of death – again, decreed by God - postponed by 15 years. He is told by Isaiah in no uncertain terms that he would die shortly, "This is what the LORD says: Put your house in order, because you are going to die; you will not recover" (2 Kings 20:1). But when Hezekiah prays to God, Isaiah is instructed to return to and give Hezekiah this message, "I have heard your prayer and seen your tears… I will add fifteen years to your life" (2 Kings 20:5-6).

Jerusalem's King rejected

Bear in mind that Matthew's gospel was written primarily for Jewish readers, [950] hence his frequent quotations from the Old Testament prophets. He continually presents Jesus as the "Son of David" which was a reference to the Messiah. If we observe the hermeneutical rule of "context" we'll discover that many of Jesus' parables had not only a spiritual and moral application, but were prophetic of the Millennium (kingdom) and the Church Age (interim kingdom).

---

[949] Jonah lived in the reign of Jeroboam II (2 Kings 14:25).

[950] Irenaeus writes (Against Heresies) that "Matthew also issued a written Gospel among the Hebrews in their own dialect." Hippolytus writes, "Matthew wrote the Gospel in the Hebrew tongue, and published it at Jerusalem…" According to Eusebius (Ecclesiastical History), Papias said "Matthew wrote the oracles in the Hebrew language, and every one interpreted them as he was able."

The parable of the fig tree

Matthew records the parable of a vineyard owner (representing God) who was unhappy with his barren fig tree (a type of Israel). He decides to give it one more chance and then destroy it, if it remains barren (Matt 13:6-9 [951]).

Figure 54: The Parable of the Fig Tree [952]

The vineyard owner, who always represents God in Jesus' parables, [953] was dissatisfied with his barren fig tree, which is a type of Israel - interpreting Scripture with Scripture, see Hosea

---

[951] Matt 13:6-9 Then he told this parable: "A man had a fig tree, planted in his vineyard, and he went to look for fruit on it, but did not find any. So he said to the man who took care of the vineyard, 'For three years now I've been coming to look for fruit on this fig tree and haven't found any. Cut it down! Why should it use up the soil?' 'Sir,' the man replied, 'leave it alone for one more year, and I'll dig around it and fertilize it. If it bears fruit next year, fine! If not, then cut it down.'"

[952] Painting by Harold Copping (1863-1932)

[953] Matt 21:28 (The parable of the 2 sons) & 21:33 (The parable of the tenants)

9:10 [954] and Jer 24:5. [955] He decides to give it one more chance and then destroy it - if it remains barren. It's interesting that in the parable, the fig tree (Israel) is given 3 more years' grace - and Jesus ministry "to the lost sheep of Israel" (Matt 15:24) lasted 3 years.

The stone the builder rejected

It was Jesus himself who taught that Jerusalem's rejection of their king, would result in the kingdom being taken away and given to another.

> *Matt 21:42-43 Jesus said to them, "Have you never read in the Scriptures: 'The stone the builders rejected has become the capstone; the Lord has done this, and it is marvellous in our eyes'? Therefore I tell you that the kingdom of God will be taken away from you and given to a people who will produce its fruit."*

And these words were spoken immediately after he rode into Jerusalem, in fulfilment of Zechariah's prophecy about the entry of Jerusalem's king into the city:

> *Shout, daughter of Jerusalem! See, your king comes to you… gentle and riding on a donkey… (Zech 9:9)*

Jesus fulfilled the above prophecy during his triumphal entry into Jerusalem, but when Pilate asks the Jews a few days later, "Shall I crucify your king?" they respond "We have no king but Caesar" (John 19:15). When Jesus had earlier approached the city, he had prophesied its future destruction because it would not recognize its king, who would bring peace to the city.

> *Matt 21:41-44 As he approached Jerusalem and saw the city, he wept over it and said, "If you, even you, had only known on this day what would bring you peace - but now*

---

[954] Hos 9:10 "When I found Israel, it was like finding grapes in the desert; when I saw your ancestors, it was like seeing the early fruit on the fig tree."

[955] Jer 24:5 "This is what the LORD, the God of Israel, says: 'Like these good figs, I regard as good the exiles from Judah, whom I sent away from this place to the land of the Babylonians."

it is hidden from your eyes... They will not leave one stone on another, because you did not recognize the time of God's coming to you."

Figure 55: Jesus enters Jerusalem as the humble king [956]

You will not see me again until...

Weeping over Jerusalem and her pending judgment, Jesus implied that he would enter the city at a later date. This time however, they would fulfil the rest of Zechariah's prophecy and say "Blessed is he who comes in the name of the Lord!"

> *Matt 23:37-39 "O Jerusalem, Jerusalem, you who kill the prophets and stone those sent to you, how often I have longed to gather your children together, as a hen gathers her chicks under her wings, but you were not willing. Look, your house is left to you desolate. For I tell you, you will not see me again until you say, 'Blessed is he who comes in the name of the Lord.'"*

Interestingly Matthew records that "the crowds that went ahead of him and those that followed" had actually shouted, "Hosanna to the Son of David!" Blessed is he who comes in the name of the Lord!" (Matt 21:9). But these were not the inhabitants of Jerusalem, who subsequently needed to inquire from his

---

[956] Courtesy of Sweet Publishing http://sweetpublishing.com

entourage as to the identity of Jesus (Matt 21:10-11 [957]). And John's gospel indicates that the crowd was actually composed of visitors to Jerusalem for the Passover Feast (John 12:12-13 [958]).

So the words of Jesus in Matt 23:37-39 imply that the inhabitants of Jerusalem had not echoed the words of his disciples, "Blessed is he who comes in the name of the Lord". And furthermore, they would not see him again until they did. The implication is that the offer of his kingship is not removed, but postponed. He in no way states that their chance of having him as king of the city is now gone forever... the date has simply shifted. Remember it is clear from the Millennial prophecies that Jesus will later reign from Jerusalem (Ps 2:6, Joel 3:17).

More parables of a rejected kingdom offer

Some have been puzzled about Jesus' reason for cursing a fig tree. Matthew relates how, immediately after the Triumphal entry, when Jesus is again approaching Jerusalem from Bethany, he cursed the fig tree (remember, a type of Israel) because it was fruitless (Matt 21:18-19 [959]). One recalls his earlier parable of the fruitless fig tree. The interim kingdom, which was not foreseen by the Old Testament prophets, would go to the Gentiles, because of the Jewish rejection of their Messiah.

---

[957] Matt 21:10-11 When Jesus entered Jerusalem, the whole city was stirred and asked, "Who is this?" The crowds answered, "This is Jesus, the prophet from Nazareth in Galilee."

[958] John 12:12-13 The next day the great crowd that had come for the Feast heard that Jesus was on his way to Jerusalem. They took palm branches and went out to meet him, shouting, "Hosanna! Blessed is he who comes in the name of the Lord!"

[959] Matt 21:18-19 Early in the morning, as he was on his way back to the city, he was hungry. Seeing a fig tree by the road, he went up to it but found nothing on it except leaves. Then he said to it, "May you never bear fruit again!" Immediately the tree withered.

1) The parable of the two sons

Matthew relates how, after cursing the fig tree, Jesus subsequently tells 3 consecutive parables, all of which are very telling, each one highlighting the fact that the offered kingdom has been rejected by Israel and will go to the Gentiles. Firstly, there is the son who initially agreed to obey (Israel) but ultimately did not - while the son who at first said he would not obey (the Gentiles), had a change of heart (Matt 21:28-31 [960]).

2) The parable of the tenants

In the second parable, the vineyard is taken from the original rebellious tenants (Israel) after they killed the heir (Jesus) and is given to others (Gentiles) to work it (Matt 21:33-41 [961]).

One of Matthew's major themes is the "kingdom of heaven" or "kingdom of God" which he refers to over 70 times. After the parable of the tenants, Jesus says, "Therefore I tell you that the kingdom of God will be taken away from you and given to a people who will produce its fruit" (v 43). In this context, he identifies himself as the "the stone the builders rejected" which "has become the capstone" (v 42), and we further read that "when the chief priests and the Pharisees heard Jesus' parables, they knew he was talking about them" (v 45).

---

[960] Matt 21:28-31 "What do you think? There was a man who had two sons. He went to the first and said, 'Son, go and work today in the vineyard.' 'I will not,' he answered, but later he changed his mind and went. Then the father went to the other son and said the same thing. He answered, 'I will, sir,' but he did not go. Which of the two did what his father wanted?" "The first," they answered.
[961] Matt 21:33-41 "... There was a landowner who planted a vineyard... Then he rented the vineyard to some farmers and went away on a journey. When the harvest time approached, he sent his servants to the tenants to collect his fruit. The tenants seized his servants; they beat one, killed another, and stoned a third... Last of all, he sent his son to them. 'They will respect my son,' he said. But when the tenants saw the son, they said to each other, 'This is the heir. Come, let's kill him and take his inheritance.' So they took him and threw him out of the vineyard and killed him. Therefore, when the owner of the vineyard comes, what will he do to those tenants?" "He will bring those wretches to a wretched end," they replied, "and he will rent the vineyard to other tenants, who will give him his share of the crop at harvest time."

Figure 56: The Parable of the Tenants [962]

3) The Parable of the Wedding Banquet

Thirdly, Jesus proceeds to tell a parable about a wedding feast where the originally intended guests (Israel) refuse the king's invitation. They mistreat and kill his servants (the prophets) and show indifference to his hospitality. They are judged and "their city" (Jerusalem) is destroyed (Matt 22:1-7 [963]). Then the wedding invitation is offered to others (the Gentiles) who accept it (Matt 22:8-10 [964]).

---

[962] Painting by Harold Copping (1863-1932)

[963] Matt 22:1-7 "The kingdom of heaven is like a king who prepared a wedding banquet for his son. He sent his servants to those who had been invited to the banquet to tell them to come, but they refused to come. Then he sent some more servants and said, '… Come to the wedding banquet.' But they paid no attention… The rest seized his servants, mistreated them and killed them. The king was enraged. He sent his army and destroyed those murderers and burned their city.

[964] Matt 22:8-10 "Then he said to his servants, 'The wedding banquet is ready, but those I invited did not deserve to come. Go to the street corners and invite to the banquet anyone you find.' So the servants went out into the streets and gathered all the people they could find, both good and bad, and the wedding hall was filled with guests.

4) The prodigal Son

Luke records the parable of the prodigal son, which is normally applied (correctly so) to personal salvation. However, I believe that the reference to the response of the second son clearly shows an intended national application on the part of Jesus. Like the previous parable of the two sons, one son represents Israel and the other the Gentiles. Jesus is alluding to his rejection by Israel - the son who was faithful initially (Israel) was offended when the father showed mercy to the repentant prodigal son (the Gentiles).

The gospel goes to the Gentiles

When Paul and Barnabas spoke in Pisidian Antioch we see that they first presented the gospels to the Jews, who rejected it. They announced that they would turn to the Gentiles instead (Acts 13:44-48 [965]). And then later in Corinth, Paul affirms that he has fulfilled his responsibility by offering the gospel to the Jews, and so will now preach to the Gentiles instead (Acts 18:6 [966]). But we know from Scripture (in particular Romans 11) that this rejection by Israel is not permanent. So Romans 11 confirms the Dispensational teaching of a postponed kingdom and an interim kingdom.

---

[965] Acts 13:44-48 On the next Sabbath almost the whole city gathered to hear the word of the Lord. When the Jews saw the crowds, they were filled with jealousy and talked abusively against what Paul was saying. Then Paul and Barnabas answered them boldly: "We had to speak the word of God to you first. Since you reject it and do not consider yourselves worthy of eternal life, we now turn to the Gentiles. For this is what the Lord has commanded us: 'I have made you a light for the Gentiles, that you may bring salvation to the ends of the earth.' When the Gentiles heard this, they were glad and honoured the word of the Lord; and all who were appointed for eternal life believed.

[966] Acts 18:6 But when the Jews opposed Paul and became abusive, he shook out his clothes in protest and said to them, "Your blood be on your own heads! I am clear of my responsibility. From now on I will go to the Gentiles."

CHAPTER 14: THE MILLENNIAL RULE

> *Ezek 37:24-25 My servant David will be king
> over them, and they will all have one
> shepherd. They will follow my laws and be
> careful to keep my decrees. They will live in
> the land I gave to my servant Jacob, the land
> where your fathers lived. They and their
> children and their children's children will live
> there forever, and David my servant will be
> their prince forever.*

Besides what we have already listed in an earlier chapter, those who hold to a Futurist Premillennial viewpoint, believe that the 1000-year golden age after Jesus returns will have the following additional characteristics, in terms of the political and religious setting.

Political rule

The prominence of Jerusalem

In the Millennium, Jerusalem will rise to become the capital of the Earth.

> *Ps 2:6 "I have installed my King on Zion, my holy hill."*
> (Also Joel 3:17 [967])

The city will be blessed by God and highly esteemed by all.

> *Jer 33:9 Then this city will bring me renown, joy, praise and honour before all nations on earth that hear of all the*

---

[967] Joel 3:17 Then you will know that I, the LORD your God, dwell in Zion, my holy hill. Jerusalem will be holy...

good things I do for it; and they will be in awe and will
tremble at the abundant prosperity and peace I provide
for it. (Also Isa 65:18-19 [968])

During its long history, Jerusalem has been destroyed 2 times,
besieged 23 times, attacked 52 times, and captured and
recaptured 44 times. [969] But this will cease during our Lord's
reign and "never again will foreigners invade her" (Joel 3:17).

> *Zech 14:10-11 … But Jerusalem will be raised up and*
> *remain in its place… It will be inhabited; never again*
> *will it be destroyed. Jerusalem will be secure.*

Jesus will reign in person on earth

In Nebuchadnezzar's dream of the statue which represented the
kingdoms of the world, the statue is finally destroyed by a rock
which subsequently fills the whole earth. Daniel explains how the
rock represents the final earthly kingdom that will be established
by God.

> *Dan 2:34-45 While you were watching, a rock was cut*
> *out, but not by human hands. It struck the statue on its*
> *feet of iron and clay and smashed them. Then the iron,*
> *the clay, the bronze, the silver and the gold were broken*
> *to pieces at the same time and became like chaff on a*
> *threshing floor in the summer. The wind swept them*
> *away without leaving a trace. But the rock that struck the*
> *statue became a huge mountain and filled the whole*
> *earth… In the time of those kings, the God of heaven will*
> *set up a kingdom that will never be destroyed, nor will it*
> *be left to another people. It will crush all those kingdoms*
> *and bring them to an end, but it will itself endure forever.*
> *This is the meaning of the vision of the rock cut out of a*
> *mountain, but not by human hands - a rock that broke the*

---

[968] Isa 65:18-19 … I will create Jerusalem to be a delight and its people a joy.
I will rejoice over Jerusalem and take delight in my people; the sound of weeping and of crying will be heard in it no more.
[969] https://en.wikipedia.org/wiki/History_of_Jerusalem

iron, the bronze, the clay, the silver and the gold to pieces."

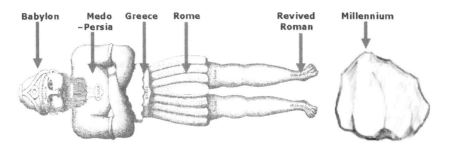

Figure 57: Nebuchadnezzar's dream of the statue

Daniel has a vision of a 'son of man' who is given authority by the Ancient of Days (God the Father) and authority over all peoples and nations.

> *Dan 7:13-14 In my vision at night I looked, and there before me was one like a son of man, coming with the clouds of heaven. He approached the Ancient of Days and was led into his presence. He was given authority, glory and sovereign power; all peoples, nations and men of every language worshiped him. His dominion is an everlasting dominion that will not pass away, and his kingdom is one that will never be destroyed.*

Both Jesus and the religious leaders of his day identified this "Son of Man" in Daniel with the Messiah (Christ) and in applying it to himself, Jesus was accused of blasphemy.

> *Matt 26:63-65 … The high priest said to him, "I charge you under oath by the living God: Tell us if you are the Christ, the Son of God." "Yes, it is as you say," Jesus replied. "But I say to all of you: In the future you will see the Son of Man sitting at the right hand of the Mighty One and coming on the clouds of heaven." Then the high priest tore his clothes and said, "He has spoken blasphemy!"*

The government on the earth will be a theocracy, with Christ as "the Son of Man" ruling. On his return, he has the titles 'King of Kings' and 'Lord of Lords' (Rev 19:16). God will reign through Jesus on earth (Zech 14:9 [970]). "He will reign on David's throne" (Isa 9:7) indicates that the reign will be based from Jerusalem and that the king is from the seed of David, something that is fulfilled in "Jesus Christ the son of David" (Matt 1:1). Let's consider the Messianic Psalm 2, quoted in the New Testament as applying to Christ.

a) The first portion refers to the Battle of Armageddon. The term "Anointed One" is 'Messiah' in Hebrew and 'Christ' in Greek.

> *Ps 2:1-3 Why do the nations conspire and the peoples plot in vain? The kings of the earth take their stand and the rulers gather together against the LORD and against his Anointed One (Messiah). "Let us break their chains," they say, "and throw off their fetters."*

b) The Father ("the One enthroned in heaven") installs the Son as King on Zion (Jerusalem).

> *Ps 2:4-6 The One enthroned in heaven laughs; the Lord scoffs at them. Then he rebukes them in his anger and terrifies them in his wrath, saying, "I have installed my King on Zion, my holy hill."*

c) V7 is quoted in Acts 13:33, [971] Heb 1:5 [972] and Heb 5:5 [973] as pertaining to Jesus.

---

[970] Zech 14:9 The LORD will be king over the whole earth.

[971] Acts 13:32-33 "We tell you the good news: What God promised our fathers he has fulfilled for us, their children, by raising up Jesus. As it is written in the second Psalm: "'You are my Son; today I have become your Father.'"

[972] Heb 1:4-5 So he (Jesus) became as much superior to the angels as the name he has inherited is superior to theirs. For to which of the angels did God ever say, "You are my Son; today I have become your Father"?

[973] Heb 5:5 So Christ also did not take upon himself the glory of becoming a high priest. But God said to him, "You are my Son; today I have become your Father."

Ps 2:7 I will proclaim the decree of the LORD: He said to me, "You are my Son; today I have become your Father."

d) V9 is quoted in Rev 12:5 [974] with regards to Christ's Millennial rule and 19:15 [975] in the context of the preceding battle of Armageddon.

Ps 2:8-9 "Ask of me, and I will make the nations your inheritance, the ends of the earth your possession. You will rule them with an iron sceptre; you will dash them to pieces like pottery."

e) The rulers of the nations are then brought into submission to the Son at the start of his Millennial rule.

Ps 2:10-12 Therefore, you kings, be wise; be warned, you rulers of the earth. Serve the LORD with fear and rejoice with trembling. Kiss the Son, lest he be angry and you be destroyed in your way, for his wrath can flare up in a moment. Blessed are all who take refuge in him.

Many prophecies state that David (a reference to Jesus, with his Messianic title being the "Son of David") will reign as king over Israel, and possibly, each nation will also have its godly king who will answer to Jesus, the King of Kings. After the time of Jacob's trouble (i.e. the Tribulation) we read that Israel "shall serve the LORD their God, and David their king whom I will raise up for them" (Jer 30:9, also Ezek 34:22-24 [976]).

---

[974] Rev 12:5 She gave birth to a son, a male child, who will rule all the nations with an iron sceptre.

[975] Rev 19:11-15 I saw heaven standing open and there before me was a white horse, whose rider is called Faithful and True. With justice he judges and makes war … his name is the Word of God. The armies of heaven were following him, riding on white horses and dressed in fine linen, white and clean. Out of his mouth comes a sharp sword with which to strike down the nations. "He will rule them with an iron sceptre."

[976] Ezek 34:22-24 I will save my flock, and they will no longer be plundered. I will judge between one sheep and another. I will place over them one shepherd, my servant David, and he will tend them; he will tend them and be their shepherd. I the LORD will be their God, and my servant David will be prince among them.

Who will reign with Christ?

There are three groups of people who will reign with Christ:

1. Old Testament saints
2. Christian saints
3. Tribulation saints

Please remember that Protestants understand the word 'saint' to simply mean 'holy', being derived from the Latin 'sanctus'. In the Bible, it is used to describe all followers of God and not a special group of holy elite people (e.g. Acts 9:13). [977]

(1) Old Testament saints

Old Testament saints will possess the kingdom and the "sovereignty, power and greatness of the kingdoms under the whole heaven will be handed over to the saints, the people of the Most High" (Dan 7:27, also Dan 7:18, [978] Dan 7:22 [979])

(2) New Testament saints

New Testament saints (i.e. Christians) will reign on the earth will Christ and "the saints will judge the world" *(1 Cor 6:2).*

> *Rev 5:9-10 "… with your blood you purchased men for God from every tribe and language and people and nation. You have made them to be a kingdom and priests to serve our God, and they will reign on the earth."*

In the letters from Jesus to the churches, he delegates some of the 'Psalm 2' authority he received from His Father to overcomers:

---

[977] Acts 9:13 "Lord," Ananias answered, "I have heard many reports about this man and all the harm he has done to your saints in Jerusalem."

[978] Dan 7:18 But the saints of the Most High will receive the kingdom and will possess it forever - yes, for ever and ever…

[979] Dan 7:22 until the Ancient of Days came and pronounced judgment in favour of the saints of the Most High, and the time came when they possessed the kingdom…

Rev 2:26-27 To him who overcomes and does my will to the end, I will give authority over the nations - 'He will rule them with an iron sceptre; he will dash them to pieces like pottery' - just as I have received authority from my Father. (Also Rev 3:21 [980])

(3) Tribulation saints

Who are the tribulation saints? They are believers who accept the Lord in the Tribulation (after the Rapture), many of whom are martyred by beheading for their refusal to participate in the Antichrist's religious, political and economic system.

> *Rev 20:4 ... And I saw the souls of those who had been beheaded because of their testimony for Jesus and because of the word of God. They had not worshiped the beast or his image and had not received his mark on their foreheads or their hands.*

And of them John writes that "they came to life and reigned with Christ a thousand years" (Rev 20:4).

The 12 apostles

The 12 apostles will judge the 12 tribes of Israel in accordance with the promise of Christ:

> *"And I confer on you a kingdom, just as my Father conferred one on me, so that you may eat and drink at my table in my kingdom and sit on thrones, judging the twelve tribes of Israel." (Luke 22:29-30)*

Judges, kings and priests

The service of the saints in the Kingdom of Christ will have three aspects - judges, kings and priests, the first two indicating political rule and the latter clerical administration.

---

[980] Rev 3:21 To him who overcomes, I will give the right to sit with me on my throne, just as I overcame and sat down with my Father on his throne.

(1) Judges

> *Rev 20:4 I saw thrones on which were seated those who had been given authority to judge…They … reigned with Christ a thousand years.*

We will judge the world and angels:

> *1 Cor 6:2-3 Do you not know that the saints will judge the world? And if you are to judge the world, are you not competent to judge trivial cases? Do you not know that we will judge angels? (Also Heb 2:5-8 [981])*

(2) Kings

We will reign with Christ.

> *2 Tim 2:11-12 Here is a trustworthy saying: If we died with him, we will also live with him; if we endure, we will also reign with him.*

We are explicitly told that we will reign "on the earth".

> *Rev 5:10 You have made them to be a kingdom and priests to serve our God, and they will reign on the earth."*

We will be given authority that is related to our demonstrated stewardship in this present age.

> *Luke 19:17 'Well done, my good servant!' his master replied. 'Because you have been trustworthy in a very small matter, take charge of ten cities.'*

The duration of the reign is 1000 years.

---

[981] Heb 2:5-8 It is not to angels that he has subjected the world to come, about which we are speaking. But there is a place where someone has testified: "What is man that you are mindful of him, the son of man that you care for him? You made him a little a lower than the angels; you crowned him with glory and honour and put everything under his feet."

Rev 20:6 Blessed and holy are those who have part in the first resurrection. The second death has no power over them, but they will be priests of God and of Christ and will reign with him for a thousand years.

Religious administration

With Satan bound in the Abyss and incapable of deceiving the nations, false religions and heresies will be a thing of the past; only the true God will be served. But as the earth begins to be progressively repopulated, these people will still need spiritual guidance. This brings us to the third role of the resurrected saints.

(3) Priests

> A priest intercedes to God on behalf of the people. This function will be fulfilled by those who were raised in the first resurrection and who have been made "to be a kingdom and priests to serve our God" Rev 5:10).
>
> > *Rev 20:6 Blessed and holy are those who have part in the first resurrection. The second death has no power over them, but they will be priests of God and of Christ...* (Also Rev 1:5-6 [982])

A restored Jerusalem temple

Once again there will be a Temple of the true God in Jerusalem, instead of the mosques dedicated to the practice of false religion that we have in this present age.

> *Ezek 37:26-28 ... I will put my sanctuary among them forever. My dwelling place will be with them; I will be their God, and they will be my people. Then the*

---

nations will know that I the LORD make Israel holy, when my sanctuary is among them forever.

As the seat of the Messiah, the Jerusalem Temple will be the centre of worship for the entire world. All nations will send representatives to Jerusalem to worship.

> *Zech 8:20-22 Many peoples and the inhabitants of many cities will yet come, and the inhabitants of one city will go to another and say, 'Let us go at once to entreat the LORD and seek the LORD Almighty. I myself am going.' And many peoples and powerful nations will come to Jerusalem to seek the LORD Almighty and to entreat him.* (Also Isa 2:2-3 [983])

Resumption of sacrifices

Several passages in the Old Testament like Isa 56:7 [984] and Jer 33:17-18 [985] indicate that there will be a resumption of animal sacrifice in the Millennium with the most extensive passage found in Ezek 43:18-46:24, where the regulations for sacrifices are stipulated. Dr. John Whitcomb writes that "Consistent dispensationalism must teach the practice of animal sacrifices for a restored and regenerated Israel in the Millennium". [986] However, critics like Amillennialist O. T. Allis view the idea of blood sacrifices re-instituted after Christ's return as incompatible with Christ's completed work and find the idea abhorrent. [987] However the theologically-savvy apostle Paul did not appear to see any contradiction between the finished work of Christ and the offering of animal sacrifice.

---

[983] Isa 2:2-3 In the last days the mountain of the LORD's temple will be established as chief among the mountains; it will be raised above the hills, and all nations will stream to it.

[984] Isa 56:7b "Their burnt offerings and sacrifices will be accepted on my altar; for my house will be called a house of prayer for all nations."

[985] Jer 33:17-18 For this is what the Lord says: 'David will never fail to have a man to sit on the throne of Israel, nor will the Levitical priests ever fail to have a man to stand before me continually to offer burnt offerings, to burn grain offerings and to present sacrifices.' "

[986] http://pre-trib.org/articles/view/ezekiel-40-thru-48-and-millennial-sacrifices

[987] Prophecy and the Church, p.248

Acts 21:26 Then Paul took the men, and the next day, purifying himself along with them, went into the temple giving notice of the completion of the days of purification, until the sacrifice was offered for each one of them.

The primary objection to the idea of animal sacrifices returning is that the Book of Hebrews teaches that Christ has come and offered a perfect sacrifice for sin, and there is therefore no need to sacrifice animals for sin (Heb 10:12-14 [988]). But we must remember that animal sacrifices in the Old Covenant never removed people's sin, but were simply a memorial, being "an annual reminder of sins" (Heb 10:1-4 [989]). As a result, many Dispensationalists view the resumed sacrifices as being only ceremonial in nature and a memorial of Christ's finished work. This will be of particular benefit to those born in the Millennium. The "Got Questions?" website puts it this way:

> To those born during the millennial kingdom, animal sacrifices will again be an object lesson. During that future time, righteousness and holiness will prevail, but those with earthly bodies will still have a sin nature, and there will be a need to teach about how offensive sin is to a holy and righteous God. Animal sacrifices will serve that purpose...[990]

John Whitcomb writes that while this might appear a step backward to some Christians, in fact from the perspective of New Covenant Israel, it is a major step forward.

---

[988] Heb 10:12-14 But when this priest had offered for all time one sacrifice for sins, he sat down at the right hand of God. Since that time he waits for his enemies to be made his footstool, because by one sacrifice he has made perfect forever those who are being made holy.

[989] Heb 10:1-4 The law is only a shadow of the good things that are coming - not the realities themselves. For this reason it can never, by the same sacrifices repeated endlessly year after year, make perfect those who draw near to worship. If it could, would they not have stopped being offered? For the worshipers would have been cleansed once for all, and would no longer have felt guilty for their sins. But those sacrifices are an annual reminder of sins, because it is impossible for the blood of bulls and goats to take away sins.

[990] https://gotquestions.org/millennial-sacrifices.html

Would such a worship system necessarily represent a great step backward for New Covenant Israel during the Kingdom age? The answer is no, for Israel will indeed be under a New Covenant program, not the Old Covenant given to Moses which was not designed to guarantee salvation. Church communion services will no longer be observed, for they have been designed only to "proclaim the Lord's death until He comes" (1 Cor. 11:26). But after He comes, animal sacrifices within a New Covenant structure, endorsed (though not performed - cf. John 4:2) by the living Lamb of God, will constitute a gigantic step forward for Israel, not a reversion to "weak and beggarly elements" (Gal. 4:9) which actually enslaved the nation because of its unregenerate misuse of the Law. [991]

Muslim nations restored to the worship of the true God

While modern Egypt and Iraq are in main, hostile to both the Gospel and to Jews, in the Millennial period both countries are mentioned as enjoying favoured-nation status.

> *Blessed be Egypt my people, Assyria the workmanship of my hands, and Israel my heritage (Isa 19:25).*

Isa 19:23-25 [992] speaks of the rebuilding of the old King's Highway from Egypt to Assyria (Iraq) and of Israel at this time.

Covenants fulfilled

Multiple covenants will see their fulfilment in the Millennium:

---

[991] http://pre-trib.org/articles/view/ezekiel-40-thru-48-and-millennial-sacrifices
[992] Isaiah 19:23-25 In that day there will be a highway from Egypt to Assyria. The Assyrians will go to Egypt and the Egyptians to Assyria. The Egyptians and Assyrians will worship together. In that day Israel will be the third, along with Egypt and Assyria, a blessing[a] on the earth. The Lord Almighty will bless them, saying, "Blessed be Egypt my people, Assyria my handiwork, and Israel my inheritance."

1. Abrahamic Covenant - Israel finally receive all the land promised.
2. Davidic Covenant - God's promise concerning David that "I will establish the throne of his kingdom forever" will be fulfilled in Jesus' (the 'Son of David') rule.
3. The New Covenant - the promise "if we endure, we will also reign with him" will be fulfilled.

Summarized support for Premillennialism

a) The Scriptures mean what they say, and should be read literally.
b) Revelation 20 literally teaches Premillennialism. The fact that the term 'thousand years' is repeated six times in Revelation 20 reinforces its literal meaning.
c) There are multiple resurrections literally taught in Scripture.
d) The apostles expected an earthly kingdom of God (Acts 1:6).
e) Christ also supported a future earthly kingdom.
f) This view is the oldest view, held by the Old Testament prophets and the early church. During the first three centuries of the apostolic Church, which was clearly Premillennial.
g) The unconditional nature of the covenants (Abrahamic and Davidic), where God made promises to Abraham, Isaac, Jacob and the twelve tribes of Israel, some of which are not fulfilled yet.
h) Premillennialism best harmonizes the Old and New Testaments.
i) We note the historic failure of Amillennialism (enforced Christian government failed in the Middle Ages). We equally note the current failure of Postmillennialism (the world is not getting better).
j) We note the historic anti-Semitism resulting from Amillennial Replacement Theology. Likewise, we note the current anti-Israel sentiment resulting from Postmillennial Replacement Theology.
k) The Bible literally teaches that the world will become more corrupt in the last days, then after the Tribulation period Christ will return and establish his Millennial kingdom. Reigning over the whole earth from Jerusalem, Israel will be

made the leader of the nations, and the Church will reign with him for a literal thousand years.

	Amillennialism	Post millennialism	Pre millennialism
Revelation 20	Allegorical	Allegorical	Literal
Duration of Millennium	Figurative	Figurative or literal 1000 years	Literal 1000 years
Beginning of 'Millennium'	Past - The Cross	Future or possibly past	Future - End of tribulation
Who reigns	Jesus in heaven	Christians on earth	Jesus with Christians on earth
State of Satan now	Bound	Bound or will be bound before 2nd coming	Free (the prince of this age)
End time apostasy	Yes - briefly before the 2nd Coming	No - world gets better	Yes - world gets more evil
Israel	Replaced by Church	Replaced by Church	Has a separate irrevocable covenant
Resurrections	One	One	Two (before and after the Millennium)
Second Coming	After the current 'Millennium'	After the current or future 'Millennium'	Before the future Millennium

Table 23: Summary of the teachings of Amillennialism, Postmillennialism and Premillennialism

l) 'Reconstructing society' was never entertained by Christ, who clearly taught "My kingdom is not of this world" (John 18:36).

m) The Church's main responsibility is evangelism and discipleship, NOT social work and political activism. While we should speak out against social evils and injustices, our primary call as believers is to change 'people' through the gospel of Jesus Christ, not to change 'society' through social reformation.
n) The Church is never commanded to subdue the earth on its own, this simply will not happen until Christ returns.
o) Peace in the world is unattainable without Jesus, 'the Prince of Peace'.

CHAPTER 15: THE RAPTURE

Historic Premillennialism and Dispensational Premillennialism

Premillennialists fall into two main categories; namely:

a) Historic Premillennialists
b) Dispensational Premillennialists

Historic Premillennialism is so called because it is the classic form which may be found in writings of some of the early church fathers, although in an undeveloped form. Dispensational Premillennialism is that form which derives from John Nelson Darby. [993]

A major difference between these 2 groups is the view of the Church in relation to Israel. Historic Premillennialists do not see so sharp a distinction between Israel and the Church as the Dispensationalists do, but instead view believers of all ages as part of one group, now revealed as the body of Christ. [994] Thus, Historic Premillennialists have no issue with the Church going through the Great Tribulation, and do not need a Pre-Tribulation Rapture of believers as the Dispensational system requires. [995] They are thus categorized as Post-Tribulationists.

> ... they see no appreciable difference in the timing of the rapture and the 'official' Second Coming. Thus they hold that Christ will not return until the end of the Great Tribulation and that Christians will suffer for the faith as they bring forth the final witness... [996]

Strictly speaking, the early church fathers would be better defined as Historic Premillennialists, although the term was not in use at that point. More recent proponents include Charles Spurgeon, George Eldon Ladd, Francis Schaeffer and Albert

---

[993] http://www.theopedia.com/premillennialism
[994] https://en.wikipedia.org/wiki/Historic_premillennialism
[995] Ibid
[996] http://www.theopedia.com/premillennialism

Mohler. [997] In contrast, classic Dispensationalists like Darby, Scofield, Larkin, Ryrie, Chafer and Lindsey are Pre-Tributationists.

> ... Pre-Tribulationists ... believe that the second coming will be in two stages separated by a 7-year period of tribulation. At the first he will return in the air to rescue those who are Christians at that time (the rapture). Then follows a 7-year period of suffering in which the Antichrist will conquer the world and kill those who refuse to worship him. At the end of the 7 years, the final witness will go out before men and angels and Christ will return to the earth. He will defeat the Antichrist, and rescue the Jews and those who have converted to Christianity during the tribulation period. [998]

Dispensationalism has also given rise to the minority view of a Mid-Tribulation Rapture.

> Mid-Tributationists ... believe that Christians will not be removed until 3 ½ years of the final 7 years have elapsed. They place the Rapture when the Temple sacrifices have been halted and ·the Antichrist has enshrined himself in the Temple, calling himself God. [999]

So Premillennialists hold 3 main views on the timing on the Rapture (Jesus' coming for his church). [1000]

1) Pre-Tribulation rapture
2) Mid-Tribulation rapture (a minority view)

---

[997] https://en.wikipedia.org/wiki/Historic_premillennialism
[998] Ibid
[999] http://www.theopedia.com/premillennialism
[1000] Another minority position is the Partial Rapture view. – "The leading advocates of the partial-rapture theory teach that all believers who fail to come to the standard necessary for participation in the Rapture will not only be left behind on earth to suffer the judgments of the Great Tribulation but that such will have no part or place in the Millennial kingdom, and therefore that they will not be raised from the dead until after the thousand years. The Redeemer's Return" — Arthur W. Pink   http://biblehub.com/library/pink/the_redeemers_return/8_because_the_partial-rapture_theory.htm

3) Post-Tribulation rapture

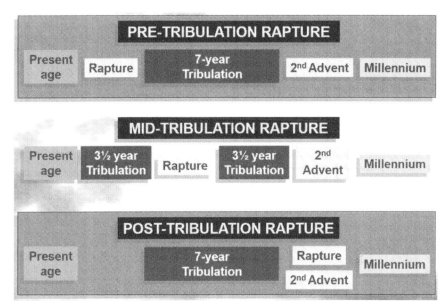

Figure 58: 3 main Premillennial views regarding the timing of the Rapture

Following is the key scripture used in the doctrine of the Rapture:

1 Thess 4:15-18 According to the Lord's own word, we tell you that we who are still alive, who are left till the coming of the Lord, will certainly not precede those who have fallen asleep. For the Lord himself will come down from heaven, with a loud command, with the voice of the archangel and with the trumpet call of God, and the dead in Christ will rise first. After that, we who are still alive and are left will be caught up together with them in the clouds to meet the Lord in the air. And so we will be with the Lord forever. Therefore encourage each other with these words.

Some critics of the doctrine of the Rapture point out that the word 'rapture' is not used in the Bible. If this supposedly invalidates a doctrine, one might wonder why the same people would endorse the doctrine of the Trinity, when the word is also not present in the Bible. In any event, while this is true of the English Bible, it is certainly not true of the Scriptures in Latin. 'Rapture', in the context of eschatology, is an English word derived from the Latin verb 'rapio', found in the Vulgate rendering of 1 Thess 4:17. [1001] The root for the Latin word 'rapiemur' is 'rapio'. 'Raptus' is the past participle of 'rapio'. The Oxford English Dictionary provides the etymology as from Latin rapere: to seize, especially abduct; it likens the words capture and rapture. [1002] 'Raptus' is Jerome's translation of the Koine Greek word harpazō, which means 'caught up' or 'taken away.' 'Harpazō' is also used in Acts 8:39 where it describes the transporting of Philip suddenly from Gaza to Azotus.

> Acts 8:39 When they came up out of the water, the Spirit of the Lord suddenly took (harpazō) Philip away, and the eunuch did not see him again…

Harpazō is used of Paul being caught up to the third heaven:

> 1 Cor 12:2 I know a man in Christ who fourteen years ago was caught up (harpazō) to the third heaven.

And again, harpazō is used of the man-child being caught up to the throne of God.

> Rev 12:5 … And her child was snatched up (harpazō) to God and to his throne.

In similar fashion, 1 Thess 4:17 tells us that we who are still alive at the time of Jesus' coming will be "caught up" (harpazō) in the clouds to meet the Lord in the air.

[1001] …deinde nos qui vivimus qui relinquimur simul **rapiemur** cum illis in nubibus obviam Domino in aera et sic semper cum Domino erimus.
[1002] http://textus-receptus.com/wiki/Rapture

There are no distinctions in the timing of this event for those who hold to the Amillennial and Postmillennial views. Like the Premillennial Post-Tribulationists, they regard the Rapture described in 1 Thess 4:15-17 as either identical to the Second Coming of Jesus as described in Matt 24:29-31, or as an event that immediately precedes the Second Coming to the earth i.e. Jesus meets his resurrected followers in the air, just before his return to earth. But the predominant view of modern Premillennialists is the Pre-Tribulation position, which distinguishes the Rapture and Second Coming as two separate events.

A recent doctrine?

Some critics of Pre-Tribulation Rapture view maintain that the belief is a recent development and that the doctrine or any semblance of it was unknown before the early 19th century and the writings of John Nelson Darby. This allegation is untrue.

As we have already noted, while in the first three centuries the Church Fathers held clear Premillennial views, their views are more easily aligned with those of Historic Premillennialists. Some like Hippolytus of Rome clearly indicate that they believed that the Church (rather than Israel) would suffer the wrath of the Antichrist. But while on the one hand they seem to indirectly advocate a Post-Tribulation Rapture; on the other hand, they sometimes refer to Christians escaping the horrors of the Tribulation (the contention of Pre-Tribulationists). Thomas Ice notes that "Since it was common in the early church to hold contradictory positions without even an awareness of inconsistency, it would not be surprising to learn that their era supports both views". [1003]

However, there is an explicit extra-Biblical reference to the Pre-Tribulation rapture in a document (Pseudo-Ephraem) dated between 374-627 AD.

[1003] http://www.pre-trib.org/articles/view/brief-history-of-rapture

> For all the saints and Elect of God are gathered, prior to the tribulation that is to come, and are taken to the Lord lest they see the confusion that is to overwhelm the world because of our sins.[1004]

This statement should change many people's historical views on the matter. But there are even earlier references to a Pre-Tribulation Rapture as well. The Shepherd of Hermas (late 1st or mid-2nd century) refers to the Pre-Tribulation concept of escaping the Tribulation.

> You have escaped from great tribulation on account of your faith, and because you did not doubt in the presence of such a beast. Go, therefore, and tell the elect of the Lord His mighty deeds, and say to them that this beast is a type of the great tribulation that is coming. If then ye prepare yourselves, and repent with all your heart, and turn to the Lord, it will be possible for you to escape it, if your heart be pure and spotless, and ye spend the rest of the days of your life in serving the Lord blamelessly. [1005]

Irenaeus refers to the church being caught up before the Tribulation:

> And therefore, when in the end the Church shall be suddenly caught up from this, it is said, 'There shall be tribulation such as has not been since the beginning, neither shall be.'" [1006]

However, like some other Church Fathers, he also saw the Church as first experiencing at least some persecution by the Antichrist. This is because they often failed to see "the saints" whom the little horn of Daniel makes war on, as being a restored Israel, but assumed that it was also a reference to the Church. Regarding the end times, Cyprian (AD 200-258), wrote:

[1004] The Rapture in Pseudo-Ephraem: Thomas Ice
[1005] The Shepherd of Hermas 1.4.2
[1006] Against Heresies 3.29.1

We who see that terrible things have begun, and know that still more terrible things are imminent, may regard it as the greatest advantage to depart from it as quickly as possible. Do you not give God thanks, do you not congratulate yourself, that by an early departure you are taken away, and delivered from the shipwrecks and disasters that are imminent? Let us greet the day which assigns each of us to his own home, which snatches us hence, and sets us free from the snares of the world and restores us to paradise and the kingdom.[1007]

Some see Cyprian's statement "by an early departure you are taken away" as a reference to a Rapture, but it's not impossible that he was actually alluding to death here.

With Amillennialism dominating the Middle Ages, we find little of Premillennialism in that period, let alone Pre-Tribulationism. And the earlier Magisterial reformers generally clung to Augustinian Amillennialism. But the concept of the Rapture, in connection with Premillennialism, was again expressed by the American Puritan father and son Increase (1639-1723) and Cotton Mather. They held to the idea that believers would be caught up in the air, followed by judgments on the earth and then the Millennium. [1008] [1009] Researcher Frank Marotta, believes that Thomas Collier in 1674 makes reference to a Pre-Tribulation rapture. But while rejecting the view himself, it does indicate his awareness that such a view was being taught in the late 17th century. [1010] Scholar Paul Benware writes:

As early as 1687, Peter Jurieu, in his book Approaching Deliverance of the Church (1687), taught that Christ would come in the air to rapture the saints and return to heaven before the battle of Armageddon. He spoke of a

---

[1007] Treatises of Cyprian

[1008] Richard G Kyle (1998) "The Last Days Are Here Again: A History of the End Times"

[1009] Paul Boyer (1992) "When Time Shall Be No More: Prophecy Belief in Modern American Culture"

[1010] Frank Marotta, Morgan Edwards: An Eighteenth Century Pre-Tributationist (1995), pp. 10-12

secretx rapture prior to His coming in glory and judgment at Armageddon…[1011]

Philip Doddridge was an English Nonconformist leader, educator and hymn writer, while John Gill was an English Baptist and Biblical scholar. The term 'Rapture' was used by Doddridge (1738) and John Gill (1748) in their New Testament commentaries, with the idea that believers would be caught up prior to judgment on the earth and Jesus' Second Coming. Both James Macknight (1763) and Thomas Scott (1792) taught that the righteous will be carried to heaven, where they will be secure until the time of judgment is over. [1012] The concept of a Pre-Tribulation Rapture was articulated by the Welsh Baptist Morgan Edwards (1722-1795) in an essay written in 1744 and later published in 1788 in Philadelphia. [1013]

> The distance between the first and second resurrection will be somewhat more than a thousand years. I say, somewhat more-, because the dead saints will be raised, and the living changed at Christ's "appearing in the air" (I Thes. iv. 17); and this will be about three years and a half before the millennium, as we shall see hereafter: but will he and they abide in the air all that time? No: they will ascend to paradise, or to some one of those many "mansions in the father's house" (John xiv. 2), and disappear during the foresaid period of time. The design of this retreat and disappearing will be to judge the risen and changed saints; for "now the time is come that judgment must begin," and that will be "at the house of God" (I Pet. iv. 17) [1014]

[1011] http://evidenceunseen.com/theology/eschatology/a-pretribulational-rapture

[1012] Paul N. Benware, Understanding End Times Prophecy: A Comprehensive Approach (Chicago: Moody Press, 1995), pp. 197-98

[1013] Wikipedia (Rapture) quoting Frank Marotta "Morgan Edwards: An Eighteenth Century Pre-Tribulationist" (1995)

[1014] http://www.pre-trib.org/articles/view/brief-history-of-rapture Thomas Ice citing Edwards - Morgan Edwards, Two Academical Exercised on Subjects Bearing the following Titles; Millennium, Last-Novelties (1788), pg 7; The spelling of all Edwards quotes have been modernized.

Baptist pastor, Joey Faust, notes that Joseph Mede (1586-1638) suggested the possibility of a Rapture before the final "conflagration" (i.e. burning of the earth) in the final days immediately before the 1000-year Kingdom. This would correspond somewhat to the final age of the Futurist (i.e. modern dispensational) system. Mede suggested that this particular burning would only be a purification and not a total annihilation of the earth - which he placed after the Millennium [1015] Notice that Mede actually used the word "rapture," as well as the analogy of Noah, which are key ideas in the modern Pre-Tribulation system.

> I will add this more, namely, what may be conceived to be the cause of this **rapture** of the saints on high to meet the Lord in the clouds, rather than to wait his coming to earth....What if it be, that they may be preserved during the Conflagration of the earth and the works thereof, 2 Pet.3:10, that as Noah and his family were preserved from the Deluge by being lift up above the waters in the Ark; so should the saints at the Conflagration be lift up in the clouds unto their Ark, Christ, to be preserved there from the deluge of fire, wherein the wicked shall be consumed? [1016] [1017]

Scottish minister, Edward Irving (1792-1834) [1018] taught a two-phase return of Christ, the first phase being a secret rapture prior to the rise of the Antichrist. [1019] The rise in belief in the Pre-

---

[1015] The Works of Joseph Mede," 1672, London edition, Book III, p.617 http://je-sus-is-savior.com/Believer's%20Corner/Doctrines/rapture_history.htm
[1016] The Works of Joseph Mede," 1672, London edition, Book IV, p.776
[1017] According to Joey Faust, "This suggestion of Mede's had considerable in-fluence on other students of the prophecies. He is later actually quoted by Wil-liam Cuninghame... as one of the earliest advocates of the pre-trib rapture view! Therefore, whether or not one agrees that Mede's quote is foundational in regard to the pre-trib rapture is beside the point. Cuninghame took it as being an early and undeveloped example of his own viewpoint and built upon it. From the point of view of the historian, Mede takes his place in history as being one of the first scholars to revive the pre-trib rapture concept."
http://jesus-is-savior.com/Believer's%20Corner/Doctrines/rapture_history.htm
[1018] Irving is generally regarded as the main figure behind the foundation of the Catholic Apostolic Church.
[1019] Wikipedia (Rapture)

Tribulation rapture is often wrongly attributed to a 15-year old Scottish-Irish girl named Margaret McDonald (a follower of Edward Irving), who in 1830 had a vision of the end times that was first published in 1840. It was published again in 1861 but two important sentences related to a Post-Tribulation Rapture were removed, namely, "This is the fiery trial which is to try us. It will be for the purging and purifying of the real members of the body of Jesus" and "The trial of the Church is from Antichrist. It is by being filled with the Spirit that we shall be kept". [1020]

John Nelson Darby's view of a Pre-Tribulation rapture was accepted among many other Plymouth Brethren in England. The Brethren Movement impacted American Christianity, primarily through their writings. [1021] Other influences included the Bible Conference Movement, starting in 1878 with the Niagara Bible Conference. These conferences led to an increasing acceptance of futurist Premillennial views and the Pre-Tribulation Rapture especially among Presbyterian, Baptist and Congregational members. [1022]

Popular books also contributed to the acceptance of the teaching. William Eugene Blackstone was an American evangelist and Christian Zionist influenced by D. L. Moody. His book "Jesus is Coming", published in 1878, sold more than 1.3 million copies [1023] and promoted the view; as did Scofield's Reference Bible and Chafer's volumes on "Systematic Theology". In the early 20th century Clarence Larkin published many books and charts illustrating Dispensational Millennialism views. In the 20th century, Dispensationalism became the most popular eschatological perspective in the US. Along with Dispensationalism came the belief in a Pre-Tribulation rapture. In 1957 John Walvoord authored a book, "The Rapture Question", that gave theological support to the views; this book eventually sold over 65,000 copies. [1024] J. Dwight Pentecost

---

[1020] Wikipedia (Rapture) citing "Margaret MacDonald's Complete Vision" (http://www.bibleprophesy.org/vision.htm)
[1021] Wikipedia (Rapture)
[1022] Ibid
[1023] Ibid
[1024] Ibid

added his support in 1958 with "Things to Come" which sold 215,000 copies. [1025] Other popular proponents of Dispensationalism and the Pre-Tribulation Rapture are Charles Ryrie (in the notes of the Ryrie Study Bible), Charles Feinberg, J. Vernon McGee, Chuck Smith, Chuck Missler, Jack Van Impe, Grant Jeffrey and David Jeremiah.

During the 1970s, the viewpoint became popular in wider circles, in part due to the movie "A Thief in the Night". It was based on the Dispensational interpretation of Matt 24:36-44 (one will be taken and one will be left). The story was about a young woman, who wakes one morning to discover that her husband has vanished - along with millions of others throughout the world. She then has to survive against a one-world totalitarian government, that will usher in the coming of the Antichrist. The movie featured the iconic Christian-rock theme song by Larry Norman, "I Wish We'd All Been Ready". The film was followed by 3 sequels (A Distant Thunder, Image of the Beast, and The Prodigal Planet) over the next decade.

The impact of popular Dispensationalist, Hal Lindsey's 1970s bestseller "The Late Great Planet Earth" also cannot be overstated. The New York Times called it the "No. 1 non-fiction bestseller of the decade". In the South African Assemblies of God, James Mullan was an ardent Pre-Tribulation Rapture adherent; as was former Congo missionary, Harold Berry; and preacher and teacher, Warren Paynter. From 1995 until present, the doctrine was further popularized by LaHaye's and Jenkins' "Left Behind" book series, which sold over 65 million copies in series and was also made into several movies. The story relates how true Christians are raptured, leaving behind a shattered and chaotic world. A politician named Nicolae Carpathia rises to become the UN secretary-general and promises to restore peace and stability to the world, but most are unaware that he is actually the Antichrist.

[1025] Ibid

Arguments for the Pre-Tribulation Rapture

Why do we believe that the Rapture and the Second Advent are two separate events and that the Rapture will take place before the 7-year Tribulation?

(a) A KNOWN day versus an UNKNOWN day

One of the best arguments in favour of a Pre-Tribulation Rapture is the prophesied element of surprise. The Bible is clear that no-one knows when Jesus will return. Jesus himself said that no-one (including the angels and the incarnate Son of God) knew the day.

> *Matt 24:36 No one knows about that day or hour, not even the angels in heaven, nor the Son, but only the Father.*

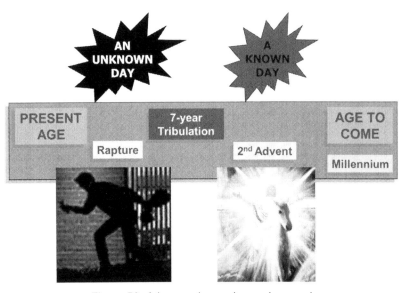

Figure 59: A known day and an unknown day

Jesus will return unexpectedly. To make this point John relates the words of Jesus saying, "Look, I come like a thief! Blessed is the one who stays awake and remains clothed, so as not to go naked and be shamefully exposed" (Rev 16:15). A thief does not announce the time of his coming, but instead comes when he is least expected. Jesus explains that the 'thief' analogy relates to the unexpected nature of his return.

Matt 24:43-44 "But understand this: If the owner of the house had known at what time of night the thief was coming, he would have kept watch and would not have let his house be broken into. So you also must be ready, because the Son of Man will come at an hour when you do not expect him."

The 'thief' comparison is again drawn by both Paul and Peter.

- ❖ *1 Thess 5:2 for you know very well that the day of the Lord will come like a thief in the night.*
- ❖ *2 Pet 3:10 But the day of the Lord will come like a thief.*

Anything other than a Pre-Tribulation Rapture view totally removes this prophesied element of surprise. If the Rapture occurs at the end or the middle of the 7-year Tribulation, then how will it be unexpected? We know that there are 2 sets of 1260 days (3 ½ years) in the Tribulation, so anyone could work it out. If Jesus comes at the end or the middle of a known 7-year Tribulation period, what possible sense would the previous passage and one like this make?

Luke 12:46 "The master of that servant will come on a day when he does not expect him and at an hour he is not aware of."

(b) 2 Second Comings?

It is often contended that Pre-Tribulationists teach a first "Second Coming" and a second "Second Coming". But remember that there were two phases to the First Coming.

1) Firstly, Jesus ministered to all until his death.
2) Secondly, after his resurrection he appeared again, but now only to believers.

The 2 phases of the First Coming were separated by the death and resurrection of Jesus.

First	Phase 1	Appears to all
coming	Phase 2	Appears only to believers

Table 24: Phase 1 and 2 of the First Coming

As with his First Coming we believe that there will be 2 phases to his Second Coming.

1) The Rapture - when Jesus appears only to believers.
2) The Second Advent - when he appears to all and comes as judge (7 years after the Rapture).

Second	Phase 1	Appears only to believers
coming	Phase 2	Appears to all

Table 25: Phase 1 and 2 of the Second Coming

(c) GOD'S WRATH versus MAN'S WRATH

Another accusation launched against Pre-Tribulationists is that their motivation for wanting to miss the Tribulation is because they do not want to suffer. The Bible plainly teaches that Christians will suffer in this present age.

> *John 16:33 (NASB) "These things I have spoken to you, so that in Me you may have peace. In the world you have tribulation, but take courage; I have overcome the world."*

However, we need to differentiate between suffering under man's (or Satan's) wrath - and suffering under God's wrath. The Tribulation is God's wrath on sinful man, not Satan's wrath in the form of persecution. In the context of the Rapture in 1 Thess 5:9 [1026] we are told that "God did not appoint us to suffer wrath". The

---

[1026] 1 Thess 5:4,9 But you, brothers, are not in darkness so that this day should surprise you like a thief... For God did not appoint us to suffer wrath but to receive salvation through our Lord Jesus Christ.

Tribulation is announced as "the wrath of the Lamb" and "the great day of their wrath", with the word "their" referring to "him who sits on the throne" and the Lamb (Jesus).

> *Rev 6:16-17 They called to the mountains and the rocks, "Fall on us and hide us from the face of him who sits on the throne and from the wrath of the Lamb! For the great day of their wrath has come, and who can stand?"*

Paul tells Christians that we are waiting for Jesus to return and that he "rescues us from the coming wrath".

> *1 Thess 1:9-10... They tell how you turned to God from idols to serve the living and true God, and to wait for his Son from heaven, whom he raised from the dead - Jesus, who rescues us from the coming wrath.*

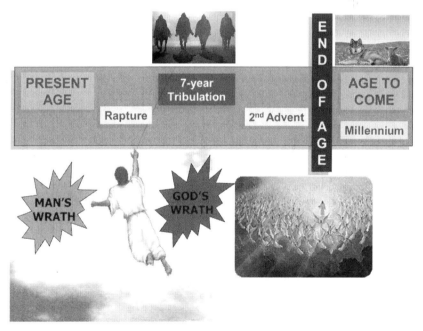

Figure 60: The righteous removed before the judgement in line with the Biblical precedents of God's judgements

Jesus promised the Philadelphian church that they will be kept from the "hour of trial" (Rev 3:10-11 [1027]). In Luke 17:26-28 Jesus compares his coming to both the judgment of the Flood and of Sodom. [1028] But Noah did not go through the Flood (God's judgment). He and his family were spared the judgement by being removed into the ark. Likewise, Lot and his family were spared the judgment on Sodom by being removed from the city. In fact, the angel told Lot with regards to fleeing to Zoar, "But flee there quickly, because I cannot do anything until you reach it" (Gen 19:22). Abraham said to God when 'negotiating' about Sodom:

> "Will you sweep away the righteous with the wicked?... Far be it from you to do such a thing - to kill the righteous with the wicked, treating the righteous and the wicked alike. Far be it from you! Will not the Judge of all the earth do right?" (Gen 18:23-25)

Like the Flood and the destruction of Sodom, the Tribulation is God's judgment on unrepentant men. Thus there is a Scriptural precedent to believe that the righteous are removed before the judgment of God.

(d) The missing church in the Book of Revelation

Pre-Tribulation adherents generally place the Rapture either between Revelation 3 and 4 or in chapter 6 (the 6th seal). You find no mention of the church in Revelation after chapter 3 until you get to Rev 22:16. There is however mention of Israel (with the 144,000 in Rev 7 and the woman in Rev 12). Also, Jerusalem as well as the Temple are featured prominently (Rev 11). Surely if the church is present during the Tribulation they should merit some mention? This is strong circumstantial evidence that the

---

[1027] Rev 3:10-11 Since you have kept my command to endure patiently, I will also keep you from the hour of trial that is going to come upon the whole world to test those who live on the earth. I am coming soon. Hold on to what you have, so that no one will take your crown.
[1028] Luke 17:26-28 "Just as it was in the days of Noah, so also will it be in the days of the Son of Man... It was the same in the days of Lot..."

church is not present and that God is once again dealing with Israel.

(e) The BLESSED HOPE versus JACOB'S TROUBLE

Israel are told that they should not long for the Day of the Lord (which we identify with the 7-year tribulation).

> *Amos 5:18-20 Woe to you who long for the day of the LORD! Why do you long for the day of the LORD? That day will be darkness, not light. It will be as though a man fled from a lion only to meet a bear, as though he entered his house and rested his hand on the wall only to have a snake bite him. Will not the day of the LORD be darkness, not light - pitch-dark, without a ray of brightness?*

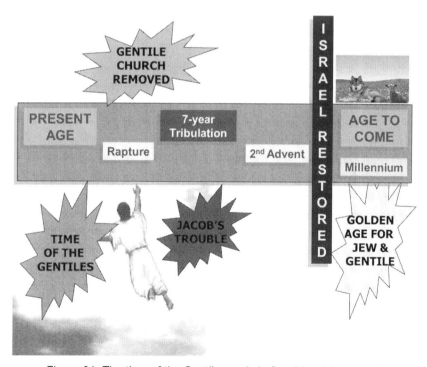

Figure 61: The time of the Gentiles ends before "Jacob's trouble"

Indeed, Jesus says of this time, "For then there will be great distress, unequalled from the beginning of the world until now - and never to be equalled again. If those days had not been cut short, no one would survive, but for the sake of the elect those days will be shortened" (Matt 24:21-22). Yet the appearing of the Lord for the Church is called "the blessed hope" (Titus 2:13). The appearing of the Lord, should it come after the Tribulation, as far as the Church is concerned, would be no blessed hope; rather, the blessed hope of church saints would be to die before the coming of the Lord, if indeed they have to go through the Tribulation. [1029]

In contrast, for Israel, who are present during the Tribulation, this period is known as "JACOB'S TROUBLE". (Jacob was renamed Israel by God and he was the father of the 12 tribes of Israel.)

> Jer 30:7 How awful that day will be! None will be like it. It will be a time of trouble for Jacob, but he will be saved out of it.

If Jesus returns after the Tribulation, then his return is not a "blessed hope" for the Church. Instead like Israel, the Church should be told "Woe to you who long for the day of the LORD!"

(f) Who repopulates the earth in the Millennium?

If the Rapture comes after the Tribulation, then all the saints, including the Jews, will be glorified, and all the wicked will be slain. [1030] The question is then, who is left to repopulate the earth during the Millennium? This causes Post-Tribulationists like Robert Gundry to place the judgment of the nations after the Millennium and, indeed, has turned many to embrace Amillennialism. [1031]

[1029] Warren Paynter: "The Pre-tribulation Rapture of the Church"
[1030] Ibid
[1031] Ibid

(g) Righteous removed

The Bible speaks of an event where the righteous are removed and an event when the wicked are removed:

- ❖ RIGHTEOUS REMOVED (Rapture):

    2 Thess 2:1-2 Concerning the coming of our Lord Jesus Christ and our being gathered to him…

- ❖ WICKED REMOVED (Second Advent):

    Matt 13:41 The Son of Man will send out his angels, and they will weed out of his kingdom everything that causes sin and all who do evil.

(h) THE LORD HIMSELF versus WITH HIS ANGELS

The Bible speaks of an event where Jesus comes alone and an event when he comes with his angels:

- ❖ COMES ALONE (Rapture): There is no need for angelic assistance because the raptured Christians shall be equal to the angels.

    1 Thess 4:16-17 For the Lord himself will come down from heaven... we who are still alive and are left will be caught up together with them in the clouds to meet the Lord in the air.

- ❖ WITH HIS ANGELS (Second Advent): The angels are required to gather the wicked for judgment.

    Matt 13:41 The Son of Man will send out his angels, and they will weed out of his kingdom everything that causes sin and all who do evil.

Expanding on 1 Thess 4:16 where Paul says that "The Lord himself shall descend from heaven", here the word translated himself (autos) is emphatic. It means "he himself and none other." "With the voice of the archangel" is better rendered "with a voice of an archangel", or in other words, "with an archangel's voice." Thus this statement does not teach that Christ will be accompanied by an archangel but that the sound of his voice, as he summons the dead in Christ from their graves, and summons them together with the living saints to meet him in the air, is like the voice of an archangel. [1032]

Paul makes it clear that the resurrection (of the righteous) and the Rapture take place at one and the same time. He writes, "The dead will be raised imperishable and we shall be changed." (1 Cor 15:52) Again, "the dead in Christ shall rise first. Then we who are alive and remain shall be caught up together with them." (1 Thess 4:16-17). Now the Lord Jesus tells us something very important about this event in Luke 20:34-36, "The sons of this age marry and are given in marriage, but those who are considered worthy to attain to that age and the resurrection from the dead, neither marry, nor are given in marriage; for they can die no more, for they are like angels, and are sons of God, being sons of the resurrection." [1033]

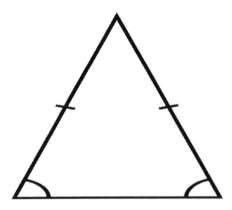

Figure 62: An isosceles triangle

The Greek word translated "like angels" is the word 'isangelos'. The prefix comes from the Greek word 'isos' which means 'equal'. (In English, an isosceles triangle is a triangle with two

[1032] Warren Paynter: "The Pre-tribulation Rapture of the Church"
[1033] Warren Paynter: "The Pre-tribulation Rapture of the Church"

sides which are equal. The first part of the word 'isos' is the Greek word for equal.) Thus Jesus said that, when the resurrection takes place, those who are resurrected, (and we know from 1 Thess 4, those who are alive at his coming) are so changed that they are now equal to angels. [1034] Thus, if we are equal to angels at the resurrection, there is no need for angelic assistance to be gathered to the Lord. However, the unrighteous at the Second Advent need to be gathered by the angels.

(i) FOR his saints versus WITH his saints

In a similar fashion, Jude speaks of an event where the Lord comes WITH his saints to execute judgement.

> *Jude 1:14-15 (KJV) And Enoch also, the seventh from Adam, prophesied of these, saying, Behold, the Lord cometh with ten thousands of his saints. To execute judgment upon all, and to convince all that are ungodly among them of all their ungodly deeds which they have ungodly committed, and of all their hard speeches which ungodly sinners have spoken against him.*

If the KJV rendering of "saints" is correct, this is clearly a reference to the Second Advent at the end of the Tribulation. At the Rapture Jesus comes FOR (not WITH) his saints. Returning seven years later, the saints are WITH him. If the Rapture and Second Advent occur at the same time, it would mean the saints are resurrected, meet Jesus in the air, and then do a U-turn to return with him.

Note: The word translated "saints" in the KJV rendering of Jude 1:14 is "hagiais" in Greek and literally means "holy ones". Thus most English versions simply render it as such, leaving it open for the reader to decide whether it refers to saints (i.e. resurrected believers) or angels. Interestingly the NASB which renders "hagiais" as "holy ones" in Jude translates it as "saint/s"

[1034] Ibid

(or a derivative) 61 times elsewhere; only 5 times does it render it as "holy one" and only this once as "holy ones". [1035]

But even if it does refer to angels instead, it still lines up with the Pre-Tribulation idea that at the Rapture Jesus comes alone, while at the Second Advent he comes with his angels, who have the responsibility for gathering the unbelievers for judgement.

The Rapture and the Second Advent

If we note these differences between the Rapture and the Second Advent, we can see it clearly in the different parables. The term "end of the age" is only applied to the Second Advent. In addition, the righteous are removed at the Rapture; but we have parables which speak of the wicked being removed, which is a reference to the Second Advent when the angels gather the wicked for the Sheep-Goat judgement.

Rapture	Second Advent
Before the Day of the Lord (i.e. Tribulation)	End of Tribulation (i.e. End of Age)
Jesus comes alone	Jesus sends out his angels
The righteous are removed	The wicked are removed
Jesus comes for his saints	Jesus comes with his saints
An unknown day	A known day

Table 26: The Rapture and the Second Advent contrasted

Second Advent parables
The parable of the wheat and tares refers, not to the Rapture, but to the Second Advent, because the term "end of the age" is used. We also see that the angels remove the wicked.

[1035] http://biblehub.com/greek/40.htm - NASB renders "hagiais": Holy (92), holy (62), Holy of Holies (1), holy one (5), holy ones (1), holy place (7), most holy (1), saint (1), saints (59), saints' (1), sanctuary (2).

Matt 13:39-42 …The harvest is the end of the age, and the harvesters are angels. As the weeds are pulled up and burned in the fire, so it will be at the end of the age. The Son of Man will send out his angels, and they will weed out of his kingdom everything that causes sin and all who do evil. They will throw them into the fiery furnace…

The parable of the net refers to the Second Advent because the term "end of the age" is used. Again, we observe that the angels remove the wicked.

Matt 13:48-50 "When it was full, the fishermen pulled it up on the shore. Then they sat down and collected the good fish in baskets, but threw the bad away. This is how it will be at the end of the age. The angels will come and separate the wicked from the righteous and throw them into the fiery furnace…"

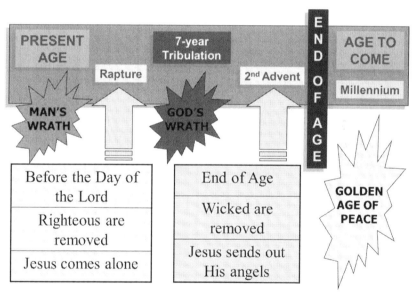

Figure 63: The Rapture and Second Advent

The teaching about the Sheep Goat judgement refers to the Second Advent because Jesus has "all the angels with him".

> *Matt 25:31 "When the Son of Man comes in his glory, and all the angels with him, he will sit on his throne in heavenly glory."*

The Rapture parables

The parable of the ten virgins refers to the Rapture because the groom comes unexpectedly to take only those wise virgins who are waiting for him.

> *Matt 25:2-13 "Five of them were foolish and five were wise… At midnight the cry rang out: 'Here's the bridegroom!' … The virgins who were ready went in with him to the wedding banquet… Therefore keep watch, because you do not know the day or the hour."*

Some have debated whether the following passage actually refers to the Second Advent. However, people are shown as being caught up in their day to day business when an unexpected return of Jesus occurs. This immediately connects it to the "thief in the night" Rapture event.

> *Matt 24:37-42 "As it was in the days of Noah, so it will be at the coming of the Son of Man. For in the days before the flood, people were eating and drinking, marrying and giving in marriage, up to the day Noah entered the ark; and they knew nothing about what would happen until the flood came and took them all away. That is how it will be at the coming of the Son of Man. Two men will be in the field; one will be taken and the other left. Two women will be grinding with a hand mill; one will be taken and the other left. Therefore keep watch, because you do not know on what day your Lord will come."*

How should we live?

Jesus cautions us to be about the business he has entrusted his servants to do, so that when he returns we will not be caught sleeping on the job!

> *Mark 13:33-37 Be on guard! Be alert! You do not know when that time will come. It's like a man going away: He leaves his house and puts his servants in charge, each with his assigned task, and tells the one at the door to keep watch. Therefore keep watch because you do not know when the owner of the house will come back - whether in the evening, or at midnight, or when the rooster crows, or at dawn. If he comes suddenly, do not let him find you sleeping. What I say to you, I say to everyone: 'Watch!'"*

Those who lose their sense of expectancy of Jesus' return might fall into sin and be punished by their returning master.

> *Matt 24:44-51 So you also must be ready, because the Son of Man will come at an hour when you do not expect him. Who then is the faithful and wise servant, whom the master has put in charge of the servants in his household to give them their food at the proper time? It will be good for that servant whose master finds him doing so when he returns. I tell you the truth, he will put him in charge of all his possessions. But suppose that servant is wicked and says to himself, 'My master is staying away a long time,' and he then begins to beat his fellow servants and to eat and drink with drunkards. The master of that servant will come on a day when he does not expect him and at an hour he is not aware of. He will cut him to pieces and assign him a place with the hypocrites, where there will be weeping and gnashing of teeth.*

Although Jesus' return is unexpected, Christians should live in a state of constant readiness and thus not be taken by surprise at his coming.

> *1 Thess 5:1-5 Now, brothers, about times and dates we do not need to write to you, for you know very well that the day of the Lord will come like a thief in the night. While people are saying, "Peace and safety," destruction will come on them suddenly, as labour pains on a pregnant woman, and they will not escape. But you, brothers, are not in darkness so that this day should surprise you like a thief. You are all sons of the light and sons of the day. We do not belong to the night or to the darkness.*

The Premillennial doctrine of imminence regarding the return of Christ adds an incentive for holy living. Norman Geisler notes:

> It is not that there are no other incentives for godliness, but certainly the imminent premillennial expectation is an added one. For no true believer wants to be caught in sin when Jesus returns. [1036]

In the words of the apostle John, "But we know that when he appears, we shall be like him, for we shall see him as he is. Everyone who has this hope in him purifies himself, just as he is pure" (1 John 3:2-3). Paul says that this "blessed hope" of Jesus' return helps in teaching us to renounce ungodliness and worldly passions. and to set apart a people "zealous for good works".

> *Titus 2:11-13 For the grace of God has appeared that offers salvation to all people. It teaches us to say "No" to ungodliness and worldly passions, and to live self-controlled, upright and godly lives in this present age, while we wait for the blessed hope - the appearing of the glory of our great God and Saviour, Jesus Christ…*

So, the expectation of Christ's soon return has a sobering effect on Christians. Speaking of the unexpected nature of Christ's return, the apostle Peter cautions:

> *The day of the Lord will come like a thief. The heavens will disappear with a roar; the elements will be destroyed*

[1036] http://normangeisler.com/the-importance-of-premillennialism

by fire, and the earth and everything in it will be laid bare. Since everything will be destroyed in this way, what kind of people ought you to be? You ought to live holy and godly lives" (2 Pet 3:10-11).

In closing, because of the expectancy of the return of Jesus, Paul also urges us to live appropriately:

1 Thess 5:6,23 So then, let us not be like others, who are asleep, but let us be alert and self-controlled... May God himself, the God of peace, sanctify you through and through. May your whole spirit, soul and body be kept blameless at the coming of our Lord Jesus Christ.

Rev 22:20 He who testifies to these things says, "Yes, I am coming soon."

Amen. Come, Lord Jesus.

CONTENTS

FIGURES

TABLES

COPYRIGHT INFORMATION

Printed in Great Britain
by Amazon